Statistics

Managing Editor
Scott Coyner, PE

Contributing Authors
David Griswold

John Hayes

Jay Hooper

Pamela Lindemer

Mary Rack

CPM Educational Program
a California 501(c)(3) nonprofit organization

Program Directors

Elizabeth Coyner   Leslie Dietiker, Ph.D.   Judy Kysh, Ph.D.   Karen Wootton

Technical Editors

Carmen de la Cruz

Sarah Maile

Technical Assistants

Brianna Atkinson

Mary Coyner

Miranda Esquivel

Michelle Lee

1 2 3 4 5 6   20 19 18 17

Printed in the United States of America   ISBN: 978-1-60328-534-6

A Note to Students:

This course was created to satisfy all of the material required for an advanced high school or first-year college level class. However, it can be adapted for use as an excellent introductory level course too. You may already have a solid background in descriptive Statistics because more and more Statistics material is being put into standard middle and high school math textbooks or perhaps you are completely new to the study of Statistics. This book is designed to take every student from their current knowledge base to a higher level of understanding of Statistics.

The most important learning will happen in class each day. Devote your energy and attention to every lesson with your study team. You will find class time to be active, participatory and challenging as you discover the concepts of Statistics. To reach your full potential, be willing to devote some time outside of class each day to review and practice the concepts you learned.

If you are reading this letter, then you have reached a point where you are making more decisions about what courses you are taking. While most of mathematics is based on universal truths ordained by nature, the applications of Statistics have been created primarily for their practical uses. In a world full of data, Statistics is becoming even more practical and hence, more important. This is likely to be the first math course you have taken which owes its existence to the usefulness of its content. We believe you made an excellent choice!

Sincerely,

The CPM Team

Statistics
Student Edition

Chapter 1 Representing Data   1

Section 1.1
1.1.1   Visualizing Information   3
1.1.2   Histograms and Stem-and-Leaf Plots   6
1.1.3   Types of Data and Variables   12

Section 1.2
1.2.1   Choosing Mean or Median   17
1.2.2   Variance and Standard Deviation   24
1.2.3   Sample Variance and Sample Standard Deviation   28
1.2.4   Investigating Data Representation   31

Section 1.3
1.3.1   Percentiles   35
1.3.2   z-Scores   41
1.3.3   Linear Transformations   46

Chapter 2 Two-Variable Quantitative Data   51

Section 2.1
2.1.1   Scatterplots and Association —   53
2.1.2   Line of Best Fit   58
2.1.3   Residuals   62
2.1.4   The Least Squares Regression Line   66
2.1.5   Using Technology to Find the LSRL   72

Section 2.2
2.2.1   The Correlation Coefficient   78
2.2.2   Behavior of Correlation and the LSRL   86
2.2.3   Residual Plots   90
2.2.4   Association is Not Causation   95
2.2.5   Interpreting Correlation in Context   100

Chapter 3 Multivariable Categorical Data — 107

Section 3.1
3.1.1 Probabilities and Two-Way Frequency Tables — 109
3.1.2 Association and Conditional Relative Frequency Tables — 115
3.1.3 Probability Notation — 121
3.1.4 Relative Frequency Tables and Conditional Probabilities — 125
3.1.5 Analyzing False Positives — 129

Section 3.2
3.2.1 Probability Trees — 134
3.2.2 Problem Solving with Categorical Data — 138
3.2.3 Simulations of Probability — 141

Chapter 4 Studies and Experiments — 145

Section 4.1
4.1.1 Survey Design I — 147
4.1.2 Samples and the Role of Randomness — 152
4.1.3 Sampling When Random is Not Possible — 158
4.1.4 Observational Studies and Experiments — 165
4.1.5 Survey Design II (optional) — 169

Section 4.2
4.2.1 Cause and Effect with Experiments — 172
4.2.2 Experimental Design I — 176
4.2.3 Experimental Design II — 181
4.2.4 Experimental Design III — 184

Chapter 5 Density Functions and Normal Distributions — 187

Section 5.1
5.1.1 Relative Frequency Histograms and Random Variables — 189
5.1.2 Introduction to Density Functions — 194
5.1.3 The Normal Probability Density Function — 200

Section 5.2
5.2.1 The Inverse Normal Function — 206
5.2.2 The Standard Normal Distribution and z-Scores — 210
5.2.3 Additional Practice Problems — 213

Chapter 6 Discrete Probability Distributions   217

Section 6.1
6.1.1   Mean and Variance of a Discrete Random Variable   219
6.1.2   Linear Combinations of Independent Random Variables   224
6.1.3   Exploring the Variability of $X - X$ 227

Section 6.2
6.2.1   Introducing the Binomial Setting   231
6.2.2   Binomial Probability Density Function   234
6.2.3   Exploring Binomial pdf and cdf   237
6.2.4   Shape, Center, and Spread of the Binomial Distribution   240
6.2.5   Normal Approximation to the Binomial Distribution   244

Section 6.3
6.3.1   Introduction to the Geometric Distribution   248
6.3.2   Binomial and Geometric Practice   252

Chapter 7 Variability in Categorical Data Sampling   257

Section 7.1
7.1.1   Introduction to Sampling Distributions   259
7.1.2   Simulating Sampling Distributions of Sample Proportions   264
7.1.3   Formulas for the Sampling Distributions of Sample Proportions   269

Section 7.2
7.2.1   Confidence Interval for a Population Proportion   275
7.2.2   Confidence Levels for Confidence Intervals   279
7.2.3   Changing the Margin of Error in Confidence Intervals   284
7.2.4   Evaluating Claims with Confidence Intervals   288

Chapter 8 Drawing Conclusions From Categorical Data   293

Section 8.1
8.1.1   Introduction to Hypothesis Testing   295
8.1.2   Hypothesis Tests for Proportions   299
8.1.3   Alternative Hypotheses and Two-Tailed Tests   304

Section 8.2
8.2.1   Types of Errors in Hypothesis Testing   310
8.2.2   Power of a Test   315

Section 8.3
8.3.1   The Difference Between Two Proportions   320
8.3.2   Two-Sample Proportion Hypothesis Tests   324
8.3.3   More Proportion Inference   329

Chapter 9 Chi-Squared Inference Procedures   333

Section 9.1
9.1.1   Introduction to the Chi-Squared Distribution   335
9.1.2   Chi-Squared Goodness of Fit   339
9.1.3   More Applications of Chi-Squared Goodness of Fit   343

Section 9.2
9.2.1   Chi-Squared Test for Independence   347
9.2.2   Chi-Squared Test for Homogeneity of Proportions   353
9.2.3   Practicing and Recognizing Chi-Squared Inference Procedures 357

Chapter 10 Drawing Conclusions From Quantitative Data   361

Section 10.1
10.1.1 Quantitative Sampling Distributions   363
10.1.2 More Sampling Distributions   369

Section 10.2
10.2.1 The Central Limit Theorem   374
10.2.2 Using the Normal Distribution with Means   378

Section 10.3
10.3.1 Introducing the t-Distribution   382
10.3.2 Calculating Confidence Intervals for μ 388
10.3.3 z-Tests and t-Tests for Population Means   392

Chapter 11 Comparing Means and Identifying Tests   397

Section 11.1
11.1.1 Paired and Independent Data from Surveys and Experiments   399
11.1.2 Paired Inference Procedures   402
11.1.3 Tests for the Difference of Two Means   406
11.1.4 Two-Sample Mean Inference with Experiments and Two-Sample Confidence Intervals   411

Section 11.2
11.2.1 Inference in Different Situations   415
11.2.2 Identifying and Implementing an Appropriate Test   419

Chapter 12 Inference for Regression   423

Section 12.1
12.1.1 Sampling Distribution of the Slope of the Regression Line   425
12.1.2 Inference for the Slope of the Regression Line   430

Section 12.2
12.2.1 Transforming Data to Achieve Linearity   436
12.2.2 Using Logarithms to Achieve Linearity   442

Chapter 13 ANOVA and Beyond!   449

Section 13.1
13.1.1 Modeling With the Chi-Squared Distribution   451
13.1.2 Introducing the F-Distribution   456

Section 13.2
13.2.1 One-Way ANOVA   461

Section 13.3
13.3.1 Sign Test: Introduction to Nonparametric Inference   467
13.3.2 Mood's Median Test   471

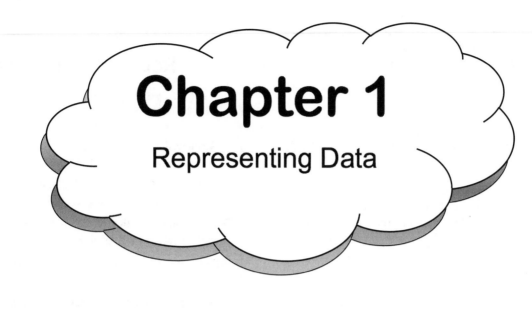

Chapter 1

Representing Data

CHAPTER 1

You may have a strong understanding of descriptive statistics from your previous math courses, or maybe none at all. Do not worry. This chapter starts at the beginning with data and how to represent it graphically and summarize it with values called statistics, then make comparisons between different sets of data. If you want to learn a branch of mathematics that only exists to be useful, you are in the right course!

Chapter Goals

Collect data and represent it using a variety of charts and graphs.

Explore the difference between quantitative and categorical data.

Discover statistics that represent the center and variation in distributions of data.

Make detailed comparisons between sets of data.

Work with measures of relative standing, percentiles, and z-scores.

Apply linear transformations to data sets and their descriptive statistics.

Chapter Outline

Section 1.1 You will create and collect a variety of data with your classmates, which are made into graphical representations including dot plots, scatterplots, stem-and-leaf plots, histograms, bar graphs, circle graphs, Venn diagrams, and two-way tables. You will discover the difference between categorical and quantitative data and their respective uses and get a preview of making predictions.

Section 1.2 You will connect the median to the IQR, and the mean to the standard deviation, and decide which is appropriate, considering the shape and outliers of the distribution. You will also distinguish between using a scatterplot or two histograms to compare two-variable data. You will compare the center, shape, spread, and outliers of two distributions and develop variance and standard deviation as methods of reporting the variability, or spread, in a distribution.

Section 1.3 You will encounter two methods of relative standing, z-scores and percentiles. You will work with ogives as a function to find percentiles and as an inverse function to find associated measurements. You will then learn how to use linear transformations to calculate appropriate statistics and parameters.

1.1.1 How can I represent information?

Visualizing Information

In this lesson, you will use different ways to visualize information. You will also consider which displays of data are better for various types of information. Your teacher will provide the necessary materials for your class to collect several pieces of data from each class member.

1-1.   DATA COLLECTION AND REPRESENTATION

Each chart is asking you to provide some information about yourself, a **variable**, information that can assume different values for each class member. For each representation (bar graph, scatterplot, dot plot, or two-way table) the class will create, be ready to answer the questions below.

a.   Was your information numerical, like a measurement, or can it only be summarized by a word like "yes," "no," or "purple"?

b.   Could you make an average from the information on each chart that gives information about its original variable(s)? If so, give examples?

c.   Working together, organize the graphs into groups of similar graphs. Your team will need to decide how many groups to make, what common features make a group, and what characteristics make each group different from the others. Be prepared to defend how your graphs are grouped.

1-2.   Collecting, organizing, analyzing, interpreting, and presenting data is part of *Statistics*. **Statistics** is an important branch of mathematics devoted to summarizing information so as to make informed decisions like choosing a college, buying a car, or even making multi-billion dollar investments.

a.   Likely you have given some thought to what you will do after high school; work, volunteer, military, or college? If you are college bound, a post-secondary education represents a large investment of time and money. It will shape the rest of your life in many ways. This may be the first big decision of your life that rests on your judgment alone. What sources of information could you use to make your choice?

b.   A friend or relative might say great things about a university they attended. Admission offices handout brochures and direct you to websites filled with photos of happy students in picture perfect settings. Are these good sources of information? Why/why not?

c.   There are 4726 degree granting institutions in the United States with a huge variation in size, style, and philosophy. It is likely you have been or will be flooded with information about prospective colleges from a wide variety of sources: friends, relatives, counselors, teachers, and college admission offices. The best fit for you may be a college you have yet to hear about. How might you go about choosing one from so many?

MATH NOTES

Statistics, statistics, Parameters and Data

The field of **Statistics** is the application of probability theory to make sense of large quantities of **data**. The study of Statistics allows us to see relationships, determine causes, and make decisions and predictions from data.

A **statistic** is a numerical fact or calculation that is formed from a sample of data. A sample mean or a correlation coefficient is a **statistic**.

When information from the entire population is available it is called a **census**. A **parameter** is a numerical fact or calculation that is formed from a **census**.

Information, often called **data** in Statistics, can have characteristics that make it untrustworthy or difficult to use.

- Data can have **bias**, which is systematically favoring certain outcomes, like an uncle telling stories from his college days while trying to convince you to go to his alma mater. Statistics has tools for detecting and avoiding bias in data, but the first rule of data is to **always consider its source**.

- Data can be overwhelming in its **quantity** or amount, like 4726 colleges all wanting your commitment at the same time. Statistics has tools for condensing and summarizing large amounts of data and techniques for using sample information to make reasonable judgments about large populations.

- There can be a large amount of **variation**, differences among and within sets of data, making comparisons difficult. Just like Universities vary widely from The Evergreen State College in Olympia Washington to The Citadel of South Carolina. Statistics provides ways to make meaningful comparisons amidst widely varying data.

1-3.   Use the bar graph at right to answer the following questions.

    a.   How many people attended the fair on Tuesday?

    b.   What was the total attendance for the week?

    c.   Compare weekend attendance to the rest of the week.

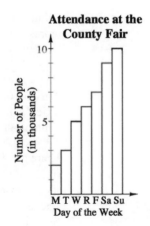

1-4. Given the data in the table at right, create a data display. Decide if a dot plot, bar graph, or Venn diagram will work best.

Mrs. McKenzie's Class Favorite Color	
Red	|||||
Orange	||
Yellow	||
Green	||||
Blue	||||| ||
Purple	|||
Brown		
Black		
Other	|||||	

1-5. Mr. Reed surveyed his class to see how many siblings (brothers and sisters) his students had. Create a graph of the data he collected, shown below. Decide if a dot plot or bar graph will work best.

1, 0, 2, 2, 3, 1, 1, 2, 0, 0, 1, 1, 1, 2, 1, 5, 1, 3, 2, 0, 1, 2, 1, 1, 1, 2, 1

1-6. For the problem below, display the data using a dot plot, bar graph, or two-way table. Decide which type of data display is best and explain why.

Appliances sold at Housemart during the month of September:

Washers: 35   Dryers: 21   Ovens: 19   Refrigerators: 27   Dishwashers: 23

1-7. Melissa collected the dates of all her friends' birthdays. The bar graph at right shows what she found.

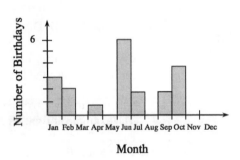

a. Make a list of the months when her friends' birthdays occur and how many birthdays there are in each month.

b. Compare the percentage of winter birthdays to the rest of the year.

1.1.2   How else can I represent data?

Histograms and Stem-and-Leaf Plots

You may have noticed that the class data charts from yesterday have been moved and separated into groups. There are also two additional charts posted that you are likely familiar with from previous math or science courses, a circle graph and a Venn diagram. Discuss with your team and be ready to share answers to the following questions.

What criteria were used to separate the charts?

Do the new charts provide any additional information?

1-8.   ESTIMATING 60 SECONDS

"Time flies", or does it?
Your Task: You will close your eyes, put your head down, and estimate when 60 seconds have passed. Your teacher will tell you when to start your estimate. When you think 60 seconds have passed, staying as quiet as possible, raise your head and determine your time from the timer approved by your teacher. When the study is finished, record your time on the sticky note provided by your teacher. This is not a contest and variation in the results is expected so be honest.

1-9.   USEFUL FORMS OF DATA

It is possible to organize items in a way that communicates information at a glance. In this problem, you will use the list of times from problem 1-8.

a.   One way to organize and display data is in a stem-and-leaf plot. The example at right represents the data 31, 31, 43, 47, 61, 66, 68, and 70. Think about how this plot is arranged and describe what you notice. For example, how would 42 be added to this plot? What about 102? Why do you think the space to the right of the 5 is blank? Be prepared to share your answers with the class.

Stem	Leaf		
3	1	1	
4	3	7	
5			
6	1	6	8
7	0		

b.   Work together to organize your class data from problem 1-8 in a similar way.

c.   What do you notice about the class data? Discuss this with your team and write down three observations you can make. Be ready to share your observations with the class and explain how you made them.

1-10.   CREATING A HISTOGRAM

A histogram is another useful way to display data. You will explore one below.

a.   In Lesson 1.1.1, you created a dot plot. Why might a dot plot not be the best choice for graphing the 60-second data?

b.   A histogram is a better type of graph for the 60-second data because it allows you to see how many pieces of data are within each interval, such as between 40 and 45 seconds. Each interval is also called a **bin**. Following your teacher's directions, place a sticky note with your time from problem 1-8 on the class histogram. Copy the histogram into your notes, using the height of bars to represent the number of sticky notes.

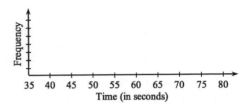

c.   Examine the graphed data. What statements can you make that describe how your class performed in the experiment? Were most students able to make a good estimate of 60 seconds? How can you tell?

1-11.   CATS AND DOGS

In the previous lesson, you may have looked at the *number* of pets that your classmates have with a dot plot. What if you want to know the *types* of pets that people have?

Assume your class is now making a bar graph and Venn diagram like the ones shown at the right, and each student in a class was given exactly one sticky dot for the bar graph and one for the Venn diagram.

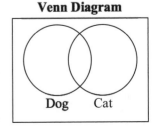

a.   Would there be anyone who had a hard time placing his or her dot on either of the graphs? Explain.

b.   What are the advantages to displaying the data in a bar graph? Venn diagram?

c.   Two categories are **mutually exclusive** if they cannot occur at the same time. Which graph is better for displaying mutually exclusive categories?

d.   Your teacher has made a Venn diagram from one of the two-way tables from yesterday's lesson. Notice how they display the same information. Draw a Venn diagram from the information in the other two-way table of class data.

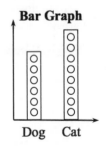

e.   In the previous lesson your class also made a Venn diagram. Try making a two-way table from the information it contains.

MATH NOTES

Displays of Categorical Data

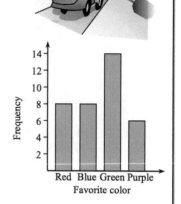

A **bar graph** is used when data has mutually exclusive categories that typically have no numerical order. The graph at right shows that green is the favorite color of 14 students.

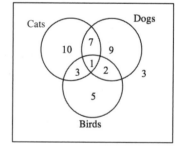

A **circle graph** is also used when data has mutually exclusive categories that typically have no numerical order. It shows the same information as a bar graph with frequencies converted to percentages.

Favorite Color

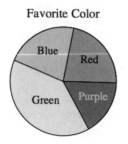

A **two-way table** is used to show overlap and relationships between variables. The two-way table is strictly limited to two variables, however each variable may have two or more response categories.

	So	Jr	Sr
Driver License	78	119	131
No License	102	53	44

A **Venn diagram** can also be used to show frequencies, relationships, and overlap. A Venn diagram is not limited to two variables, but each variable is limited to two responses, typically yes and no.

MATH NOTES

Displays of Quantitative Data

A **dot plot** is a way of displaying data that has an order and can be placed on a number line. Dot plots are generally used when the data is discrete (separate and distinct) and numerous pieces of data fall on most values. Examples: the number of siblings each student in your class has, the number of correct answers on a quiz, or the number rolled on a die (the graph at right shows 20 rolls)

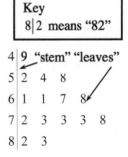

A **histogram** is similar to a dot plot except that each bar represents data in an interval of numbers. The intervals for the data are shown on the horizontal axis. The frequency (number of pieces of data in each interval) is represented by the height of a bar above the interval. Each interval is also called a bin.

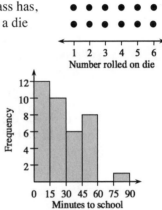

The labels on the horizontal axis represent the lower end of each interval. The histogram shows that 10 students take at least 15 minutes but less than 30 minutes to get to school.

A **stem-and-leaf plot** is similar to a histogram except that it shows the individual values from a set of data and how the values are distributed. The "stem" part of the graph represents all of the digits in a number except the last one. The "leaf" part of the graph represents the last digit of each of the numbers. Every stem-and-leaf plot needs a "key." The key determines the place value of the entries. This is important because $8\,|\,2$ could mean 82 or 8.2.

Example: Students in a math class received the following scores on their tests: 49, 52, 54, 58, 61, 61, 67, 68, 72, 73, 73, 73, 78, 82, and 83.

```
Key
8 | 2  means "82"
```

```
4 | 9   "stem"  "leaves"
5 | 2   4   8
6 | 1   1   7   8
7 | 2   3   3   3   8
8 | 2   3
```

A **scatterplot** displays paired data. Each data pair is represented by a point on a two dimensional graph. Actual data seldom follow the perfect lines and curves seen in other mathematics courses. The graph at right compares the gas mileage to the weight of numerous vehicles.

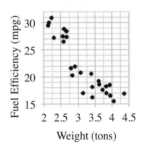

1-12.   Lynn asked some of her classmates how many people are normally at home for dinner. She recorded her results in the histogram shown at right.

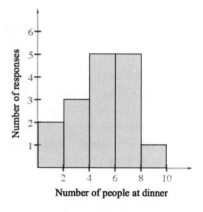

a.   How many classmates were surveyed?

b.   How many classmates have eight or nine people at home for dinner?

c.   Can you tell which is the most common number of people at home for dinner? Why or why not?

1-13.   Copy and complete the stem-and-leaf plot at right for the following set of data: 64, 87, 52, 12, 17, 23, 45, 88, 45, 92, 62, 76, 77, 34, and 53.

Key
1|2 means 12

```
1 | 2 7
2 |
3 |
4 |
5 |
6 |
7 |
8 |
9 |
```

1-14.   What is the best way to display the data below? Why? Display the data using the method you chose.

Daily high temperature for Honolulu, Hawaii in December of 2009:

83, 83, 81, 82, 80, 83, 81, 82, 79, 83, 84, 82, 81, 81, 80, 81, 84, 80, 80, 81, 81, 82, 80, 79, 78, 80, 84, 82, 82, 81, 83

1-15. Given the data in the table at right, copy and complete the histogram below to represent families of various sizes. Remember that data falling on a tick mark (3, 6, 9, …) goes in the bin to the right of that mark. What range do most families fall between? Do any families appear to be much larger or much smaller than other families?

Student	# of Family Members
LaTrese	4
James	8
Phu	7
Byron	3
Evan	2
Diamond	11
Jackie	5
Antonio	5
Shinna	6
Ryan	8

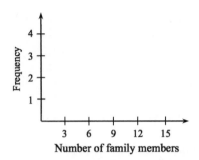

1-16. Ruth's brother, Ethan, planted a garden for her as a surprise while she was away. He planted seeds for vegetables in 50% of the garden. He also planted flowers and herbs.

The entire circle in the graph at right represents the area of Ruth's garden. If the lightly shaded portion represents flowers, estimate what percentage of the garden could be herbs. Explain your estimate.

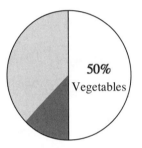

50%
Vegetables

1.1.3 How can I compare data representations?

Types of Data and Variables

In this lesson, you will identify characteristics of various types of data and choose the most descriptive ways to display and interpret it.

1-17. COMPARING WAYS TO REPRESENT DATA

Use the golf-tournament data below to complete parts (a) through (e).

Ages of golfers participating in a golf tournament: 25, 28, 29, 30, 32, 33, 34, 34, 35, 35, 37, 38, 40, 42, 43, 43, 43, 44, 44, 45, 45, 46, 47, 48, 50, 51, 57, 60, 63

a. Use the data to create a dot plot.

b. Create a stem-and-leaf plot for the data.

c. Use the stem-and-leaf plot to create a histogram for the data.

d. What are the most effective ways to represent this data? Why?

e. What range of ages do most golfers fall between? Do you see any ages that are much larger or smaller than other ages?

1-18. JUMPING FROG JUBILEE

A famous frog-jumping contest takes place each May in Calaveras County, California. For more than 90 years, contestants have been entering large bullfrogs into the contest. The frogs measure at least 4 inches long! The purpose of the contest is to see which frog can move the farthest in three hops.

Each year, people travel from around the country (and sometimes the world) to see the frogs jump.

When it is time to compete in the Jumping Frog Jubilee, the frog is put on a starting pad. The frog hops three times. Then the distance is measured from the center of the starting pad to the end of the third hop. This measurement is the official jump length.

Problem continues on next page →

1-18.   *Problem continued from previous page.*

Look carefully at the histogram. Use it to answer the questions below.

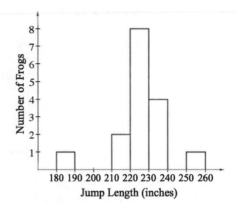
Jump Length (inches)

a.   Between which two numbers on the graph did the most frogs jump?

b.   Typical frogs jump between what two jump lengths?

c.   Were there any unusually long or short jumps?

d.   How many frogs are represented on this histogram?

e.   Half the frogs jumped less than how many inches?

MATH NOTES

Describing Shape (of a Data Distribution)

Statisticians use the words below to describe the shape of a data distribution

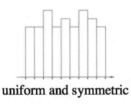

uniform and symmetric

positively skewed or
skewed to the right

symmetric and bell shaped

negatively skewed or
skewed to the left

1-19.   AN ASSOCIATION?

The Collectable Card Club wants to take a trip to their State's Card-a-Con. Felisia is trying to gather information to order club t-shirts in either male or female cuts, and arrange carpools, so she takes a census of the club's members.

31 males, 9 females, 13 members with cars, 27 without cars. She also notices that only one third of the girls have cars.

a.   Use her census information to make an appropriate chart or graph.

b.   Felisia is convinced there is a relationship between the variables "gender" and "having a car." Do you agree with Felisia? Justify your reasoning.

1-20.   In previous lessons you learned how to create dot plots, bar graphs, histograms, and stem-and-leaf plots. Which of these representations would best display the data given below? Use that representation to display the data.

Boot sizes of the Math Marching Team:
10, 8, 12, 10, 10, 9, 10, 11, 12, 8, 8, 9, 10, 11, 10, 9, 11, 11, 12, 11, 10, 11, 8, 10, 12, 8

1-21.   Jay, the manager at Housemart, is looking over data for the number of appliances sold for the month of August, but he spilled his coffee on the report and lost the number for the dishwashers category.

Washers: 27   Dryers: 18   Ovens: 14   Refrigerators: 31   Dishwashers:

Total: 113

a.   Help out Jay and recover the number of dishwashers sold in August:

b.   Jay tells you the average number of sold appliances for August is 22.6, so then the average appliance must be between a dryer and a dishwasher. Explain to Jay what is wrong with his interpretation by providing some examples of trying to average categories.

c.   What meaning can you assign to Jay's average of 22.6?

MATH NOTES

Types of Data and Variables

	Categorical	**Quantitative**	
Descriptions	The information collected is counted in named categories with no numerical order. Responses are often yes/no or true/false and are used to find percentages, proportions, or probabilities	The information collected is numeric in nature, usually a measurement with units of some kind.	
		Discrete responses are limited so you expect much of the data to have the same values: 0, 1, 2, 3, 4… pets	**Continuous** data is usually only limited by the precision of the tool or units used to make the measurement: 3.625, 3.630… cm
Example Questions	What percentage of students identify themselves as Jewish? Will the Governor's education bill pass?	What is the average number of children per household, or students per class?	What is the average income per household? What is the seasonal rainfall in Tulsa?
One-Variable Displays	bar graphs circle graphs	dot plots stem-and-leaf plots	histograms boxplots
Two-Variable Displays	two-way tables Venn diagrams	scatterplots	scatterplots

1-22.   Use the histogram at right to answer the following questions. The histogram contains the amount of snowfall in Urbana, IL during winter from 1990 to 2009.

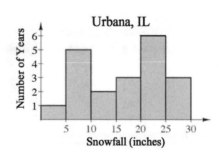

a.   Which range of snowfall measurements occurred most often?

b.   Were there any years with unusually high or low snowfall amounts?

c.   Half of the years had snowfall amounts above how many inches?

1-23.   The stem-and-leaf plot below contains the age of each of the United States presidents (as of 2016) at the time of their inauguration. Use it to answer the questions that follow.

        4│2 3 6 6 7 7 8 9 9
        5│0 1 1 1 1 1 2 2 4 4 4 4 4 5 5 5 5 6 6 6 7 7 7 7 8
        6│0 1 1 1 2 4 4 5 8 9

    a.   How old was the oldest president at the time of inauguration?

    b.   How old was the youngest?

1-24.   On your paper, copy the histogram at right, which represents some of the data about U.S. presidents from problem 1-23.

    a.   Fill in the missing bar. How did you decide how tall the bar should be?

    b.   How many U.S. presidents were younger than 50 years old at the time of their inauguration?

    c.   How many U.S. presidents are represented by this data?

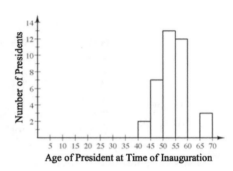

Age of President at Time of Inauguration

1-25.   Look at the two histograms below. They give you information about the heights of players on two basketball teams, the Tigers and the Panthers. Use the histograms to answer the following questions.

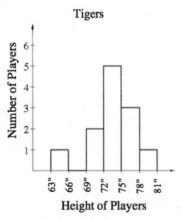

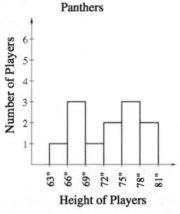

    a.   Which team has taller players? Which has shorter players? Explain your thinking.

    b.   Which team has heights that vary more? Explain your thinking.

    c.   Which team has more players that are about the same height?

1.2.1 What is a typical value?

Choosing Mean or Median

You are exposed to a huge amount of information every day in school, in the news, in advertising, and in other places. What you can learn from data? Today you will turn your attention to developing tools to be able to understand what the data means. Is there a typical value that can be used to describe the data?

1-26.   JUMPING FROG JUBILEE

In Lesson 1.1.3, you examined some results of the Calaveras County frog-jumping contest.

With your team, brainstorm ways that you could compare the two groups of frogs. Recall some of the measures of central tendency from previous courses.

2008		2009	
Frog Name	**Jump Length**	**Frog Name**	**Jump Length**
Skeeter Eater	231.5 in	For the Sign	252 in
Warped	230 in	Alex Frog	236.5 in
Greg Crome Dome	229 in	Shakit	231.5 in
R.G.	227 in	Six-Mile Shooter	226.75 in
The Well Ain't Dry	221.5 in	Spare the Air Every Day	223.25 in
Winner	220.5 in	Hooper	223.25 in
7 lb 8 oz. Baby	217 in	Jenifer's Jumper	222.25 in
Delbert Sr.	216.5 in	Dr. Frog	185.25 in

a.   Your first job is to make a graphical representation of the data. Many statisticians say that the first and most important step in analyzing any data is to make a graphical representation. How can a graphical representation help you analyze the data?

b.   Use the Univariate Data Explorer eTool to create histograms of the data, or look at the ones that your teacher displays for you. The bin size of each histogram should be 10 inches. Why is a histogram a better choice than a dot plot for this data?

c.   What was more obvious when you looked at the histograms compared to looking at the list of data? Is there information that is easier to see on the histograms?

d.   The eTool shows the mean and the median of the data below the histogram. However, if the mean and the median were not labeled, would there be a way to determine the median or mean from a histogram alone? Explain.

1-27.   Use the list of data in problem 1-26 or the histograms that you or your teacher made to continue to analyze and compare the frog jumps for 2008 and 2009. Answer the following questions.

    a.   What was the range of the jumps in each year? What does this tell you about the frog jumps?

    b.   What was the most typical jump length of the frogs each year? How did you find this value?

    c.   Were the jumps all about the same, or were some jumps outliers? Name any outliers and explain why you think they are outliers.

    d.   Compare as completely as you can the 2008 jumps to the 2009 jumps. Compare the center, shape, spread (range), and outliers. Then draw a conclusion: were one year's frogs a better group of jumpers than the other? How do you know?

1-28.   CHOOSING MEAN OR MEDIAN

    It is important to look at the distribution of the data when deciding whether to use the mean or the median.

    a.   In 2008, which represents a typical jump better, the mean or the median?

    b.   What if the 9th place jump in 2008 was very small, such as 160 inches? Redraw your histogram from problem 1-26 and include this new jump.

    c.   Without using a calculator, make a prediction. How does adding this outlier affect the mean and the median of the 2008 data?

    d.   Use a calculator to test your prediction from part (c).

    e.   Look at your histogram from part (b). Does the mean or does the median better represent a typical jump in 2008?

    f.   When does the median represent a typical jump better than the mean does?

1-29.   Even though there are outliers in the data, the mean and the median in 2009 are almost the same. Why?

1-30.   What if the 8th place jump length for 2009 was 222 inches instead? How would the mean and the median change? To answer this question, first make a prediction without using a calculator. Then test your prediction with a calculator.

1-31.   Efren has been keeping data on the Calaveras County
        frog-jumping contest for several years. Look carefully at
        the stem-and-leaf plot he made for the top 8 jumpers in
        2007, shown at right.

    a. What is the **minimum** (smallest) value? What is the
        maximum (largest) value?

    b. Are there any outliers in the data?

    c. Is it possible to find the median of the data from the
        stem-and-leaf plot? If so, find the median. If not,
        explain why not.

    d. Is it possible to find the mean with the stem-and-leaf
        plot? If so, calculate it and explain what the mean
        tells you about the frog jumps in 2007. If not,
        explain why not.

    e. Which represents a typical jump for 2007 better,
        the mean or the median?

    f. Create a new stem-and-leaf plot for the 2006 data
        at right. What is a typical jump for 2006?

**2007 Frog Jump Winners
Stem-and-Leaf Plot**

Note: 22 | 1 means 221 inches

22	1 2 5 8
23	4 8
24	5
25	6

2006

Frog Name	Jump Length
Clausenn's Cuzor	235 in
Whipper	222 in
Me Me Me Me	212 in
Haren's Heat	212 in
Midnight Croaker	209 in
Alex's Hopper	208 in
Oh Sweet Sue	205 in
Humpty Jumpty	204 in

1-32.   A visitor to the frog-jumping contest told stories about another contest he attended. He made
        the statements below. Find a possible set of data that would satisfy all of his statements.

    •   The measures of the jumps of the seven frogs were all integers and had a median of
        14 meters.

    •   The minimum jump length was 11 meters, and the maximum was 15 meters.

    •   The value 11 meters appears more often than any other value.

MATH NOTES

Measures of Central Tendency

Numbers that locate or approximate the "center" of a set of data are called the **measures of central tendency**. The mean and the median are measures of central tendency.

The **mean** is the arithmetic average of the data set. One way to compute the mean is to add the data elements and then to divide the sum by the number of items of data. The mean is generally the best measure of central tendency to use when the set of data is symmetric and without outliers.

The **median** is the middle number in a set of data arranged numerically. If there is an even number of values, the median is the average (mean) of the two middle numbers. The median is more accurate than the mean as a measure of central tendency when there are outliers in the data set or when the data is either not symmetric or skewed.

When dealing with measures of central tendency, it is often useful to consider the distribution of the data. For symmetric distributions with no outliers, the mean can represent the middle, or typical value, of the data well. However, in the presence of outliers or non-symmetrical distributions, the median may be a better measure.

Examples: Suppose the following data set represents the number of home runs hit by the best seven players on a Major League Baseball team:

$$16, 26, 21, 9, 13, 15, 9$$

The mean is $\frac{16+26+21+9+13+15+9}{7} = \frac{109}{7} \approx 15.57$.

The median is 15, since, when arranged in order (9, 9, 13, 15, 16, 21, 26), the middle number is 15.

MATH NOTES

Interquartile Range and Boxplots

Quartiles are points that divide a data set into four equal parts (and thus, the use of the prefix "quar" as in "quarter"). One of these points is the median. The **first quartile (Q1)** is the median of the lower half, and the **third quartile (Q3)** is the median of the upper half.

To find quartiles, the data set must be placed in order from smallest to largest. Note that if there are an odd number of data values, the median is not included in either half of the data set.

Suppose you have the data set: 22, 43, 14, 7, 2, 32, 9, 36, and 12.

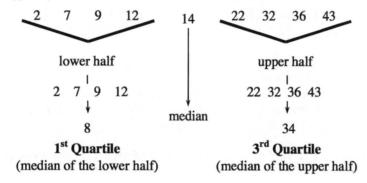

The **interquartile range (IQR)** is the difference between the third and first quartiles. It is used to measure the spread (the variability) of the middle 50% of the data. The interquartile range is $34 - 8 = 26$.

A **boxplot** (also known as a box-and-whisker plot) displays a five number summary of data: minimum, first quartile, median, third quartile, and maximum. The box contains "the middle half" of the data and visually displays how large the IQR is. The right segment represents the top 25% of the data and the left segment represents the bottom 25% of the data. A boxplot makes it easy to see where the data are spread out and where they are concentrated. The wider the box, the more the data are spread out.

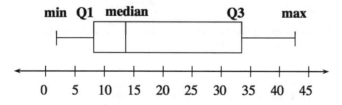

MATH NOTES

Comparing Boxplots and Showing Outliers

When comparing data with graphics, the representations should be drawn above the same scaled axis. When two boxplots are drawn on the same axis, they are called **parallel boxplots**. An example is shown at right.

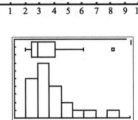

Outliers are any data values that are far away from the bulk of the data distribution. Identifying outliers is important because often they require additional inquiry. "Why does a student have 19 pets? Did they follow the class definition? Was it a calculation or recording error?" In the example at right, data values in the right-most bin are outliers. Outliers are marked on a **modified boxplot** with a dot.

For convenience statisticians have created several ways to mathematically identify how far-out a data point is before it is considered an outlier. None of them are effective in all situations. For guidance this course will use one of the most widely used rules called the "**1.5 IQR Rule**," which holds that:

Points greater than Q3 + (1.5)(IQR) or less than Q1 – (1.5)(IQR) are worthy of consideration as outliers.

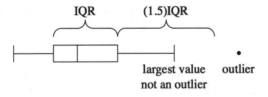

Review & Preview

1-33. A sample of 23 newborns at the Dallas University Health Center had the following lengths in centimeters. The measurements have been sorted from lowest to highest.

46.4, 46.9, 47.7, 48.1, 48.5, 48.5, 48.8, 49.0, 49.3, 50.0, 50.1, 50.4, 50.6, 51.1, 51.4, 51.8, 52.4, 52.5, 53.2, 53.8, 54.4, 55.1, 55.9

Find the **five number summary** of the lengths of the newborns. A five number summary includes the minimum, first quartile, median, third quartile, and maximum. Do not use a calculator. For help with quartiles, see the Math Notes box above.

1-34.   The GPAs of a sample of 26 community college applicants were selected and
          listed in ascending order below. Do not use a calculator for this problem.

          1.58   1.87   2.32   2.44   2.46   2.46   2.50   2.63   2.69
          2.72   2.78   2.81   2.83   2.99   3.10   3.16   3.30   3.42
          3.46   3.49   3.54   3.67   3.75   3.87   3.89   4.29

   a.   Find the five number summary of the GPAs of these
          applicants.

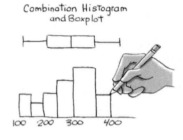

Combination Histogram
and Boxplot

   b.   On grid paper, create a combination histogram and
          boxplot. Use an interval of 0.5 on the x-axis. (A
          combination histogram and boxplot starts with a
          histogram. Then place a boxplot on top of the
          histogram. Help with creating a boxplot is in the
          Math Notes box for this lesson. Use the same x-axis
          scale for both the histogram and the boxplot.)

   c.   Describe the center, shape, spread, and outliers. To review descriptions of "shape," see
          the Math Notes box in the next lesson. To describe "spread" use the IQR, reviewed in the
          Math Notes box in this lesson.

1-35.   The weights of 19 hummingbirds are given below in ounces. Create a histogram for the data
          and use it to justify whether the mean or the median is a better choice for a typical
          hummingbird's weight and calculate it.

          $4, 5, 7, 8, 8, 9, 9, 9, 9, 10, 10, 10, 10, 10, 10, 10, 11, 11, 11$

1-36.   Mrs. Sakata is correcting math tests. Here are the scores for the first fourteen tests she has
          corrected: $62, 65, 93, 51, 55, 12, 79, 85, 55, 72, 78, 83, 91,$ and 76. Which score does not seem
          to fit in this set of data? Without calculating, explain how the outlier score affects the mean
          and the median of the data?

1.2.2 How can I measure variability?

Variance and Standard Deviation

In the previous lesson you considered whether it is more appropriate to use the mean or median to describe the central tendency of a particular data set. Today you will look at variability and choose the best statistic to represent the spread of a particular data set.

1-37.   Assume a biologist is trying to determine which sugar is more successful in growing a particular eukaryotic cell. She collected the data below (diameter in micrometers (μm)).

Sugar W: 10, 32, 32, 34, 34, 36, 37, 39, 39, 40, 41, 43, 43, 44, 45, 46, **46, 49, 70**

Sugar P: 10, 10, 15, 20, 25, 28, 30, 32, 35, 40, 45, 48, 50, 52, 55, 60, 65, 70, 70

a.   Make a combination histogram and boxplot for each sugar. (Use an interval of 10 to 80 with a bin width of 10.)

b.   Find the mean and median of both collections of data.

c.   The two sets of data are obviously not the same. Which statistic(s) differentiate between these two data sets? You do not need to calculate the statistic. If the biologist wants to consistently grow large cells, which sugar should she use?

1-38.   MEASURING SPREAD

a.   One way to measure the spread of data is to calculate the **range** (maximum minus minimum). What range of cell sizes did each sugar grow? Why is the range often not a useful measure of spread?

b.   Another method for measuring the spread is the average distance to the mean, called the **mean absolute deviation**. Find the distance each value is to the mean (remember to use absolute value because distances are positive!), and find the mean distance. Compare the mean absolute deviation of Sugar W to Sugar P.

c.   A mean absolute deviation should not be calculated if the data has outliers or is not symmetric. Why?

d.   When the data is not symmetric or has outliers, the interquartile range (IQR) can be used to measure spread. Compare the IQR of the two sugars. If you need a reminder, read the Math Notes box about calculating IQR at the end of Lesson 1.2.1.

1-39. **VARIANCE AND STANDARD DEVIATION**

Statisticians prefer to make numbers positive by squaring them instead of using the absolute value. From algebra you know the inverse function of a square root is a quadratic. Quadratics are relatively easy to work with in higher mathematics while the inverse of an absolute value function cannot be expressed as a function at all which causes complications.

The variance is a measure of how much variability there is in a data set. The **variance** is the average of all the distances to the mean, after the distances have been made positive by squaring.

The **standard deviation** is yet another measure of how much variability there is in a data set. The standard deviation is simply the square root of the variance. What advantage is there in reporting the standard deviation instead of the variance?

1-40.   Without using a graphing calculator, find the variance and standard deviation of each sugar in problem 1-37. Compare the variability (the spread) of the two sugars.

1-41.   Your teacher will demonstrate how to find the standard deviation using a calculator. Verify the standard deviations of the two sugars in problem 1-40 using a calculator.

1-42.   An environmental engineering group has collected data on top soils at 26 sites to determine the levels of lead contamination in parts per million (ppm). The sorted results are as follows:

100, 100, 150, 200, 250, 300, 310, 320, 340, 350, 360, 390, 400, 400, 430, 440, 450, 450, 460, 500, 500, 550, 600, 650, 650, 690   *checksum: 10340*

Determine if the mean and standard deviation is an appropriate way to summarize this data. If so, find the mean and standard deviation with a calculator. If not, use the median and IQR.

MATH NOTES

Describing Spread (of a Data Distribution)

A distribution of data can be summarized by describing its center, shape, spread, and outliers. You have learned four ways to describe the spread.

Interquartile Range (IQR)
The variability, or spread, in the distribution can be numerically summarized with the interquartile range (IQR). The IQR is found by subtracting the first quartile from the third quartile. The IQR is the range of the middle half of the data. IQR can represent the spread of any data distribution, even if the distribution is not symmetric or has outliers.

Standard Deviation $= \sqrt{\text{variance}}$
Either the variance or standard deviation can be used to represent the spread if the data is reasonably symmetric and has no strong outliers. The standard deviation of a population is the square root of the average of the distances to the mean, after the distances have been made positive by squaring.

$$\sigma_x = \sqrt{\frac{\sum_{i=1}^{n}(x_i-\mu)^2}{n}}$$

Informally, the standard deviation represents a typical distance one could expect to find a data value from the mean.

Where n = the number of data points, x_i is a data point, and μ is the population mean, Σ is an uppercase Greek sigma which represents a summation.

For example, for the data 10 12 14 16 18 kilograms:

- The mean is 14 kg.
- The distances of each data value to the mean are $-4, -2, 0, 2, 4$ kg.
- The distances squared are $16, 4, 0, 4, 16 \text{ kg}^2$.
- The sum of those squared distances is 40 kg^2.
- The mean distance-squared is 8 kg^2.
- The square root is 2.83 kg. The standard deviation is 2.83 kg.

Range
The range (maximum minus minimum) is usually not a very good way to describe the spread because it considers only the extreme values in the data, rather than how the bulk of the data is spread.

1-43.   There are five students of different ages. Their
median age is 13 years.

a.   What are two possibilities for the ages of
the three oldest students?

b.   If each student is a different age, how
many students must be younger than 13?

c.   In complete sentences, describe what a
median is to another student in the class. Pretend that the student was absent the day you
learned about medians.

1-44.   Match the histogram to its corresponding boxplot.

a.   b.   c.   d.   e.

i.   ii.   iii.   iv.   v.

1-45.   You previously created a five number summary of the lengths of 23 newborns at the Dallas
University Health Center. The measurements, in centimeters, were:

46.4, 46.9, 47.7, 48.1, 48.5, 48.5, 48.8, 49.0, 49.3, 50.0, 50.1, 50.4, 50.6, 51.1, 51.4, 51.8, 52.4,
52.5, 53.2, 53.8, 54.4, 55.1, 55.9   *checksum: 1165.9*

Determine if it is appropriate to summarize the data with the mean and standard deviation. If it
is appropriate, justify your reasoning and find the mean and standard deviation. If it is not
appropriate, explain why not, and find the median and IQR. Consider the precision of the
measurements when giving the result.

1.2.3 How can I measure sample variability?

Sample Variance and Sample Standard Deviation

One of the purposes of Statistics is to make decisions with sample information and one of the dangers of sampling is the introduction of bias. Bias can creep in unexpected places and one of those is the variance and standard deviation. The next two problems are an unlikely example with very simple data, but can be extended to all cases of sampling.

1-46.   The Planet Claire has pink air and some unusual inhabitants. Every citizen of Planet Claire has either one or five pet rocks. You may assume there are equal numbers of 1-rock and 5-rock citizens and the overall population of Planet Claire is in the millions.

   a.   Find the mean pet rock ownership of a citizen of Planet Claire.

   b.   Find the population variance of the pet rock ownership.

1-47.   NASA has sent a deep space probe to Claire to survey its citizens about pet rock ownership. Space travel is very expensive and the probe only has the capacity to survey two citizens at random on the planet.

   a.   There are 4 equally likely outcomes of pet rock ownership the NASA probe could find in its random survey of two citizens. List them.

   b.   Calculate a variance for each sample listed in part (a).

1-48.   If NASA were able to send many of these probes what would be the average value for the variance in pet rock ownership?

   a.   Compare the population variance you found in part (b) of problem 1-46 with the mean of the variances found in the samples. Summarize the bias in variance calculations shown in this example.

   b.   Now repeat your four variance calculations from part (b) of problem 1-47, this time dividing the sum of squared differences by $(n - 1)$ or 1 instead of n or 2. This adjustment to the denominator makes each resulting value a **sample variance**.

   c.   What is the average of these new sample variances? How does it compare to the population variance in part (b) of problem 1-46?

MATH NOTES

Two Types of Variance and Standard Deviation

An important distinction between parameters and statistics is in how the data and calculations will be used.

	Population Parameters	**Sample Statistics**
Descriptions	Parameters are for making statements or comparisons about the set of subjects that were measured directly.	Sample statistics may be used to make inferences or predictions about the populations they came from.
Variance	$$\sigma_x^2 = \frac{\sum\limits_{i=1}^{n}(x_i - \mu)^2}{n}$$	The **sample variance** is an unbiased estimator of the population variance. $$s_x^2 = \frac{\sum\limits_{i=1}^{n}(x_i - \bar{x})^2}{n-1}$$
Standard Deviation	$$\sigma_x = \sqrt{\frac{\sum\limits_{i=1}^{n}(x_i - \mu)^2}{n}}$$	$$s_x = \sqrt{\frac{\sum\limits_{i=1}^{n}(x_i - \bar{x})^2}{n-1}}$$

Inference from samples is very common in the field of Statistics. When you are asked to calculate a variance or standard deviation in this course, you may assume the sample statistics are most appropriate.

1-49.   The speeds (in miles per hour) of a sample of motorists ticketed during one day on a five-mile stretch of highway are sorted and listed below.

70, 70, 71, 72, 73, 73, 74, 75, 75, 80, 80, 83, 84, 85, 85, 86, 88, 88, 89, 89 mph
checksum: 1590

Make a combination histogram and boxplot, starting at 70 mph with a bin width of 4 mph. Describe the center, shape, spread, and outliers. Use the mean and standard deviation if appropriate.

1-50.   Eleanor is an avid gardener, but rabbits keep eating her prize vegetables! She begins to research the rabbits, and is trying to decide on a dog or a cat to help keep them away. She want to make sure that her dog or cat will be fast enough, so she measures the speed (in miles per hour) of a random sample of rabbits as they run away.

a.   Use the graphical displays at right to describe the distribution of rabbit speeds. Apply an appropriate rule to justify the presence of outliers.

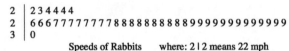

Speeds of Rabbits (mph)

b.   What is one feature of the data that is easily seen in the stem-and-leaf plot that is missing in the boxplot?

```
2 | 2 3 4 4 4 4
2 | 6 6 6 7 7 7 7 7 7 7 8 8 8 8 8 8 8 8 8 9 9 9 9 9 9 9 9 9 9 9 9
3 | 0
```

Speeds of Rabbits   where: 2 | 2 means 22 mph

c.   What is one feature of the data that is seen in the boxplot that is not easily seen in the stem-and-leaf plot?

1-51.   Eleanor's friend Kaimana is just as annoyed with rabbits and is keeping similar data. Kaimana's data is displayed in the histogram at right.

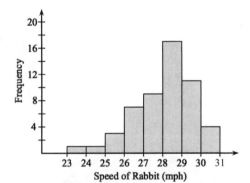

a.   Use the histogram to calculate an accurate estimate for the mean speed of rabbits from Kaimana's sample. Show your work!

b.   Estimate the median speed. Explain how you obtained your answer.

c.   Estimate the sample variance and standard deviation. You may use appropriate technology to obtain your answer.

d.   Explain, in this context, the meaning of the standard deviation you found in part (c).

1-52.   A school survey showed that 153 students owned πPods, 53 students owned πPhones, 17 students owned both, and 246 students owned neither.

a.   What is the ratio of πPod only owners to πPhone only owners?

b.   What is the ratio of πPhone only owners to those that have neither a πPhone nor a πPod?

c.   What would be the best way to display this data? Review Lessons 1.1.1 and 1.1.2 for the types of data displays you have learned about in this course. Justify your answer.

1.2.4 How do I compare data?

. . . .

Investigating Data Representations

In this lesson you will continue your study of one-variable quantitative data by modeling a golf tournament.

1-53.   THIRTY SIX HOLES OF GOLF

The Hookenslise Corporation is having its annual charity fundraising event. In order to encourage donors to attend, the Hookenslise organizes a fun game called "Thirty Six Holes of Golf" and gives away prizes.

Each team plays thirty six holes of golf. There is a prize for the team that is consistently closest to the hole. Your teacher has set up a "hole." Your team will "swing" thirty six pennies toward the "hole." You will then represent your data on a graph and with numerical statistics. Analyzing the statistics will help you decide which team was the most consistently close to the hole.

Your Task:

- Your teacher will give you nine pennies. Have one team member stand 7 feet (215 cm) from the "hole." That team member will toss all nine pennies. No "do-overs" and no practice shots are allowed. Then record the distance from the center of each penny to the "hole" (to the nearest centimeter), even if the penny rolled far away.

- Repeat with different team members until 36 pennies have been tossed. Do not take turns tossing pennies—each team member should toss all their pennies, one at a time. Then the next team member can take their turn.

- When directed by the teacher, return to the classroom. Decide how you want to represent your data in your presentation: dot plot, boxplot, circle graph, scatterplot, histogram, or bar graph.

- Decide the four most important facts you wish to report about your team's golf shots and add them to your presentation.

- Record your team's data in a safe place. You will need it in the next lesson.

- Your teacher will direct you on how to compare your team's results with the other teams. Which team was most consistently close to the hole?

MATH NOTES

Comparing Distributions of Data

A comparison of data sets is not just a list of statistics. Numbers must be given context and contrasted between the samples. It should be clearly understood if read on its own by someone with limited knowledge of formal statistics.

Black swans are native to Australia and New Zealand. While in the Southern Hemisphere describing encroached upon preserves of black swans, assume Daniella studied measurements from two geographically distinct samples of swans and gave the following comparison of swan lengths:

Provide a meaningful graphical comparison of the data sets such as parallel box plots or histograms made on the same scale.

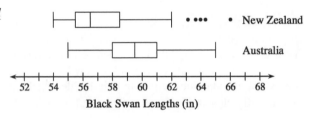

Black Swan Lengths (in)

Compare the shapes of the distributions, including significant gaps or clusters.

The distribution of black swan lengths in the first sample appears to be right (or positively) skewed with a cluster of longer swans between 63 and 65 inches, while the shape of the second sample is nearly symmetric and perhaps bell shaped.

Compare the centers in context using appropriate units. Do not simply list statistics.

A median Australian black swan is about 59.5 inches long, even longer than the 3rd quartile New Zealand black swan, and about 3 inches longer than the median New Zealand black swan in the samples.

Compare the spread of the data and discuss outliers, if appropriate.

There was a larger range of lengths among the sample of New Zealand black swans because of several large outliers. However the interquartile ranges of both sample is about three inches, meaning the middle half of all swans in each sample are within three inches in length.

1-54.   Megan is an industrial engineer for Coyner Cola Company. She takes a random sample of cola cans from the production line each day to determine if the product meets various specifications. One of the measurements she records is the mass (in grams) of the filled cans. The following sorted data are from of a sample of 30 regular and diet cola cans.

Note: The data is sorted so it is easy to use without a statistical calculator.

Regular

361	362	363	365	366	366	367	367	367	368
368	368	369	369	369	369	370	370	370	370
371	371	371	371	373	375	375	376	376	380

checksum: 11083

Diet

349	349	350	351	353	353	353	354	354	354
354	355	355	355	356	357	358	361	361	361
361	361	361	362	362	363	364	365	366	366

checksum: 10724

a.   Find the five number summary (minimum, third quartile, median, first quartile, maximum) for each soda.

b.   Make a combination histogram and boxplot for each type of soda. Include the five number summary. Scale the an *x*-axis from 348 to 384 grams and use a bin width of 4 grams.

c.   Describe the center, shape, spread, and any outliers, of each histogram.

d.   Compare the two samples.

e.   Each can is marked as containing 12 fluid ounces. 12 ounces is about 341 grams. Why is there so much variation from 341 grams in the samples?

1-55.   The Toronto Hawks football team is having a meeting with fans to discuss salaries. The team president says, *"We cannot afford to be any more generous because our average salary is almost $2,000,000 a year."* A fan replies, *"Nonsense. Your average player only makes $850,000 a year—you can easily afford a raise."* If they are using the same set of data, how can their averages be different? How could such a large difference have occurred?

1-56.   The owner of Universal Widgets has two teams of employees and
wants to know which team is working the "best." The assistant
manager gathered data for the number of widgets made per team
member on various days. He presented the data to the owner as
two boxplots, shown at right. The owner is confused.

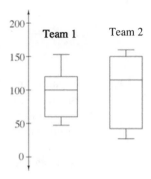

a.   Help the owner decide which team is working the "best"
by comparing center, shape, spread, and outliers.

b.   Which team had a smaller standard deviation? Explain.

1.3.1 Where do I stand?

Percentiles

Data is often not meaningful unless it is compared to other data. What interest is your batting average or free throw average if you are the only person who has one? What interest is your SAT score if there are no other scores to compare to?

1-57.   DO COLLEGE ATHLETES EARN MORE?

A 2005 study at the State University of New York looked at college athletes' earnings six years after graduation to determine if college athletes tended to earn more in their full-time jobs than non-athletes. The data is below.

Annual Earnings (in thousands of dollars)	Number of Non-Athletes	Number of Athletes
$0 to $27	11	7
$27 to $54	9	8
$54 to $81	28	25
$81 to $108	26	27
$108 to $135	16	21
$135 to $162	6	6
$162 to $189	2	4
$189 to $216	1	1
$216 to $243	1	1

a.   How many athletes were interviewed? How many non-athletes?

b.   By looking at your data representation, estimate the five number summary for non-athletes and athletes.

c.   The U.S. median household income was around $54,000 at the time of the survey. What percentage of non-athletes and athletes made less than the median household income?

d.   Someone can be considered wealthy if they make over $216,000 per year. What percentage of non-athletes made less than $216,000? What percentage of athletes made less than $216.000?

1-58.   ESCAPE IN MINNEAPOLIS

Cory, Jamison, and Harper love puzzles of all kinds,
so when they heard about a new escape room
business in Minneapolis they were excited to try it.
An escape room is an elaborate puzzle where teams
of participants are "locked" into a room and need to
solve a series of problems and riddles in order to
escape. Teams can compete against one another by
getting scored based on a function with a domain that
includes the time it took to escape and the number of
clues required to do it. After overcoming all of the mental challenges and earning their
freedom from a room called *The Library*, the Puzzle Master congratulated each of them and
said, *"Your team score is 55."* Cory, Jamison, and Harper are now staring blankly at the
Puzzle Master, beginning to wonder if this is yet another challenge.

a.   If you were in this trio and could ask the Puzzle Master two questions about the team's
score, what would they be?

b.   The Puzzle Master sees their blank stares and says, *"You did well. About 300 teams have
tried to escape from The Library and the average team score for that particular escape
room is 43."* Harper then remembers seeing the top scores for each room posted at the
front desk when they arrived. The top team score for *The Library* was 84 points. Cory
then asks, *"Did we get the second highest score ever?"* Is that possible? Explain your
thinking to Cory.

c.   The Puzzle Master can tell that the information she has given them about their team score
is only leading to more questions, so she goes to her desk and hands them the following
chart, saying, *"Here is the ogive,"* (pronounced oh-jive) before leaving abruptly.

Score Ogive

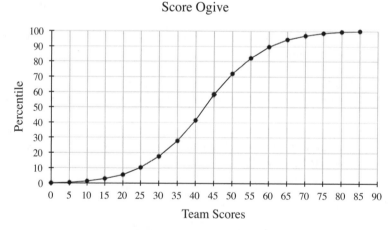

After some thought Cory reasons that the ogive is a graph of a function that uses scores
and converts them to percentile rankings. Use Cory's idea and the ogive to read the
approximate percentile corresponding to their team score of 55?

d.   If there were about 300 teams scored for this escape room, about how many did they
outscore? About how many teams did better?

Problem continues on next page →

Statistics

1-58.   *Problem continued from previous page.*

    e.   Jamison notices that the chart can be read "backwards" as an inverse function that inputs percentiles and outputs team scores. Use Jamison's observation and the ogive to approximate the team score corresponding to the 10th percentile.

    f.   Use the ogive to estimate a five number summary for all of the scores.

1-59.   THE DISTRIBUTION OF INCOME AMONG COLLEGE ATHLETES

Revisit the data from problem 1-57, this time focusing just on the athlete's column.

    a.   Without using a calculator, sketch a histogram of the income data for athletes. Scale the *x*-axis from 0 to 243 (thousand dollars) and use a bin width of 27 (thousand dollars).

    b.   Divide the frequencies of each bin by the total number of athletes in the survey so each bin now has a corresponding proportion. These proportions are called **relative frequencies**. Make a **relative frequency histogram** by scaling the height of the histogram bars with the relative frequencies. Compare it to the histogram you made in part (a). What do you notice?

    c.   Using the same *x*-scale for yearly earnings, use the relative frequencies to make an ogive of the income of the athletes. Keep in mind that an ogive is also known as a cumulative relative frequency chart.

    d.   Using the ogive estimate the percentile ranking of an athlete who made $100,000 per year? What income corresponds to the 10th and 90th percentiles?

MATH NOTES

Relative Frequency Histograms and Ogives

Examine this temperature data assumed to be collected from a sample of classroom temperatures at Buena High School.

Room Temps (°F)	Rooms (f)
55 to 60	0
60 to 65	3
65 to 70	11
70 to 75	16
75 to 80	9
80 to 85	1
total	40

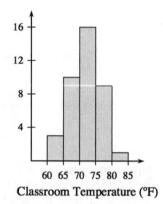

Here the relative frequencies have been computed and **the** histogram converted to a **relative frequency histogram**. Notice that only the scale of the *y*-axis has changed.

Room Temps (°F)	Rooms (f)	Relative f ($f \div 40$)
55 to 60	0	0
60 to 65	3	0.075
65 to 70	11	0.275
70 to 75	16	0.4
75 to 80	9	0.225
80 to 85	1	0.025
total	40	1

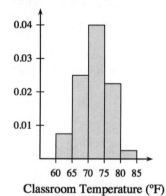

Now the **cumulative relative frequencies** are added and the ogive created. In fact, ogives are often called **cumulative relative frequency graphs**.

Room Temps (°F)	Rooms (f)	Cumulative Relative f
55 to 60	0	0
60 to 65	3	0.075
65 to 70	11	0.35
70 to 75	16	0.75
75 to 80	9	0.975
80 to 85	1	1

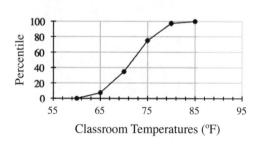

1-60. A principal made the histogram at right to analyze how many years that teachers had been teaching at her school.

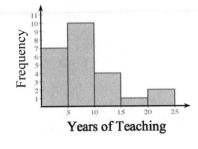

Years of Teaching

a. How many teachers work at her school?

b. If you chose a teacher at random, what is the probability the teacher has been there for fewer than 5 years?

c. Convert the information shown in the histogram to a cumulative relative frequency table and ogive.

d. Use the ogive to estimate the IQR of the data.

1-61. Eduardo's 12 friends guessed how many jelly beans were in a jar at his birthday party. Here is an ogive of their guesses:

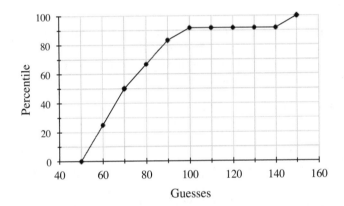

Use the information from the ogive to create a histogram of the original data.

1-62. Duncan is testing two types of memory chips (W and Z) for performance and reliability. One test involves a measurement of the maximum electrical current in milliamperes required by the chip when storing and retrieving 14 different data sets. A lower required current means greater energy efficiency.

Data Set

	A	B	C	D	E	F	G	H	I	J	K	L	M	N
Chip W	130	130	132	132	133	133	133	134	135	135	135	137	137	137

checksum: 1873

	A	B	C	D	E	F	G	H	I	J	K	L	M	N
Chip Z	129	131	131	132	132	132	133	133	133	133	134	137	138	140

checksum: 1868

a. When Duncan is trying to summarize the data, he finds the IQR for chip W is larger, but the standard deviation for chip Z is larger. Both are measures of spread. How can they be conflicting? Use combination histogram and boxplots in your explanation.

b. Which chip should Duncan recommend to the manufacturer? Justify your choice.

1-63. Jet Set claims that they are more "on time" than National Airways because National was delayed over an hour a couple times. Arin did not believe Jet Set was more "on time" so he looked up the data for both airlines during the last two weeks. Below is the data he found for departure delays. Negative numbers indicate that a flight departed earlier than scheduled.

National Airways:
69, 22, –3, –7, 2, 25, 7, 0, –3, 14, –4, 0, –1, –9, –2, 4, 12, 25, 65, –10 *checksum: 206*

Jet Set:
6, –5, 33, 4, 37, 10, 23, 5, 21, 31, 2, –5, 35, 42, 19, –8, 25, 15 *checksum: 290*

a. Compare the center, shape, spread, and outliers of the data sets. Use the values you calculate to make an argument as to which airline is on time more often. Use a bin width of 10 minutes on your histograms.

b. Arin wants to summarize his findings with just two numbers: the center and spread. Can he use mean and standard deviation, or should he use median and IQR? Justify your choice, then summarize the data for Arin.

1.3.2 Where else do I stand?

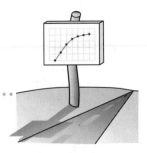

z-Scores

As you learned in the previous lesson, data is often not meaningful unless it is compared to other data.

1-64. ESCAPE IN MINNEAPOLIS II

Cory, Jamison, and Harper are back in another escape room in Minneapolis. After another round of overcoming all of the mental challenges and earning their freedom a room called *The Basement,* they sat waiting to get their score and perhaps another ogive. The Puzzle Master soon congratulated each of them again and said, *"Your score is 203 points. The mean score for The Basement is 140 with a standard deviation of 35."* Cory, Jamison, and Harper now again staring blankly at the Puzzle Master, are beginning to wonder if she is actually a Statistics teacher.

Cory, Jamison, and Harper then spot their classmates Latavia, McKenna, and Kirk emerging from a different escape room called *The Apartment,* looking victorious. *"We just dominated that room!"* shouted McKenna. The Puzzle Master arrives and tells them simply *"Your score was 220 and the average for the Apartment is 140 with a standard deviation of 45."* Kirk begins some kind of spasmodic victory dance and Latavia asks, *"How did you guys do?"*

a. Because the six classmates all know each other and have a passion for puzzling, a spirited argument erupts over what team has the most skill. Which team displayed more evidence of their problem solving prowess today? Explain your thinking.

The Puzzle Master hears the commotion and says, *"One way to compare scores from different rooms is by standardizing. A standardized score, also called a z-score, is the number of standard deviations above or below the mean your team score is."*

b. Determine the z-score for each team. Show your work. Which team wins the day?

c. If another team had a z-score of –2 for the *The Basement* room, what was their team score? Show your work.

d. In this problem a higher z-score is "better." Think of at least two situations where a lower z-score would be desirable.

1-65.   Live oak wood is heavy but very strong. The frame of the USS Constitution was constructed from southern live oak. Imani is in Alabama researching principal supplies of southern live oaks. Imani believes the distribution of oak specific gravities have a mean of 0.854 (unitless ratio) and a standard deviation of 0.053.

a.   What is the standardized z-score of a southern live oak specific gravity of 0.788?

b.   What is the specific gravity of a southern live oak sample with a standardized z-score of 1.54?

c.   What is more <u>unusual</u>, a southern live oak sample with a z-score or of –1.253, or a sample with a z-score of 1.714? Explain your thinking.

1-66.   I'M MELTING!

Granite is one of the oldest known industrial building materials. Valentina is in Utah investigating natural supplies of granites. Valentina believes the distribution of granite melting temperatures have a mean of 1239°C and a standard deviation of 15.7°C.

a.   A particular sample melts at 1204°C. What is its standardized z-score?

b.   She melts a particular sample and calculates its standardized score to be $z = -1.554$. What was its melting point?

c.   Further investigations by Valentina revealed a granite sample which melted at 1272°C, while Imani from the previous problem has a southern live oak sample with a specific gravity of 0.701. Which one is the more unusual find? Explain.

MATH NOTES

Standardized Scores (z-Scores)

A **standardized score** represents the number of standard deviations away from the mean a particular observation lies. It is a *unitless* quantity that can be used as a measure of relative standing for both population and sample data.

$$z = \frac{x - \mu}{\sigma}$$

parameter

$$z = \frac{x - \bar{x}}{s_x}$$

statistic

While working at his school's 5K fun-run fundraiser, Deion found all of the runner's times had a mean of 24.55 minutes and a standard deviation of 2.29 minutes. Then he sketched a histogram of the all of the race time results.

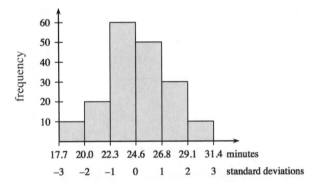

Deion's little sister Janette won the 6th grade category with a time of 26.55 minutes and his friend Giselle set a personal record in the high school girls category with a time of 22.83 minutes. He calculated their z-score as follows:

$$z_J = \frac{26.55 - 24.55}{2.29} = 0.873 \qquad z_G = \frac{22.83 - 24.55}{2.29} = -0.751$$

Deion notes that sometimes a negative z-score is more desirable like in a timed race where the lower time represents a better ranking. He is proud of his sister and friend but notices in the context of all of the runners their times are fairly ordinary, both being within one standard deviation of the mean. The larger the magnitude of a z-score, the more unusual its corresponding data point.

1-67.   The ice cream consumption in a sample of several countries is given in the table at right.

a.   How many countries are represented?

b.   Display the data in a histogram. Make the bins 4 liters per person wide (0 to 4, 4 to 8, etc.).

c.   Calculate the mean. Why is it an appropriate measure of center for this data?

d.   Measure the spread (variability) of the data by finding the sample standard deviation.

e.   Find the z-score for Chile's per capita ice cream consumption.

f.   Find the countries with the highest and lowest z-scores. Which represents the more unique score?

Ice Cream Consumption (2007)	
Country	Liters per Person
Australia	18.0
Canada	8.7
Chile	5.6
China	1.9
Denmark	8.7
Finland	14.0
Ireland	9.0
Italy	9.2
Japan	0.01
Malaysia	2.0
New Zealand	22.5
Sweden	11.9
United Kingdom	6.0
United States	18.3

1-68.   The city of Waynesboro is trying to decide whether to
         initiate a composting project where each residence would
         be provided with a dumpster for garden and yard waste.
         The city manager needs some measure of assurance that
         the citizens will participate before launching the project,
         so he chooses a random sample of 25 homes and provides
         them with the new dumpster for yard and garden waste.
         After one week the contents of each dumpster is weighed
         (in pounds) before processing. The sorted data is shown
         below:

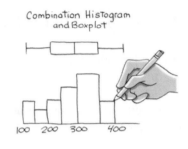

Combination Histogram
and Boxplot

0.0	0.0	0.0	0.0	1.7	2.6	2.9	4.2	4.4
5.1	5.6	6.4	8.0	8.9	9.7	10.1	11.2	13.5
15.1	16.3	17.7	21.4	22.0	22.2	36.5		

checksum: 245.5

a.   Create a combination boxplot and histogram. Use an interval of 0 to 42 pounds on the
      x-axis and a bin width of 6 pounds.

b.   Describe the center, shape, spread, and outliers.

c.   What is a better measure of center for this distribution the mean or median and why?

d.   What is a better measure of spread the standard deviation or IQR and why?

e.   The city can sell the compost, and engineers estimate the program will be profitable if
      each home averages at least 9 pounds of material. The city manager sees the mean is
      nearly 10 pounds and is ready to order dumpsters for every residence. What advice would
      you give him?

1-69.   SAVED BY THE STATS

         Mr. Temp was working with a spreadsheet when his computer suddenly shutdown. Ugh, darn
         batteries! After a recharge he was shocked to find that he lost all of the critical expense data
         from January AND the first week from every month! Temp's ranting attracted the attention of
         some coworkers. Tex Avie, the computer guy, said electronic recovery was not possible but
         Stacy Istic took one look and said it was no big deal.

         What is she thinking? Recover Mr. Temp's data if possible.

Critical Expense Report ($1000)

wk	Jan	Feb	Mar	Apr	May	Jun	Jul	Aug	Sep	Oct	Nov	Dec	tot
1													
2		71	76	54	67	35	90	49	93	61	45	91	787
3		80	94	96	53	68	63	77	58	76	42	84	853
4		87	80	80	42	42	97	36	41	55	59	40	734
tot		318	310	305	249	182	315	214	275	240	222	264	3106

1.3.3 What if I change the units of measure?

....

Linear Transformations

Today you will learn how various statistics respond when the all of the data has been transformed by a linear equation.

Ollie and Caspar love baseball and baseball statistics. During a night game seventh inning stretch, Ollie asked Caspar if he knew the average career length for a Major League Baseball (MLB) player. Caspar used his smartphone to check on baseball statistics for first-year players and discovered that a rookie might play approximately 5.6 years, less than half of the rookies actually last to play a fifth year, and most are retired before the age of 30.

Now Ollie wants to know how many MLB players had long careers. Caspar checked the statistics website again and found 34 retired ball players whose last seasons ranged from 1897 to 2012. Some had careers that lasted up to five decades and retired at ages 45 and upward, which shows once again that age is not anything but a number!

Caspar wants to make a Statistics problem out of the data he collected on the phone and wants Ollie to guess the mean retirement age of the 34 retired MLB players. Ollie says that Caspar needs to collect more than his one guess. Caspar, ignoring the fact that the data might be biased due to a convenient data collection method, asks more baseball fans in the bleachers around him to guess the mean retirement age of the 34 players so that he can quickly make a dot plot before the eighth inning begins.

1-70.   Each member of your team needs to guess the mean age at which he/she believes the 34 oldest ball players retired. Your teacher will record and display each guess on a dot plot.

   a.   Record this dot plot on your graph paper. Label it "Mean Age of Retirement Guesses."

   b.   Describe the distribution (shape, center, and spread.)

   c.   Record any extreme values that you notice.

   d.   Is the dot plot symmetric or skewed?

1-71.   Let X be a random variable that represents the guesses in the previous problem. Let the constant value a represent the correct mean age of retirement. We will transform each guess by subtracting a from each guess $(X - a)$ and create a second dot plot showing the distribution of the guessing errors.

   a.   Record this dot plot below the first dot plot. Label the second dot plot "Guessing Errors for the Age of Retirement."

   b.   What do you notice about the two graphs? What has stayed the same? What has changed? How has a changed the measures of center and spread?

   c.   What would the dot plot look like if we transformed each guess by adding a?

   d.   Summarize your findings about how subtracting (or adding) the same positive number a affects measures of center and spread.

1-72.   Changes in the temperature of the water in volcanic hot springs can be a sign of changing volcanic activity. Assume a geologist at the University of Wyoming studying volcanic activity around Yellowstone National Park took the following temperature measurements in degrees Centigrade from a sample of springs in and around the park. She then converted them to Fahrenheit using the relationship $F = 32 + 1.8(C)$ and computed the following summary statistics:

Centigrade	53	42	30	14	34	36	44	45	63	22
Fahrenheit	127.4	107.6	86.0	57.2	93.2	96.8	111.2	113.0	145.4	71.6

	Mean	Median	Standard Deviation	IQR
Centigrade	38.3	39.0	14.4	15.0
Fahrenheit	100.9	102.2	25.9	27.0

   a.   Compare the corresponding summary statistics and explain how changing the units of measurement changed measure of center and spread.

   b.   Her partner brought back the following summary statistics:

	Mean	Median	Standard Deviation	IQR
Centigrade	61.9	60.2	25.3	32.9

   Convert them to degrees Fahrenheit.

MATH NOTES

Why not $y = mx + b$?

Linear transformations and predictions in statistics are not limited to just two variables and can be expressed in this general form:

$$\hat{y} = a + b(X_1) + c(X_2) + d(X_3) + e(X_4) + \ldots + \beta(X_n)$$

In this particular course we limit this type of analysis to two quantitative variables $\hat{y}$ and X that shortens this general form to:

$$\hat{y} = a + b(X)$$

In two-variable statistical analysis *a* **is the y-intercept** and *b* **is the slope.**
Notice statistical notation is different from $y = mx + b$ where b is the y-intercept.

To transform measures of center such as the mean and median:
$$\overline{x}_{\text{new}} = a + b(\overline{x}_{\text{original}})$$

For measures of spread such as standard deviation and IQR:
$$s_{\text{new}} = b(s_{\text{original}})$$

1-73.   Ranger Adriana is warning the park tourists about the dangers of getting too near the thermal areas. Assume that she got the following information from a team of geologist about water temperatures in a particular thermal area:

	Mean	Median	Standard Deviation	IQR
Fahrenheit	205	199	18.7	33.1

She realizes she is speaking to tour group from outside the U.S. who do not use temperatures in degrees Fahrenheit. She knows the formula $C = \frac{5}{9}(F - 32)$ for converting to degrees Centigrade. Help her give the information to the tour group in their familiar units. (Hint: The formula $C = \frac{5}{9}(F - 32)$ needs some simplification to be represented by $X_{\text{new}} = a + b(X_{\text{original}})$.)

1-74.   Each team member in the team will record the number of letters in their middle name on a sticky dot. The Recorder/Reporter in each team will attach these values on the dot plot on the board.

Record this dot plot on your graph paper. Name this dot plot "Middle Name Lengths."

a.   Describe the distribution of the sticky dots.

b.   Enter the class data set into a calculator and compute the one-variable summary statistics (mean, median, IQR, range, and standard deviation). Record the summary statistics below the dot plot.

c.   Pretend everyone's middle name is too short! Multiply your original middle name length by a constant value b equal to 2 and write the new number on a sticky dot.

The Recorder/Reporter in each team will attach these new values on the dot plot on the board. Describe the new distribution of the sticky dots.

d.   Enter the transformed (multiplied) class data set into a calculator and compute the one-variable summary statistics for the class data set. Record the summary statistics for the sticky dots below the summary statistics in part (b). Compare the two sets of summary statistics. What has changed? What has stayed the same?

1-75.   The table at right shows the ages of the 34 oldest MLB players at retirement.

a.   Describe the distribution of the dot plot.

b.   Are there any extreme values or outliers in the data set? If so, what are they?

c.   Is the dot plot symmetrical or skewed? If it is skewed, which way is it skewed?

d.   Is the mean to the left or right of the median? How do you know?

45	Cap Anson	46	Nolan Ryan
45	Roger Clemens	46	Sam Thompson
45	Carlton Fisk	48	Johnny Evers
45	Fred Johnson	48	Deacon McGuire
45	Ted Lyons	48	Phil Niekro
45	Gaylord Perry	48	Gabby Street
45	Sam Rice	49	Julio Franco
45	Pete Rose	49	Hughie Jennings
45	Omar Vizquel	49	Arlie Latham
45	Tim Wakefield	49	Jamie Moyer
46	Jimmy Austin	49	Hoyt Wilhelm
46	Dan Brouthers	50	Jack Quinn
46	Charlie Hough	54	Jim O'Rourke
46	Tommy John	56	Minnie Miñoso
46	Randy Johnson	57	Nick Altrock
46	Hod Lisenbee	58	Charley O'Leary
46	Jesse Orosco	59	Satchel Paige

1-76.   Ms. Frances gave her AP Statistics class of fourteen students a free-response test for Chapter 1. When the tests were returned, many students groaned because the average score was 23%.

Ms. Frances wants the average score (mean) to be 70% (a C Minus). She decides to grade on a curve.

a.   Use the linear transformation equation to calculate the new scores for the class. Let $a = 24$ and $b = 2$.

Original Score (%)	16	22	24	27	21	18	32	28	19	23
New Score (%)										

b.   Find the average score and standard deviation for the original scores.

c.   Using the statistics you calculated in part (b), find the mean and standard deviation for the new transformed scores.

d.   How does adding a to x when $b = 1$ affect the original mean?

e.   How did b affect the original standard deviation and the range?

1-77.   When vapor under high pressure is released into the air, the resulting noise can severely damage people's hearing. This is a concern for large industrial facilities like power plants and factories. To help control this noise pollution companies install silencers, which work on the same principles as car mufflers. Hector is an engineer for Vapor Kinetics. He is testing two different models of silencers, the Hush Puppy and the Quiet Down, by measuring the sound energy in decibels (dB) each silencer is producing at various temperatures and pressures. The data has been sorted and is shown below:

Hush Puppy
19.7	22.8	26.3	27.4	29.5	38.8	39.3	44.5	46.7	50.0
51.2	52.4	53.4	56.6	58.0	58.6	60.7	62.3	66.4	67.0
68.6	69.6	70.1	70.9	71.3	72.9	76.4	76.5	76.7	79.5

checksum: 1664.1

Quiet Down
14.2	16.3	19.3	24.6	26.0	30.5	35.8	37.4	39.9	40.0
40.1	47.3	52.9	53.5	53.7	56.0	56.6	56.7	59.1	59.8
61.3	62.6	63.3	64.3	66.5	67.1	71.8	95.7	101.2	102.1

checksum: 1575.6

a.   Create a combination boxplot and histogram for each silencer. For the histograms, scale the *x*-axis from 12 to 108 and use a bin width of 12 dB.

b.   Describe the center, shape, spread, and outliers for each silencer. Make sure your results have the same level of precision as the measurements.

c.   Hector needs to recommend one design for production. Which one do you suggest and why?

d.   The decibel scale is logarithmic, not linear. For example, a 105 dB sound is 1000 times more intense than a 75 dB sound. This is roughly the difference in noise between running a kitchen blender and running a chain saw. Does this information change your answer to part (c)? Why or why not?

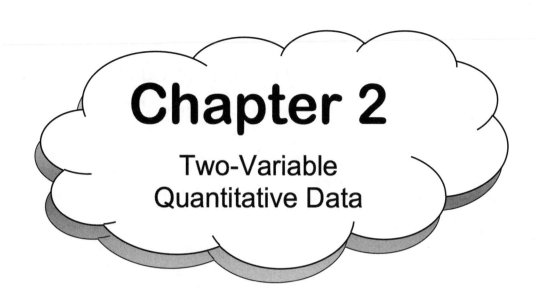

Chapter 2

Two-Variable
Quantitative Data

CHAPTER 2 — Two-Variable Quantitative Data

Chapter Goals

Learn techniques for finding a line of best fit between two quantitative variables.

Interpret the slope and *y*-intercept of the model in the context of two quantitative variables.

Quantify variability using residuals and residual plots.

Describe the association between two quantitative variables—the form, direction, strength, and outliers.

Calculate and interpret the correlation coefficient and coefficient of determination R^2.

Understand why association is not the same as causation.

In your previous math courses the points on a graph were all on a line or perhaps a smooth curve such as parabola. In Statistics the points on a graph represent actual data and are much less orderly. When looking at a scatterplot you might ask: *Do the two quantitative variables have a relationship? Is it curved, linear? If so, how strong is it, and in which direction is the relationship? Can the relationship be used to make predictions?*

Chapter Outline

Section 2.1 You will review how to make scatterplots and learn the technical terms for describing associations between two quantitative variables visible in a scatterplot. Interpret the slope and *y*-intercept of the model in the context of two quantitative variables. You will explore the limitations of the models when they are extrapolated far from the edges of the actual data. You will begin learning to quantify variability using residuals and learn a consistent way of creating lines of best fit—by creating the least squares regression line.

Section 2.2 You will begin describing the association between two quantitative variables—the form, direction, strength, and outliers—in terms that are more mathematical. You will calculate and graph calculate residuals, find the correlation coefficient, coefficient of determination R^2, and interpret these quantities in the context of the situation. You will also understand why association is not the same as causation.

2.1.1 How can I describe relationships?

Scatterplots and Association

Most of the work in the previous chapter had to do with *single-variable* situations, where you looked at the distribution of one set of categorical or quantitative data. What if you want to *compare* two or more variables? In this chapter you will begin exploring this idea by looking at the specific case of using scatterplots to compare two quantitative variables.

2-1.   Coach Johnson, head football coach for Tinker Toy Tech (TTT) is getting ready for recruitment season. He is looking at all of the data for his former first-year offensive players, trying to look for patterns that will give him additional information to help him recruit great players. Below is a snippet of his data for 12 such players from previous years:

Data gathered at recruitment time			Data gathered later, during season	
Weight (lb)	GPA	100 m dash run time (sec)	Average yards run per game	Average points scored per game
210	2.7	12.3	112	6.5
230	3.2	13.7	68	1.9
180	2.6	15.2	70	3.2
185	3.3	12.9	99	4.2
210	4.0	13.1	101	5.9
180	2.3	13.6	85	2.2
195	2.1	15	75	2.4
190	3.0	14	98	3.7
200	2.9	13.4	92	5.1
190	2.7	12.2	142	7.7
230	2.2	12.6	92	5.9
250	3.1	14.2	75	5.9

His assistant coaches have different opinions about this data. Coach Griswold thinks that weight is a good piece of information to help predict the number of points per game a player will make. *"Heavier players will be able to push aside more defenders, so they will score more points!"* Coach Faulder, on the other hand, thinks that the 100 meter dash time will be the best predictor. *"Faster players, who have lower times on the 100 meter dash, will be able to avoid defenders more and score more points."* Looking at the data, do a *gut check*: do you agree with one or both of the coaches? Explain your reasoning.

2-2.   To make it easier to see relationships between variables like these, you can use a scatterplot. When making a scatterplot, the first question to ask is: which is the **explanatory variable** and which is the **response variable**? The response variable is the variable you are hoping to make predictions about, while the explanatory variable is the variable you are hoping to use to help make those predictions. Some situations do not have explanatory or response variables, so in those situations the choice is arbitrary!

What are the explanatory and response variables for the situations described by Coaches Faulder and Griswold in problem 2-1?

2-3.   In a statistical scatterplot, the explanatory variable is placed on the *x*-axis and the response variable is placed on the *y*-axis. Scales can start and end anywhere, but tick marks must be equally spaced, just as in algebraic graphs.

Below are the scatterplots for the data in both Coach Griswold's and Coach Faulder's comparisons. Figure out which scatterplot goes with which scenario, then copy sketches or trace the scatterplots into your notes and add appropriate titles, axis labels, and numbers to represent the scale.

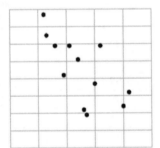 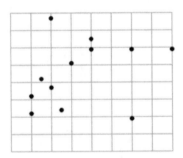

2-4.   Look at the scatterplots and decide, for each scenario: does the scatterplot support the coach's theory? That is, does there appear to be a relationship between the variables? If so, how would you describe the relationship? If you were Coach Johnson, which variable, weight, or 100 m dash time, would you pay more attention to?

2-5.   Read the Math Notes box on the next page on describing association in scatterplots, then describe the relationship in the scatterplot at right, also from Coach Johnson's data. Does this scatterplot demonstrate a useful relationship for recruitment season? Why or why not?

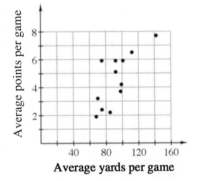

2-6.   Make a prediction: do you think there will be an association between player GPA and points scored? Explain your reasoning.

Statistics

2-7.   Make a scatterplot comparing GPA to points scored. Label the axes and scale and describe any association you see.

MATH NOTES

Describing Association

Form, direction, strength, and outliers describe an association (relationship) between two quantitative variables.

The shape of the pattern is called the **form** of the association: this course focuses on linear and nonlinear. Sometimes you get **clusters** or **gaps** within the form of the data, which should be mentioned.

If the variables tend to increase together, the **direction** is said to be a **positive association**. If one variable increases as the other variable decreases, there is said to be a **negative association**. If there is no apparent relationship in the scatterplot, then the variables have **no association**.

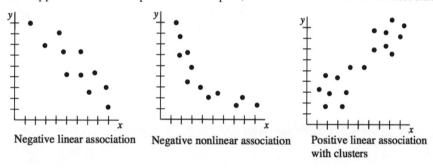

Negative linear association   Negative nonlinear association   Positive linear association with clusters

Strength describes how much scatter there is in the data away from the general pattern. It can help to draw an "envelope" around the data—thinner envelopes are stronger. See some examples below.

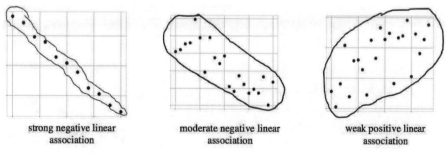

strong negative linear association   moderate negative linear association   weak positive linear association

An **outlier** is a piece of data that does not seem to fit into the overall pattern. There is one obvious outlier in the association graphed at right.

outlier →

2-8.   Fully describe the associations in each of the example scatterplots below.

a.   Height vs. specific gravity of live oaks

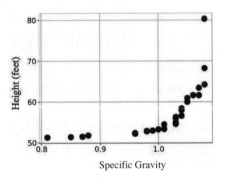

b.   Study time vs. score earned on math test

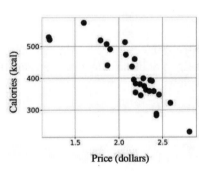

c.   Price vs. calories of bear claws

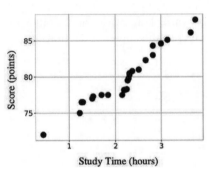

d.   Height vs. age of feral burros

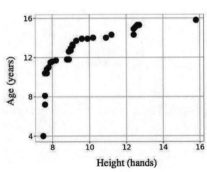

2-9.   Assume a sample of seven random albatrosses produced the following data on mass and wingspan:

Wingspan (cm)	256	264	274	288	312	314	322
Mass (kg)	0.45	0.50	0.54	0.62	0.65	0.61	0.64

a.   Sketch and fully label a scatterplot for this data and describe the association.

b.   Use your "gut," the data, and the scatterplot to make predictions: what would you expect the mass of an albatross with a wingspan of 280 cm to be? What would be the lowest and highest masses you would find surprising for that wingspan?

2-10.   The auto repair shop is concerned about the reliability of its lathe. A lathe is a rotating piece of equipment used in restoring parts. The shop's owner measured the rotations per minute at various times over the course of a month. These are his sorted measurements:

250, 251, 253, 253, 253, 254, 257, 257, 259, 259, 261, 263, 265, 270, 291 RPM

a.   On grid paper, draw a combination histogram and boxplot.

b.   Describe center, shape, spread, and outliers.

c.   When reporting the center of this data, or the "typical RPM," which would be more appropriate, the mean or the median? Why?

2-11.   A farmer wonders if his crops grow better in sun or in shade. He measures the amount of fruit gathered from a sample of 50 trees growing in full sun and from a sample of 50 trees growing in mostly shade. The five number summaries (minimum, Q1, median, Q3, maximum) follow:

Amount of fruit gathered from sunny trees: 10.8, 13.3, 22.1, 58.1, 100 bushels

Amount of fruit gathered from shady trees: 10.9, 18.5, 29.3, 61.5, 127 bushels

a.   On the same set of axes on grid paper, create a boxplot for each type of tree. Compare the center, shape, spread, and outliers of amount of fruit from sunny trees to the amount from shady trees.

b.   The farmer wants to summarize the amount of fruit per tree from each type of orchard with a mean and standard deviation. Is that appropriate? Explain.

2.1.2 How can I make predictions?

Line of Best Fit

The championship is on the line between Coach Johnson's Tinker Toy Tech (TTT) and City College. Robbie plans to attend TTT next fall and desperately wants to see the game, which has been sold out for weeks.

Surveying the exterior of the stadium, Robbie has discovered a small drainage pipe that has a direct view of the field. The stadium is being prepared for the big game and a maintenance van is currently blocking the view from the pipe, but the van will be removed prior to the game.

2-12. The south end of the field is 50 yards from the end of the pipe and the field runs from north to south. The total length of the playing field, including the end zones, is 120 yards. The pipe will be at the center of the south end of the field. The width of the field is 53.3 yards (160 feet). Investigate how much of the field Robbie will be able to see when he looks through the pipe at game time.

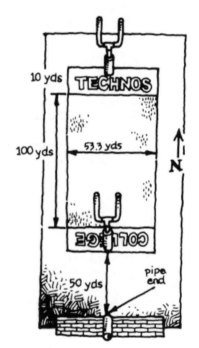

a. To assist Robbie with this problem you will need to create a model to collect data. Obtain the view tube that has the same dimensions as the pipe through which Robbie will be looking.

Record the length and diameter of your team's view tube. Then gather eight sets of data points by measuring two distances: from the end of your "pipe" to the wall (in inches) and the width of the field of view, how much of the wall you can see (in inches).

Length of tube:

Diameter of tube:

Distance from wall (inches)	Width of field of view (inches)

b. Make a scatterplot of your data. Describe the association between the field of view and distance from the wall. If you need a reminder about how to describe associations, see the Math Notes box in Lesson 2.1.1.

c. Draw a line of best fit that models your data and will allow you to make predictions. What is the equation of your line of best fit?

d. What do the slope and y-intercept represent in the context of the problem?

2-13.   Predict how wide (in yards) Robbie's field of view will be at the south end of the field. How wide will it be at the north end in yards?

2-14.   On your paper, sketch the football field, including the end zones and label the dimensions. Using a different color, shade the part of the field that Robbie can see.

   a.   Find the area of the field of view.

   b.   What percent of the football playing field will Robbie be able to see?

   c.   The game comes down to the final play in the fourth quarter with TTT driving towards the north goal line. The end zones are 10 yards deep, so the north goal line is 10 yards before the north end of the playing field. What is the probability Robbie sees the touchdown?

2-15.   Sam collected data by measuring the pencils of his classmates. He recorded the length of the painted part of each pencil and its mass. His data is shown on the graph at right.

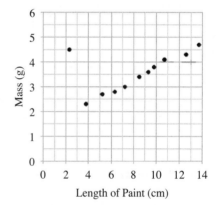

   a.   Describe the association between mass and length of the pencil. Remember to describe the form, direction, strength, and outliers.

   b.   Make a conjecture (a guess) about why Sam's data had an outlier.

   c.   Sam created a line of best fit: $\hat{m} = 1.4 + 0.25l$ where $\hat{m}$ is the predicted mass of the pencil in grams and l is the length of the paint on the pencil in centimeters. What does the slope represent in this context?

   d.   Sam's teacher has a pencil with 11.5 cm of paint. Predict the mass of the teacher's pencil.

   e.   Interpret the meaning of the y-intercept in context.

MATH NOTES

Line of Best Fit

A **line of best fit** is a line that represents, in general, data on a scatterplot, as shown in the diagram. This line does not need to touch any of the actual data points, nor does it need to go through the origin. The line of best fit is a model of numerical two-variable data that helps describe the data in order to make predictions for other data.

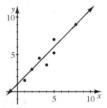

To write the equation of a line of best fit, find the coordinates of any two convenient points on the line (they could be lattice points where the gridlines intersect, or they could be data points, or the origin, or a combination). Then write the equation of the line that goes through these two points.

When writing the equation for a line of best fit, use the hat symbol to represent the explanatory variable, e.g. $\hat{y} = a + bx$ or $\hat{y} = b_0 + b_1 x$. You can read this "y-hat." Statisticians generally put the y-intercept first and the slope second.

2-16.   Sam wanted to spend a little time exploring the data he collected in problem 2-15 more thoroughly. (If you have not completed problem 2-15, do it first).

a.   Use the scatterplot to create a data table that shows (approximately) the data points in the graph. Mark the outlier on your data table.

b.   Sam wants to find the average length and the average mass of pencils in his class. Should he include the outlier in his data? Why or why not?

c.   Find the mean and sample standard deviation of the length values and the mass values (you may include the outlier or leave it out, based on your answer to part (b)). Make sure to include units and reasonable symbols to represent these values.

d.   If you were to add a dot that represents the "perfectly average" pencil, based on your calculations from part (c), where would it appear? If that pencil existed, would Sam's line of best fit ($\hat{m} = 1.4 + 0.25l$) do a good job of predicting its mass from its length? How far off would his model be?

2-17.   In problem 2-1, you looked at data for the stats of various
football players at TTT. An association was found between
100 m dash times and average points scored per game. A
copy of the scatterplot for that model is shown at right.

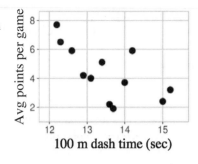

a.   Copy this scatterplot onto your paper and add a
best-fit line.

b.   Estimate an equation for the line.

c.   Use your line to predict the points scored by a player
with a 14.5 second 100 m dash time.

d.   A new player with a 14.5 second 100 m dash time averages 6.5 points per game. Would
you consider this student an outlier? Explain.

2-18.   ALDEN'S SODA

Alden created a boxplot for the calories in 11 different brands of sodas, as shown below.

a.   Is this data quantitative or categorical? Explain

b.   According to this graph, give as complete a description about the
calories of the 11 brands of soda as you can. Consider the center,
shape, spread, and outliers.

2.1.3 How close is the model?

Residuals

Today you will investigate **residuals**. A residual is the difference between what actually occurred and what your best-fit model predicted.

2-19.   Battle Creek Cereal is trying a variety of packaging sizes for their Crispy Puffs cereal. At right is a list of six current packages.

Packaging Cardboard (in^2)	Net Amount of Cereal (g)
34	21
150	198
218	283
325	567
357	680
471	1020

Make a scatterplot of the data then write a few sentences to the executives of Battle Creek Cereal that describe the association. Give an equation to the executives they can use to predict the net amount of cereal based on the amount of cardboard used for the package. Tell the executives how much cereal a new experimental "green" package that uses 260 in^2 of cardboard is expected to hold.

2-20.   A residual can be calculated by subtracting the predicted value from the actual value.

residual = actual – predicted

The 260 in^2 box from problem 2-19 will actually hold 355 g of cereal.

Your Task: Discuss with your team how you can indicate the residual for the 260 in^2 box as a distance on your scatterplot from problem 2-19. Be prepared to share what you discuss with the class.

Discussion Points

What is the residual for the 260 in^2 box?

What is the difference between a positive and a negative residual in the context of this problem?

How could graphing the actual and predicted data points help?

2-21.   What is your residual for the 471 in^2 box? Mark the residual on your scatterplot. Be sure to include units for your residual.

2-22.   The warehouse store wants to offer a super-sized 600 in^2 box.

    a.   The residual for this box is 1005 grams. What is the actual amount of cereal in a 600 in^2 box?

    b.   Why do you suppose the residual is so large?

    c.   Interpret the meaning of the slope and y-intercept of your model in the context of this problem. Does the y-intercept make sense in the context of the problem?

MATH NOTES

Interpreting Slope and y-Intercept on Scatterplots

The **slope** of a linear association plays the same role as the slope of a line in algebra. Slope is the amount of change expected in the response variable ($\Delta\hat{y}$) when changing the explanatory variable (Δx) by one unit. When describing the slope of a line of best fit, always acknowledge that you are making a prediction, as opposed to knowing the truth, by using words like "predict," "expect," or "estimate."

The **y-intercept** of an association is the same as in algebra. It is the predicted value of the response variable when the explanatory variable is zero. Be careful. In statistical scatterplots, the vertical axis is often not drawn at the origin, so the y-intercept can be someplace other than where the line of best fit crosses the vertical axis in a scatterplot.

Also be careful about **extrapolating** the data too far—making predictions that are far to the right or left of the data. The models you create can be valid within the range of the data, but the farther you go outside this range, the less reliable the predictions become. Often, the y-intercept itself is extrapolation, so make sure to consider whether it makes sense when interpreting it!

When describing a linear association, you can use the slope, whether it is positive or negative, and its interpretation in context, to describe the *direction* of the association.

2-23.   Armen was concerned about the amount of sugar in his diet, so he went to the store and collected data from several cereal boxes. Armen used the data to create a model that related the sugar in cereal to calories:

$$\hat{s} = -16.9 + 0.23c$$

where s is the amount of sugar in grams and c is the number of calories in one cup of cereal.

a.   What would a negative residual mean in this context? Is a cereal with a positive or negative residual better for Armen's diet?

b.   Interpret the meaning of the slope and y-intercept in the context of the problem. Does the y-intercept make sense in the context of the problem?

2-24.   The price of homes (in thousands of dollars) is associated with the number of square feet in a home. Home prices in Smallville can be modeled with the equation $\hat{p} = 150 + 0.041a$ where p is the price of the home in thousands of dollars and a is the area of the house in square feet. Home prices in Fancyville can be modeled with the equation $\hat{p} = 250 + 0.198a$. Ngoc saw a real estate advertisement for a 2800 square foot home that was selling for $280,000. Which city should she predict that the home is in?

2-25.   In problem 2-17, you wrote the equation for a best-fit line comparing 100 m dash time to points scored by TTT football players. Find (or re-write) the equation.

a.   Interpret the meaning of the slope and y-intercept in the context of the problem.

b.   Find and interpret the residual of a player who runs the 100 m dash in 14.5 s and averages 6.5 points per game.

2-26.   Lucy and Marissa each designed a boxplot to represent this data set:

16 18 19 19 25 26 27 32 35

Their plots are shown in part (a) below.

a.   Which plot is scaled correctly and why? Explain the mistakes in the incorrect plot.

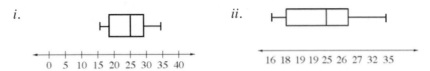

i.   *ii.*

0 5 10 15 20 25 30 35 40   16 18 19 19 25 26 27 32 35

b.   Determine the first and third quartiles, the median, and the interquartile range (IQR) for this data set.

d.   Is this data discrete or continuous?

2-27.   It is reasonable to think there may be an association between the power of a car's engine and its fuel efficiency, measured in miles per gallon (or mpg). A random selection of 10 cars found the following data comparing the horsepower of the cars' engines to their earned mpg.

hp	mpg
197	16
170	24
166	19
230	15
381	13
438	20
170	21
326	11
451	10
290	15

a.   Create a scatterplot of the data.

b.   Estimate a line of best fit and determine its equation.

c.   Interpret the slope and y-intercept in context.

d.   Describe the association between the variables.

e.   Find the residual for the vehicle with 381 horsepower and interpret in context. Would a car owner prefer a positive or a negative residual?

2.1.4 How can we agree on a line of best fit?

The Least Squares Regression Line

In previous problems, each team drew a slightly different line of best fit. Today your class will learn about a special kind of best fit line that can be calculated and agreed on for any situation.

2-28. The following table shows data for one season of the El Toro professional basketball team. El Toro team member Antonio Kusoc was inadvertently left off of the list. Antonio Kusoc played for 2103 minutes. You will predict how many points he scored in the season.

Player Name	Minutes Played	Total Points Scored in a Season
Sordan, Scottie	3090	2491
Lippen, Mike	2825	1496
Karper, Don	1886	594
Shortley, Luc	1641	564
Gerr, Bill	1919	688
Jodman, Dennis	2088	351
Kennington, Steve	1065	376
Bailey, John	7	5
Bookler, Jack	740	278
Dimkins, Rickie	685	216
Edwards, Jason	274	98
Gaffey, James	545	182
Black, Sandy	671	185
Talley, Dan	191	36

a. Obtain a Lesson 2.1.4 Resource Page. Draw a line of best fit for the data and then use it to write an equation that models the relationship between total points in the season and minutes played.

b. Which data point is an outlier for this data? Whose data does that point represent? What is his residual?

c. Would a player be more proud of a negative or positive residual?

d. Predict how many points Antonio Kusoc made.

2-29.   Different people will come up with different models for the relationship between total points and minutes played in the previous problem. They will also have different estimates for the number of points for Antonio Kusoc.

Your Task: Discuss with your team how you can decide which equation models the data the best. Calculate any values for your data that you think will be useful for comparing to others.

Discussion Points

What do you think about when deciding where to place a line of best fit?

What makes one line a better model than another line?

Do we have any calculations from earlier lessons that could allow us to decide which line for the same data is the best?

2-30.   An option for a "best" line of best fit is one that minimizes the standard deviation of the residuals. Recall, that the standard deviation of a one-variable dataset can be interpreted as a "typical" distance a value is from the mean. The formula for the sample standard deviation of a one-variable dataset is

$$s_x = \sqrt{\frac{\sum (x_i - \bar{x})^2}{n-1}}$$

The **standard deviation of the residuals** (represented with the letter S) can be interpreted as a "typical" vertical distance a point will found from the line of best fit. The formula for the sample standard deviation of a two-variable dataset is

$$S = \sqrt{\frac{\sum (\text{residual})^2}{n-2}}$$

a.   Since $n - 2$ is a fixed value for all possible lines of best fit, you can simplify your goal: what number would be easier to calculate which you could minimize to the same effect?

b.   Why do you think the line you are going to find might be called the **least squares regression line (LSRL)**?

2-31.   Technology aids in giving a visual understanding of a "least residual square sum". Open the LSRL regression line eTool for this problem by going to student.desmos.com and entering the code provided by your teacher.

a.   At first, only the scatterplot is visible. Click the circle next to "My Line of Best Fit" and drag the red points to create a fit line that you like. What is your equation? (You can see the slope and y-intercept of the line by clicking the arrow next to "Fit Line Values.")

b.   Click the circle next to "Residual Squares" to turn on their visual. This shows a visual image of the squares of the residuals: the total area of all of these squares is the "sum of the squared residuals." Manipulate your line until that total area looks as small as you can get it: that is the goal of the LSRL. What points are you using now, if they changed?

c.   Click the arrow next to "Best Fit Sums" to see your lines' two "scores"—the sum of squared residuals and the standard deviation of the residuals. Use those numbers to manipulate your graph again to get the smallest value for those numbers you can. What is the smallest squared residual sum you can get?

d.   Click the circle next to "Least Squares Regression Line" to turn on the least squares regression line and *its* residual squares, then uncheck the arrow next to LSRL Sums and compare the LSRL values to your line's values. How close did you get? Can you find another line that is as low or lower than the LSRL? (Hint: If the screen is too visually overwhelming, you can turn off the blue squares for your own line.)

e.   Finally, click the circle next to "Mean Lines". This plots two purple lines: a horizontal one at the mean of the y-values and a vertical one at the mean of the x-values. If you added a point where those two lines cross, what would that point represent?

f.   What do you notice about the LSRL and the means? Explain why this makes sense.

g.   If time permits, feel free to move the points around by dragging them, or by directly editing their values in the "Data Points" folder to continue exploring this concept.

2-32.   Consider the simple data set and graph shown at right:

Joe proposes the best-fit line $y = 10 + 1.5x$.
Kristen proposes the best-fit line $y = 11 + 1.2x$.

x	y
1	12
3	13
4	16
5	17

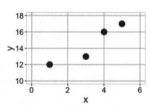

a.   Copy the scatterplot on to your paper and sketch both lines of best fit on top. Which one do you think is better?

b.   Calculate a value to decide which person's model is mathematically better.

c.   The LSRL for this situation is $y = 10.2 + 1.3x$. Calculate the sum of the squared residuals and confirm that this line is better than Joe's or Kristen's.

MATH NOTES

Residuals and Their Standard Deviation

How far a prediction made by your model is from an actual observed value is a **residual**:

residual = actual − predicted

A residual has the same units as the *y*-axis. A residual can be graphed with a vertical segment that extends from the point to the line or curve made by the best-fit model. The length of this segment (in the units of the *y*-axis) is the residual. A positive residual means that the actual value is greater than the predicted value; a negative residual means that the actual value is less than the predicted value.

It is often interesting to have an estimate of how "close" a line of best fit is to the points in a graph. One way to calculate this is to use the **standard deviation of the residuals**, *S*:

$$S = \sqrt{\frac{\sum (y_i - \hat{y}_i)^2}{n-2}} = \sqrt{\frac{\sum (\text{residual}^2)}{n-2}}$$

where *n* − 2 is degrees of freedom for this calculation. *S* has the same units as the *y*-axis and can be interpreted as "the *typical* distance in the *y*-direction between a point and the line of best fit" or equivalently "the typical difference between an *actual* value of the response variable and the *predicted* value." Visually, you can think of *S* as being the width of an interval drawn around a line of best fit that captures the *majority* of the points.

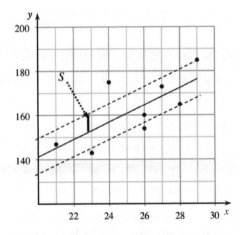

2-33. Charlie's friend is visiting from Texas and asks him, *"What does a hamburger cost in this town?"* This caused Charlie to wonder because the price of a hamburger seems to be different at every eatery. Charlie thinks there may be an association between the amount of meat in the patty and the cost of the hamburger. He made the following data table and used a computer program to find the LSRL graphed below right.

Meat (oz)	Cost ($)
1.6	1.00
2	2.10
3	3.20
3.2	2.80
4	3.10
4	3.30
4	2.80
4	2.70
5.3	5.50
6	4.10
7	4.30
8	5.10
8	5.30
8	7.50
10.7	8.90

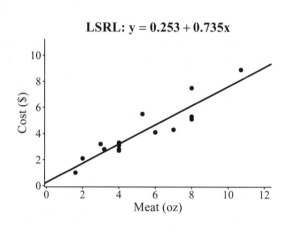

LSRL: y = 0.253 + 0.735x

a. Sketch a version of the scatterplot that includes a visual representation of the "sum of squared residuals."

b. Fully describe the association between meat and cost.

c. Interpret the slope and *y*-intercept of the LSRL in context. Does the *y*-intercept make sense in this situation

d. What is the residual for the hamburger with the 3-ounce patty? What does it mean in context?

e. The sum of the squared residuals in this problem is 8.923. Use this value to find the standard deviation of the residuals, and interpret it.

f. Charlie's friend says that in his hometown he can buy a 1-pound hamburger for $14.70. Would this be a reasonable price in Charlie's town? Show how you know.

g. Verify that the LSRL regression line passes through the "perfectly average" point by finding the means of the weights and costs and plugging in.

h. A new burger joint opens in Charlie's town that sells a free-range, organic, grass-fed burger. It has a 10-oz patty and costs $12. If Charlie adds this burger to his data set, what will be the effect on the slope of the LSRL? What will be the effect on *S* and the strength of the association?

2-34.   How do boxplots help compare data? Think about this question as you compare the data at right that shows the ages of students at three schools.

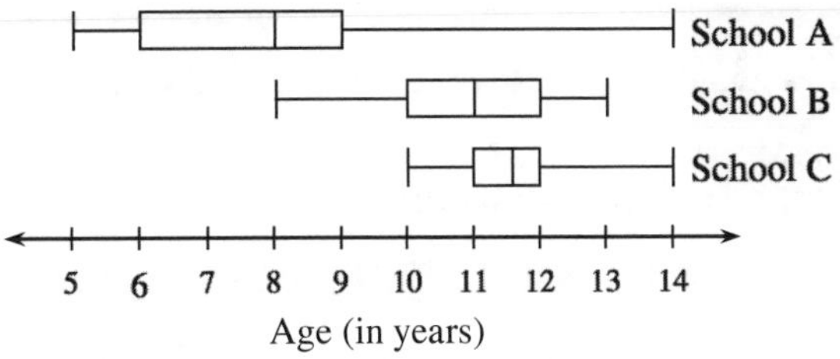

School A
School B
School C

Age (in years)

a.   Which school is a K-8 school? How do you know? Does that school have more students in grades K to 2, 3 to 5, or 6 to 8? Why?

b.   What does the boxplot for School C tell you about 11-year-old students at that school?

c.   How many students attend School C?

d.   Make a conjecture about how the data for these plots was collected.

e.   What statements can you make about the students at School B based on its boxplot? Consider the center, shape, spread, and outliers.

2.1.5 How can we find the LSRL?

Using Technology to Find the LSRL

In a later lesson you will see how the LSRL can be calculated by hand, but in practice it is much more common to find the line using technology. In this lesson you will practice making a least squares regression line using technology tools.

2-35.   Use the Scatterplot Generator eTool to calculate and interpret the least squares regression line.

Jacob is studying the radiation given off by a very small sample of radium. He collects the following data:

Distance from sample (cm)	Radiation (mrad/s)	Distance from sample (cm)	Radiation (mrad/s)	Distance from sample (cm)	Radiation (mrad/s)
20.76	80.7	21.51	78.3	22.74	77.2
20.87	79	21.56	78.1	22.83	76.3
21.18	78.9	21.73	78	23.13	75.7
21.29	78.6	22.41	77.9	23.16	75.3

a.   Select the Comma radio button under "Delimeter?". Enter the data in the eTool in the "Data" section. You will put your headers on the first row, separated by a comma, and then the data points one per row, also separated by commas, like below:

```
Distance from sample (cm), Radiation (mrad/s)
20.76,80.7
20.87,79
...
```

If you prefer, you can also write the header and data in Excel or Google Sheets first then copy and paste it in: change the "Delimeter?" option to "Tab" if you do that. Once the data is entered, fully describe the scatterplot that appears.

b.   To add the regression line, simply click the "Show Regression Line" checkbox in the "Graph Behavior and Sizing" section. You can also uncheck "Automatically set scales" to modify the look of the graph by manually setting the scales. Play around with these settings for a minute or two. Estimate the slope of the regression line from the picture.

c.   By default, the regression line does not give you an equation or any other data. Click the "Regr. Output" box to get various pieces of data about this regression. Interpreting this data can be tricky, but is a common question on the AP exam! There are lots of numbers there: which one appears like it might be the slope, based on your estimate from part (b)?

d.   If you remember from your study of polynomials, in a polynomial such as $y = a + bx$, b is called the coefficient of the variable x while a is called the constant coefficient. How does that connect to your table? Use this connection to find the y-intercept.

Problem continues on next page →

2-35.   *Problem continued from previous page.*

     e.   Write the LSRL down and interpret the slope and *y*-intercept in this context.

     f.   Most of the remaining numbers on this table are not something you know how to interpret yet (and some of them you will not know until Chapter 12), but there should be one other value you can interpret. Find it and do so.

     g.   Finally (for now), if you click the "Resid Table" option on the right, you will get a table of residuals. Find and interpret the largest residual in the list.

2-36.   A study was done for a vitamin supplement that claims to shorten the length of the common cold. The data the scientists collected from ten patients in an early study are shown in the table below.

Number of months taking supplement	0.5	2.5	1	2	0.5	1	2	1	1.5	2.5
Number of days cold lasted	4.5	1.6	3	1.8	5	4.2	2.4	3.6	3.3	1.4

     a.   Your teacher will show you how to use a calculator to make a scatterplot of this data. (Graphing calculator instructions for some models can also be downloaded from cpm.org.)

     b.   Your teacher will show you how to find the LSRL and graph it on a calculator. Sketch your scatterplot and LSRL on your paper.

     c.   Your teacher will show you how to find the residuals for the LSRL using a calculator. What is the sum of the squares of the residuals of the LSRL the calculator found? What is the standard deviation of the residuals (S)? Interpret S in context.

     d.   How long a cold does the LSRL predict for someone who has taken supplements for 2 months? Is this a reasonable prediction?

     e.   How long a cold does the LSRL predict for someone who has taken supplements for 6 months?

2-37.   Use the Desmos graphing calculator at desmos.com. (Works on computers or mobile devices. It is also available as a dedicated app on many phones and tablets).

Darius is working at his neighborhood dental office researching procedures involving gold crowns. A stratified sample of 24 crowns revealed the following summary regarding the relationship between cost and preparation time. His data table is shown at right.

Cost ($)	Prep Time (mins)
360	17.3
367	17.9
383	20.2
384	20.5
390	20.5
392	21.1
394	21.5
399	21.7
399	22.3
408	22.4
412	22.4
415	22.7
417	22.8
419	23
419	23.2
422	23.2
422	23.4
423	23.5
425	24.5
429	25.1
430	25.3
439	26.1
447	26.3
460	28.6

a.   Open a new Desmos calculator screen. To enter the data, click the [+▾] button in the upper left and choose [▦] table . Enter your data. A scatterplot should appear! You can also copy and paste data from many sources, including Excel and Google Sheets, so if you would prefer you can type your data in one of those sources first.

b.   Click the [✏] button in the upper right corner and set your x-axis and y-axis to reasonable values. Add labels at the same time. You should now have a good scatterplot! Describe the association you see in the graph.

c.   Your table headers should be named "x_1" and "y_1" by default. If they are not, that is okay, just change the names on the next command. On the left, click the line under the table and type "**y1 ~ a+bx1**". When you type it, the 1's will automatically subscript to give you $y_1 \sim a + bx_1$. You can find the squiggly line (called a "tilde") in the upper-left of your keyboard. This is your least squares regression line.

d.   Look at the information that appeared under your $y_1 \sim a + bx_1$ line. Some of those numbers you will talk about later. If you click the [plot] button next to the variable that says "Residuals", your residuals will get added to your table of values! Use the list to find the residual for the $384 crown and interpret it in context.

e.   Use the values under "parameters" to write your equation for the line of best fit, and interpret the slope and y-intercept in context.

f.   Joe says, *"This data is really strongly associated! If I were a dentist, I would charge less, because that would make my prep time lower and I would have more time to watch TV."* What is wrong with this statement?

g.   Desmos does not calculate S for you, but if you are feeling like you want it you can get it by typing "sqrt(total(e1^2)) / (length(e1)-2). As you type, Desmos will convert this until it looks like $\sqrt{\frac{\text{total}(e_1^2)}{\text{length}(e_1)-2}}$. (This is assuming your regression list is named e_1). Do you understand how this formula works? Use it to find and interpret the standard deviation of the residuals in this context.

2-38.   Robbie's class collected the following view tube data in
         problem 2-12.

Distance from wall (in)	Width of field of view (in)
144	20.7
132	19.6
120	17.3
96	14.8
84	13.1
72	11.4
60	9.3

a.   Use an eTool as suggested by your teacher or a calculator
      to make a scatterplot and graph the least squares
      regression line (LSRL). Sketch the graph and LSRL on
      your paper. Remember to put a scale on the *x*-axis and
      y-axis of your sketch. Write the equation of the LSRL
      rounded to four decimal places.

b.   With your tool, find the list of the residuals. Make a table with the *distance from wall
      (inches)* as the first column, and *residual (inches)* in the second column. What is the sum
      of the squares of the residuals?

c.   Use the sum of squared residuals from part (b) to find and interpret *S*. (If your graph tool
      already calculated *S* for you, confirm it by hand).

MATH NOTES

Least Squares Regression Line

There are two reasons for modeling scattered data with a best-fit line. First, the best-fit line
allows the trend in the data to easily be described to others without giving them a list of all the
data points. Second, it lets predictions be be made about points for which you do not have actual
data.

A unique best-fit line for data, the **least squares regression line** (LSRL), can be found by
determining the line that makes the sum of the squared residuals as small as possible. Using
technology, one can find the LSRL quickly. Statisticians prefer the LSRL to some other best-fit
lines because there is one unique LSRL for any set of data. All statisticians, therefore, come up
with exactly the same best-fit line and can use it to make similar descriptions of, and predictions
from, the scattered data.

2-39.   Fabienne is working at marketing research company and has discovered a linear relationship
         between the price of coffee-based beverage and the level of customer satisfaction on a scale of
         1 to 10.

    a.   Do you think that the association would be positive or negative? Strong or weak?

    b.   Assume Fabienne found the LSRL to be $g = 6.11 + 0.42c$ where g is the customer
          satisfaction rating and c is the cost of the beverage. Interpret the slope of Fabienne's
          model in context.

    c.   Fabienne found the standard deviation of the residuals to be 1.30. Explain this value in
          context.

    d.   A customer just paid $5.93 for a super sized espresso and her residual was –2.10 points,
          what was her customer satisfaction rating?

2-40.   In problem 2-27, you looked at data comparing a random sample of 10 cars
         of various models and the engine horsepower and city gas mileage is
         recorded for each one.

hp	mpg
197	16
170	24
166	19
230	15
381	13
438	20
170	21
326	11
451	10
290	15

    a.   Create a scatterplot and calculate the LSRL using an eTool or
          calculator. Compare this to the equation $\hat{m} = 29.5 - 0.05h$ from
          problem 2-27. Why are the slope and y-intercept so different?

    b.   The standard deviation of the residuals for the LSRL is 3.898.
          Interpret this number in context.

    c.   What do you predict will happen to the LSRL and standard deviation
          of the residuals if you remove the outlier and recalculate?

    d.   Remove the outlier at (438, 20) from your data set and calculate the LSRL again. Were
          your predictions in part (c) correct? (You may have to estimate S visually if your
          preferred tool does not calculate it.)

2-41.   Levi used the boxplot below to say, "*Half of the class walked more than 30 laps at the walk-a-thon.*" Levi also knows that his class has more than 20 students.

Number of Laps per Person

a.   Do you agree with him? Explain your reasoning. If you do not agree with him, what statement could he say about those who walked more than 30 laps?

b.   Levi wants to describe the portion of students who walked between 20 and 30 laps (the box). What statement could he say?

c.   How could you alter a single data point and not change the graph? How could you change one data value and only move the median to the right?

d.   Can you determine how many students are in Levi's class? Explain why or why not.

2.2.1 How can I compare strengths?

The Correlation Coefficient

You may recall that the equation of the LSRL minimized the sum of the squares of the residuals, and, by association, the standard deviation of the residuals. The smaller the sum of the squares, the closer the data was to the line of best fit. However, the magnitude of the sum of squares and the residuals depends on the *units* of the variables being plotted. Therefore the sum of squares cannot be compared between different scatterplots—it is not a good way to compare the strength of various associations.

Today you will look at another way to describe the *strength* of an association and fit line, a way that does not rely on units.

2-42.　Consider the two very small data sets and scatterplots shown below. One of them compares average study time to test scores for 5 students, while another compares percentage of absences to test scores for 5 different students.

Dataset A

Study Time (minutes)	Average Test Score
10	71
32	81
68	85
60	93
80	88
Mean: 50	Mean: 83.6
SD: 28.5	SD: 8.29

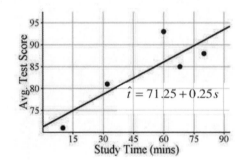

$\hat{t} = 71.25 + 0.25s$

Dataset B

Absence (%)	Average Test Score
0	83
1.2	91
3.2	71
5.6	74
10.1	61
Mean: 4.02	Mean: 76
SD: 4.00	SD: 11.49

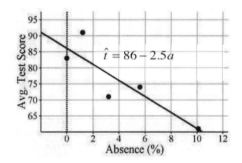

$\hat{t} = 86 - 2.5a$

a.　Why might it be interesting to know which association is stronger?

b.　Compare and contrast these scatterplots. Which appears stronger?

2-43.   For this problem you want to compare completely different variables; luckily, you already have a technique available to use that might help us compare values with different units and scales: standardization, using z-scores!

a.   Recall the formula for standardizing a data point x_i is $z_{x_i} = \frac{x_i - \bar{x}}{s_x}$. Maria is the student who was absent 1.2% of the time. Use the mean and standard deviation provided to find and interpret the z-score of her absence percentage.

b.   When standardizing bivariate data, you standardize the x-values and the y-values *separately*. Find and interpret the z-score for Maria's average test score (relative to the others in her study).

c.   Explain why it makes sense in this situation for a student with a negative z-score on the first variable to have a positive z-score on the other variable.

d.   In which variable, absence or test score, is Maria more "out of the ordinary?"

e.   Since Maria is more out of the ordinary in one variable than the other, that means you could not have predicted her position perfectly. If you had a **perfect** linear graph, meaning one variable was a perfect predictor of the other, what would you expect to be true about Maria's scores?

2-44.   The standardized data, fit lines, and scatterplots for these data sets are shown below.

Standardized Dataset A

Study Time (z)	Avg. Test Score (z)
−1.40	−1.52
−0.63	−0.31
0.63	0.17
0.35	1.13
1.05	0.53
Mean: 0	Mean: 0
SD: 1	SD: 1

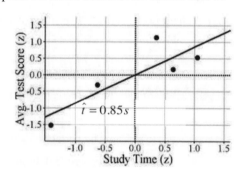

Standardized Dataset B

Absence % (z)	Avg. Test Score (z)
−1.00	0.61
−0.70	1.31
−0.20	−0.44
0.39	−0.17
1.52	−1.31
Mean: 0	Mean: 0
SD: 1	SD: 1

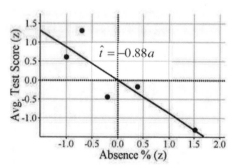

a.   What do you notice about all of the means and standard deviations? Explain.

b.   Compare and contrast these scatterplots to the scatterplots of the original data.

c.   Why does it make sense that the origin, $(0, 0)$, is near the center of these graphs?

d.   Why do you think both lines of best fit go through the origin $(0, 0)$?

2-45.   Statisticians love to multiply things and add them together. When they only have one variable to look at, they tend to square it, but in this case they have two. One number you can calculate using this technique is called the **correlation coefficient, *r*.** It can be found by multiplying the *standardized x* and *y*-values of each point, add them all up, then dividing by good old $(n-1)$.

That is, $r = \frac{\sum z_{xi} z_{yi}}{n-1}$, where z_{xi} and z_{yi} represent the coordinates of the *standardized* data points.

a.   If you calculate *r* for the data sets above, would you expect them to be positive or negative?

b.   Summarize: how do you expect the *sign* of *r* to relate to the graph?

c.   Calculate *r* for both datasets. (This is probably the only time you will ever do this by hand!)

d.   Your teacher will show you how to use an eTool or calculator to find *r* if you did not already learn how. Enter the ORIGINAL (not standardized!) data for one of the data sets and find *r* for that data set. What do you notice?

e.   Look back at your graphs: What is the relationship between *r* and the LSRL of the standardized dataset?

2-46.   If you have it available, use the eTool provided by your teacher to explore the correlation coefficient. Try to answer the following discussion points with your team, making sure you agree on all points. (If the eTool is not available, use the "Further Guidance" section below to answer these questions using a calculator)

Discussion Points

What happens to *r* as the points get closer to the line of best fit?

What is the largest *r* that is possible? The smallest?

Can *r* be negative? Can *r* be zero? What does that mean?

What does *r* reveal about the strength of the linear association?

Is *r* resistant to outliers?

2-47. For parts (a) through (e), use a calculator to make a scatterplot and find the LSRL. Make a sketch of each graph in your notebook, and record the value of the correlation coefficient r. Your teacher will show you how to use a calculator to find r.

a. Start by graphing any two points that have integer coordinates and a positive slope between them. Each member in your team should choose a different pair of points. Compare your results with your team.

b. Each member of your team should choose two new points that have a negative slope between them. Compare your results with your team.

c. What happens when you have more than two data points? Use your original two points from part (a), and add an additional third point that results in $r = 1$. How can you describe the location of *all* possible points that result in $r = 1$?

d. Start again with your original two points from part (a). Enter a third point that makes the slope of the LSRL negative. What happens to r?

e. Start again with your original two points from part (a). Choose a third point that makes r close to zero (say, r between -0.2 and 0.2).

f. Work with your team to discuss the following questions, and record all of your conclusions about the value of r.

- What is the largest r can be? The smallest?

- What do the scatterplot and LSRL look like if $r = 1$? $r = -1$? $r = 0$?

- What does a value of r close to 1 mean, compared to a value of r close to zero?

———————   *Further Guidance*   ———————
section ends here.

2-48. Given the maximum "perfect" absolute value of r you found in your exploration, which of the two datasets you began with has a stronger linear association?

2-49. The following scatterplots have correlation $r = -0.9$, $r = -0.6$, $r = 0.1$, and $r = 0.5$. Which scatterplot has which correlation coefficient, r?

a.

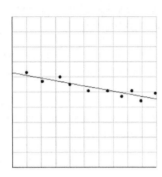

b.

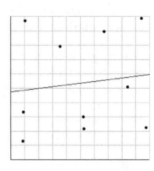

c.

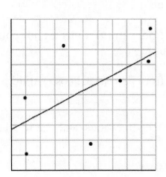

d.

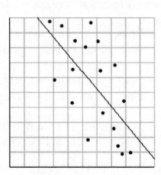

MATH NOTES

Computer Regression Output

Many statistics packages output the data from linear regression using a fairly standard format that needs to be interpreted, as shown below:

Regression Output for Happiness vs. Time Without Math

Predictor	Coef	SE Coef	T	P
Constant	1.79	0.13	13.52	0.00
Time	−0.21	0.05	−4.20	0.00

S = 0.01131   R-Sq = 39.55%   R-Sq(Adj) = 37.31%

Eventually you will understand nearly every number on this output, but for now the important numbers are:

- The coefficient of the explanatory variable −0.21 (in this case "Time without math". This is the slope of the LSRL.

- The constant coefficient 1.79 is the y-intercept of the LSRL.

- S, the standard deviation of the residuals

- R^2, which is the square of the correlation coefficient r (this number has its own name, the coefficient of determination, explained in a later lesson.) You can use R^2 to find r, if asked, by taking the square root then using the slope's sign to decide if r should be positive or negative.

Review & Preview

2-50.   In problem 2-12, you completed an investigation that helped Robbie use a viewing tube to see a football game. Typical data is shown in the table below. The LSRL is $y = 1.66 + 0.13x$.

Distance from wall (in)	Width of field of view (in)
144	20.7
132	19.6
120	17.3
96	14.8
84	13.1
72	11.4
60	9.3

   a.   Use an eTool or calculator to create a scatterplot and find the correlation coefficient. Is the association strong or weak?

   b.   Describe the form, direction, strength, and outliers of the association. Include numbers when possible to back up your description.

   c.   Based on the LSRL calculated with this data, how many inches of wall would you expect to see if you were 600 inches away? Is this a meaningful number?

2-51.   Live Oak wood is heavy but very strong. The frame of the USS Constitution was constructed from southern live oak. Demone is in South Carolina investigating precious supplies of southern live oaks. An SRS of 26 oaks produced the following statistical information regarding the relationship between specific gravity and height.

Regression Output for Height (ft) vs. Specific Gravity

```
Predictor      Coef      SE Coef       T           P

Height        103.80      12.27       8.46        0.00

Specific      -48.60      13.98      -3.48        0.00
Gravity

S = 4.018      R-Sq = 33.49%     R-Sq(Adj) = 30.72%
```

a.   Find the equation of the LSRL and use it to predict the height of a tree with specific gravity of 0.78.

b.   "R-Sq" stands for "r-squared", the square of the correlation coefficient (you will explore this more in a later lesson.) Using that value and the slope, find r.

c.   Interpret S in the context of this problem.

d.   Assuming the form is linear and there are no outliers, use this information to describe the association between height and specific gravity of live oak trees.

2-52.   In your own words, why is it sometimes valuable to standardize the x-values and y-values of bivariate data sets?

2-53.   Anscombe's quartet is a very famous group of datasets. Statistician Francis Anscombe constructed them in 1973 as an education tool to demonstrate the importance of graphs. The scatterplots and part of the computer regression output for each dataset is shown below. Explain what is interesting about these sets, why they demonstrate the importance of graphing data, and what it tells us about the limitations of r.

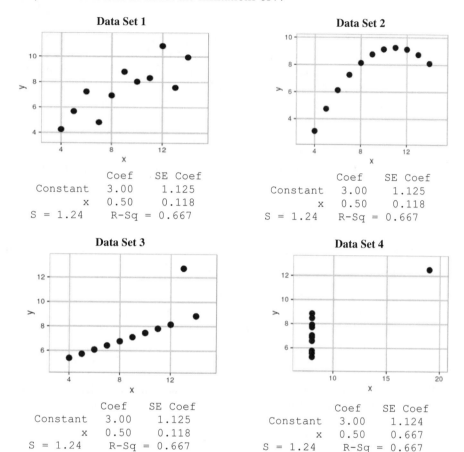

2-54.   Jerome is keeping track of how many books he and his friends have read during the first 100 days of school. The numbers of books are 12, 17, 10, 24, 18, 31, 17, 21, 20, 14, 30, 9, and 25. Help Jerome present the data to his teacher.

a.   How many pieces of data, or observations, does Jerome have?

b.   Make a stem-and-leaf plot of the data.

c.   Jerome wants to present the data with a plot that makes it possible to calculate the mean and the median. Can he do this with a stem-and-leaf plot? He is not asking you to calculate them, but he wants you to tell him if it is possible and why.

d.   Use the stem-and-leaf plot to describe how the data is spread. That is, is it spread out, or is it concentrated mostly in a narrow range?

e.   Would it be helpful for Jerome to create a dot plot to display and analyze the data? Why or why not?

2.2.2 How can a LSRL connect to correlation?

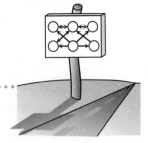

Behavior of Correlation and the LSRL

You might be wondering some or all of the following: how does the computer go about calculating the least squares regression line? Why does the slope of the standardized LSRL equal the correlation? Does the slope of the non-standardized LSRL connect to correlation too? Why is the correlation the same whether you standardize or not? What if you switch the variables or change units? If you are wondering why any of those things are true (or just love algebra!) this is the lesson for you.

2-55.   The correlation coefficient is an interesting value for many reasons, with many interesting behaviors. Many of these behaviors can be understood simply by analyzing the formula carefully.

Recall the formula is $r = \dfrac{\sum z_{xi} z_{yi}}{n-1}$.

a.   Convert this formula to a process: if you had a list of data, how would you compute the correlation coefficient using this formula?

b.   Look at that formula and think: does it matter which variable in the original dataset you call x and which you call y? Why or why not? What does this mean about r if you switch the explanatory and response variables?

c.   Explain why r is the same for the original data and standardized data.

d.   If the correlation between finger length in cm and height in inches is 0.78, what will be the correlation between finger length in inches and height in meters? Why?

e.   Summarize: what matters about a scatterplot in determining correlation?

2-56.   You saw in problem 2-45 that the slope of the LSRL with *standardized data* is equal to r, and you also saw that the LSRL always passes through $(0, 0)$ on the standardized graph. (Proving this will come later, for those interested; for now, trust it.)

a.   In terms of x_z, y_z, and r, write the equation for the standardized LSRL. (z_x is a standardized x-value, z_y is the corresponding standardized y-value.)

b.   Use the formulas for x_z and y_z to rewrite this in terms of $x, y, s_x, s_y, \bar{x}, \bar{y}$, and r. *Carefully* solve for y. This equation is fairly messy, but is easier if you focus only on finding the *slope*—the y-intercept comes in part (c).

c.   The y-intercept is easiest to find in terms of the slope. Given that the LSRL passes through $(0, 0)$ in the standardized form, what point does it always pass through in non-standardized form? (Your answer will contain symbols.)

d.   Use the facts from part (d) to solve for the y-intercept in terms of the slope and the means.

2-57.   While working at her grandfather's math tutoring center researching the level of comprehension of the students, Sophia researched a stratified sample of 27 students which showed the following information regarding the relationship between test preparation time and test score.

The mean the student test preparation time is 2.423 hours with a standard deviation of 0.676 hours. The mean test score is 79.33% with a standard deviation of 8.684. The correlation coefficient is 0.567.

a.   What is the strength and direction of this association?

b.   Find the equation for the LSRL in this equation and interpret the slope and y-intercept of the equation.

c.   Anna prepares for 4 hours and earns an 85% on the test. Calculate and interpret her residual.

2-58.   In this problem, you will be guided through the derivation of the formulas for the least squares regression line. For now, assume you are finding the regression line for standardized data. Assume that the least squares regression line will pass through the intersection of the means, which is $(0, 0)$ in the standardized plot. In other words, the y-intercept of the standardized LSRL will be 0! Therefore, you only need to prove what you already noticed: the slope of the standardized LSRL is r.

a.   You will do this by *working backwards*. Let us call the slope of our line m. And let us use the symbol x_z for the standardized x-values and y_z for the standardized y-values. What is the equation for our standardized line?

b.   You want to find the slope that makes the sum of the squared residuals as small as possible. Using only the variables y_{zi}, x_{zi}, and m, write a formula for the sum of the squared residuals. It should start "SSR=…"

c.   You should have a squared binomial as part of your answer from part (b). Expand that binomial to get a new version of the formula.

d.   When you have a summation symbol of sums, like $\sum (ax_i + bx_i^2 + c^2 y_i)$, you can pull constants out and break up the summation to rewrite it as $a\sum x_i + b\sum x_i^2 + c^2 \sum y_i$. Use this fact to break up and simplify your squared residuals formula.

e.   The formula $\frac{\sum z_{yi}^2}{n-1}$ is the formula for the variance of our standardized y-values. What is the numeric value for this variance? Why?

f.   Divide each term in your expression for the SSR (sum of squared residuals) by $(n - 1)$, and simplify anything that is a variance equal to 1.

g.   At this point, you might notice that this is starting to look like a quadratic expression in m. The expression $\frac{\sum z_{xi} z_{yi}}{n-1}$ should look familiar. What is it?

Problem continues on next page →

2-58.   *Problem continued from previous page.*

h.   Simplify your expression by putting *r* where it belongs.

i.   Since you do not know what *m* is, you can think of it as a variable. You want to find the value of *m* that gives the smallest possible value for SSR (and therefore $\frac{SSR}{n-1}$). If you were to graph the function you found, replacing $\frac{SSR}{n-1}$ with *y* and *m* with *x*, what kind of graph would you get?

j.   Complete the square or use the vertex formula to find the coordinates of the *vertex* of your parabola in terms of *r*.

k.   Almost there: the vertex of the parabola is the spot that minimizes the *y*-value. So what slope *m* minimizes the SSR with standardized data? Proof complete!

2-59.   Bianca plays lacrosse for her high school team. She loves to look at the ratings of lacrosse teams that play in her area. Bianca looked at the difference in ratings between the two teams. She wondered if she could predict the differences in the final scores when the two teams played each other. Bianca drew the following scatterplot by hand.

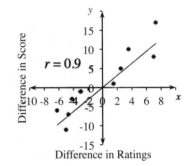

a.   Discuss the association, including an interpretation of slope and *r*.

b.   Predict the outcome of the game if Novato (rating 74.27) played Marin Catholic (rating 76.61).

c.   The difference in rating between Woodbridge and Lakeside was 5.00. When they played, their residual was 7. What was the difference in their scores in this game?

d.   The standard deviation of the score differences in this dataset is 5.2 points. Use this fact to find and interpret the standard deviation of the ratings differences.

2-60.   Darlene collects data on her classmate's heights and shoe size, measuring heights in inches. She finds a LSRL of $\text{height} = 54 + 1.5(\text{shoe size})$ models this relationship well, with a correlation of $r = 0.85$. Fill in each statement below with "decrease", "increase," "stay the same", "stay the same.", or "behave unpredictably."

   a.   If she changes her height unit to cm, the slope will _____.

   b.   If she changes her height unit to cm, the y-intercept will _____.

   c.   If she changes her height unit to cm, the correlation coefficient r will _____.

   d.   If she changes her height unit to cm, the standard deviation of the residuals will _____.

   e.   If she switches her explanatory and response variables, her slope will _____.

   f.   If she switches her explanatory and response variables, her y-intercept will _____.

   g.   If she switches her explanatory and response variables, her correlation coefficient will _____.

2-61.   Mark each of the statements below as "always," "sometimes," or "never" true. If sometimes, explain when it does or does not happen if you can.

   a.   The correlation coefficient is resistant to outliers.

   b.   The correlation coefficient increases when a new point is added.

   c.   The equation of the LSRL changes when a new point is added.

   d.   The standard deviation of the residuals can be compared across datasets.

   e.   The correlation coefficient can be compared across linear datasets.

   f.   An association with $r = 0.8$ is a stronger linear association than a dataset with $r = 0.6$.

2-62.   The carbon content in iron compounds determines the strength and hardness of steel. Jose is an engineering student at Northern Arizona University investigating the carbon content of steel. An SRS of different 68 steel types gave the following carbon content information:

   The shape of the distribution of steel carbon contents appears to be nearly symmetric and perhaps bell shaped. A typical steel carbon content is near 0.95%. The steel carbon contents range from 0.47% to 1.36%. There is an outlier at 0.47%.

   a.   Based on this information create a reasonable representation of a of histogram beginning at 0.4% with a bin width of 0.2% carbon.

   b.   Is this data discrete or continuous? Explain.

2.2.3 When is my model appropriate?

· ·

Residual Plots

In this lesson, you will create residual plots to help you visually determine how well a LSRL fits the data.

2-63.   In problem 2-12, you completed an investigation that helped Robbie use a viewing tube to see a football game. Typical data is shown in the table at right.

Distance from wall (in)	Width of field of view (in)
144	20.7
132	19.6
120	17.3
96	14.8
84	13.1
72	11.4
60	9.3
checksum: 816	*checksum: 122.4*

a.   Use an eTool or calculator to create a scatterplot and LSRL, finding r. Sketch the graph on your paper. What is the equation of the LSRL and the value of r?

b.   When entering the data, Amy accidentally entered (144, 10.7) for the first data point. Make this change to your data and sketch the new point and new LSRL in a different color. Would you consider this point an outlier?

c.   What is the impact of the outlier? Will Amy's predictions for the field of view be too large or too small? How do you know?

2-64.   Giulia's father would like to open a restaurant, and is deciding how much to charge for the toppings on pizza. He sent Giulia to eight different Italian restaurants around town to find out how much they each charge. Giulia returned with the following information:

	# Toppings on Pizza (not including cheese)	Cost ($)
Paolo's Pizza	1	10.50
Vittore's Italian	3	9.00
Ristorante Isabella	4	14.00
Bianca's Place	6	15.00
JohnBoy's Pizza Delivery	3	12.50
Ristorante Raffaello	5	16.50
Rosa's Restaurant	0	8.00
House of Pizza Pie	2	9.00

a.   Based on her findings, Giulia needs to describe to her father what he should charge for pizzas with various numbers of toppings. Discuss with your team what elements Giulia's complete two variable quantitative statistical analysis should contain.

b.   Perform the complete analysis you described in part (a), and predict what Giulia's father should charge for a two-topping pizza.

2-65.   You have seen numeric ways to back up statements of strength and direction, but not form. A **residual plot** can help you determine if a linear model is the best fit for a set of data. Whenever a LSRL line is drawn on a scatterplot, a residual plot can also be created. A residual plot has an *x*-axis that is the same as the scatterplot, and a *y*-axis that plots the residual.

   a.   Match each scatterplot below with its corresponding residual plot.

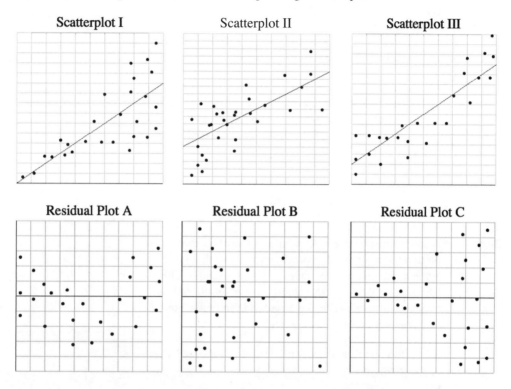

   b.   For which of the scatterplots does a linear model fit the data best? How does the residual plot help you make that decision?

2-66.   Help Giulia analyze the residuals for the pizza parlors in problem 2-64 as described below:

   a.   Mark the residuals on the scatterplot you created in problem 2-64. If you want to purchase an inexpensive pizza, should you go to a store with a positive or negative residual?

   b.   What is the sum of the residuals? Are you surprised at this result?

   c.   Use an eTool or calculator to make a residual plot, with the *x*-axis representing the number of pizza toppings, and the *y*-axis representing the residuals. Interpret the scatter of the points on the residual plot. Is a linear model a good fit for the data?

2-67. Dry ice (frozen carbon dioxide) evaporates at room temperature. Giulia's father uses dry ice to keep the glasses in the restaurant cold. Since dry ice evaporates in the restaurant cooler, Giulia was curious how long a piece of dry ice would last. She collected the following data:

# of hours after noon	Weight of dry ice (oz)
0	15.3
1	14.7
2	14.3
3	13.6
4	13.1
5	12.5
6	11.9
7	11.5
8	11.0
9	10.6
10	10.2

a. Sketch and describe the scatterplot and LSRL of this data and find the correlation coefficient.

b. Use an eTool or calculator to make a residual plot to determine if a linear model is appropriate. Make a conjecture about what the residual plot tells you about the shape of the original data Giulia collected.

c. Conclude: is the correlation coefficient a good measure of the linearity of a data set?

2-68. A study by one state's Agricultural Commission plotted the number of avocado farms in each county against that county's population (in thousands). The LSRL is $f = 9.37 + 3.96p$ where f is the number of avocado farms and p is the population in thousands. The residual plot is shown at right.

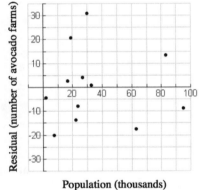

a. Do you think a linear model is appropriate? Why or why not?

b. What is the predicted number of avocado farms for the county with a population of 62,900 people?

c. Using the residual plot, estimate the actual number of avocado farms in the county with 62,900 residents.

2-69. Sophie and Lindsey were discussing what it meant for a residual plot to have random scatter. Sophie said that the points need to be evenly scattered over the whole plot. Lindsey heard her dad say that stars in the night sky can be considered to be randomly distributed even though the stars sometimes appear in clusters and sometimes there are large expanses of nothing in the sky.

Your teacher will show you how to make a scatterplot with random points on it. Share your random plot with your teammates. Then make another random scatterplot or two so that you observe several different random scatterplots.

Write a note to Sophie and Lindsey telling them what you discovered about random scatter plots.

2-70.   Sam collected data in problem 2-15 by measuring the pencils of his classmates. He recorded the length of the painted part of each pencil and its mass. His data is listed in the table below.

Length of paint (cm)	13.7	12.6	10.7	9.8	9.3	8.5	7.2	6.3	5.2	4.5	3.8
Mass (g)	4.7	4.3	4.1	3.8	3.6	3.4	3.0	2.8	2.7	2.3	2.3

Analyze the data using an eTool or calculator.

a.   Sketch the scatterplot on your paper.

b.   What is the equation of the LSRL? Sketch it on your scatterplot.

c.   Create a residual plot and sketch it on your paper.

d.   Interpret your residual plot. Does it seem appropriate to use a linear model to make predictions about the mass of a pencil?

e.   The teacher's pencil, when it was new, had 16.8 cm of paint and a mass of 6 g. What was the residual? Consider the precision of the original data and use an appropriate number of decimal places.

f.   What does a positive residual mean in this context?

2-71.   While working at his brother's coffee shop describing the production of donuts, Isaac researched a random sample of 22 donuts, which showed the following information regarding the relationship between price and calorie count.

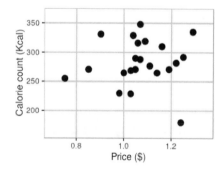

The mean donut price is $1.071 with a standard deviation of $0.131. The mean calorie count is 282.864 Kcal with a standard deviation of 39.67 Kcal. The correlation coefficient is 0.0568.

a.   Find the equation of the LSRL from the given information.

b.   Describe the association completely.

c.   If the correlation coefficient is close to 0, the slope of the LSRL should also be close to 0. Explain why the slope of this LSRL does not seem to be close to 0.

2-72.   Come up with your own scenarios that you would expect exhibit the following relationships. If the relationship is impossible, explain why.

    a.   High positive value of r, LSRL slope greater than 10.

    b.   Low positive value of r, LSRL slope greater than 10.

    c.   Value of r very close to -1, LSRL slope between 0 and -0.5.

    d.   Value of r very close 0, LSRL slope "more negative" than -10.

    e.   Value of r of about -0.5, LSRL slope greater than 1.

2-73.   Raquel is an engineering student at Fresno State University studying high levels of greenhouse gases in air samples. An SRS of 62 samples produced the following CO_2 percentage results:

Mean	Stdev
0.0379	0.0044

Low	Q1	Median	Q3	High
0.031	0.034	0.038	0.042	0.045

Describe the data in context. Remember to include center, shape, spread, and outliers.

2.2.4 Why can't studies determine cause and effect?

Association is Not Causation

A study found that the more hours students spent on activities outside school, the higher their grades tended to be. Does that mean if you go sign up for more activities, your grades will go up?

Another study found a link between how often you brush your teeth and a reduction in heart disease. Does that mean if you brush your teeth twice a day, your heart will be healthier?

As a consumer of statistical information, you need to be aware of the difference between association and causation. Today's investigation will explore that difference.

2-74.   Fire hoses come in different diameters. How far the hose can shoot water depends on the diameter of the hose. The Smallville Fire Department collected data about their fire hoses. The residual plot for the data is shown at right.

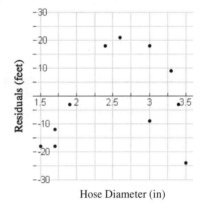

a.   What does the residual plot tell you about the LSRL model the fire department used?

b.   Find the worst prediction made with the LSRL. How different was the worst prediction from what was actually observed? Explain why in context.

c.   Make a conjecture about what the original scatterplot might have looked like and sketch it. Label both axes.

2-75.   The mayor of Smallville finds the following graph in the town's annual financial report.

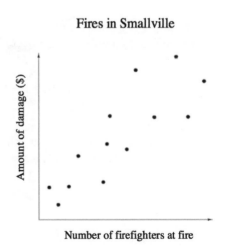

Fires in Smallville

a.   Describe the association, if any, in the scatterplot.

b.   The mayor immediately orders the fire department to send fewer firefighters to each fire so that there is less damage. Why do you think the mayor said this? Do you agree with the mayor's decision? Explain why or why not.

2-76.   A dietician studying the benefits of eating spinach surveyed a large sample of individuals. She recorded the amount of spinach they ate and their physical strength. The dietician found the spinach eaters to be much stronger than the non-spinach eaters. The next day the newspaper headline was, *"Popeye was right! Eating spinach makes you stronger!"*

   a.   Do you agree with the newspaper? Do you agree that if you eat more spinach, you will grow stronger muscles and increase your strength?

   b.   The dietician correctly found an association. What could explain this association other than spinach makes you stronger?

2-77.   **Confounding variables** are a common problem when looking for causation because they are strongly associated with the response variable, but may not part be of the study. The size of the fire in problem 2-75 and the amount people workout in problem 2-76 are confounding variables.

   A medical study found a strong link between the numbers of hours high school students wear a helmet and the number of concussions (head injuries). However, it is unlikely that wearing helmets causes head injuries. Can you think of a confounding variable that might explain this association?

2-78.   A web of confounding variables can get complex and be difficult to unravel. Consider a medical study focused on hearing loss. It may associate variables like eating prunes to hearing loss as strongly as it associates an actual cause like long-term noise exposure to hearing loss.

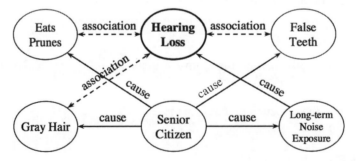

   Here are some newspaper headlines from actual observational studies. Each of them found an association. Some even imply a cause and effect relationship.

   Problem continues on next page →

2-78.   *Problem continued from previous page.*

Assume the associations are true, but determine at least one plausible confounding variable that could be the actual cause.

a.   Calcium in Diet May Cut Risk for Some Cancers, Study Finds

b.   Study: Family Time Declines as Web Use Booms

c.   Chocolate is Linked to Depression

d.   Study: Kids Who Were Spanked Have Lower IQs

e.   Lack of Health Insurance Kills 45,000 a Year

2-79.   Come up with your own original news headlines. The first sentence should contain a reasonable link between two variables. The second statement should be a clear misinterpretation of the link. Two examples are given below.

1st Statement: Facial Tissue Linked to Colds and Flu.
2nd Statement: Surgeon General Calls For a Shift to Paper Towels!

1st Statement: Bathing Suits Tied to Sunburn.
2nd Statement: Doctors Recommend: Swim Naked!

MATH NOTES

Residual Plots

 A **residual plot** is created in order to analyze the appropriateness of a best-fit model. A residual plot has an *x*-axis that is the same as the independent variable for the data. The *y*-axis of a residual plot is the residual for each point. Recall that residuals have the same units as the dependent variable of the data.

If a linear model fits the data well, no interesting pattern will be made by the residuals. That is because a line that fits the data well just goes through the "middle" of all the data.

A residual plot can be used as evidence that the description of the *form* of a linear association has been made appropriately.

2-80.   A human resources manager recorded the experience and hourly wage for a sample of 10 technology workers.

Experience (years)	1	2	3	4	5	6	7	8	9	10
Hourly Wage ($)	12.00	13.25	14.00	16.00	17.00	18.00	19.50	21.00	22.00	23.25

Use an eTool or calculator to analyze the data.

a.   Sketch a scatterplot showing the association between the wage and the years of experience. Describe the association.

b.   Sketch the residual plot. Is a linear model appropriate?

c.   What is the correlation coefficient? What does it tell you?

2-81.   Marissa went with her friends to the amusement park on a beautiful spring day. The park was crowded. Marissa wondered if there was an association between the weather and attendance. From data she received at the theme park office, Marissa randomly picked ten Saturdays and analyzed the data.

a.   Marissa calculated the least squares regression line $a = -14 + 0.41t$, where a is the attendance (in 1000s) and t is the high temperature (°F) that day. Interpret the slope in this context.

b.   The residual plot Marissa created is shown at right. On days when temperatures were in the 80s, would you expect the predictions made by Marissa's model to be too high, too low, or pretty accurate?

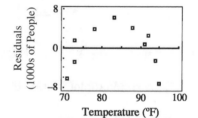

c.   What was the actual attendance on the day when the temperature was 95°F?

d.   Marissa drew the upper boundary line at $a = -7 + 0.41t$ and the lower boundary line at $a = -21 + 0.41t$. What are the upper and lower bounds for the predicted number of people attending when the temperature is 80°F?

e.   Would you rely on this model to make predictions? Why or why not?

2-82.   While in the Indian Ocean investigating vulnerable ranges of barracudas, Alejandra observed a stratified sample of 25 barracudas which produced the following information regarding the relationship between weight and speed burst.

The mean barracuda weight is 12.02 lbs with a standard deviation of 1.85 lbs. The mean speed burst is 23.78 mph with a standard deviation of 3.16 mph. The correlation coefficient is –0.8305.

a.   Decide which variable is explanatory in this situation, then find the equation of the LSRL for this scenario from the provided data. Interpret the slope and y-intercept in context.

b.   The standard deviation of the residuals, S, is 1.8. Interpret this number in context.

c.   An unlabeled residual plot is shown below. Given the values above, make some reasonable guesses for the values of the labels. Make a sketch of this plot on your paper, adding labels and reasonable guesses for your scale. Explain how you found your scale estimates.

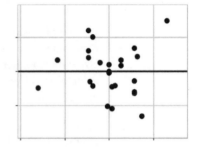

d.   Using all information available, fully describe this association.

2-83.   Most mallard ducks spend a majority of their day in the water. Gabriela is in the state of Washington studying marshy habitats of mallards. An SRS of 63 mallards lengths yielded the summary ogive below:

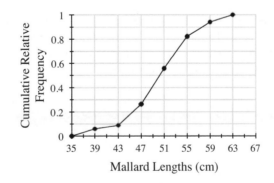

a.   Create a reasonable representation of a histogram of mallard lengths beginning at 35.0 cm with a bin width of 4 cm.

b.   Is this data quantitative or categorical? Explain.

2.2.5 What does the correlation mean?

. . . .

Interpreting Correlation in Context

Although the correlation coefficient is widely used to describe the amount of scatter in a linear association, unfortunately it is an arbitrary computation. Correlation does not have a direct real-world meaning. In this lesson, you will learn a way to make sense—in context—of the correlation coefficient by finding a related number: the coefficient of determination.

2-84.   Kerin is curious whether height is associated with foot size.

Shoe size	Height (cm)
6	153
8	160
7	158
8.5	161
8	168
8	166
9	167
7.5	162
8	162
7.5	166
8.5	167
6.5	159

a.   It was not practical for Kerin to measure her classmates' feet, so Kerin collected the following shoe-size data from her (female) classmates. Use an eTool or calculator to find the LSRL and r. Find the mean height as well, which you will use in a moment.

b.   A new student, Marsha, is joining Kerin's class the next week. She decides to use her data to predict the students' height. Based on her data, what is her best guess for the student's height at this point?

c.   Kerin, as the class ambassador, has the new student's email, and she decides this is a perfect time for an experiment. She emails Marsha and ask her shoe size. Marsha replies, *"I wear a size 9."* Based on the new information, what is Kerin's best guess for Marsha's height?

d.   When Marsha arrives, Kerin immediately measures her, and finds her to be 166.1 cm tall. How many inches better was the line of best fit at predicting Marsha's height than the mean? Try to express your answer as a percentage, as in "Kerin's guess using the LSRL was _____% better than using the mean."

2-85.   Kerin's classmate Louis realizes that this technique could be used to describe the strength of a line of best fit! *"If the line is perfect,"* he says, *"then we could say it always results in a 100% improvement in our predictions; if the line is meaningless, then it would be a 0% improvement on average. We just need a way to calculate how far off we are that takes into account all of the points, not just one!"*

a.   What are some ways you can calculate how far away the height values are *in general* from the line of best fit?

b.   What are some ways you can calculate how far away the height values are *in general* from the mean?

c.   As always, statisticians love squaring and summing things. In this case, the classic calculation of "offness" is using the sum of squared differences.

You will calculate the "percent improvement" by first calculating two values: first, the sum of the squared residuals (the same one minimized with the LSRL) will give us a measure of how "wrong" the LSRL is in total. Calculate that value.

d.   Next, you need a measure of how "wrong" you would be in general if you guessed using the mean. This is the top part of the variance calculation: the sum of the squared differences from the mean. This value is sometimes called the "total square error." Calculate the value for our data.

e.   Using the two numbers from parts (c) and (d), fill in the blank: "Overall, using the LSRL instead of the mean improves our estimates by _____."

f.   The preferred way of stating this relationship is "_____% of the variation in (the explanatory variable) can be explained by the linear association between (response variable) and (explanatory variable)." Use this form to interpret your value from part (e) in context.

g.   Confirm that this value is equal to r^2 (within rounding error).

It probably seems odd that this reasonable and explainable measure of strength as a "percent improvement" happens to be equal to r^2 and it is pretty odd! Actually, it was proved in problem 2-58 in the y-coordinate of the parabola vertex $(r, 1 - r^2)$! Using standardized data, the "best" slope is r, and the smallest sum of squared errors is proportional to $1 - r^2$. Before continuing, read the Math Notes at the end of this section.

2-86.   Suppose Alyse collected the following data for five random students in her class:

Shoe size	Height (cm)
6	154
7½	160
8	162
8½	164
10	170

a.   What is the correlation coefficient? Why is the data unusual? In the context of this problem, what does the correlation coefficient tell Alyse about the association between height and shoe size for these very unusual students?

b.   What can Alyse say about the variability in height in her unusual class? What can she say about predicting height for a student?

c.   What is the value of S, the standard deviation of the residuals, in this problem? How does that interpretation fit the interpretation of R^2?

2-87.   Holly created the scatterplot shown at right for the girls in her class.

a.   What do you notice about the pattern of this data? What do you suppose the correlation coefficient is? Write a sentence about the variability in girls' height in Holly's class.

b.   The best prediction Holly can make is that a girl has average height no matter what her test score was. Holly calculated the average height of the girls in her class to be 162 cm. What would the line of best fit look like? What is the equation of the line of best fit?

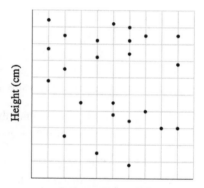

Score on Chapter 5 Test

2-88.   When Giulia went around town in problem 2-74 comparing the cost of toppings at pizza parlors, she gathered this data.

	# toppings on pizza (not including cheese)	Cost ($)
Paolo's Pizza	1	10.50
Vittore's Italian	3	9.00
Ristorante Isabella	4	14.00
Bianca's Place	6	15.00
JohnBoy's Pizza Delivery	3	12.50
Ristorante Raffaello	5	16.50
Rosa's Restaurant	0	8.00
House of Pizza Pie	2	9.00

a.   What is the LSRL? Interpret the y-intercept in context.

b.   What are the correlation coefficient and R^2?

c.   In problem 2-64 you wrote an analysis describing this association. Now improve upon the report by making it more mathematical. Use slope when describing the "direction," and use a sentence about R^2 when describing "strength."

2-89.   Giulia's father finally opened his pizza parlor. He charges $7.00 for each cheese pizza plus $1.50 for each additional topping.

a.   Choose four or five points and make a scatterplot of the cost of pizza versus the number of toppings at Giulia's father's pizza parlor. What is the LSRL? Interpret the slope and y-intercept in context.

b.   What is r? R^2? Write a sentence about the variation in cost of pizza at this parlor. Explain, in context, the difference between this R^2 and the one that you calculated in problem 2-98.

2-90.   A researcher wanted to see if there was an association between the number of hours spent watching TV and students' grade point averages. He found $r = -0.72$. Interpret the researcher's results.

2-91.   Suppose you found that the correlation between the life expectancy of citizens in a nation and the average number of TVs in households in that nation is $r = 0.89$. Does that mean that watching TV helps you live longer?

MATH NOTES

Correlation Coefficient

The **correlation coefficient**, $r = \frac{\sum z_{xi} z_{yi}}{n-1}$, is a measure of how much or how little data is scattered around the LSRL; it is a measure of the strength of a linear association. The correlation coefficient can take on values between -1 and 1. If $r = 1$ or $r = -1$ the association is perfectly linear. There is no scatter about the LSRL at all. A positive correlation coefficient means the trend is increasing (slope is positive), while a negative correlation means the opposite. A correlation coefficient of zero means the slope of the LSRL is horizontal and there is no linear association whatsoever between the variables.

The correlation coefficient does not have units, therefore it is a useful way to compare scatter from situation to situation regardless of the units of the variables. The correlation coefficient does not have a real-world meaning other than as an arbitrary measure of strength.

The value of the correlation coefficient squared, however, does have a real-world meaning, **R-squared**. This coefficient of determination, is written as R^2 and expressed as a percent. R-squared means that "$R^2\%$ of the variability in the dependent variable can be explained by a linear relationship with the independent variable." It can also be found using the formula

$$R^2 = 1 - \frac{\sum (y_i - \hat{y})^2}{\sum (y_i - \bar{y})^2} \; .$$

For example, if the association between the amount of fertilizer and plant height has correlation coefficient $r = 0.60$, you can say that 36% of the variability in plant height can be explained by a linear relationship with the amount of fertilizer used. The rest of the variation in plant height is explained by other variables: amount of water, amount of sunlight, soil type, and so forth.

The correlation coefficient, along with the interpretation of R^2 and the standard deviation of the residuals S, is used to describe the *strength* of a linear association.

2-92.   Make a conjecture about what r is for the following
          scatterplot. Make a conjecture about what the LSRL
          equation might be.

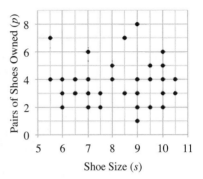

2-93.   Here are some more news headlines from real observational studies. Just as you did in
          problem 2-78, determine at least one plausible confounding variable that could explain the
          cause and effect. Remember, do not argue about the link expressed in the headline. Accept the
          association or link as true. Your task is to find the other variable(s) that could be the actual
          cause(s).

          a.   Teens With Own Cars More Likely to Crash

          b.   Bottled Water Linked to Healthier Babies

2-94.   Caleb is working at his brother's pizzeria researching the preparation of different pizza dough recipes. A cluster sample of 27 recipes revealed the following information regarding the relationship between cost and preparation time.

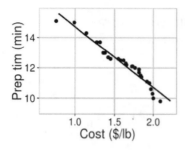 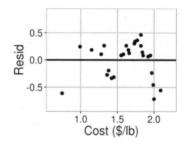

Regression Output for Preparation Time vs. Cost

Predictor	Coef	SE Coef	T	P
Constant	18.7095	0.0634	295.31	0.0
Cost	-3.9967	0.0384	-104.0	0.0

S = 0.033   R-Sq = 94.24%   R-Sq(Adj)= 94.009%

a.   Interpret the slope and y-intercept of the regression line in context.

b.   Calculate r. Interpret $S, r,$ and R^2 in the context of the problem.

c.   Comment on the residual plot.

2-95.   Ms. Anderson is looking at test scores from her U.S. History class. She wants to display them to her class but does not know what kind of representation she should use. She knows that each representation shows different kinds of information.

Explain to her what measures of central tendency or other information will be easily read from each kind of graph listed below.

List the information that will not be easy to obtain. Justify your answers.

a.   Histogram

b.   Stem-and-leaf plot

c.   Boxplot

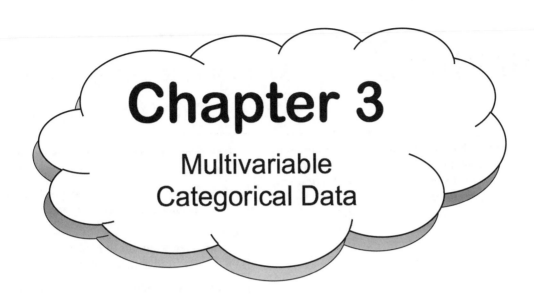

Chapter 3

Multivariable Categorical Data

85	68	153
6	20	26
91	88	179

CHAPTER 3　Multivariable Categorical Data

Chapter Goals

In Chapter 2 you studied associations between two quantitative variables. Categorical variables are used to determine proportions and probabilities. *What is an association of categorical variables? What does it look like and how can it be identified? What if there are more than two categorical variables?*

Explore conditional probability to determine association between categorical variables.

Understand the impact of false positives on testing and detection systems.

Use a variety of tools such as two-way tables and tree diagrams to model complex probability problems.

Create simulations to estimate complex probabilities.

Investigate the concept of natural variation in samples and how that variation can be controlled through sample size.

Chapter Outline

Section 3.1　You will start by extending what they learned about statistical association between two variables previewed in Chapter 1 and use probability to determine association between *categorical* variables represented on a two-way conditional relative frequency tables. Any system designed to detect rare events may be highly accurate but still have problems with false positives. You will look at several such systems, such as HIV and drug tests, and decide whether the social cost of false positives is greater than the benefits of true positive results.

Section 3.2　This section introduces probability tree diagrams as a tool for solving and conceptualizing situations involving more than two categorical variables and makes comparisons between two-way tables and trees as strategies for solving probability problems. You will then learn how to use simulations to estimate complex probabilities and investigate the concept of natural variation in samples and how that variation can be controlled through sample size.

3.1.1 What can I find with categorical data?

Probability and Two-Way Frequency Tables

Often data is collected as counts in named categories. Categorical data incudes your gender, what courses you are taking, what type of shoe you are wearing, and what brand of hamburger you prefer—anything that cannot be graphed on a number line. Categorical data is often collected from surveys.

In the past you may have used Venn diagrams to show relationships between categorical variables. A Venn diagram showing the relationship between variables *A* and *B*, is illustrated at right. Before determining probabilities from categorical data, it is important to organize the information into events where each outcome may only be counted once, or in other words, into **mutually exclusive** events. It is important to notice that while variable A and variable B overlap and are not mutually exclusive, the events (A), (A and B), (B), (not A not B) are mutually exclusive. Every possible event is included and each outcome is included exactly once.

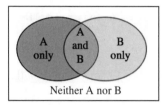

3-1.   Pham is conducting a survey for the school newspaper. He surveyed 175 students at his school and found that 28 students had the new πPhone, 44 students had a πPad computer, and 110 students had neither. Pham then made a Venn diagram to illustrate the information.

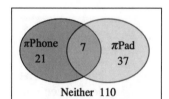

   a.   How did Pham determine the number of students who have both πPhones and πPads?

   b.   How many students have πPhones or πPads? How did he find this?

   c.   Recall that 28 students had the new πPhone and 44 students had a πPad. Why cannot Pham just add 28 + 44 to get the answer to part (b)? Explain.

3-2.   Raul said he could not figure out how to put the data from problem 3-1 into a Venn diagram because it was hard to find the number of students with both πPhones and πPads, so he put the information into a table like the one below.

	πPad	no πPad	totals
πPhone			28
no πPhone		110	
totals	44		175

a.   Copy and complete Raul's table to figure out the number of students in the missing cells.

b.   This type of table is called a two-way frequency table and is often used to organize information and calculate the probabilities. How is it similar to and different from a Venn diagram? What are its advantages or disadvantages?

c.   Assume that Pham's survey is from a random sample of students in his school:

i.   What is the predicted probability that a student at his high school has a πPhone *or* a πPad? $P(\pi\text{Phone } or \text{ a } \pi\text{Pad}) =$ _____

ii.   What is the predicted probability that a student has a πPhone *and* a πPad? $P(\pi\text{Phone } and \text{ a } \pi\text{Pad}) =$ _____

3-3.   A survey of 200 recent high school graduates found that 170 had driver licenses and 108 had jobs. 21 graduates said that they had neither a driver license nor a job.

	Job	No job	
License	99	71	170
No license	9	21	30
	108	92	200

a.   Draw a two-way frequency table to represent the situation.

b.   If one of these 200 graduates is randomly selected, what is the probability that he or she has a job and no license?

c.   If the randomly selected graduate is known to have a job, what is the probability that he or she has a license?

3-4.   At Cal's Computer Warehouse, Cal wants to know the probability that a customer who comes into his store will buy a computer or a printer. He collected the following data during a recent week: 233 customers entered the store, 126 purchased computers, 44 purchased printers, and 93 made no purchase.

a.   Draw a Venn diagram to represent the situation.

b.   Based on this data, what is the probability that the next customer who comes into the store will buy a computer or a printer?

c.   Cal has promised a raise for his salespeople if they can increase the probability that the customers who buy computers also buy printers. For the given data, what is the probability that if a customer bought a computer, he or she also bought a printer?

3-5.   A soda company conducted a taste test for three different kinds of soda that it makes. It surveyed 200 people in each age group about their favorite flavor and the results are shown in the table below.

Age	Soda A	Soda B	Soda C
Under 20	30	44	126
20 to 39	67	75	58
40 to 59	88	78	34
60 and over	141	49	10

a.   What is the probability that a participant chose Soda C or was under 20 years old?

b.   What is the probability that Soda A was chosen?

c.   If Soda A was chosen, what is the conditional probability that the participant was 60 years old or older?

3-6.   An airline wants to determine if passengers not checking luggage is related to people being on business trips. Data for 1000 random passengers at an airport was collected and summarized in the table below.

	Checked baggage	No checked baggage
Traveling for business	103	387
Not traveling for business	216	294

If a traveler were selected at random from this sample:

a.   What is the probability that a passenger did not check baggage?

b.   What is the probability that a passenger checked a bag or was traveling for business?

c.   If a passenger is traveling for business, what is the probability that the passenger did not check baggage?

3-7.   Mr. McGee is the manager of the washer and dryer department of an appliance store. He wants to estimate the probability that a customer who comes to his department will buy a washer or dryer. He collected the following data during one week: 177 customers came to his department, 88 purchased washers, 64 purchased dryers, and 69 did not make a purchase.

a.   Make a two-way frequency table. Using Mr. McGee's data, what is the probability that the next customer who comes to his department will purchase a washer or a dryer?

b.   Mr. McGee promises his sales people a bonus if they can increase the probability that the customers who buy washers also buy dryers. What is the conditional probability that if a customer bought a washer, he or she also bought a dryer?

MATH NOTES

Probability Vocabulary and Definitions

Outcome: Any possible or actual result of the action considered, such as rolling a 5 on a standard number cube or getting tails when flipping a coin.

Event: An outcome or group of outcomes of interest (often called a statistical success), such as rolling a total of seven with two standard number cubes.

Sample space: All possible outcomes of a situation. For example, the sample space for flipping a coin is heads and tails; rolling a standard number cube has six possible outcomes (1, 2, 3, 4, 5, and 6).

Probability describes:

The likelihood that an event will occur.

> Probabilities may be written as fractions, decimals, or percentages. An event that is guaranteed to happen has a probability of 1, or 100%. An event that has no chance of happening has a probability of 0, or 0%. Events that "might happen" have probabilities between 0 and 1 or between 0% and 100%.

The long term. The ratio of successful outcomes to all outcomes after many, many trials under the same conditions.

$$P(\text{success}) = \frac{\text{number of successful outcomes}}{\text{total number of outcomes}}$$

> When a meteorologist says there is a 60% chance of rain in Houston tomorrow, that means that given the same conditions, repeated over and over again, rain would fall in Houston tending toward a ratio of 0.6 rainy days per day.

The future only. If an event is in the past, it can only be described as having a probability of 1 or 0, regardless of one's personal knowledge of the event.

> It is incorrect to say, *"There is a 60% chance it rained in Houston yesterday."* Because it either rained or it did not rain yesterday. The correct way to express an already determined event is to use the word "certain" or "confident." For example, *"I am 60% confident it rained in Houston yesterday."*

3-8.   The graph at right shows a comparison of the length of
several gold chain necklaces (including the clasp) to the
total mass.

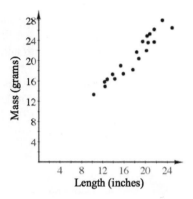

  a.   Estimate a line of best fit and then write an equation
        for the line of best fit.

  b.   Based on your equation, what would you expect to
        be the mass of a 17-inch chain?

  c.   Would you be confident using this data to predict
        the mass of a 3-inch bracelet? Explain.

3-9.   The graph at right compares the gas mileage to the
weight of numerous vehicles.

Describe the association between these two quantities.

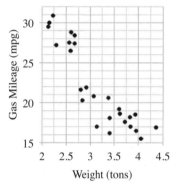

3-10. Cactuses are succulents, meaning they have thickened, fleshy parts adapted to store water. While in Arizona investigating natural supplies of cactuses, Grace described a random sample of 22 cactuses which showed the following example results regarding the relationship between root length and root diameter.

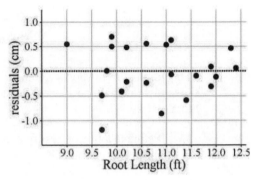

The mean root length is 10.79 feet with a standard deviation of 0.96 feet. The mean root diameter is 5.04 cm with a standard deviation of 1.14 cm. The correlation coefficient is 0.8911.

a. Determine the LSRL equation and label the variables in context.

b. Describe the slope and its meaning in the context of this sample.

c. Use the LSRL to predict the root diameter of a cactus whose root length is 9.40 feet.

d. Calculate the residual for the point $(9.90, 4.80)$.

e. Is a linear model the most appropriate? How do you know?

3-11. The giant panda is China's national symbol. Julia is in China investigating thriving habitats of giant pandas. Assume a stratified sample of 23 pandas showed the following statistical information regarding the relationship between giant panda mass and tail length.

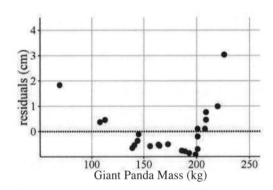

The mean giant panda mass is 172.13 kg with a standard deviation of 40.20 kg. The mean tail length is 11.67 cm with a standard deviation of 1.96 cm. The correlation coefficient is 0.8738.

a. Describe the association between mass and tail length of giant pandas as seen in the sample.

b. Determine r^2 and explain what it tells you about the relationship between giant panda mass and tail length.

3.1.2 Can I find association in categorical data?

Association and Conditional Relative Frequency Tables

In previous lessons, you determined whether there was an association between numerical variables and how to describe that association. You studied the numerical variables of distance from a wall, forearm length, points scored in basketball, and number of pizza toppings, among others. But often data is collected in categories instead.

Probability can be used to help detect whether there is an **association** between categorical variables. Remember, association is not the same as causation. Variables are associated if knowledge of the state of one variable gives you at least some knowledge of the state of another.

3-12. Recall the data from Raul's survey in problem 3-2:

	πPad	no πPad	
πPhone	7	21	28
no πPhone	37	110	147
	44	131	175

Is there an association between owning a πPad and owning a πPhone? In other words, if you own a πPad are you more or less likely to own a πPhone? Investigate this question by calculating the probability that a πPad owner owns a πPhone. Then compare to the probability of a non-πPad-owner owning a πPhone.

3-13. There are 145 students enrolled in senior-level fitness class at Cooper High School; 116 boys and 29 girls. 24 of the boys and 7 of the girls earned As for their first semester.

   a. Create a two-way frequency table to display the counts (the numbers of students) in each category.

   b. Is there an association between gender and the grade received? In other words, is it more likely for a boy to receive an A than a girl?

   c. Comparing percentages is easier in a **conditional relative frequency table** that displays percentages instead of counts. Enter the percentages you calculated in part (b) into a conditional relative frequency table like the one to the right; note that often totals are not included on conditional relative frequency tables. Fill out the missing two values.

3-14.   A researcher suspected that some blood types are more susceptible
to the DapT genetic defect than other blood types. The researcher
collected the following data to investigate. Make a conditional
relative frequency table to determine whether there is an association
between blood type and the presence of the DapT defect.

	# people (in millions)	
	has DapT	no DapT
Type O	0.30	137
Type A	0.28	131
Type B	0.07	31
Type AB	0.03	12

All the two-way tables in this lesson are displayed, for convenience, with the variable across
the top as the explanatory variable. That means that you calculate percentages for columns.
The percentages in a column should add up to 100%.

3-15.   Is there an association between chores and curfews? In other words, do
students who do more chores also have a stricter curfew?

a.   The data for 27 students in the two-way frequency table below is
fabricated ("made up") to make a point.

	early curfew	late curfew
does chores	9	0
does not do chores	9	9

Assume that curfew is the explanatory variable. That means that you should find the total
number of students having early curfew (or late curfew) when you create a conditional
relative frequency table. Then the columns of "curfew" will add up to 100%.

b.   Is there an association between chores and curfew? Explain based on the conditional
relative frequency table you made.

c.   Does doing chores depend on whether you have an early or late curfew, or does having
an early or late curfew depend on whether you do chores or not? Does it matter? Explore
those questions. This time, assume that chores is the explanatory variable. Make a new
conditional relative frequency table, by finding the totals of doing or not doing chores.
Interchange the rows and columns since chores is the explanatory variable.

Does changing the explanatory variable change your conclusion about there being an
association?

d.   Now consider this new group of 30 fabricated
students. Is there an association if curfew is
the explanatory variable? Is there an
association if doing chores is the explanatory
variable? Make conditional relative frequency
tables for both situations.

	early curfew	late curfew
does chores	6	4
does not do chores	12	8

e.   What is interesting about the conditional relative frequency tables that have no
association?

Statistics

3-16.   According to the U.S. Census Bureau, of the 312.59 million people living in the U.S. in 2011, the number of people living alone is given in the two-way frequency table below (in millions). Obtain the Lesson 3.1.2 Resource Page for a copy of this table that you can write on.

	Age						
	Under 25	25 to 34	35 to 44	45 to 54	55 to 64	65 to 74	Over 75
Living alone	1.45	4.16	3.55	5.57	6.69	4.81	6.50
Living with others	109.67	37.41	36.28	38.37	30.28	16.59	11.26

a.   Why do you think this is called a two-way frequency table?

b.   What is the probability of living alone?

c.   What is the probability of being 65 or over?

d.   What is the probability of being under 65?

e.   What is the joint probability of being under 35 years of age *and* living alone?

f.   To find the probability of being under 35 years of age *or* living alone, Qui added the total number of people in the first two columns to the total number of people in the first row. What did Qui do wrong?

g.   Is there an association between age and living alone?

MATH NOTES

Two-Way Frequency Vocabulary

The relationships between two categorical variables can be displayed in a **two-way frequency table** like the one below. In the example below, one variable is the gender of the student, and the other variable is the class level of that student.

	Freshman	Sophomore	Junior	Senior	
Male	53	34	40	49	176
Female	50	61	68	60	239
	103	95	108	109	415

When entries in the table are frequencies (counts), the table is a **frequency table**. The entries in a two way-table are called **joint frequencies**. The sum of a row or column on a frequency table is the **marginal frequency** or **marginal distribution**.

In the two-way frequency table above, the joint frequency of senior males is 49 students, and the marginal frequency of freshman is 103 students.

A **relative frequency table** shows the joint frequencies as proportions or percentages of the entire sample as opposed to counts.

	Freshman	Sophomore	Junior	Senior	
Male	0.1277	0.0819	0.0964	0.1181	0.4241
Female	0.1205	0.1470	0.1639	0.1446	0.5759
	0.2482	0.2289	0.2602	0.2627	**1.0000**

The conditional relative frequency table shows proportions or percentages with respect to a particular variable. For example, the chance of selecting a female, given that she is a junior, is P(female given junior) = $\frac{68}{108} \approx 63\%$.

	Freshman	Sophomore	Junior	Senior
Male	51	36	37	45
Female	49	64	63	55
	100%	**100%**	**100%**	**100%**

3-17. Delenn is re-examining the difference in backpacks among different grade levels at her school. She has collected a random sample of 100 students to see if there are categorical relationships between carrying backpacks and graduating classes.

	Freshmen	Sophomore	Junior	Senior
Backpack	8	16	18	19
No Backpack	3	6	14	16
	11	22	32	35

a. Based on her sample, what relative frequency of students do not carry a backpack at school?

b. If a junior is chosen, what is the conditional probability of selecting a person carrying a backpack?

c. If a randomly selected student is not carrying a backpack, what is the conditional probability they are a junior or senior?

d. Is there a relationship between graduating class and carrying a backpack at school? Show your evidence.

3-18. Assume an analysis of data collected for a study of a vitamin supplement that claims to shorten the length of the common cold is shown in the scatterplot at right and the table below:

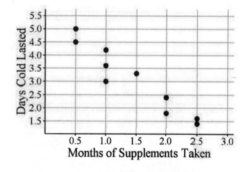

Regression Output for Days Cold Lasted
vs. Months of Supplements

```
       Predictor       Coef      SE Coef       T          P

       Constant        5.3531    0.2902     18.4469    0.0000

       Months of
                      -1.5608    0.1791     -8.7140    0.0000
       Supplements
```

S = 0.4094   R-Sq = 0.9047   R-Sq(Adj) = 0.8928   r = -0.9512

a. Find a LSRL. Define any variables you use.

b. Is a linear model appropriate? Provide evidence.

c. Interpret R^2 and the standard deviation of the residuals in context.

d. Describe the association. Make sure you describe the *form* and provide evidence for the form. Provide numerical values for *direction* and *strength* and interpret them in context. Describe any *outliers*.

3-19. Unlike most members of the cat family, tigers like water. They are good swimmers and often cool off in pools or streams. Assume that while in Mongolia collecting data on protected habitats of Siberian tigers, Olivia investigated an SRS of 23 tigers which produced the following results regarding the relationship between weight and length.

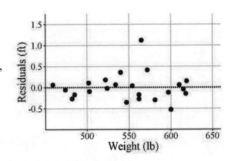

Regression Output for Length vs. Weight

```
Predictor    Coef     SE Coef      T           P

Constant    10.23      0.17     59.55       0.00

Weight      0.012      0.00      4.27       0.00


S = 0.337        R-Sq = 0.0380        R-Sq(Adj)= -0.0078
```

a. Describe the *association* between the weight and length of Siberian tigers as seen in the sample.

b. Determine r^2 and its meaning in the context of this sample.

c. Discuss the standard deviation of the residuals and its meaning in the context of this sample.

3.1.3 How can I express probabilities?

Probability Notation

You may have noticed that there are many reoccurring words in probability problems like "and," "or," and "not." Just like you have been using $P(\ )$ notation to express probabilities, there are symbols commonly used to represent these various events. Some of them are shown here in the context of a relative frequency table:

3-20.   APPLES AND BANANAS

Let event "A" represent a randomly selected high school student ate an apple at lunch and event "B" represent the student ate a banana at lunch. The event did NOT eat an apple is then $\overline{A}$ and did NOT eat a banana is $\overline{B}$.

	B	$\overline{B}$	
A	0.20	0.10	0.30
$\overline{A}$	0.45	0.25	0.70
	0.65	0.35	

The right notation can save a lot of explaining. For example, answer each of the next two questions in a <u>complete sentence</u>:

a. $P(B) = $ _____

b. $P(\overline{A}) = $ _____

The symbol $\cup$ stands for the "**union**" and represent the "**or**" condition, while the symbol $\cap$ stands for "**intersection**" and represents the "**and**" condition. Often the symbol "$|$" is used to represent "**given that**." $P(G \mid H)$ represents the probability of G given that H has occurred.

Convert the following language to probability notation and find the probabilities associated with randomly selecting a high school student who

c.   ate a banana and an apple at lunch.

d.   ate a banana or did not eat an apple at lunch.

e.   did not eat a banana and ate an apple at lunch.

f.   ate a banana given that they ate an apple at lunch.

Here is the apples and bananas table with the relative frequencies removed. Some of the relative frequencies have been replaced with their associated probability notations.

g.   Fill in the other missing relative frequencies with the correct probability notation.

	B	$\overline{B}$	
A			$P(A)$
$\overline{A}$		$P(\overline{A} \cap \overline{B})$	
	$P(B)$		

3-21. In a recent survey of college freshman, 35% of students checked the box next to "exercise regularly," 33% checked the box next to "eat five or more servings of fruits and vegetables a day," and 57% checked the box next to "neither." Use the appropriate probability notation in following questions.

    a. Draw a two-way relative frequency table to represent this situation.

    b. What is the joint probability of randomly selecting a surveyed freshman who exercises regularly *and* eats 5 servings of fruits and vegetables each day?

    c. What is the probability of selecting a freshman who exercises regularly *or* eats 5 servings of fruits and vegetables each day?

    d. Is there an association between eating fruits and vegetables and exercise? Create a conditional relative frequency table to help answer this question.

3-22. Lately there have been a number of times when the sound quality of the news interviews on the school's video station has been unfit to broadcast. One source of the sound problem might be that one of the microphones is not working well. Brendan collected the following data from the last broadcast season:

Interview Sound was:	Mic A	Mic B	Mic C
Good	27	49	33
Unacceptable	6	10	7
TOTAL	33	59	40

    a. Among all of the interviews, what is the probability that a randomly selected interview will have an unacceptable sound quality? Good sound quality?

    b. Is there an association between the sound quality and the microphone used? Make a table with the conditional relative frequencies for each microphone. Should Brendan keep searching for the source of the sound problem or has he found it?

    c. Compare the probabilities in part (a) and part (b). Use your comparison to make a conjecture about a simple test for association.

3-23. Here is the *Apples and Bananas* table again with all of the relative frequencies removed and replaced with their associated probability notations.

	B	$\bar{B}$	
A	$P(A \cap B)$	$P(A \cap \bar{B})$	$P(A)$
$\bar{A}$	$P(\bar{A} \cap B)$	$P(\bar{A} \cap \bar{B})$	$P(\bar{A})$
	$P(B)$	$P(\bar{B})$	

Using only probability notation, (no numbers) create expressions which represent the events shown in parts (a) through (d). You should not have to use the $\bar{A}$ or $\bar{B}$ symbols for any of the following:

    a. $P(B \mid A) =$ b. $P(A \mid B) =$

    c. $P(A \cup B) =$ d. $P(\bar{A} \cap \bar{B}) =$

MATH NOTES

Association and Independence

Statistics is concerned with determining **association** and **independence**. As you have seen so far, if variables (quantitative or categorical) are associated, one variable can be used to change predictions about the other. The attendance secretary knows there will be more absent students on Mondays because the variables school attendance and day of the week are associated. Conversely, demonstrating independence is showing that any apparent correlation between variables can be attributed to chance variations. Showing independence can be as important as demonstrating innocence in a court of law, where an attorney tries to show that the defendant's "variables" are not associated enough with the events of a crime scene to rule out chance variation.

In a logical sense association and independence are complements of each other. If variables are associated, then they are <u>not</u> independent. Likewise, if you determine variables are <u>not</u> associated, then they are independent.

There are some simple rules to check for independence (or association) as long as you keep in mind that chance variation may come with any kind of sampling. Consider the following relative frequencies from two independent samples:

<table>
<tr><td></td><td colspan="2">**Conjecture:**
Independent Variables</td><td></td><td></td><td colspan="2">**Conjecture:**
Associated Variables</td><td></td></tr>
<tr><td></td><td>Left
Handed</td><td>Not Left
Handed</td><td></td><td></td><td>Over
6 ft Tall</td><td>Not Over 6
ft Tall</td><td></td></tr>
<tr><td>Male</td><td>0.04</td><td>0.35</td><td>$P(M) = 0.39$</td><td>Male</td><td>0.14</td><td>0.31</td><td>$P(M) = 0.45$</td></tr>
<tr><td>Female</td><td>0.06</td><td>0.55</td><td>$P(F) = 0.61$</td><td>Female</td><td>0.05</td><td>0.50</td><td>$P(F) = 0.55$</td></tr>
<tr><td></td><td>$P(L) =$
0.10</td><td>$P(\bar{L}) =$
0.90</td><td>1.00</td><td></td><td>$P(> 6) =$
0.19</td><td>$P(\leq 6) =$
0.81</td><td>1.00</td></tr>
</table>

Verifying the conditional probabilities for association in each sample above:

$P(M \mid L) = \frac{0.04}{0.10}$, $P(M \mid \bar{L}) = \frac{0.35}{0.90}$, $P(M) = 0.39$ $P(M \mid > 6) = \frac{0.14}{0.19}$, $P(M \mid \leq 6) = \frac{0.31}{0.81}$, $P(M) = 0.45$

$\qquad\qquad 0.400 \approx 0.389 \approx 0.390$ $0.737 \neq 0.383 \neq 0.450$

   Small variation. Likely due to random chance.   **Large variation. Could not just be chance.**
      Conclusion: Independent, No Association   **Conclusion: Not Independent, Associated**

The relationships you have been using to find association can be generalized to the following:

$P(A) \approx P(A \mid B)$ then A and B are **independent variables (not associated)** or

$P(A) \cdot P(B) \approx P(A \cap B)$ then A and B are **independent variables (not associated)**

3-24. In Canada, 92% of the households have televisions. 72% of households have televisions and internet access. 5% have neither. Use appropriate probability notation to answer the following:

  a. Create a relative frequency table of this situation.

  b. What is the probability of selecting a Canadian house at random that has internet access but no television?

  c. What is the conditional probability of selecting a house that has internet given that it has a television?

  d. Of the houses that do not have television, what is the conditional probability of selecting one that has internet access?

  e. Without doing any further calculations, give evidence in a complete sentence that there is an association between television ownership and internet access in Canadian homes.

3-25. Scientists hypothesized that dietary fiber would impact the blood cholesterol level of college students. They collected data and found $r = -0.45$ with a scattered residual plot. Interpret the scientists' findings in context.

3-26. Chris got a summer job at an environmental sciences lab. He was using a microscope to measure the length of a particular organelle in tree phloem cells and the diameter of the cell itself. Chris collected the following data. A "μm" is a micrometer or one millionth of a meter.

Length of Organelle (μm)	2	9	7	4	4	9	6	2
Diameter of Cell (μm)	46	34	36	42	46	36	42	45

  a. What would you include in a mini-report that fully describes all aspects of a linear association? Make as detailed a list as you can.

  b. Using an eTool or calculator, perform the following analysis. Fully describe all aspects of the linear association in context. Include appropriate graphs.

3-27. Craig is practicing his baseball pitching. He kept track of the speed of each of his throws yesterday, and made the histogram at right.

  a. Is this data categorical or quantitative? Explain.

  b. Can you tell the speed of Craig's fastest pitch? Explain.

  c. Between what speeds does Craig usually pitch?

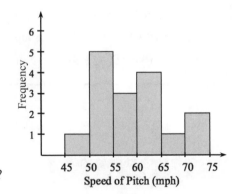

  d. Based on this data, what is the probability that Craig will pitch the ball between 70 and 75 miles per hour?

3.1.4 What if I am given conditional probabilities?

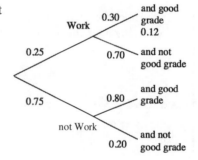

Relative Frequency Tables and Conditional Probabilities

3-28. **APPLES AND BANANAS** (the remix)

Here is the relative frequency table from problem 3-20.

Find the conditional probability that a randomly selected high school's student did not eat a banana for lunch given that they did not eat an apple. Use appropriate $P(\ )$ notation and show your work.

	B	$\bar{B}$	
A	0.20	0.10	0.30
$\bar{A}$	0.45	0.25	0.70
	0.65	0.35	

Express your result in part (a) in probability symbols only (no numbers). For example the equation: $P(A \cup B) = P(A) + P(B) - P(A \cap B)$ is in symbols only.

Now consider a case where you were given a conditional probability such as $P(A \mid B)$ along with $P(B)$. Show symbolically how you could get the joint probability $P(A \cap B)$.

3-29. There is a 25% chance that Claire will have to work tonight and cannot study for the big math test. If Claire studies, then she has an 80% chance of earning a good grade. If she does not study, she only has a 30% chance of earning a good grade. Claire made the adjacent tree diagram to help find her chances of getting a good grade.

- a. Using the tree diagram, determine the joint probabilities and draw a two-way relative frequency table to represent this situation.

- b. Calculate the probability of Claire earning a good grade on the math test.

- c. If Claire earned a good grade, what is the probability that she studied?

3-30. At McDougal's Giant Hotdogs 15% of the workers are under 18 years old. The best shift for those under 18 is 4 to 8 p.m., so 80% of the workers under 18 years old have that shift. 30% of the workers who are 18 years or older have the 4 to 8 p.m. shift.

- a. List the given probabilities with appropriate notation.

- b. Represent these probabilities in a two-way relative frequency table. (You may find a tree diagram to be helpful.)

- c. What is the probability that a randomly selected worker is 18 or over and does not work the 4 to 8 p.m. shift?

- d. What is the probability that a randomly selected worker from the 4 to 8 p.m. shift is under 18 years old?

3-31. Are Timmy's pitching style and Brandon's chance of getting a base hit when batting independent? Brandon batted 32 times when Timmy was pitching. Brandon got a base hit eight times. Timmy used his fastball 12 times, but Brandon got only three base hits when Timmy used his fastball. Make a two-way frequency table and a conditional relative frequency table, then decide whether pitching style and getting a base hit are independent variables for these two athletes.

MATH NOTES

Bayes' Theorem and the Addition Rule

Because variables are often associated, many probability calculations involve conditional probabilities. Through the use of two-way relative frequency tables you have developed the following relationship for determining conditional probabilities: $P(A \mid B) = \frac{P(A \cap B)}{P(B)}$ which is an abbreviated version of **Bayes' Theorem**, commonly written as: $P(A \mid B) = \frac{P(B \mid A)P(A)}{P(B)}$.

Consider the probabilities given in the table below. Assume you wish to find the probability of selecting a female given that the person is over six feet tall.

$$P(F \mid > 6) = \frac{P(F \cap > 6)}{P(> 6)}$$

$$P(F \mid > 6) = \frac{0.05}{0.19} = 0.2632$$

	Over 6 ft (> 6)	Not over $(\overline{> 6})$	
Male	0.14	0.31	0.45
Female	0.05	0.50	0.55
	0.19	0.81	1.00

You have also considered several problems which asked for the **union** of two events. For example, finding the probability of randomly selecting a female **or** someone not over 6 feet tall. From the table you can easily see the joint probabilities which make-up the event:
$P(\overline{> 6} \cup F) = 0.31 + 0.05 + 0.50 = 0.86$.

This same result can be found without needing all of the joint probabilities by using the **general addition rule**. $P(A \cup B) = P(A) + P(B) - P(A \cap B)$

$$
\begin{aligned}
P(\overline{> 6} \cup F) &= P(\overline{> 6}) + P(F) - P(\overline{> 6} \cap F) \\
&= 0.81 + 0.55 - 0.50 \\
&= 0.86
\end{aligned}
$$

3-32. Of the students who choose to live on the East Coast College campus, 10% are seniors. The most desirable dorm is the newly constructed OceanView dorm, and 60% of the seniors who live on campus live there, while 20% of the rest of the on-campus students live there.

   a.   Represent these probabilities in a graphical display (tree, and/or relative frequency table).

   b.   What is the probability that a randomly selected resident of the OceanView dorm is a senior?

3-33. Mary helps prepare food in the Tiger Café. Mary notices that sales of fresh fruit cups seem to vary widely from day to day. This is a problem because preparing too many cups results in wasted fruit and making too few results in lost sales. She decides that the daily weather may have a strong association with demand. Mary chooses 5 days at random from last semester and pairs each day's high temperature with the number of fresh fruit cups sold each day.

Temp (°F)	# of Cups
89	150
52	85
72	136
65	101
72	122

Use an eTool or calculator to perform the following analysis.

   a.   Sketch a scatterplot of this data and describe the association.

   b.   Find the LSRL and define your variables.

   c.   Find all five residuals and interpret the one of the largest magnitude.

   d.   Calculate the standard deviation of the residuals for this line and interpret it in context. Use it to create a reasonable range of values for the number of cups the café will sell when it is 75°F.

   e.   What could Mary do to potentially lower the standard deviation of her residuals?

3-34. Gracie loves to talk on the phone, but her parents try to limit the amount of time she talks. They decided to keep a record of the number of minutes that she spends on the phone each day. Here are the data for the past nine days: 120, 60, 0, 30, 15, 0, 0, 10, and 20.

   a.   Find the mean and median for the information.

   b.   Which of the two measures in part (a) would give Gracie's parents the most accurate information about her phone use? Why do you think so?

3-35.   Okapi have large ears that help them to detect any disturbances and long tongues for stripping leaves from various plants. Demarco is in the Democratic Republic of the Congo collecting data on threatened habitats of okapi. Observations from two independent okapi populations produced the following tongue length results:

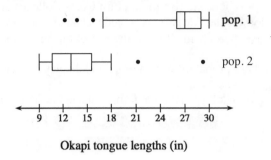

Okapi tongue lengths (in)

Compare the two samples.

3.1.5 How can I explain the counterintuitive?

Analyzing False Positives

In today's problems you will have the opportunity to see how probability can play an important role in decision-making. In *Midnight Mystery*, the results of your investigation will shed light on the accusation that one of the Measleys is guilty of the curling trophy prank, and in *Testing for HIV*, your results can be used in an argument about mandatory testing. There are many other similar applications.

3-36.   SHIFTY SHAUNA

Shauna has a bad relationship with the truth—she does not usually tell it! In fact, whenever Shauna is asked a question, she rolls a die. If it comes up 6, she tells the truth. Otherwise, she lies.

a.   If Shauna flips a fair coin and you ask her how it came out, what is the probability that she says "heads" and is telling the truth? Use a tree diagram and/or a relative frequency table to solve this problem and carefully record your work. Be ready to share your solution method with the class.

b.   Suppose Shauna flips a fair coin and you ask her whether it came up heads or tails. What is the probability that she says "heads"? (Hint: The answer is not $\frac{1}{12}$!)

3-37.   MIDNIGHT MYSTERY

Each year, the students at Haardvarks School randomly select a student to play a prank. Late last night, Groundskeeper Lily Smilch saw a student steal the school's National Curling Championship trophy from the trophy case. All Lily can tell the headmaster about the crime is that the student who stole the trophy looked like he or she had red hair.

Unfortunately, of the 100 students at Haardvarks, the only ones with red hair are your friend Don Measley and his siblings. Groundskeeper Smilch insists that one of the five Measleys committed the crime and should be punished. Don is incensed: *"We Measleys would never play such a stupid prank! Groundskeeper Smilch claims to have seen someone with red hair, but it was so dark at the time and Smilch's eyes are so bad, there is no way she could have identified the color of someone's hair!"*

The Headmaster is not convinced, so he walks around with Lily at night and points to students one by one, asking her whether each one has red hair. Lily is right about the hair color 4 out of every 5 times.

This looks like bad news for Don, but Professor McMonacle agrees to take up his defense. *"I think,"* McMonacle says, *"that the thief probably was not one of the Measleys."*

Problem continues on next page →

3-37.   *Problem continued from previous page.*

Your Task: Develop the basis for McMonacle's argument as follows:

a.   Model the probabilities in this situation with a tree diagram and/or a relative frequency table. The two chance events in your model should be "The thief is/is not a redhead" and "Lily is/is not correct about the thief's hair color."

b.   If you performed this experiment with 100 students, how many times would you expect Lily to say the student had red hair and be correct about it?

c.   Suppose that to help make Don's case, you perform the following experiment repeatedly: you pick a Haardvarks student at random, show the student to Lily late at night, and see whether Lily says the hair is red or not. If you performed this experiment with 100 students, how many times would you expect Lily to say the student had red hair? Which part(s) or your diagram can you use to answer this question?

d.   If you performed this experiment with 100 students, what percentage of the students Lily *said* had red hair would *actually* have red hair?

e.   How can you use these calculations to defend the Measleys? Is it likely that a Measley was the thief?

f.   Have you *proven* that none of the Measleys stole the Curling Trophy?

3-38.   TESTING FOR HIV

An understanding of probability is valuable in relation to important policy issues that are often decided for political reasons. As the issues get more complicated, knowledge of probability and statistics could make a big difference in the decisions each of us will help to make. For example, with the growing number of AIDS cases, some people have called for mandatory testing of healthcare professionals (doctors, dentists) for the HIV virus, with public disclosure of the results. Others argue that mandatory testing jeopardizes the lives and livelihood of many people who do not have the disease and is therefore an unwarranted and unjust invasion of their privacy. Furthermore, they argue that if results are not ever made public for anybody, more people who are not required to test (like health technicians) will volunteer for testing, increasing the likelihood of identifying and helping people who do have the disease.

In order to explore these issues further, you will consider a hypothetical situation. Suppose that the currently used test for HIV is 99% accurate, and suppose that in the population to be tested (in this case it is doctors, dentists, and other health practitioners) 100 out of 100,000 people actually are HIV positive. The question is: what is the probability that a health practitioner would be identified as having the HIV virus who actually did not?

a.   Make a tree diagram and/or a frequency table for this situation.

b.   How does the number of people who are HIV positive compare with the number of people who will be told they are HIV positive but really are not?

Problem continues on next page →

3-38. *Problem continued from previous page.*

    c.   If a randomly tested health practitioner's test comes back positive, what is the probability that he is *not* actually HIV positive? (This is called a **false positive**.) In other words, if you are told that you are sick, what is the conditional probability that you are not sick?

    d.   Write up your statistical conclusions about mandatory testing of health practitioners. How might your statistics change if the study was about subjects in the general population who volunteered for testing?

    e.   Are the test results mathematically independent of the fact that the person tested does or does not have HIV? How could you check this? Explain.

MATH NOTES

Base Rate Fallacy

To overly focus on the accuracy of a test without considering the rarity of the event it is testing is called the **base rate fallacy**. To visualize these situations, think about false alarms. Nearly all alarm systems do an excellent job of warning if there is a specific threat. Car alarms protect cars, smoke alarms protect against fires, and burglar alarms protect homes and businesses, with very high probabilities of detecting the problems they were designed to guard against. However, the frequency of these kinds of threats is thankfully very low, so alarm systems sound more often in response to more common and less exciting events (false alarms). This makes for statements that sound similar but have very different probabilities.

$P(A \mid B)$ can be much greater than $P(B \mid A)$

Very High Probability	*Much Lower Probability*	*Some False Alarm Causes*
Given that a car has been broken into, its alarm system would detect it.	Given that you hear a car alarm go off, the car has been broken into.	Loud noises or music, a large truck driving by, a cat climbs on the hood.
Given that there is a fire the smoke/fire detector will sound.	Given you hear a smoke/fire alarm, there is a fire.	Steamy showers, burning toast, inexperienced chemistry teacher doing a lab, scheduled fire drills.
Given that there is an unwelcome intruder, the security system will call the police.	Given that a security system has called police, there is an unwelcome intruder.	Pets wandering inside the home, someone watering your plants when you are on vacation, a cousin pays a surprise visit.

3-39.   Any system that is responsible for detecting relatively rare events is going to have problems with false positives. You saw this in problem 3-38 regarding testing for HIV. Consider other cases such as burglar alarms, smoke detectors, red light cameras, and drug testing for athletes. All of these systems have proven accuracy and all have a persistent problem of false positives (false alarms).

Consider a hypothetical situation. Suppose that rare event A occurs with a frequency of $\frac{1}{1000}$. Suppose that a detection system for event A responsible for sounding an alarm is 96% accurate. The question is: if the alarm is sounding, what is the probability that event A has not occurred (false alarm)?

a.   Make a tree diagram and/or a relative frequency table for this situation.

b.   If the alarm has been activated, what is the probability that it is false?

c.   Are the test results mathematically independent of whether event A occurs or not? How could you check this? Explain.

3-40.   It seems reasonable that there would be a relationship between the amount of time a student spends studying and their GPA. Suppose you were interested in predicting a student's GPA based on the hours they study per week. You were able to randomly select 11 students and obtain this information from each student.

Hours	GPA
4	2.9
5	3.3
11	3.9
1	2.2
2	1.8
10	4.6
6	2.9
7	2.2
0	3
7	3.3
9	4.5

a.   Without a calculator, make a scatterplot.

b.   Estimate a line of best fit (use a ruler and "eyeball" it), and determine its equation.

c.   Interpret the slope and y-intercept in context.

d.   Describe the association.

3-41. Many people believe that students who are strong in music are also strong in mathematics. The principal at University High School wonders if that same connection exists between music students and English students. The principal went through the records for the past year and found 10 students who were enrolled in both Advanced Placement Music and Advanced Placement English. He compared their final exam scores.

Final Exam Scores	
AP Music	AP English
88	63
74	96
82	86
64	90
97	68
90	90
82	78
72	74
78	96
62	79

Use an eTool or calculator to perform the following analysis.

a. Create a scatterplot of the data.

b. Determine the LSRL and define your variables.

c. Interpret the slope and y-intercept in context.

d. Describe the association.

3-42. Josh is just starting a round of golf. This first hole is 130 yards long. He needs to decide which club to use for his first shot. He has kept careful records about how close his first shots came to the hole, all from this same distance. His records include data from his use of two different golf clubs, a 3-wood and an 8-iron, over the past year.

3-wood: 0, 1, 2, 2, 3, 5, 7, 15, 22, 25 yards

8-iron: 3, 5, 7, 8, 8, 10, 10, 11, 11, 12, 12, 13, 19, 20 yards

a. Create a histogram and boxplot for each of the clubs. Place the boxplot above the histogram on the same number line for each club to make a combination plot. Use a bin width of 5 yards.

b. To find the "typical" distance that Josh hits the ball from the hole with a 3-wood, is the mean or the median a better choice? Find the typical distance Josh hits the ball from the hole with a 3-wood and compare it to the typical distance he hits the ball with an 8-iron.

c. Advise Josh which club to use. Explain your thinking.

3-43. It is just as important to consider the spread of the data as it is to consider the center when comparing data sets.

a. Calculate the interquartile range (IQR) for each golf club in the previous problem. With which club is Josh more consistent?

b. If Josh decided to use the 8-iron, he could "typically" expect to hit the ball so that it lands between 8 and 12 yards from the hole. This is indicated by the box on the boxplot display and corresponds with the IQR. If Josh decided to use the 3-wood, what is a "typical" interval of distances from the hole he could expect the ball to land?

c. Compare the typical interval of distances for the 8-iron with the interval you found for the 3-wood. Do you wish to modify your advice to Josh? Explain.

3.2.1   What if I have more than two variables?

Probability Trees

Today you will explore more ways to use tree diagrams.

3-44.   Chopper the cheerful chipmunk is storing nuts for the winter in his hillside burrow. A map of the tunnels in his burrow is shown at right. Nuts are stored in Dens A, B or C. If every time Chopper comes to a fork in a tunnel he is equally likely to choose any path in front of him, determine the probability of him ending up in each of the three dens? The *conditional* probabilities of choosing each tunnel are provided.

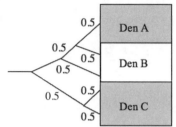

3-45.   SEEING THE PROBABILITIES THROUGH THE TREES

Assume a fair coin is flipped four times and the numbers of heads and tails recorded. Since each flip represents a new variable, a tree diagram is a good choice for representing this situation. The first flip has only two possibilities: heads (H) or tails (T). From each branch, split again into H or T. Continuing this for each flip of the coin. The final number of branches at the end tells us the total number of outcomes after four flips of the coin. In this example there are 16 possible outcomes. The conditional probabilities are not shown on the branches but can be assumed to all be 0.5 because the coin is fair.

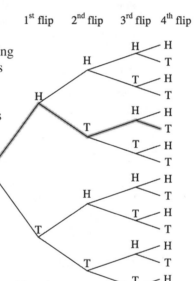

a.   What is the probability of getting all tails? $P(TTTT) = ?$

b.   Determine $P(HTHH)$.

c.   What is the probability of getting at least one tail? The **at least one** condition is common in statistics. The best way to solve this condition is to realize that there is only ONE situation that does NOT qualify. In this problem $P(\text{at least one tail}) = 100\% - P(\text{all heads})$.

d.   What is the probability of flipping a fair coin four times and having tails come up exactly two of those times? Using the "paths" along the branches, how many ways are there to get exactly two Ts? *The path consisting of HTHT is highlighted.*

e.   If the coin was tossed 10 times determine the number of branches needed to show the entire sample space. Show your work, but not the tree.

f.   Sometimes the concept of the tree is more important than a physical representation. Like when you are interested in just one specific branch. If the coin was tossed 10 times calculate $P(HHHTHTHTTT)$? Show your work, but not the tree.

3-46.   Chopper's cousin Violet the vole is also gathering food for
        winter. A map of the tunnels in her burrow is shown at right.
        Seeds are stored in Dens A, B or C. If every time Violet
        comes to a fork in a tunnel she is three times more likely to go
        upward than downward, what is the probability of her ending
        up in each of the three dens?

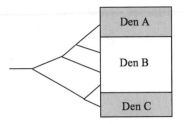

3-47.   Scott's job at Crazy Creations Ice Cream Shop is to design new ice cream
        flavors. The company has just received some new ingredients and Scott
        wants to be sure to try all of the possible combinations. He needs to
        choose one item from each category to create the new flavor.

Base flavor	Chunky mix-in	Fruit swirl
Vanilla	Hazelnuts	Apricot
Chocolate	Sprinkles	Plum
	Toffee bits	Berry
		Grape

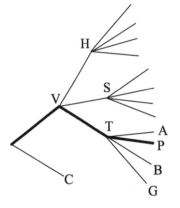

a.   Because there are more than two variables, a
     probability table is challenging. Creating a probability
     tree to show the different combinations. A probability
     tree, like the one started at shows the different
     possibilities branching off each other. In this case, the
     two segments on the left show the base flavors. Each
     different mix-in choice branches off of the base flavor,
     and each fruit swirl branches off each mix-in choice.
     The first letter of each choice is used to label this
     diagram.

     The bold line in the diagram shows the combination
     vanilla, toffee bits, and plum swirl. Complete the probability tree to show all of the
     possible combinations.

b.   How many different flavor combinations are possible? Where do you look on the
     diagram to count the number of complete combinations?

c.   Use your probability tree to help you find the probability that Scott's final combination
     will include plum swirl.

d.   What is the probability that his final combination will include hazelnuts?

e.   Scott's sister will always choose hazelnuts and Scott's little brother will always choose
     grape. List all of the outcomes in Scott's sister's event. List all the outcomes in Scott's
     little brother's event.

f.   Two events are **mutually exclusive** if they have no outcomes in common. Do Scott's
     sister and little brother have mutually exclusive events?

g.   What would two mutually exclusive events in the Crazy Creations Ice Cream Shop be?

3-48.   Anton is ordering shirts for the environmental club. The shirts come in three colors, (red, green, and yellow) and two sizes (large and medium). Anton knows from years past that about 60% of club members ask for the large size. Half of the people who want a large shirt then ask for the color green and half of the people who want a medium shirt then ask for yellow. The other members seem to have no particular color preference so Anton decides to split them equally between the other colors.

   a.   Express the given probabilities using appropriate notation.

   b.   Help Anton determine the T-shirt order by completing a tree diagram and/or two-way relative frequency table of the situation.

   c.   What percentage of the shirt order should be large and yellow?

   d.   If a red shirt is selected from the order, what is the likelihood it came from the medium stack?

3-49.   Battle Creek Cereal was considering a variety of packaging options for Toasted Oats cereal. They wish to predict the net amount of cereal based on the amount of cardboard used for the package. At right is a list of six current packages.

Packaging cardboard (in^2)	Net Amount of cereal (g)
34	21
150	198
218	283
325	567
357	680
471	1020

   a.   The scatterplot, residual plot, and computer output for this data are shown below. Describe the association completely.

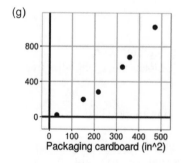 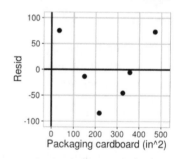

Regression Output for Net Amount of Cereal (g) vs. Packaging Cardboard (in^2)

```
Predictor              Coef      SE Coef      T          P

Constant           -132.1022   60.2567    -2.1923    0.0934

Packaging           2.2904      0.2035    11.2556    0.0004
Cardboard (in²)

S = 71.39      R-Sq = 0.9694      R-Sq(Adj)= 0.9617
```

   b.   Interpret the y-intercept of the LSRL in the context of this problem.

3-50.   Ms. Whitney has thirteen students who did extra credit assignments to raise their grades. The scores on the assignments were 96, 45, 89, 100, 100, 77, 67, 84, 98, 33, 60, 97, and 100.

   a.   Is this data discrete or continuous, quantitative or categorical? Explain.

   b.   Make a stem-and-leaf plot of this data.

   c.   Find the median, and the first and third quartiles.

3-51.   Use the numbers $0, 1, 2, 2\frac{1}{2}, 3, 7, 7\frac{1}{2}, 9$, and 10 to answer each of the following questions. Note that you may use each number as many times as you like.

   a.   List five numbers with a mean of 5.

   b.   List five numbers with a mean of 5 and a median of $2\frac{1}{2}$.

   c.   If a list of five nonnegative numbers has a mean of 5, what is the largest median that this set of data can have?

3-52.   Badgers prefer to live in open grasslands. While in Indiana studying the environment of American badgers, Sienna investigated a stratified sample of 77 badgers which produced the following home range results:

   a.   Create a reasonable representation of a boxplot using the same scale.

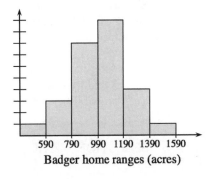
Badger home ranges (acres)

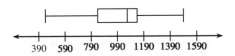

   b.   Is this data discrete or continuous? Explain.

3.2.2 What if I have different situations?

. . . .

Problem Solving with Categorical Data

Today you will use the probability tools you have learned and apply intuition and reasoning to model outcomes from different kinds of categorical variable situations. Show your work!

3-53.   FIND THE QUEEN OF HEARTS

Your friend makes a large fan from a shuffled deck of 52 playing cards and asks you to choose a card. She has you place the card facedown without looking at its face value and tells you the winner will have the Queen of Hearts (QH). While she is looking at all of the card faces, she selects one card and places it face down next to yours. She then shows you the value of every other card in the deck to verify that one of the facedown cards must be the QH. Two cards remain, yours and hers, and one must be the QH. You turn them over to reveal the winner.

a.   Using probability explain to her why this is not a fair game at all.

She offers to play the same game with a three card deck, the QH and two other cards. You agree with the condition that you have the option of switching cards with her before turning them face-up.

b.   After the selecting is done from the 3 card deck, again there are two cards facedown. Should you keep your card, switch cards? Does it matter? Backup your choice with probabilities.

3-54.   SELECTION WITHOUT REPLACEMENT

In five-card poker games having all five cards be the same suit is called a flush. Assume you have been dealt five cards from a shuffled deck of 52 cards.

a.   Find the probability all five cards in your hand will be hearts.

b.   Find the probability of being dealt at least one heart.

c.   Find the probability all five cards are the same suit.

3-55.   A homework answer can be found on shortcut.edu 72% of the time, 55% of the time on cheater.edu, and on both websites 40% of the time. Show whether finding the answers on the two websites are associated.

3-56.   A concierge is a hotel employee who finds food and entertainment for hotel guests. Suppose a concierge makes dinner reservations at three different restaurants with one third of the guests choosing restaurant R1, half choosing R2, and the rest choosing R3. Past experience has shown that three-quarters of those who go to R1 are married, two thirds of those who choose R2 are married, and one half of those who choose R3 are married. If you know one of the reservations is for a married couple, what is the probability that they went to R3?

3-57.   The probability that a student is on-time to class is 0.1 and the probability he is on-time or marked tardy on the attendance roster is 0.9. What is the probability he will be marked tardy if the events on-time and marked tardy are:

    a.   mutually exclusive?

    b.   independent?

3-58.   Platelets provided by blood donors are needed to save the lives of people who are sick or injured. Platelets also vary in healthy adults from 450 to 150 thousand per microliter. Assume the probability of a randomly selected blood donor having not enough platelets in their blood to be a donor is 0.05. The test to measure the number of platelets a potential donor is subject to variation. The probability the test will be negative (indicating the person has to few platelets) is 0.98 given that the potential donor has too few platelets, and 0.02 for a potential donor with enough. If a randomly selected person is tested and the test result is negative, what is the probability they actually have sufficient platelets to be considered a donor.

3-59.   Suppose that only 8.9% of the population has a certain rare blood type. If ten people are chosen at random, what is the probability that at least one has that very rare blood type?

3-60.   Assume $P(A) = 0.13$, and $P(B) = 0.31$. If both events are

    a.   mutually exclusive, find $P(A \text{ or } B)$.

    b.   independent, find $P(A \cap B)$.

    c.   mutually exclusive, find $P(A \text{ and } B)$.

    d.   independent, find $P(A \cup B)$.

3-61.   In speed golfing an athlete's score is determined by adding the number of strokes to complete a course to the minutes required to finish. For example, 90 strokes in 51 minutes would be a score of 141. The lower the score, the better. Diego wants to see if there is a relationship between the time, t, it takes for him to complete a speed golfing match and the number of strokes, s, he takes in the same match. If so, perhaps focusing on running faster will also reduce the number of strokes.

Time, t	Strokes, s
56	86
92	90
56	80
58	91
45	77
50	86

a.   Create a scatterplot with pencil and paper. Determine Diego's best score and circle the point representing Diego's best total score.

b.   Discuss what you can about the association from observation of the scatterplot.

c.   Diego recalls that he was suffering from seasonal allergies that slowed his running on a particular course. Cross out that point. Then use your intuition and draw a line of best fit from the remaining points.

d.   Estimate the slope of your trend line and interpret it in the context of the problem.

e.   Should Diego train to reduce his time so that he sees a decrease in his golf score?

3-62.   Valentina is investigating potential relationships between hybrid car ownership and gender of the owner. Assume a survey of 100 persons revealed:

- The probability of selecting a person who does not own a hybrid car is 0.315.

- If a person does not own a hybrid car, the probability they are female is 0.516.

- If a person owns a hybrid, the probability they are male is 0.435.

a.   Construct a probability tree and/or relative frequency table.

b.   If you were to choose a person at random from the sample, determine the probability they have:

i.   a hybrid car.

ii.   a hybrid car given that they are male.

iii.   male gender.

iv.   a hybrid car or male gender.

v.   a hybrid car and male gender.

3.2.3 How can I estimate complex probabilities?

Simulations of Probability

If you toss a coin ten times, what is the probability of having a run of three or more "heads" in a row?

When 67 people get cancer in the 250 homes in a small town, could that be chance alone, or is polluted well water a more likely explanation of the cluster of cancer cases?

When the mathematics becomes too complex to figure out the theoretical probability of certain events, statisticians often use **simulations** instead. Simulations can also be used to check statistical computations, or they can be used in place of a study that is too expensive, time-consuming, or unethical. A simulation is a model—often computer-based—that uses the probabilities of a real-life situation.

All simulations require random numbers. Random numbers have no pattern; they cannot be predicted in any way. Knowing one random number in no way allows you to predict the next random number.

Complex simulations, such as those that model the weather, traffic patterns, cancer radiation therapy, or stock market swings, require tens of billions of random numbers and a large computer that runs for hours or even days. However, many simpler simulations can be done with graphing calculators.

3-63.   A GIRL OR ALL BOYS?

Mr. and Mrs. Sittman want to have children and would love to have a girl, but they do not want to have more than four children. They want to figure out the chances of having a girl if they have children until they have a girl, or until they have four children, whichever comes first. Since a coin has a 50% chance of landing on "heads," a coin can be used to model the real-life probability that a girl is born.

a.   Talk with your team about how you can use flipping a coin to determine the probability of a couple having a daughter if they try until the first girl or the fourth child is born, whichever comes first.

b.   Once your class has planned the simulation and found a method for tallying results, run the simulation and tally the results until your team has modeled 25 possible families (25 trials).

c.   Combine your results with those of rest of the class. According to your class's simulation, what is the couple's probability of having a girl in this situation?

3-64.   In the simulation for problem 3-63, do you think that more trials would lead to a better estimate of the probability? Tossing coins can become tedious, but you can use a calculator or computer to complete many more trials.

   a.   Your teacher will show you how to use a calculator to randomly generate a family of four children. You can use "**0**" to represent a boy, and "**1**" to represent a girl. Since they will stop having children after their first girl, you can ignore all the digits in the family after the first girl. For example, "0101" would represent a family with one boy and one girl, and you would mark "Girl in Family" on the tally sheet.

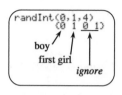

   b.   Be prepared to share your team results with the rest of the class. Use the class results to estimate the probability of a couple having a girl if they try until they have a girl, or until they have four children, whichever comes first. Do you think this result is a better estimate of the theoretical probability than the result in problem 3-63? Why or why not?

3-65.   For the situation you simulated in problems 3-63 and 3-64, the theoretical probability is not too complicated to work out. Work with your team to calculate the theoretical probability for the problem posed by Mr. and Mrs. Sittman in problem 3-63.

3-66.   According to a mathematical principal known as the **Law of Large Numbers**, the more times you run your simulation, the closer your result will come to the theoretical value. Was this what happened when you compared results from problem 3-63 with problem 3-64? Were you close to the expected theoretical value from problem 3-65?

3-67.   HOW MANY GAMES IN A WORLD SERIES?

   In baseball's World Series, the first team to win four games wins the championship. The series might last four, five, six, or seven games. A fan who buys tickets would like to know how many games, on average, he can expect a championship series to last. Assume the two teams are equally matched, and set aside such potentially confounding factors as the advantage of playing at home. Fans want to know the expected value for the number of games that will be played in the World Series.

   a.   Simulate a World Series on a calculator or computer. Let a "**1**" represent Team 1 winning a game, and a "**2**" represent Team 2 winning. You will simulate seven "games," but as soon as one team wins four games the World Series is over and you have to ignore any results that follow that. See below for an example.

   Record how many games it took to win the series. In the example at right, it took 5 games.

   Repeat the simulation at least 25 times. Each time, record the number of games it took to win the World Series. You do not care *which team* won, you only care *how long* the series took.

   b.   Based on your simulation, what is the average number of games a World Series lasts?

3-68.   Dana is looking for clear wood (without knots) to make furniture. The chair he has designed requires four 3-foot boards of clear wood. If there is a 20% chance of a knot being in a particular foot of wood, on average, how many boards will Dana have to sort through to get enough clear wood for one chair?

To simulate each 3-foot board, you can use a calculator or random number table to produce random digits in sets of three from 0 to 9. Consider each digit to be a foot of wood within the "board" where "0" and "1" represent knots (20% of the digits). Simulated boards would look like {6 0 3}, {9 9 5}, {1 4 7}, etc., with each "foot" having a 20% chance of having a "knot".

Continue generating your simulated boards, counting the number created in order to get four sets without a 0 or 1.

Repeat this process enough times to get a meaningful average.

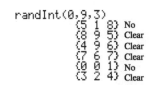

```
randInt(0,9,3)
    {5 1 8} No
    {8 9 5} Clear
    {4 9 6} Clear
    {7 6 7} Clear
    {0 0 1} No
    {3 2 4} Clear
```

3-69.   Mitchell likes to study the weather. He is fascinated by the sophistication of the computer models used to make weather predictions. Mitchell wonders if he can make his own model to predict the next day's high temperature in his area based only on today's high temperature. He selects 11 days at random and gets the temperatures from the Internet. The results from his computer spreadsheet are at right.

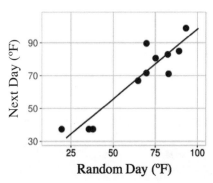

Regression Output for Next Day (°F) vs. Random (°F)

Predictor	Coef	SE Coef	T	P
Constant	13.1758	7.9286	1.6618	0.1309
Random Day (°F)	0.8524	0.1142	7.4607	0.0000

$S = 8.72$ R-Sq = 0.8608   R-Sq(Adj)= 0.8453

a.   Write a few sentences that describe the association. Include interpretations of slope, y-intercept, and S.

b.   Use the graph to estimate and interpret the largest residual.

c.   Mitchell puts his plan in action: he looks up today's high temperature, and it was 68°F. Using the model and the standard deviation of the residuals, S, use Mitchell's model to estimate the temperature tomorrow with a reasonable margin of error. Is Mitchell's model ready to be be used by the local news?

3-70.   Jahna measured the heights of the sunflowers growing in her backyard. Here are the heights that she found (in inches): 34, 39, 48, 52, 56, 61, 61, 61, 61, 76, 76, 79, 81, 83, 84, and 88.

   a.   Is this information categorical or quantitative? Explain.

   b.   Find the mean and median of the heights.

   c.   Create a histogram to represent this data. Use a bin width of 15 inches.

3-71.   Would it be easier for Dana from problem 3-68 to find a single 12-foot board of clear wood rather than four clear 3-foot pieces? Use a simulation to estimate the average number of 12-foot boards he would have to consider.

```
randInt(0,9,12)
{1 2 2 5 4 3 5 ...
{3 9 8 2 8 6 5 ...
{6 8 9 6 3 2 4 ...
{1 3 4 6 4 9 4 ...
{5 6 2 2 3 5 4 ...
{0 3 1 4 9 7 2 ...
```

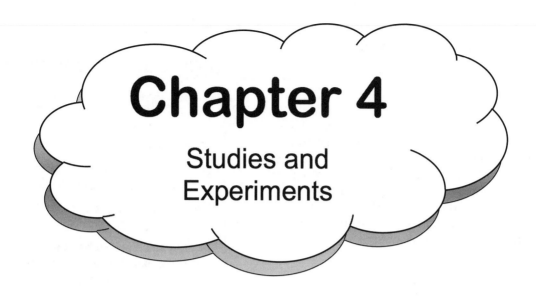

Chapter 4

Studies and
Experiments

CHAPTER 4

Observational studies and experiments are two designs researchers use to collect data and draw conclusions. *What is the difference between them? What conditions are necessary for each design?* In Chapter 2 when looking for associations between quantitative variables you learned that confounding variables make it difficult to determine actual cause and effect. *Can cause ever be determined? How so?*

Chapter Goals

Know how to avoid bias in surveys.

Understand the necessity for randomness in data collection.

Use a variety of techniques for random selection.

Identify situations where observational studies or experiments are appropriate and explain why.

Investigate ways to control confounding variables.

Create a well-designed observational study or experiment for a given situation.

Chapter Outline

Section 4.1   You will begin with an overview of survey design and consider bias in surveys. You will discover that random selection in sampling is necessary to produce a sample that is representative of the population and experiment with different methods of sampling and consider the strengths and weakness of each. You will compare and contrast observational studies and experiments as you think critically about and analyze the conclusions for various real and fictitious studies.

Section 4.2   You will consider what makes a well-designed experiment. You will discover that random assignment is necessary to produce treatment groups that have similar attributes and explore other features of experimental design as you attempt to control confounding variables.

4.1.1 What questions will I ask?

··

Survey Design I

Have you heard statements like the ones below?

- *"81% of public school students are not satisfied with the food provided by their schools."*

- *"The President has an approval rating of 72%."*

- *"The average American household in 2015 consisted of 2.54 people."*

How do news sources get this information? Do they ask every public school student? Do they ask every citizen? What questions do they ask? How reliable are their results? Do you believe them?

In this chapter, you will learn some of the methods used by statisticians to justify claims such as these. You will also apply these methods to investigate your own questions.

4-1.   WHAT DO WE WANT TO KNOW?

Before you can figure out a way to find information, you need to know what information you are looking for! Work with your team to brainstorm research questions that you find interesting. A research question should be complex enough need several survey questions to answer. Be clear about the **population** (the entire group) in which you are interested. The bulleted questions below are examples of research questions, while the numbered questions would be examples of survey questions:

- What do voters in this town think about a raise in taxes?

    1.   If taxes were raised, are there particular improvements you would expect to see the money used for such as schools, road repair etc.?

    2.   If taxes were raised, how do you think the tax would best be collected, users fees for parks, income tax, sales tax etc.?

- How many students at your school restrict their consumption of animal products and what are their beliefs and practices?

    1.   Do you restrict your intake of animal products?

    2.   Do you subscribe to a specific diet such as vegan, or ovo-lacto vegetarian?

    3.   What reasons would you share for restricting meat consumption, concern for animal wellbeing, religion, allergies, or other health concerns?

a.   Work with your team to brainstorm research questions that might be investigated with a short survey.

b.   Next, as a team, discuss your ideas and decide on one research question that you will investigate together. When you have made a decision, call your teacher over to confirm that your question will work.

c.   Talk with your team about how you might go about gathering information about your question. Write down your ideas and be prepared to share them with the class.

4-2.   BIAS IN SURVEY QUESTIONS

Shortly, you will write survey questions for your own investigation. However, before you do that, it is important to understand how the questions that you ask can favor some results, creating bias. Consideration must also be given to how individual responses may be influenced by the interviewer, respondent, measurement instrument, or method of data collection. A poor measurement process can result in unwanted **measurement error**, creating bias and rendering the results useless.

Discuss each of the following survey questions with your team. For each one,

- Look for ways in which the question may create bias. Make sure to mention which outcomes you think will be favored.

- Rewrite the question to reduce the bias you found.

- Be prepared to share your ideas with the class.

a.   Do teenagers worry about getting poor grades?

b.   Do you support the Governor's education plan that ensures that students will be more successful in school?

c.   Does the frequent occurrence of brutal violence in movies and video games have a negative affect on the young people exposed to them?

d.   Do you believe the current movie ratings system is effective?

e.   Should your teachers be paid more?

f.   Moderate exercise is necessary to stay healthy. Do you exercise regularly?

4-3.   Consider the following descriptions of common sources of bias in survey questions. Look back at the survey questions in problem 4-2 to see if you can find any of these types of bias in those questions. Note that some of these questions may refer to bias that you already identified, while some may help you see new sources of bias.

a.   **Question Order:** Sometimes two questions are asked in an order such that the first question suggests an answer to the second. Which of the poll questions uses the biased question order technique? Why would you expect it to influence responses?

b.   **Preface:** Some questions start with statements that can bias the result of the question that follows. Which of the survey questions presented to your class uses this technique? Why would you expect such statements to influence responses?

Problem continues on next page →

4-3. *Problem continued from previous page.*

    c.   **Two Questions in One:** This technique involves asking two questions at once. Survey respondents may agree with one part and disagree with another part, but they are only allowed to give one answer. Which of the survey questions presented to your class uses this technique?

    d.   **Biased Wording:** By using pleasing or unpleasant words, the surveyor can influence results. Which of the survey questions presented to your class uses this technique?

    e.   **Desire To Please:** Research shows that many survey takers will answer in the ways that they perceive will please the surveyor. Which of the survey questions presented to your class are likely to create bias in this way? Are some more likely to do so than others?

4-4.   CREATING BIAS

You and your team members have been asked by the U.S. Department of Education to survey people about the President's new proposal to extend the school year from the current length of 180 days to 200 days. A survey question might be, "Do you think students should attend school for 180 days as they do now, or for 200 days?"

Work with your team to rewrite this question in as many ways as you can to *introduce* bias. For each new question you write, note in which direction the bias is likely to influence responses.

4-5.   A recent survey asked the question: *"What is your arm span?"*

    a.   Why might this information be valuable?

    b.   This question resulted in a number of responses that were half of the expected length. Why do you think this might have happened?

    c.   If the survey were distributed internationally, what problem might occur when analyzing the data?

    d.   How would you rewrite the question in order to avoid the problems described in parts (b) and (c)?

4-6.   In the United States, an average of 2.58 people make up a household in 2010. In order to arrive at this figure, the U.S. Census Bureau asked the question, *"How many people were living or staying in this house, apartment, or mobile home April 1, 2010."*

    a.   Why might this information be valuable?

    b.   Why did the Census Bureau not ask for the number of people in this household or in this family?

4-7.   DESIGNING YOUR SURVEY

Now you and your team will write your own survey questions.

a.   Work with your team to write a short survey that you could use to investigate the research question that you selected in problem 4-1. Do your best to minimize bias due to measurement error in your questions.

b.   Trade survey questions with another team. Read their questions and decide whether you see bias in any of them. If so, write a brief explanation of what type of bias you see and offer suggestions for rewording the questions to reduce bias.

c.   Get your survey questions back from the team that offered you feedback. Consider their feedback and make any revisions that you decide will help improve your survey.

4-8.   Consider the following two survey questions:

Question 1: What superpower would you most like to have?

Question 2: What superpower would you most like to have?
     Invisibility   Telepathy   Super Strength   Fly   Freeze Time

a.   Discuss these two ways of asking people about their superpower preferences. What are the possibilities and limitations of each question?

b.   Question 1 is an example of an **open question**, while Question 2 is a **closed question**. Open questions allow respondents to offer any response they like, while closed questions limit them to some set number of responses from which to choose. Discuss these question types with your team. Is one type likely to give more accurate information? Why? Is one type likely to be more convenient? Why? When might you want to choose to ask an open or a closed question?

c.   Review your survey questions with your team and then make changes to your survey questions so that you have *at least one* open question and *at least one* closed question. Be careful! Changing the format of a question can introduce new kinds of bias.

Store your survey questions in a safe place. They will be needed later in this chapter.

4-9.   For each question listed below, identify the variable of interest and describe the population. Then state whether a census is practical or whether it makes more sense to take a sample. Justify your response.

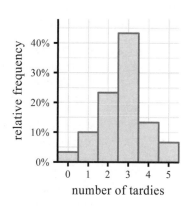

   a.   What is the average time it takes U.S. employees to commute to work?

   b.   What is the average bedtime for students in your math class?

   c.   How much Vitamin A is in an average carrot?

   d.   What is the public approval rating of the Governor?

   e.   How much weight can an elevator cable support?

   f.   What are your friends' favorite movies?

4-10.   Mo and Lana want to gather data on the proportion of students who have cheated on a test during high school. Examine the survey designs below and identify the potential for bias in each. Be sure to explain thoroughly.

   a.   All 1st hour teachers will ask for a show of hands (students raise their hands during class if they have cheated on a test).

   b.   Students will be asked to complete a one-question survey: *"Cheating on a test can get you kicked out of college. Have you ever cheated on a test in high school? Circle one: Yes No"*

4-11.   In a survey of 200 pet owners, 76 claimed to not own a cat and 63 indicated they did not own a dog. 82 responded that they own both a cat and a dog. Make a two-way table displaying the counts in each category. Is there an association between cat and dog ownership?

4-12.   Some students at North City High are abusing the privilege of being allowed to leave campus for lunch. The number of students tardy to Mrs. Greene's period after lunch is too high. For each of the last 30 school days, she recorded the number of tardy students shown in the relative frequency histogram at right.

   a.   Describe the distribution of tardy students.

   b.   How many days were 3 or more students tardy?

   c.   What percent of the days were no students tardy?

4.1.2 Whom should I survey?

Samples and the Role of Randomness

4-13.   Who wrote the *Federalist Papers*? Was it Alexander Hamilton, John Jay, or James Madison? Were the works attributed to William Shakespeare actually written by Sir Francis Bacon, Edward de Vere, Christopher Marlowe, or William Stanley? And who wrote the books of the Bible? The science of statistics is often used to analyze text when authorship is disputed or anonymous. One technique is to look at the average length of words in a passage and compare that with a text written by a known author.

The following is an excerpt from the *Emancipation Proclamation* by President Abraham Lincoln that became effective on January 1, 1863:

> *Whereas, on the twenty-second day of September, in the year of our Lord one thousand eight hundred and sixty-two, a proclamation was issued by the President of the United States, containing, among other things, the following, to wit:*

> *"That on the first day of January, in the year of our Lord one thousand eight hundred and sixty-three, all persons held as slaves within any State or designated part of a State, the people whereof shall then be in rebellion against the United States, shall be then, thenceforward, and forever free; and the Executive Government of the United States, including the military and naval authority thereof, will recognize and maintain the freedom of such persons, and will do no act or acts to repress such persons, or any of them, in any efforts they may make for their actual freedom."*

Your task is to analyze the length of words in the *Emancipation Proclamation*.

a.   Look at the passage above and quickly, *without talking to anyone*, estimate the length of an average word.

b.   Contribute your estimate to the class's histogram. Sketch the histogram on your paper and describe its attributes, including the center, shape, spread, and the presence of any outliers.

4-14.   Is there another way to estimate the length of a typical word in the *Emancipation Proclamation*? Follow the instructions below to take a sample.

a.   Again, *without talking to anyone*, pick ten "typical" words from the passage above and count the number of letters in each. Write down the length of each word and then calculate the mean. Do you think this result is a better estimate of the length of a typical word than the one you estimated in problem 4-13? Why or why not?

b.   Again, follow your teacher's instructions and contribute your calculated mean to the class's new histogram. Sketch the histogram on your own paper and describe how this histogram compares to the histogram of the class's estimates from problem 4-13.

c.   In general, which set of estimates is more accurate? How can you tell? Be sure to use your comparison of the histograms to help justify your answer.

Statistics

4-15.   A classmate suggests that you put each word from the passage on a separate notecard and place them in a hat. He suggests that you first mix the numbers in the hat and then draw a word to include in your sample. Once you have recorded the length of the word, repeat the process nine more times, until you have ten words. This is a reasonable method of obtaining a **simple random sample** (or **SRS**) where every possible sample of nine words has an equal chance of being selected, but you are not looking forward to writing out notecards for 139 words. You and your teammates agree that it is time to ask for assistance.

a.   Your teacher will instruct you on how to use the table of random digits on Lesson 4.1.2B Resource Page to randomly select 10 words. Calculate the mean length of the words in your sample.

b.   Again, follow your teacher's instructions to contribute your calculated mean to the class's new histogram of randomly selected words. Sketch the histogram on your own paper and describe how this histogram compares to the histograms of the class's estimates from problems 4-13 and 4-14.

c.   Your teacher will provide you with the actual mean length of the words in the Emancipation Proclamation. Which sampling method seems to produce the best estimate of the length of a "typical" word? How can you tell?

4-16.   In order to decide whether you like a particular ice-cream flavor, do you need to eat the whole container? Usually, you can make a certain decision about an ice-cream flavor by taking a small taste, or a sample.

When conducting a study, it is usually not possible to survey every person or object in the population in which you are interested (for example, all the residents of the United States, all the students at your school, or all teenage shoppers). However, just as you can learn about the flavor of ice cream with a small taste, you can learn about a population by *sampling* instead of taking a census.

Sometimes statisticians are restricted to sampling strategies based on who is available to them, a practice known as **convenience sampling**. When this sampling technique is used, it is often impossible to make responsible claims about the original population.

Delilah is a pollster and she wants to know what American voters think about a possible federal income tax increase to fund education. She stands outside of a grocery store one evening and surveys every adult who is registered to vote. 62% of the voters Delilah surveyed support the tax increase.

a.   Can Delilah claim that this result is representative of American voters in general? Be sure to justify your thinking.

b.   With your team, think about the population that Delilah is actually finding information about. Whom can she responsibly claim her 62%-in-favor result represents?

Problem continues on next page →

4-16.   *Problem continued from previous page.*

c.   Delilah's sample does not adequately represent all American voters. Errors due to **unrepresentative samples** create bias when the sampling frame (the pool of elements from which the sample is drawn) does not match up with the population of interest. How might Delilah improve her sampling technique to better represent the population of American voters? Discuss this with your team and be prepared to share your ideas with the class.

4-17.   For each of the following sampling methods, consider the actual population it could represent. What sorts of biases might you expect from these groups about Delilah's question from problem 4-16? What biases might you expect them to have about your own team's research question? Be prepared to share your ideas with the class.

a.   A call-in survey on a morning television talk show.

b.   Questionnaires mailed to addresses found in an online phone list.

c.   A phone survey using random digit dialing is conducted on a Tuesday between the hours of 10 a.m. and 2 p.m.

4-18.   **Voluntary response samples** are made up of people who choose to be a part of the survey. Which of the sampling methods in the previous question involve voluntary samples?

4-19.   **Nonresponse errors** occur when respondents do not have an answer, refuse to answer, or cannot be reached. Outline a plan for Delilah's survey that involves conducting interviews over the phone while addressing the concern of nonresponse.

4-20.   CHOOSING YOUR SAMPLE

Talk with your team about what it would mean to randomly choose a sample from the population in your survey. How might you do that? Will it be possible to survey a simple random sample? Why or why not?

Store your survey questions in a safe place. They will be needed later in this chapter.

MATH NOTES

Sources of Bias

Recall that **bias** occurs when data systematically favors some outcomes over others. There are many possible sources of bias in data.

Measurement error occurs when careless or inaccurate processes are used to measure the outcome of a variable. For example, this could come from using a poorly calibrated scale or ruler. If the error is consistent and systematic, this can result in bias.

Sampling bias or **selection bias** occurs when a sample used to gather data is not representative of the population. There are several common types of selection bias.

- **Convenience sampling bias** occurs when a sample is chosen based on ease, rather than through a random process. A common example is choosing the first fifty people available to answer a survey. This makes confounding variables far more likely.

- **Voluntary response bias** occurs when the sample used to gather data is made up purely of volunteers. Online polls or surveys sent out to all customers are classic examples of this design. This is a type of convenience sample, and often results in bias because only those with time, energy, and passion respond to the survey.

- **Undercoverage** is bias created when some members of the population will never be reachable by the design study. Convenience samples often create undercoverage, but it can also arise in other ways. A common example is telephone surveys; anybody who does not have a phone will never be reachable by such a survey. A good survey design minimizes undercoverage as much as possible.

- **Nonresponse bias** occurs when participants are unable or refuse to participate in a study, even if they are reached. This can create problems similar to voluntary response, but is harder to avoid. It can be a major problem for *all* surveys involving humans.

Response bias is bias created by wording or psychological factors. Some possible causes of response bias you have discussed are question order, prefaces to questions, two questions in one, biased wording, and desire to please. Response bias is only a problem when the individuals being studied are humans.

Whenever you are considering potential sources of bias in a study, you should make sure to mention exactly how you think the data is biased—that is, explain which outcomes seem to be favored by the question or design.

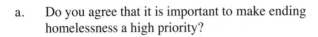

4-21.   Consider each of the following survey questions. For
each one, explain any bias you find. If you think the
question is unbiased (or fair), explain why.

a.   Do you agree that it is important to make ending
homelessness a high priority?

b.   Which of the following factors is most important
to address in order to slow global climate change?

   A.   Car emissions   B.   Airplane emissions

   C.   Pollutants from private industry   D.   Dependence on oil

c.   How important is it to raise teacher salaries?

4-22.   Consider each of the following research conditions. For each one, write a research question
that would be subject to such conditions.

a.   Sampling must be used because the population is too large to measure.

b.   Sampling must be used because measuring the population would destroy it.

c.   A census can be used because the population is measurable.

d.   A census can be used, even though the population is very large.

4-23.   A bag contains 4 blue marbles and 2 yellow marbles. Two marbles are randomly chosen (the
first marble is NOT replaced before drawing the second one).

a.   What is the probability that both marbles are blue?

b.   What is the probability that both marbles are yellow?

c.   What is the probability of one blue and then one yellow?

d.   If you are told that both selected marbles are the same color, what is the probability that
both are blue?

4-24.   A random sample of competitive cyclists had their maximum sustainable power output (watts) versus VO_2max tested. Their data is shown in the table to the right. Note: VO_2max, also called "aerobic capacity," is a measure of how much oxygen your body uses when exercising at a maximal effort for an extended period of time.

VO_2max (ml/kg/min)	Power (watts)
54	292
51	362
49	280
43	293
53	280
59	413
64	358
58	293
56	342
55	335
checksum: 542	*checksum:* 3248

a.   Create a model by finding the LSRL. Sketch the graph and the LSRL.

b.   What power does the model predict for the cyclist that has a VO_2max of 43 ml/kg/min? Consider the precision of the measurements in the table and use an appropriate precision in your result.

c.   Find the residual for the cyclist in part (b).

d.   Find the correlation coefficient and interpret it.

e.   Describe the association. Provide numerical values for *direction* and *strength* and interpret them in context.

4.1.3 What if a simple random sample is not possible?

Sampling When Random is Not Possible

In Lesson 4.1.2, you learned that random selection of observational units tends to produce samples that represent the population and all of its diverse characteristics more closely than samples that do not use random selection of subjects. If random selection is used to reduce bias, is taking a simple random sample always the best method? Consider the following questions with your team as you work today:

> Are there other sampling methods that use random selection?

> What are the benefits of using a particular sampling method?

> What are the drawbacks of using a particular sampling method?

4-25. David is attending a dog show hosted by the local kennel club and wonders, *"What is the weight of a typical dog at the show?"* David is currently taking AP Statistics at school and has decided to use what he knows about sampling to determine the average weight.

a. David decides to begin by taking a simple random sample of dogs at the show by using his calculator's ability to generate random numbers. Your teacher will give you instructions to make sure that the calculator you use generates different random numbers from other calculators.

Follow your teacher's instructions and use a calculator to randomly select fifteen unique numbers. Each member of your team should generate his or her own set of random numbers.

b. Obtain a copy of Lesson 4.1.3A Resource Page which contains information on all 118 dogs at the show. The dogs that correspond to the 15 numbers you generated using a calculator will make up your SRS. Find the mean weight for your sample.

c. Combine your results with those of your classmates to make a histogram of the sample mean weights. How does your estimate compare with those of your classmates? Sketch the histogram in your notes and describe the distribution of mean weights.

4-26. David's SRS resulted in a mean weight of 75.9 pounds. While he cannot be certain, David thinks this mean is too large and believes that his sample may contain a bigger proportion of large dogs than the population of dogs at the show. He remembers discussing stratified sampling as a way to control variation in samples, and decides that it may be the solution to his problem. David begins by dividing the dogs into groups, or strata (plural *stratum*), by size: small, medium, and large. He now plans to take a random sample of 5 small, 7 medium, and 3 large dogs from the strata.

    a.   Why does David not just take 5 dogs from each stratum?

    b.   Obtain a copy of Lesson 4.1.3B Resource Page, which contains information on all 118 dogs at the show, sorted by size category. Using David's sample sizes, take a stratified sample of 15 dogs at the show and find the mean weight.

    c.   Add your statistic to the class histogram of mean weights found using stratified random sampling. Locate the parameter on this histogram. How does it compare?

4-27. David remembers talking about cluster sampling in class and decides that the seven groups for the dogs will form the clusters. He plans to take a random sample of two clusters from the seven available and then use all dogs in those clusters as his sample.

    a.   Take a cluster sample and find the mean weight.

    b.   Combine your sample mean with the rest of your class to create a histogram. Locate the true mean weight of a dog at the show on this histogram. How does it compare?

    c.   David recalls that cluster sampling is often used when other methods are too difficult or costly. He also remembers that cluster sampling is most successful when the attributes of each cluster mirror the attributes of the population. What concerns do you have about the cluster samples you and your classmates generated to estimate the weight of a typical dog at the dog show?

4-28. David plans to take a systematic sample of dogs by randomly selecting a number between 1 and 6, inclusive. Using the alphabetized list of dogs, David will select the dog that corresponds to that number. He will then include every 8th dog on the list in his sample.

    a.   Why did David choose to use a random number between 1 and 6 to start the sample?

    b.   Take a systematic sample of dogs and find the mean weight.

    c.   Combine your sample mean with the rest of the class in a histogram. How do these estimates compare to the true mean?

4-29.   Multi-stage sampling involves combining sampling methods. David decides that he wants to begin by using 5 clusters of the 7 dog groups. He then plans to take a systematic sample by choosing the 3rd dog in an alphabetical list of dogs in each cluster.

a.   Take your own multi-stage sample following David's plan and find the mean weight.

b.   Create another histogram with your classmates and compare the resulting distribution to the true mean weight of all dogs at the dog show.

c.   Of the sampling methods you have used, which seems to be most useful for predicting the weight of a typical dog at the dog show? Why might that be? Which method seems the least useful for predicting? Why might that be?

4-30.   CHOOSING A SAMPLING METHOD AND CONDUCTING YOUR SURVEY

When your team conducts the survey you have been designing, it may not be possible for you to survey every person in your **population** of interest, such as *all* female teenage shoppers or *all* of the students at your school. Statisticians often collect information about a **sample** (a portion of the population) to gain knowledge about the population itself. However, finding a **representative sample** (a sample that well represents the whole population) is not easy.

Consider the methods you have explored in this section as you make a plan for sampling. Consider the following questions and be prepared to share your plan with your teacher.

- What is the population you are interested in?

- How will you select a sample of your population? How can you incorporate some degree of randomness into your selection process?

- How can you justify your sample is representative of your population?

Submit your survey proposal to your teacher. Be sure to justify your decisions in your proposal. It should include:

1.   Research Question

2.   Sampling Instrument

3.   Sampling Method

4.   Plan for Conducting Your Survey

4-31.   David was not really interested in the mean weight for a sample of dogs. He actually wanted to be able to generalize his findings to all dogs at the dog show. Consider the sampling methods below. To what populations can you reasonably generalize the outcome of the study?

Method of Sampling	Description of Actual Population
Call every hundredth name in the phone book.	People with phones who also have their numbers listed
Survey people who come to the "Vote Now" booth at the high school football game.	
Ask every tenth student entering a high school football game.	
Haphazardly survey students during the morning break.	
Text response to an online "instant" poll.	
Hand out surveys in the library before school.	
Survey all students in Period 1 English classes.	

MATH NOTES

Types of Samples from a Population

When taking a survey, the **population** is the group of people about whom the information is to be gathered. For example, if you wanted to conduct a survey about what foods to serve in the cafeteria, the population would be the entire student body. Since it is not usually convenient to survey the total population, different kinds of samples may be used.

Non-random samples should not be used, as they easily create bias. One type of non-random sample is a **convenience sample**, where a subgroup of the population is selected that is easy to survey or measure. Only sampling your friends would be convenient but would seldom accurately represent the your entire school. Another example is a **voluntary response sample**, which contains only the sample of the population that actively chose to respond. Examples include suggestion boxes and text or online surveys. The resulting sample may not accurately represent the opinions of the population of interest by over representing those most passionate about a specific topic.

A **representative sample** is a subgroup of the population that matches the general characteristics of the entire population. If you choose a sample of students at a school, ideally you would include an equivalent fraction of students from variables such as grade level, gender, ethnicity, etc., as the students appear in the larger population of the school. To achieve the most representative sample, your sampling frame should coincide with the target population. Randomness should be used at some level to achieve a representative sample.

A **simple random sample,** or SRS, is more than just giving every subject the same chance of being included. It is a sample selected in such a way that every possible sample of the same size has an equal chance of being selected. Place the name of every student in a hat, mix the names and then draw a subset of (n) names to include in your sample. This would give every possible group of size (n) an equal chance to be included.

A **cluster sample** is most successful when the population is naturally divided into clusters whose attributes closely match those of the population. Randomly selecting a given number of homerooms within the school and including all students in those homerooms in your sample is a cluster sample. It may be more convenient than an SRS, but the resulting sample will only be representative of the student body if the homerooms are similar to random samples of the student body.

A **stratified random sample** involves dividing the population into strata that share a common attribute associated with a large variation in the sample results, and then taking a random sample from each stratum. Taking an SRS from each grade level would ensure that your sample includes a representative portion of students from each grade in a situation where grade level could be responsible for a great amount of variation among samples without stratification.

A **systematic sample** involves choosing a random starting point and then selecting every n^{th} member of the population as subjects. Standing at the door before school and surveying every 27th student to walk in requires less work than other sampling methods.

Multistage sampling combines different methods when selecting a sample. For example: You might decide to take a cluster sample of homerooms and then stand at the door of each class before homeroom and survey every third student to walk through the door.

4-32.   Label each of the following questions as either "open" or "closed."

a.   How often do you exercise?

   A.   Every day

   B.   Once a week or more

   C.   Less than once a week

b.   What is your favorite way to exercise?

c.   What is your favorite time of year?

d.   In which country were you born?

4-33.   For each question in problem 4-32 that you decided is open, give examples of answers that might be difficult to compare and quantify. For each question that you decided is closed, explain how the information you get from an answer may not be as accurate as it could be.

4-34.   Kendra has programmed her cell phone to randomly show one of six photos when she turns it on. Two of the photos are of her parents, one is of her niece, and three are of her boyfriend, Bruce. Today, she will need to turn her phone on twice: once before school and again after school.

a.   Create an area model to represent this situation.

b.   Given that the before-school photo was of her boyfriend, what is the conditional probability the after-school photo will also be of her boyfriend?

c.   What is the probability that neither photo will be of her niece?

d.   Given that neither photo was of her niece, what is the conditional probability that the before-school photo was of her parents?

4-35.   Brett is working in the chemistry lab trying to
          determine if he can predict the volume of three
          different gases (nitrogen, oxygen, and carbon
          dioxide) based upon the pressure applied to them.
          He kept all other characteristics of the gases
          constant. Brett performed the following analysis:

| | | Volume | |
Pressure	Nitrogen	Oxygen	CO_2
2	11.94	12.45	9.45
3	7.71	7.37	8.56
4	6.62	5.09	5.79
5	5.2	5.83	4.9
6	4.51	4.9	3.61

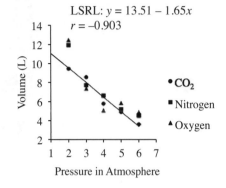

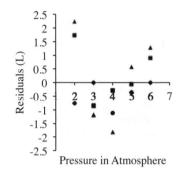

a.   Discuss the association, including slope and R^2.

b.   What is the residual with the greatest magnitude and what point does it belong to?

c.   Using the LSRL model, estimate the volume of a gas at 2.5, 4.5 and 6.5 atmospheres. Use
     an appropriate precision.

d.   How well would this linear model work in predicting more extreme pressures? Support
     your answer.

4-36.   The Kennedy High School cross-country running team ran the following
          distances in recent practices (in miles):

          3.5, 2.5, 4, 3.25, 3, 4, and 6.

          Find the mean and median of the team's distances.

4.1.4 How can I answer the question?

· ·

Observational Studies and Experiments

In an **observational study**, data is collected by observing a subject or unit without imposing any kind of change. The surveys and sampling techniques you have learned in this chapter are part of performing observational studies.

Observational studies are often plagued by confounding variables. A confounding variable may be the true cause of an association, but may not part be of the study. Consider the headline *"International students outperform U.S. students on the math portion of the SAT."* Does this mean that international students are better at math? Not necessarily. The SAT is taken each year by a wide variety of students in the United States as they seek to gain entrance into a college or university. The only international students who take the SAT are those who plan to study in the United States, a very select group of students. In this case, the confounding variable is the level of a student's mathematical education.

You will often see headlines in everyday life announcing the results of some statistical study. Today you will critically analyze the possible meanings of such headlines.

4-37.   For each of the parts (a) through (e) below, discuss, decide, and record:

- Does a census or sample make more sense in this situation?

- If an observational study is possible, explain how you would carry out the study. How would you get a representative sample from the population?

- If surveys are necessary, list a potential source of bias in the question(s).

- If an observational study claims an association between variables, discuss the effects of at least two possible confounding variables.

a.   Is there a relationship between the amount of physical activity a person gets and their self perceived level of stress?

b.   What is the mean of the 2015 SAT math scores for the state of Arizona? Is it higher than the corresponding mean score for West Virginia?

c.   What percentage of high school students would be willing to donate $10 or an hour of time to help a local food bank?

d.   What is the mean weight of backpacks carried on college campuses? Is it different than the mean weight of backpacks carried on high school campuses?

e.   Would wearing neckties increase standardized test scores for boys in middle school?

Problem continues on next page →

4-37.   *Problem continued from previous page.*

    f.   What is the average number of absences for the freshman class at your school?

    g.   What proportion of refurbished cell phones are defective?

    h.   How much cholesterol is in a chicken egg?

    i.   Do the seniors at your school do less homework than the sophomores?

MATH NOTES

Design of Experiments

Because observational studies can only find associations between variables, often **experiments** are conducted to determine cause and effect. In a **completely randomized design**, volunteers are randomly assigned to two or more groups, and **treatments** (explanatory variables of interest) are imposed on at least one of the groups Then response variables are measured and compared between the groups. Randomized experiments can be used to determine cause and effect because the influence of confounding variables has to a great extent been equalized by the randomization among all the groups. If there is a difference among groups, it is most likely due to the treatment since everything else is virtually the same. Often times one of the treatments is a **placebo**, or neutral treatment used to measure the impacts of the knowledge a person has of potentially receiving an actual treatment.

A simple experimental design diagram

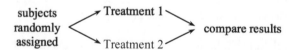

Experiments are usually more difficult and expensive to perform than observational studies. Experiments involving humans require **subjects**, volunteers who have specifically consented to participate, making random sampling nearly impossible. Also, if the treatments are potentially harmful to the subjects, the experiment may be unethical or even illegal.

4-38.   Look back at the research questions in parts (a) through (i) of problem 4-37 and document the following:

    i.   Determine if an experiment would be a reasonable option.

    ii.   If an experiment would be suitable, describe a possible experimental design in context.

Example: *Does homework improve math test scores?* This can be done as an experiment. Randomly assign student volunteers to the homework or no-homework groups. Apply homework and no homework for two weeks. Give the students the same math test and compare the results between the groups.

4-39. Consider these actual newspaper headlines. If an observational study was done, explain how. Explain why an experiment was not possible. If the observational study shows an association between variables, discuss the effects of at least two possible confounding variables. If you believe an experiment was done, state so, and outline a possible experimental design including a placebo if possible. If surveys were necessary, list a potential source of bias in the question(s), and a potential difficulty in getting a representative sample from the population.

a. STUDY STICKS IT TO TRADITIONAL BACK CARE. Acupuncture—real and fake—gets better results for pain than the usual treatments.

b. MARITAL STRIFE A HEART WRECKER? Bad marriage can increase risk of coronary disease, researchers say.

c. BREASTFEEDING MAY CUT BREAST CANCER RISK. Women with a family history of breast cancer who have ever breastfed reduce their risk of getting premenopausal breast cancer by nearly 60%, according to a new study.

d. STUDY: ORAL DRUG BETTER THAN LOTION TO KILL LICE… A new study has found that in tough cases, a (new) oral medication kills the parasites more effectively than a prescription lotion applied to the scalp.

4-40. Suppose you were conducting a survey to determine what portion of voters in your town supports a particular candidate for mayor. Consider each of the following methods for sampling the voting population of your town. State whether each is likely to produce a representative sample and explain your reasoning.

a. Call one number from each page of an online phone listing for your town between noon and 2 p.m.

b. Survey each person leaving a local grocery store.

c. Survey each person leaving a local movie theater.

d. Walk around downtown and survey every fourth person you see.

e. Could you make a representative sample by surveying a few people from each of the situations described in parts (a) through (d) above? Explain, and consider what problems might still remain.

4-41.   Consider this question: *"Does a traditional classroom SAT preparation course improve scores more than an online study course?"*

Design an experiment that could help to answer this question. Refer to problem 4-37 for ideas.

4-42.   Alligators are the official state reptile of three states: Florida, Louisiana, and Mississippi. Sophia is in Florida studying endangered habitats of alligators. A stratified sample of 25 alligators yielded the following summary regarding the relationship between mass and length.

The mean alligator mass is 353.3 kg with a standard deviation of 43.5 kg. The mean length is 402.1 cm with a standard deviation of 15.8 cm. The correlation coefficient is 0.9348. A scatterplot of the data is shown at right.

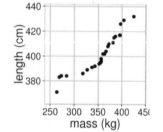

a.   Find and interpret the slope of the LSRL.

b.   Completely describe the association between mass and length of alligators, including an interpretation of R^2.

4-43.   Calculate the probability of randomly entering each room in the maze shown at right.

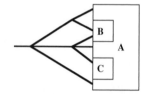

a. $P(A)$ b. $P(B)$ c. $P(C)$

4-44.   If $P(A) = 0.43$ and $P(B) = 0.34$, what is $P(A \text{ or } B)$ if A and B are independent?

4-45.   Mandrills live in very large groups. While in Cameroon investigating robust communities of mandrills, Hannah described a random sample of 56 mandrills, which revealed the maturity age ogive shown below:

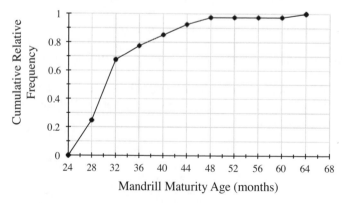

Create a modified boxplot from this data showing outliers if appropriate.

4.1.5 Is there a relationship?

Survey Design II

Today you and your classmates will have the opportunity to hear about a variety of different surveys. As you listen, keep the following questions in mind:

What are the explanatory and response variables?

How was randomization used in the study?

What sampling method was used?

Do you have any concerns about the outcome of the survey being generalized to the population of interest?

4-46.   Legend has it that four university students missed their Statistics final because they were out late the night before but claim their absence was due to a flat tire. The professor allowed them to make up the exam and sent them into separate rooms to take it. The last question on the exam, worth 80% of the entire grade, was *"Which tire?"*

   a.   Without talking to anyone, record your answer to the question on a sheet of paper. Combine your results with the rest of the class and create an appropriate visual display. Comment on any relationships it suggests.

   b.   Assuming that students randomly choose a tire, what is the probability that they would choose the right front tire? How many students in this class would you expect to choose the right front tire? How does this compare with the results from the survey in part (a)?

   c.   Use simulation to estimate the number of students in this class who would randomly choose right front tire. Run your simulation 3 times and combine your results in a class dot plot. Describe the distribution of simulated results.

   d.   Are students in this class more likely to respond "right front"? Use your work from parts (b) and (c) to justify your response. Do you feel comfortable generalizing the results of this study to all students in the United States?

4-47.   What did you learn from planning your own survey? Are there questions that you still have about sampling and survey design?

4-48.   The principal at Parkview Middle School is interested in finding out how much time students spend doing homework each night.

a.   Why might you want to take a stratified sample instead of an SRS?

b.   Explain in detail how you would go about taking a stratified sample of 60 students at Parkview Middle School.

4-49.   For each question below, describe a realistic method to collect information to answer the question. Be sure to indicate whether you would use a sample or census and whether your results would be parameters or statistics.

a.   What percentage of American League baseball players had a batting average above .300 this season?

b.   How much pressure can be exerted on a chicken egg before it breaks?

c.   How many hours of television does a high school student watch per day?

4-50.   A number of states are considering legislation that calls for people to get mandatory drug testing in order to qualify for public assistance money. Some argue that mandatory testing of welfare recipients would jeopardize the livelihood of many people who do not have substance abuse problems and is therefore an unwarranted invasion of their privacy.

Consider a hypothetical situation. Suppose that the currently used test for illegal drugs is 99% accurate, and suppose that in the population to be tested (in this case it is the population of people on public assistance of a given state) 2300 out of 100,000 people are substance abusers. The question is: what is the probability of a "false negative"? That is, the probability that the test identifies a person on public assistance as using drugs when they actually do not use drugs?

a.   Make a diagram or chart for this situation.

b.   How does the proportion of people who are using drugs compare with the proportion of people who will be told they are using drugs but really are not?

c.   If a randomly tested recipient's test comes back positive, what is the probability that he or she is *not* actually using drugs?

d.   Write up your statistical conclusions.

e.   Are the test results mathematically independent of using or not using drugs? How could you check this? Explain.

4-51.   Nicholas is a studying biology at the University of Nevada, Reno. He conducted a field survey to focus on the habitat of the Steller's Jay, specifically at what altitudes they are found in the Sierra Nevada mountains. He created the boxplot below.

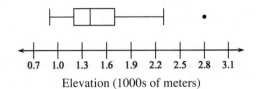

Elevation (1000s of meters)

Create a reasonable representation of a histogram using the same scale.

4.2.1 What is the cause?

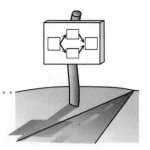

Cause and Effect with Experiments

If our goal is to establish a cause and effect relationship, it is important to plan and conduct a well-designed experiment. As you work today, consider the following questions with your teammates:

Are there variables other than the explanatory and response variables that may have an effect on the results of the experiment?

How will these other variables be controlled?

4-52.   Age, time of day, amount of sleep, eating breakfast, there so many variables that can effect short term memory it can be difficult to measure the effect of a particular treatment. Today, you will be asked to take part in a memory experiment. Your teacher will give you instructions for the experiment. Please keep them upside down until you are told to turn them over.

   a.   Make class histograms and boxplots for the two treatment groups.

   b.   As a class, compare the histograms and boxplots, discuss your results, and write a brief conclusion.

4-53.   Suppose your results from problem 4-52 were seriously confounded by a variable which is not one of the treatments. Using proper experimental procedures can defeat the effects of this confounding variable. As a team, brainstorm improvements that could be made to the testing procedures. Be ready to share you ideas with the class.

4-54.   Your instructor will repeat the experiment using the revised testing procedures you have identified.

   a.   Create histograms and boxplots for the improved experiment.

   b.   Write a conclusion to the experiment.

   c.   How did randomization defeat the confounding variable the class identified and any other confounding variables?

   d.   This experiment was **blind**, (at least in the first trial) meaning that the subjects did not know there were two different versions of the treatment. How might have this be beneficial?

   e.   This experiment could use a placebo group. How could it be done and what would be the benefits?

4-55.   You have just been hired to test the effectiveness of a new pain relief medication. There are 60 patients who routinely suffer from headaches that are available for your study.

a.   The control group in a medical trial may receive an existing treatment or a placebo. In this experiment, a placebo might be a sugar pill that has no medical benefits. Why might you want to incorporate a placebo in this experiment?

b.   Describe a placebo controlled, completely randomized design for an experiment to test the new pain medication. Be sure to include a diagram.

c.   Neither the subjects nor the researchers know which treatment is being administered in a **double-blind experiment**. Why might you want this drug test to be double-blind?

4-56.   Some clinical trials do not have a group that receives a placebo. For example, an experiment that was testing how effective a new surgical technique would not use a placebo group. Explain why this experiment would not use a placebo group.

4-57.   Research suggests that a midday power nap increases focus and productivity. The biggest question is: How long? Most researchers agree that power naps are less than 50 minutes. Consider designing an experiment to determine the most optimal length for a power nap.

a.   Identify the experimental units and the explanatory and response variables.

b.   Create a diagram to outline a completely randomized experiment.

c.   After the word recall experiment, you are concerned about possible confounding variables. Identify some other variables could have an effect on focus and productivity.

4-58.   Design an experiment to answer each of the questions below. Be sure to address the following:

- Explanatory and response variables
- Random assignment
- Possible blinding
- Possible placebo control
- Comparisons

a.   Does a new pain medication reduce the chronic pain caused by fibromyalgia?

b.   Does a new diet patch help people lose weight?

c.   Does drinking green tea reduce the risk of developing Alzheimer's?

MATH NOTES

Blind and Double-Blind Experiments

Incorporating a comparison group into an experiment may control confounding variables. Sometimes, the control group receives a placebo, or neutral treatment. Experiments that use a placebo are often **blind**, that is, the subject is not aware of the treatment group they belong to. In the case of a drug trial, the subjects do not know if they have been assigned to take the new drug, the placebo, or an existing drug. In a **double-blind** experiment, neither the subject nor the researchers in the drug trial who are monitoring the responses to treatments are aware of which pill the subjects are receiving.

The **placebo effect** occurs when a subject has a positive response to a placebo due to the subject's belief in the treatment. If subjects are randomly assigned to treatments in a blind experiment, then the placebo effect should affect all groups equally and any differences among the responses should be due to the explanatory variable. In every drug trial, subjects experience positive psychological benefits by being part a part of the study, regardless of the treatment they are receiving.

4-59. Consider the headlines below. Is there a confounding variable that that could be responsible for the observed relationship? Explain your thinking.

a. Record ice cream sales lead to an unprecedented number of drownings!

b. Wearing jewelry can make you a better communicator.

c. Better reading comprehension linked to larger shoe sizes.

4-60. Does taking Vitamin C reduce the severity and duration of the common cold? How much Vitamin C is enough?

a. Why might you want to incorporate a placebo into an experiment designed to answer these questions?

b. What problems might occur if the researchers were allowed to decide which pill a subject received? Explain how this might lead to an incorrect conclusion and suggest how to avoid this problem.

4-61. Is there an association between a voter's political party and whether the voter supported the ballot proposition or not? The data at right was collected.

	Republican	Democrat
supported proposition	234	286
did not support proposition	162	198
undecided	54	66

4-62. Coach Ron has 15 athletes trying out for 12 openings on the varsity basketball team. As part of the tryout he has each player run a mile and Ron records their time and heart rate as they finish. Coach Ron made a scatterplot as follows.

	Min	BPM
A	5.76	164
B	5.83	153
C	6.04	158
D	6.13	140
E	6.22	172
F	6.27	178
G	6.62	161
H	7.12	152
I	7.18	166
J	7.23	162
K	7.53	166
L	7.82	173
M	7.84	142
N	7.95	135
O	8.20	137
P	8.33	182

LSRL $y = 173 - 2.0x$ $r = -0.119$

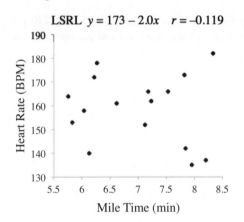

a. Describe the association to Coach Ron in detail.

b. Ron's assistant Cheryl believes they can still find something useful in the results. She proposes that if heart rates could be considered the level of effort given, some athletes may stand out as more or less desirable for the team.

Cheryl divided the scatterplot into four quadrants and put the new labels on the axes. She also labeled each point. She drew the scatterplot at right.

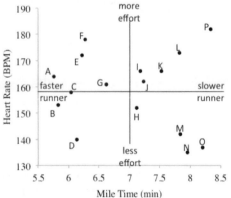

Coach Cheryl believes that the farther a player is from the center, the more they help or hurt the team. Give specific advice to Coach Ron about players D, F, N, O, and P.

4.2.2 How can I reduce variability?

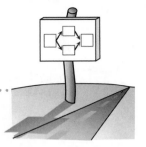

Experimental Design I

Sales of workout apps on mobile devices, designed to help people improve their fitness, are experiencing phenomenal growth. Companies boldly claim that their products will improve cardiovascular health and running speed, help with weight loss, and even increase happiness. But are they as good as people say?

4-63.   BioNomial is one of the fastest growing producers of workout training apps. They are currently under investigation for over-exaggerating the gains that people can expect by using the BioNomial app. Many people claim a popular free training app will work just as well. The BioNomial has hired your team to conduct an experiment comparing the effectiveness of the BioNomial app to the popular free app in increasing the overall fitness of participants, as measured using a formula that combines resting heart rate, body fat percentage, full-effort running speed, and various other factors into a "fitness score."

   a.   Outline a completely randomized design to test the claim that using the BioNomial training app increases fitness scores more than the popular free training app. What are the explanatory and response variables? What specifically will be measured and how will the treatments be compared?

   b.   You conduct a completely randomized experiment with 200 volunteers and make side-by-side boxplots of the change in fitness test scores for the two groups, as shown below. Based on this graph, do you think this experiment gives convincing evidence that the BioNomial app would work better than the free app on average in the larger population?

   c.   Unhappy with your results (and rolling in money), the BioNomial asks you to conduct the experiment again. When you do, you get the following pair of boxplots. Do these boxplots make a more compelling case? Explain.

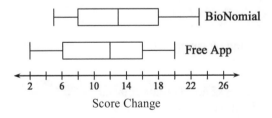

   d.   If you can, open the eTool. This allows you to simulate this experiment yourself with many different populations of volunteers. Click "Generate volunteers" to generate a random group of 200 imaginary volunteers. Leave all of the checkboxes blank (they will be addressed soon!) and click "Randomize Treatments and run experiments" to randomly assign volunteers to groups and create boxplots. Sketch your result. Does it appear to be good evidence for the effectiveness of the app?

   e.   Click "Randomize Treatments and run experiment" ten more times. For each one, decide if it is good evidence or not. What percentage of experiments appear to be strong evidence? Do you ever get a boxplot that seems to show the free app is doing better?

Problem continues on next page →

Statistics

4-63.   *Problem continued from previous page.*

    f.   Note that when you click "Randomize Treatments and run experiment", your volunteers stay the same—only their assignments to the *treatments* are randomized again. What then is the source of all the variation confusing the results?

    g.   Click the "Generate sample" button again to generate a new sample and try again. In general, what seems to be true about the *variability* in this experiment?

    h.   Think of a way you might control the variation seen in repeated trials of this experiment?

4-64.   Assuming that the BioNomial app is actually better than the free app, your team considers a few possible *confounding variables* that could be leading to the high variability.

    a.   Mary thinks that the age of the participant could be a confounding variable. *"Older people may not be able to improve their fitness as rapidly as young people, so a group with both younger and older people would have high variability, which makes it hard to see what is happening."* Test Mary's idea: using the eTool, select the "Age range" checkbox, then click "Randomize Treatments."

        The eTool is now doing what is called a **blocked experiment**; it separates the original volunteers into three groups based variables associated with variation like the subjects' age and basically conducts three smaller experiments within those groups.

        If Mary is right, then the BioNomial app should show up as better more consistently. Does it? Feel free to randomize many times if desired, or even generate new volunteer groups.

    b.   Joan says, *"I think a major thing that matters is the attitude of the volunteers. They all know they are in an experiment since there is no way to make this blind, and some people are going to be more focused on improving than others. What if we sort the volunteers into people who claim to have a 'competitive nature' and those who do not and try blocking by that?"* Use the eTool to test Joan's theory. What happens if you block by Competitive Nature?

    c.   Play around with other blocking variables and combinations of two blocking variables. What blocking variables or combination of two blocking variables results in the least variability?

4-65.   Can you walk and text at the same time? Is it possible that texting and walking can be dangerous and even life threatening? An experiment designed to test this claim randomly assigned 60 participants to three treatments: walking, reading and walking, and texting and walking. Participants were asked to engage in the treatment for a distance of 30 feet. Data was collected on the length of their stride and the time it took them to walk 30 feet. When the results were analyzed, no significant difference among the treatments was found. Despite what the data suggests, the researchers were still convinced that a difference exists.

    a.   How might the results of this experiment been made insignificant because of variability from confounding variables? Give at least two specific examples.

    b.   Design a better experiment to test whether or not there is a difference among the three treatments.

4-66.   Read the Math Notes box at the end of this lesson and work with your teammates to design an experiment to answer each of the questions below. Be sure to consider, document, and justify the following in each case:

      i.   explanatory and response variables

      ii.   blind or double-blind

      iii. placebo control group

      iv. blocking of confounding variables or using a matched-pairs design

   a.   Does the smell of sunscreen reduce blood pressure?

   b.   Does listening to music while you study improve learning?

   c.   Does eating slow digesting carbs, like whole grains, for breakfast and lunch improve endurance for an afterschool workout?

MATH NOTES

The Randomized Block Design and Matched Pairs

If the goal of an experiment is to establish cause and effect, then when you look at the results you hope to find variability between treatments that reveals a relationship. Unfortunately, other variables can confound the results and cause variability within treatment groups that distorts the relationship between the explanatory and response variables.

In a **randomized block design**, experimental units that are similar with respect to this other variable are grouped together to form blocks. Blocking reduces the variability among subjects, before the treatments are applied. The effects of each treatment should then stand out more clearly within each block. In a drug trial, researchers who believe that males and females will respond differently to a new medication would form blocks based on gender. Parallel experiments are then carried out within each block to control the variation in results brought on by gender differences.

A **matched pairs design** is a special type of randomized block design. In a matched pairs design there are a large number of blocks. However, each block only contains as many subjects as there are treatments. In the case of a drug trial, researchers may believe that subjects will respond differently based on the severity of their symptoms. If the experiment has two treatments, then each subject will be paired with another subject who has nearly identical symptoms to form a block. Parallel experiments will then be carried out within each block and the difference between the paired subjects recorded. In another version of the matched pairs design, each subject becomes their own block and experiences all treatments. The change in each subject is the response variable and randomization is used to determine the order in which each treatment will be administered. In a drug trial, each subject would take both drugs in the order they are randomly assigned and the difference in effects of the drugs recorded.

Well-designed experiments use blocking to control variation from variables that can be anticipated and randomization to limit bias from those that cannot.

4-67. Is it easier to learn how to play the guitar by taking lessons from a live instructor or from a computer program? Does whether or not you already play an instrument have an influence on which method you find easier? Outline a well-designed experiment to answer the question.

4-68. It has been an extremely difficult winter and you have missed 16 days due to poor weather conditions. A local newspaper puts a survey online asking the question: *"Should students be required to make up the school days they missed due to bad weather?"* Can you predict the outcome of the survey? Explain your thinking clearly.

4-69. Eddie told Allison, *"I'll bet if I flip three coins, I can get exactly two heads."* Allison replied, *"I'll bet I can get exactly two heads if I flip four coins!"* Eddie scoffed, *"Well, so what? That's easier."* Allison argued, *"No, it's not. It's harder."*

Who is correct? Show all of your work and be prepared to defend your conclusion.

4-70. You have previously explored the relationship between the amount of time a student spends studying and their GPA in problem 3-47. Data from the random selection of students is shown, as well as the computer output from a computer regression run on the data.

Hours	GPA
4	2.9
5	3.3
11	3.9
1	2.2
15	4.1
2	1.8
10	4.6
6	2.9
7	2.2
0	3
7	3.3
9	4.5

Regression Output for GPA vs. Hours

```
Predictor    Coef     SE Coef      T          P

Constant    2.2493    0.3417     6.5825     0.0001

Hours       0.1521    0.0445     3.4156     0.0066

 S = 0.6496      R-Sq = 0.5384      R-Sq(Adj)= 0.4923
```

a. Find the residual for the student who studied 10 hours, and interpret it in context. Would a student prefer a positive or a negative residual?

b. Interpret *S* in the context of this data.

c. Use any reasonable method to predict upper and lower bounds for a student who studies 8 hours per week. Is your prediction useful?

4-71. Anna surveyed 50 students in her school and asked the how many hours they spent on Facegram, Twillerpage, and Instant Book during 3 different months October, November, and December. To the right is a segmented bar graph of her results.

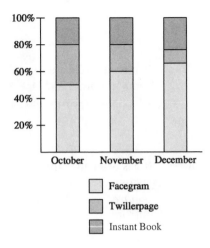

a. Describe the results of her survey.

b. Create a conditional relative frequency two-way table for this graph.

4.2.3 How can I improve the design?

Experimental Design II

Today you will use what you have learned to critically analyze an experiment and suggest possible improvements to the design. Consider the following questions as you work with your teammates:

> Does the design incorporate ways of a controlling variation, randomized assignment of treatments, and a sufficient sample size?
>
> Are there confounding variables that have not been accounted for?
>
> What could be added to the design that would improve the experiment?

4-72. Your teacher will conduct an experiment to determine if one hand reacts quicker than the other. Analyze the results from the experiment by creating a visual display. Comment on any relationship the graph reveals.

4-73. Work with your teammates to redesign the experiment. Be sure to clearly explain why you would recommend each change. Be prepared to share your ideas with the class.

4-74. Your teacher will now conduct the experiment again, incorporating many of the changes suggested. Analyze the results from the experiment. Create a visual display and comment on any relationship the graph reveals.

MATH NOTES

Principles of Experimental Design

When attempting to show cause and effect, it is essential to carefully consider the question to be answered before an experiment is conducted. In addition, it is important to identify possible sources of variation among experimental units. A well-designed experiment is planned in such a way that the effects of confounding variables are controlled so that an association between the explanatory variable and the response variable can be established.

Control helps to reduce the effects of variables other than the explanatory and response variables, which you suspect may cause variation in the results. If you did an experiment involving heart health, you would be wise to control for the variable smoker, non-smoker. A strength experiment might control for the variables age and gender.

It is not possible to anticipate and control <u>every</u> troublesome variable so **randomization** is used to suppress bias associated with uncontrolled variables. Randomization refers to the practice of using chance to assign subjects to treatment groups. Random assignment tends to create treatment groups that have a similar mix of uncontrolled variables, which allows changes in the response variable to be attributed to the treatment.

Replication involves applying the treatments to multiple experimental units. This allows your results to standout against the effects of chance variation that always occurs when sampling from a population. When combined with randomization, replication helps ensure that treatment groups are representative of the population of interest.

4-75.　Whether you are up late studying for a test, working out hard at the gym, or trying to stay alert during first period, most of us have been grateful for the boost offered by an energy drink. These drinks claim to increase energy, sharpen concentration, and improve athletic performance. You have just formulated a new energy drink that you believe is better than anything currently available. Is your formula really better than all the rest? How would you test it? Discuss these questions with your team and record your ideas.

4-76.　Look at your ideas for testing the claim that your new energy drink is the best. How did you address the three principles of experimental design? Be prepared to share your ideas with the class.

4-77.　Does wearing socks to bed improve sleep? Outline a well-designed experiment to address the question. What are the explanatory and response variables? Are there other variables that may affect the outcome of your experiment? Explain.

4-78.   Suppose you want to figure out the insurance coverage in the city of Grand Rapids, population 187,800, by taking a sample of households.

   a.   Explain how you would take a simple random sample of 100 households.

   b.   Why might you want to take a cluster sample instead?

   c.   Explain how you would go about taking a cluster sample of households in the city.

4-79.   A survey of 155 recent high school graduates found that 130 had driver's licenses and 58 had jobs. 21 said they had neither a driver's license nor a job. Is there an association between having a driver's license and a job among the recent graduates?

4-80.   In problem 3-48 you explored the connection between Music and English by looking at final exam scores in AP Music and AP English scores earned by 10 random students at University High School. The principal at the school was not satisfied with his eyeballed line of best fit, and asked you for help! Use the data and computer output to answer his questions below.

Final Exam Scores

AP Music	AP English
88	63
74	96
82	86
64	90
97	68
90	90
82	78
72	74
78	96
62	79

Regression Output for AP English Final Exam vs. AP Music Final Exam

Predictor	Coef	SE Coef	T	P
Constant	112.0863	26.6729	4.2023	0.0030
AP Music	-0.3813	0.3350	-1.1382	0.2880

   a.   A new student entered the school with a perfect score of 100 on the English exam with a residual of 20 points. What was her predicted English score? What was her music score?

   b.   Assume $S = 11.28$. Interpret S in the context of this data and use it to decide if this a useful association for prediction.

4-81.   Mt. Rose Middle School collected canned food to donate to a local charity. Each classroom kept track of how many cans it collected. The number of cans in each room were 107, 55, 39, 79, 86, 62, 65, 70, 80, and 77. The principal displayed the data in the boxplot at right.

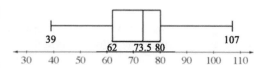

   a.   What is the interquartile range of the data?

   b.   The main office staff collected 55 cans, the counseling staff collected 89 cans, and the custodial staff collected 67 cans.

   On grid paper, make a new boxplot that includes this data. Clearly label the median and the first and third quartiles.

4.2.4 How does blinding work?

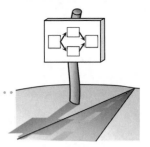

Experimental Design III

Today you and your classmates will have the opportunity to examine several different experiments. Consider the following questions for each:

What are the explanatory and response variables?

How were control, randomization, and replication incorporated into the design?

Do you have any concerns about the outcome of the experiment being generalized to the population of interest?

4-82.   Can students tell the difference between tap water and bottled water? You will take part in a blind taste test today to answer this question. You will be presented with three cups of water to sample. Two of the cups will contain the same kind of water while the third cup will contain a different kind of water. It is your job to identify the cup that is different.

    a.   Assuming that students randomly choose a cup of water, what is the probability that they correctly choose the cup of water that is different? How many students in this class would you expect to choose correctly?

    b.   Use simulation to estimate the number of students in this class who would randomly choose the correct cup of water. Run your simulation 3 times and combine your results in a class dot plot. Describe the distribution of simulated results.

    c.   Can students in this class distinguish the difference between tap water and bottled water? Use your work from parts (a) and (b) along with the results from the experiment to justify your response. Do you feel comfortable generalizing your conclusion to all high school students in the United States?

4-83.   Consider this question: *"Does a new type of motor oil improve gas mileage?"* Assuming this new motor oil was already available to the public, you could survey some car owners who use the oil and some who do not and compare their mean gas mileages.

    a.   What problems might arise from using this method? What are some confounding variables that could affect the outcome of the study?

    b.   Design an experiment to help decide whether the new motor oil improves gas mileage. Include a placebo control group.

4-84.   In what ways did you incorporate control, randomization, and replication in your design from problem 4-83? Are there questions that you still have about experimental design?

4-85. Does counting sheep help you fall asleep?

    a.   Is a census or a sample most appropriate for answering this question? Explain.

    b.   What are the explanatory and response variables?

    c.   What other variables might have an effect on falling asleep?

    d.   Design an experiment to answer the question. Control for at least one of the variables you identified in part (c).

4-86. A health club wants take a survey about extending their hours of operation. Describe in detail a method for taking a simple random sample of 50 from the club's 2735 members.

4-87. The owner of Taco Shack saw reviews online complaining that there was not enough cheese on his tacos. Without identifying himself, he randomly purchased 250 tacos from his own stores and from his competitor. He weighed the amount of cheese on each taco. His results are below:

	Taco Shack	Competitor
< 15 grams cheese	15	11
between 15 and 25 g cheese	82	68
> 25 grams cheese	41	33
	138	112

Is there an association between the amount of cheese and where a taco was purchased? Should the owner of Taco Shack adjust the amount of cheese based on what his competitor is doing?

4-88. A study comparing the mass (kg) to length (cm) of alligators found the LSRL
$\widehat{\text{length}} = 125 + 0.5(\text{mass})$.

    a.   Interpret the LSRL.

    b.   A particular alligator is 500 cm long and has a residual of 60 cm. Find the mass of the alligator.

4-89.   Elvin found the boxplot below in the school newspaper.

Number of hours spent watching TV each week

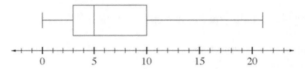

a.   Based on the plot, what percent of students watch more than 10 hours of television each week?

b.   Based on the plot, what percent of students watch less than 5 hours of television each week?

c.   Can Elvin use the plot to find the mean (average) number of hours of television students watch each week? If so, what is it? Explain your reasoning.

d.   Describe the distribution.

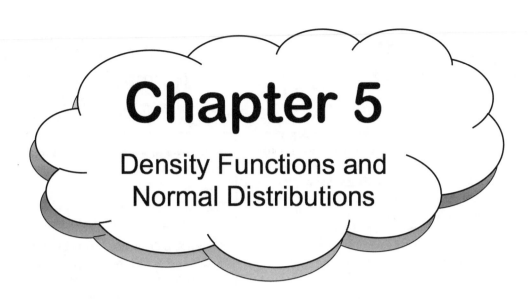

Chapter 5

Density Functions and Normal Distributions

CHAPTER 5

Density Functions and
Normal Distributions

Chapter Goals

Because the field of Statistics is based on practical use, it has a number of rules made by consensus rather than theory, such as the 1.5 IQR rule for outliers. However, there are important elements of Statistics that rely on universal theorems and patterns in nature. Perhaps the most foundational of these is the normal probability density function. This chapter will answer: *What is a probability density function and how can it be used? What is the standard normal distribution and where does it apply?*

Discover probability density functions through the use of relative frequency histograms.

Use a uniform probability distribution as a model for simple situations.

Investigate the normal probability density function as a way to find probabilities and percentiles from normally distributed populations.

Identify situations and use an inverse normal function to find measurable values from probabilities.

Explore the Empirical Rule for quick and efficient estimations of normal probabilities based on z-scores.

Chapter Outline

Section 5.1   You will explore different types of density functions: uniform and bell-shaped. You will create a bell-shaped mathematical model of data called normal probability density function. Much of the real life data that is encountered in science, business, and industry can be modeled with a normal probability density function. You will explore and discuss the similarities and differences between a relative frequency histogram as a way to represent a sample and the normal distribution as a model for the population represented in the sample.

Section 5.2   Every normal density function has an inverse. You will use normal density inverse functions to convert probabilities and percentiles into values of a random variable, then explore and discuss the standard normal probability distribution and z-scores.

5.1.1 How can I show percentages for quantitative data?

Relative Frequency Histograms and Random Variables

As you saw in Lesson 1.3.1, when the frequencies (counts of numbers or values) listed in a frequency table are divided by the total number of data points, the frequencies become ratios, and the frequency table becomes a relative frequency table.

Histograms display the information from frequency tables and **relative frequency histograms** display information from relative frequency tables. A relative frequency histogram helps you find the proportion of the population with a certain characteristic or compare distribution characteristics when working with very different sample sizes.

5-1.   VISORS FOR RUNNERS, Part 1

The Style & Comfort Headgear Company makes printed visors as gifts for women running in charity marathons. Marathons in different cities have different numbers of participants. S & C Headgear needs a method for deciding how many visors of each size to print for each event. The company collected the data below for women's head circumference by measuring 40 randomly selected runners at charity events.

Sorted Head Circumferences (cm)

51.2	52.2	52.7	53.0	53.1	53.7	53.9	55.2
51.4	52.2	52.7	53.1	53.2	53.7	54.3	55.3
51.9	52.3	52.8	53.1	53.2	53.7	54.5	55.4
51.9	52.5	52.9	53.1	53.3	53.7	54.6	55.4
51.9	52.6	53.0	53.1	53.4	53.8	54.8	55.5

checksum: 2133.3

a.   What are the mean head circumference and standard deviation for these women?

b.   Make a histogram of the distribution of women's head circumferences and sketch it. Use an interval from 50 cm to 57 cm with a bin width of 1 cm.

c.   Hat size is determined by the whole-number portion of a woman's head circumference. For example, a woman with a head measuring 55.8 cm would need a size 55 hat. According to your histogram, how many women in this sample need a size 52 hat?

d.   What percent of the women in this sample have a hat size less than 54?

5-2.   Questions about percentages, like those in part (d) of problem 5-1 above, are easier to answer if you make a table of **relative frequencies**. Relative frequency is the **proportion** of hats in that size out of the total 40 hats, written as a decimal.

a.   Copy and complete the table at right.

Women's hat sizes

size interval	frequency (# of hats)	relative frequency (proportion of hats)
50 to 51	0	0
51 to 52	5	0.125
52 to 53	9	0.225
53 to 54	17	
54 to 55		
55 to 56		
56 to 57		

b.   Make a **relative frequency histogram** from the table above. Sketch the relative frequency histogram. Label the top of each bar with its relative frequency. What do you notice about the shape of the relative frequency histogram?

c.   Relative frequency histograms make percentages easier to visualize. Use the histogram to compute the percent of hats in this sample between size 52 and 55.

d.   What percent of hats in this sample are below size 56? Show a computation.

5-3.   CHARITY RACE TIMES, Part One

In Chapter 1 you learned that the sample variance was an unbiased estimator of the population variance, so the sample standard deviation is calculated by taking the square root of the sample variance in order to reduce bias in the estimation.

The 40 women in the sample recorded their race times in various charity 5K races in the table at right. Keeping the data from problem 5-1 in the calculator, add the adjacent race times to another list.

Sorted Race Times (min)

20.6	22.5	22.7	23.0	23.3	23.3	23.6	24.4
21.3	22.5	22.8	23.1	23.3	23.4	23.9	24.5
21.6	22.5	22.8	23.1	23.3	23.5	24.1	24.7
22.2	22.6	22.9	23.1	23.3	23.5	24.4	24.9
22.3	22.6	23.0	23.2	23.3	23.5	24.4	25.7

checksum: 928.7

a.   Find the mean and standard deviation of the race times to four decimal places. Justify your choice of standard deviation and use the proper notation.

b.   Create a relative frequency histogram. Use an interval from 19 to 27 with a bin width of 1. Label the top of each bar with its relative frequency.

c.   Use the relative frequencies on your histogram to calculate the percentage of racers in this sample that had a time faster than 22 minutes. Remember, smaller times are faster.

d.   What percentage of racers in this sample completed a race between 22 and 25 minutes? What is the relationship between the area of the bars and the percentage of the population?

In Chapter 1 you learned that an ogive can be a useful representation of a function that converts data to percentiles and also the inverse function that turns percentiles into data values. Using a random variable provides a convenient way to refer to a set of outcomes and express its probability. A **random variable** is a quantifiable value, which is subject to a probability of occurrence. Just like the quantitative outcomes random variables represent, they can be classified as **discrete random variables** (based on a set of countable data) or **continuous random variables** (limited only by the precision of the tool used in the measurement).

5-4.   MEANWHILE BACK IN MINNEAPOLIS

The intrepid trio of Cory, Jamison, and Harper had more questions about the ogive from the escape room called "The Library." Jamison asked, *"What is the probability of selecting a team at random with a score less than 50 points?"* Then Harper suggests, *"Let's simplify this by calling a team's score a random variable X. Then the entire question is reduced to P(X < 50) = ?"*

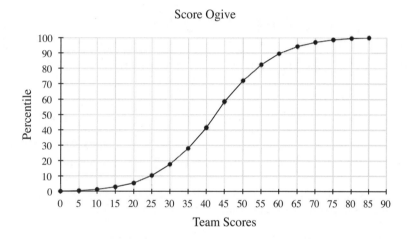

a.   Convert the following statements to $P(X)$ notation using a random variable X and then find the associated probabilities on the ogive:

    i.   What is the probability of selecting a team at random with a score less than 35 points?

    ii.   What is the probability of selecting a team at random with a score more than 65 points?

    iii.   What is the probability of selecting a team at random with a score between 30 and 60 points?

    iv.   What is the probability of selecting a team at random with a score between 0 and 90 points?

b.   Estimate the 50th percentile score. Remember to answer with random variable notation.

5-5.   Caspar and Ollie took their physics test today. Caspar took his physics test during period 2 and Ollie took his physics test during period 6. Caspar scored a 91 on his test. Period 2 had a class mean of 89 and a standard deviation of 2. Ollie scored a 94 on his test. Period 6 had a class mean of 88 and the standard deviation was 3. Caspar and Ollie are arguing over who had the best score relative to their classmates.

   a.   Transform Caspar's raw score to a z-score.

   b.   Transform Ollie's raw score to a z-score

   c.   Who had the better score? Explain why.

   d.   Jasper, a student in period 6, scored an 85. Compute Jasper's measure of relative location.

MATH NOTES

Symbols for Standard Deviation

In Statistics, standard variables are used to represent the mean and standard deviation.

The population parameters are written using lower-case Greek letters such as μ (pronounced "myoo") for the mean, and σ (pronounced "sigma") for the population standard deviation

When the data are a sample, $\bar{x}$ (pronounced "x-bar") represents the sample mean, and s is used to represent the sample standard deviation.

The number of values in a data set is often represented with n.

Review & Preview

5-6.   Coastal redwoods are considered the tallest terrestrial organisms in the world. While in California investigating majestic inventories of mature coastal redwoods, Maria investigated a stratified sample of 25 redwoods, which revealed the relative frequency histogram shown at right:

Convert the following questions to notation using a random variable X and estimate the associated probabilities from the relative frequency histogram:

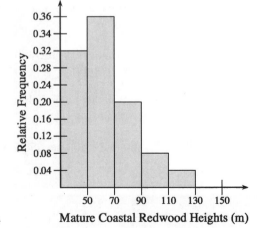

Mature Coastal Redwood Heights (m)

Problem continues on next page →

5-6.   *Problem continues from previous page.*

    a.   What is the probability of selecting a tree from the sample greater than 70 meters tall?

    b.   What is the probability of selecting a tree from the sample less than 60 meters tall?

    c.   What is the probability of selecting a tree from the sample between 80 and 120 meters tall?

    d.   What is the probability of selecting a tree from the sample between 30 and 130 meters tall?

5-7.   Lana believes that students at her school who arrive late to class are more likely to receive lower grades on tests than their peers who arrive on time.

    a.   Should an observational study or an experiment be carried out to answer the question? Explain.

    b.   Describe how you would carry out the study.

5-8.   Agatha is a big fan of chicken nuggets and decided to do some comparison shopping at local restaurants. She went to several chains that sold chicken nuggets and compared the number of nuggets in a pack and the cost of the nuggets. The resulting data were used to create the residual plot at right and computer regression output below.

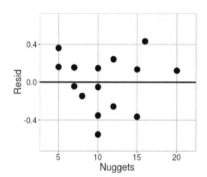

Regression Output for Price vs. Nuggets

```
Predictor     Coef     SE Coef       T          P

Constant    -0.1845    0.2135    -0.8642     0.4031

Nuggets      0.2026    0.0185    10.9748     0.0000

S = 0.2956     R-Sq = 0.9026     R-Sq(Adj) = 0.8951
```

    a.   Does a linear model seem appropriate for this data?

    b.   What is the (approximate) actual cost of the container with 16 nuggets?

    c.   Agatha goes out later that day to Chikns-R-Yum and finds they have a 30-pack of chicken nuggets for $2.99. How will adding this point to the data affect r?

5-9.   Mr. Dobson is planning to give a quiz to his class tomorrow. Unfortunately for his students, Mr. Dobson is notorious for writing quizzes that seem to have no relevance to the subject. With this in mind, his students know that their efforts will be purely guesswork. If the quiz contains ten questions that the students will have to match with ten given answers, what is the probability that Rodney Random will get all ten questions matched correctly?

5.1.2 How can I find probabilities using continuous random variables?

Introduction to Density Functions

Today's lesson will help you develop skills and build knowledge about **probability density functions**, commonly called **probability distributions**, which are tools for finding probabilities based on counts or measurements for random variables.

A density function is an idealized mathematical model for continuous probability distributions. You must remember to differentiate between sample statistics such as ($\bar{x}$, s_x) from idealized parameters of the population (μ, σ).

Density functions take on the same kinds of shapes you learned from frequency distributions in Chapter 1 including symmetric, uniform, and skewed.

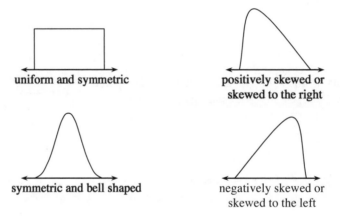

Density functions are useful to describe the overall shape of a distribution. These curves are always located on or above the horizontal axis. The total area under the curve is equal to 100%, or as a decimal, equal to 1.00.

The areas under the density function represent the relative frequencies of observations. Alternatively, the area under the curve for an interval of a random variable is the proportion of all observations that are located in that interval.

5-10.   THE WEAKEST LINK

Steel cables are used for supporting heavy structures like bridges but are also flexible enough to be used with pulley systems for applications like elevators and cranes. Periodically, random samples of cables are tested to provide assurance that they are as safe and strong as advertised. Assume a 50 cm piece of cable will be loaded until it breaks and the break has an equal chance of occurring anywhere along the length of the cable. For the sake of this example assume the cable does not stretch.

a.   Let X be a random variable representing where along its 50 cm length the cable breaks. Convert the following statements to notation using a random variable X and estimate the associated probabilities:

   i.   What is the probability of the cable breaking at a point between 0 and 25 cm?

   ii.   What is the probability of the cable breaking at a point between 0 and 50 cm?

   iii.   What is the probability the cable breaks somewhere in the first 10 cm?

   iv.   What is the probability of the cable breaking at a point between 37.5 and 50 cm?

   v.   What is the probability of the cable breaking exactly at 17.531 cm?

b.   If you were to perform this same strength test with many similar sections of cable, what would the relative frequency histogram look like? Sketch it and include the correct relative frequency on the y-axis.

c.   The relative frequency histogram you made in part (b) most resembles which probability density function?

d.   What would be the mean of the random variable X in the relative frequency histogram you made in part (b)?

MATH NOTES

Uniform Probability Density Function

The **uniform probability density function** has no mode, no peaks, and no clusters. The mean and the median are the same value. The uniform distribution is symmetric and the relative frequencies distributed evenly across the histogram. The shape of the idealized uniform density function is a rectangle.

Every outcome in the sample space is equally likely to occur in a uniform distribution (which means the probabilities for the outcomes are equal), so the area of the rectangle represents all possible outcomes hence and equals 1 or 100%. The uniform distribution can be discrete or continuous.

In the continuous form, the variable X is evenly distributed over a horizontal interval of length $X_{max} - X_{min}$. The height of the distribution is $\frac{1}{X_{max} - X_{min}}$.

For all continuous probability density functions, areas under the curve represent probability. Since there is no area below any single value of $P(X)$, the probability for any distinct value of a random variable X is zero. $P(X = k) = 0$.

The following is an example with a continuous random variable X representing distance in kilometers:

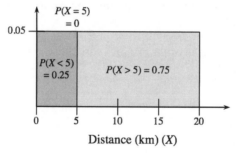

5-11.   The relationship between the magnitude, total number, and time between earthquakes in any given region is called the Gutenberg-Richter law. Assume that in Shakeyton, USA the time period between earthquakes of at least magnitude 5.2 follows a uniform probability density function with a mean of 20 years.

   a.   Sketch this density function. Include the height of the rectangle.

   b.   What is the probability of an earthquake with at least 5.2 magnitude happening within 15 years?

   c.   What is the probability of an earthquake with at least 5.2 magnitude happening within 32 years?

   d.   What is the probability of an earthquake with at least 5.2 magnitude happening in any 25 year period?

   e.   What is the probability of an earthquake with at least 5.2 magnitude happening in exactly 1 year from this moment?

   f.   There is a 0.30 probability that a magnitude 5.2 earthquake will happen before how many years have past?

5-12.   Enrique shares the old family minivan with his brother and sister. It seems like every time he goes to use it, the gas tank is nearly empty. Assume however that the minivan has an 18 gallon tank and everyone who drives it refills the tank when the red light on the dashboard turns on (indicating there are 2 gallons remaining). The amount of fuel in the tank when Enrique goes to drive then follows a uniform distribution ranging from 2 to 18 gallons.

   a.   Sketch the uniform probability distribution of the random variable gasoline in the tank (X). Include the height of the rectangle.

   b.   What is the probability there is less than half a tank of gas (9 gallons) when Enrique starts a trip?

   c.   What is the probability there is less than a quarter of a tank of gas when Enrique starts a trip?

   d.   What is the probability there are exactly 14 gallons of gas in the tank when Enrique starts a trip?

   e.   75% of the time there is less than how much gas in the tank when Enrique starts his trip? Shade in the first 0.75 of the rectangle you made in part (a). What is the corresponding value of X?

   f.   40% of the time there is less than how much gas in the tank when Enrique starts his trip?

5-13.   Caspar and Ollie brainstormed examples of a discrete probability distributions and listed them below:

- Raffle tickets: Participants purchase n raffle tickets and each raffle ticket is a random variable X that has the same probability of being the winning ticket. $P(\text{win}) = \frac{1}{n}$.

- Rolling a die: Each random variable X on a six-sided die has the same probability of being rolled. $P(\text{each outcome}) = \frac{1}{6}$.

Caspar and Ollie brainstormed examples of continuous probability distributions and listed them below:

- The location on a bicycle tire where a puncture might occur.

- The location on a baseball diamond where the ball will bounce or fall.

With your team, brainstorm *at least* two other examples of a continuous probability distribution and *at least* two other examples of a discrete probability distribution. Explain your thinking in writing.

5-14.   Katelyn owns a 24-hour coffee shop in front of a downtown office building. She recorded the number of cups of coffee sold each hour during a 48-hour time period.

Katelyn sorted the data and made the following histogram:

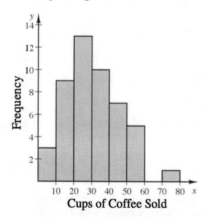

Cups of Coffee Sold		
1	22	37
5	22	38
7	23	38
12	24	40
12	25	41
12	26	41
12	26	42
12	29	47
14	29	47
16	30	49
17	30	51
19	31	52
20	32	55
21	33	55
21	35	59
22	36	76
checksum: 1444		

a.   Using the sorted data from the table and the histogram, find the five number summary (minimum, first quartile, median, third quartile, maximum) without using a calculator.

b.   Describe the distribution of coffee sales per hour.

5-15.   Governments and security companies are coming to rely more heavily on facial recognition software to locate persons of interest.

Consider a hypothetical situation. Suppose that facial recognition software can accurately identify a person 99.9% of the time, and suppose the suspect is among 200,000 facial images available to a government agency. When the software makes a positive identification, what it the probability that it is not the suspect?

a.   Make a model for this situation.

b.   If a person has been identified as the suspect, what is the probability that he or she is *not* actually the suspect?

5-16.   Does reading to dogs improve reading fluency in children? The local library decides to pilot a program in which children read to dogs. They contact a random sample of patrons with children and ask if they would be willing to participate in a study. Of the 60 families that agree, 33 choose to bring their child to the library three times a week where they will read to a well-trained dog. The other 27 families agree to have their child read to a family member three times a week. The children will take a test of reading fluency before and after the treatment phase of the experiment and the change in test scores will be recorded. The average change in scores for the two groups will be compared.

a.   Identify the experimental units and the explanatory and response variables.

b.   Identify elements of control, randomization, and replication in the experiment.

c.   The amount of time the children spent reading each week is a confounding variable. Explain.

5.1.3 How can I make predictions?

The Normal Probability Density Function

By creating a mathematical model of data, you can describe the data to others without giving them a list of all the data, and you can make predictions based on the data. In previous courses you created a model when you drew a line of best fit as a model for data in a scatterplot. Using the line of best fit, you were able to describe the association in the data, and you were able to make predictions from the model.

Much of the real data that is encountered in science, business, and industry can be modeled with a bell-shaped curve, called a **normal probability density function**. This function is given by the following mathematical formula:

$$f(x) = \frac{1}{\sqrt{2\pi\sigma^2}} e^{-\frac{(x-\mu)^2}{2\sigma^2}}$$

Although this looks intimidating, technology tools can draw the graph very easily based on the mean and standard deviation of the data.

5-17. CHARITY RACE TIMES, Part Two

Reread problem 5-3, *Charity Race Times*, from Lesson 5.1.1. Quickly recreate the relative frequency histogram, and record the mean and standard deviation. Use an interval from 19 to 27 with a bin width of 1.

Your teacher will demonstrate a normal probability density function ("**normal distribution**") fit to the histogram using technology. Sketch the normal curve on your histogram.

How well does your model represent the data? What are the strengths and weaknesses of your model?

5-18.   If you wanted to use the relative frequency histogram to find the percent of women in this sample that have run times between 22.5 and 24.5 minutes, you would add up the bars between 22.5 and 24.5. But since your histogram is not drawn conveniently with those bins, you would have to redraw the histogram. However, your model of the data comes to the rescue!

a.   The height of the bars between 22.5 and 24.5 can be modeled with the area under the normal distribution between 22.5 and 24.5, as shaded black in the diagram at right.

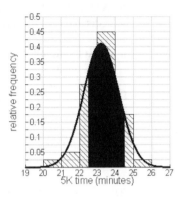

Your teacher will show you how to use the normalcdf function on a calculator to find the area under the curve between 22.5 and 24.5. In general, on a TI-83/84+ calculator, you enter [2nd] [DISTR] normalcdf(*lower limit, upper limit, mean, standard deviation*) to have the calculator find the proportion for the interval.

What percent of women in this sample have running times between 22.5 and 24.5 minutes?

b.   The normal model represents the percentages of women in the sample that have various run times. But it does much more than that—since the sample of 40 randomly selected women represents the whole population of women that run in 5K races, the normal model can tell you about percentages in the whole population. (You will refine these techniques in later chapters.) If the normal model represented the whole population, what percentage of all women that run 5K races have race times between 20 and 25 minutes?

c.   Even though the fastest (smallest) time in the sample of 40 women was 20.6 minutes, the model that you chose (the normal probability density function) starts at negative infinity and goes all the way to positive infinity. What percentage of all women in the population run faster than 26 minutes according to your model? Since the calculator may not have an infinity key, instead enter -10^{99} for the lower limit.

d.   Using the normal model, make a prediction for the percentage of women that fall below the mean running time. Does your answer make sense?

5-19.   VISORS FOR RUNNERS, Part 2

The Style and Comfort 5K Race for Charity is coming up. The
Style and Comfort Headwear Company expects 775 racers. Based
on a model for hat size distributions for all women, they will need
to order hats for the event.

a.   Recreate the relative frequency histogram for the 40 women's
hat sizes in problem 5-2. Use an interval from 50 cm to 57 cm
with a bin width of 1.

b.   Find the mean and standard deviation of the hat sizes.

c.   Your teacher will again demonstrate a normal probability density function ("**normal
distribution**") fit to this data. Sketch the normal curve on your histogram from part (a).

d.   Using the normal model to represent all women running 5K races, determine what
percentage of women racers wear a size 51 hat. Shade this proportion on a new sketch of
the model, and calculate the proportion using normalcdf on a calculator using
$\bar{x} = 53.3$ cm, $s = 1.12$ cm. How does the percentage predicted by the model compare to
the percentage observed in your sample?

e.   How many size 51 hats should Style and Comfort order for the anticipated 775 racers at
the Style and Comfort 5K Race for Charity?

f.   Use the normal model to predict how many of the racers at the Style and Comfort 5K
Race for Charity are expected to have a hat size below 51. Sketch these proportions on a
new sketch of the model.

g.   How many racers would you expect to have a hat size over size 56? Between 51 and 56?

h.   Does your answer to part (f) make sense when compared to
the answers from part (e)?

i.   What percentage of racers does your normal
distribution model predict have hat sizes between
negative infinity and infinity? Does the prediction
seem reasonable?

MATH NOTES

Normal Probability Density Function

For many situations in science, business, and industry, data may be represented by a bell-shaped curve. In order to be able to work mathematically with that data—describing it to others, making predictions—an equation called a **normal probability density function** is fitted to the data. This is very similar to how a line of best fit is used to describe and make predictions of data on a scatterplot.

The normal probability density function ("normal distribution") stretches to infinity in both directions. The normal distribution can be thought of as modeling the heights of the bars in a scaled relative frequency histogram where the area of the bars is 1. However, instead of individual bars, a curve is drawn that represents the tops of an infinite number of bars. Like the sum of the bar heights on a relative frequency histogram represent the portion of the population within an interval, the <u>area</u> under the normal distribution (shaded in the diagram below) represents the portion of the population within an interval.

The total area under the curve is 1, representing 100% of the population. The peak of the normal distribution is at the mean and the resulting symmetry makes the mean equal to the median.

The spread of the normal distribution is determined by the standard deviation (the variability) of the population under study. The **Empirical Rule** (also known as the **68-95-99.7 Rule**) states that approximately 68% of the observation of the normal random variable will be within one standard deviation of the mean. Two standard deviations from the mean will capture about 95% of the observations and three standard deviations each side of the mean will contain approximately 99.7% of the occurrences of the random variable.

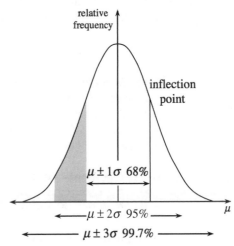

5-20.   The diet of martens consists of squirrels, mice, rabbits, birds, fish, insects, and eggs, and they will also eat fruit and nuts. While in upstate New York investigating encroached upon environments of martens, Anton investigated a random sample of 90 martens, which yielded the following relative frequency histogram:

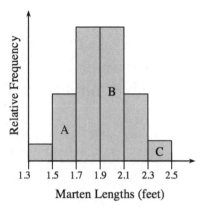

If the distribution is normally distributed with a mean of 1.9 feet and a standard deviation of 0.20 feet, by the Empirical Rule the area of the bars from 1.7 to 2.1 feet is 0.68. Use the Empirical Rule and the symmetry of the normal distribution to estimate the area of

   a.   bar A.

   b.   bar B.

   c.   bar C.

5-21   Ravens are the largest perching birds in North America. If raven wingspans are normally distributed with a mean of 4.363 ft and a standard deviation of 0.339 ft. Sketch the normal probability density function. What is the probability of selecting a raven wingspan less than 4.236 ft?

5-22.   Half-liter soda bottles are filled with cola at a bottling plant. The equipment used to fill the bottles is not capable of putting exactly 500 mL in each bottle, so it is adjusted such that the amount of cola placed in the bottles follows a normal distribution with a mean of 502 mL and a standard deviation of 1.8 mL. Answer the following questions, including a sketch of the normal distribution and appropriate random variable $P(X)$ notation for each one.

   a.   What proportion of bottles will have more than 502 mL of cola in them?

   b.   What proportion of bottles will have between 500 and 502 mL in them?

   c.   What proportion of bottles are under-filled (hold less than 500 mL)?

   d.   What percentile corresponds to 503 mL?

   e.   What percentile corresponds to 505 mL?

5-23.   Curious about the relationship between the food tastes of kids and their parents, Kesha asked 50 kids between 10 and 12 and their parents to rank their enthusiasm for 25 different food items. The average of each food's kid ranking and parent ranking is below. (For example, one of the dots represents roasted Brussels sprouts and another represents boxed macaroni and cheese.) A scatterplot with regression line is shown below.

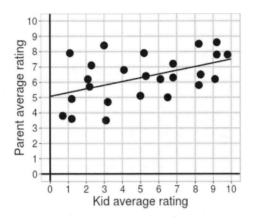

a.   Describe the association as well as you can.

b.   Estimate the equation for the least-squares regression line and interpret the slope.

c.   Mark each statement as true or false:

  i.   Higher-rated foods by kids tend to be higher-rated by parents as well.

  ii.   Parents tend to rate foods lower than kids.

  iii.   Parents tend to rate foods more in the middle than kids.

  iv.   There are some foods that kids hate and parents like.

  v.   There are some foods that kids love that parents hate.

d.   Which point do you believe is the roasted Brussels sprouts? Which point do you believe is the macaroni and cheese from a box? Pick any other point and make a guess as to what food it might be. Explain.

5-24.   Coach Pham claims that his new six week agility program will increase an athletes' vertical leap by 10 centimeters more than traditional workouts.

a.   Design an experiment to test the coach's claim.

b.   If the group using Coach Pham's techniques improved their leaping significantly more than the group using traditional methods, would this provide evidence that the new agility program is the cause?

5.2.1 How can I convert percentiles to measurements?

The Inverse Normal Function

From this lesson forward the expectation is that every student will provide a sketch of the normal distribution and use appropriate *P(X)* notation for every problem in which they use a normal probability function or its inverse whether asked for in the problem or not.

You have previously converted percentiles or probabilities to values of a random variable using ogives and also with continuous uniform probability distributions. Likewise, one may start with an area under the Normal curve and use an inverse normal probability function to get the corresponding value of the random variable. On a TI-83/TI-84+ calculator use: invNorm*(area, mean, standard dev)*.

5-25. The ACT is a test that colleges use to help make admissions decisions for potential students. Nationwide, the scores are normally distributed, with a mean score of 21 (out of a possible 36) and a standard deviation of 4.7.

    a. Adèle scored 25 on the ACT. With your team, explore how well she did. Remember your normal distribution is a model for the bars of a histogram. Make a sketch of the normal distribution for all ACT scores and shade the "bars" (the area under the normal distribution) for all the scores below Adèle's score. What percent of scores are below Adèle's score? Round to the nearest whole number.

    b. Rémy scored better than two thirds of test-takers. You can say Rémy scored at the 67th percentile on the ACT. What was Rémy's actual score? Start with a sketch of the normal distribution and shade in the area where approximately 67% of the scores are lower.

    c. Rémy's sister Antoinette took the ACT as a sophomore and scored at the 26th percentile on the ACT. What was Antoinette's actual score? Start with a sketch of the normal distribution and shade in the area where approximately 26% of the scores are lower.

    d. Leonard scored at the 50th percentile on the ACT. *Without a calculator*, make a sketch of the scores below Leonard on a normal distribution and indicate what he scored on the ACT.

                                                            Statistics

5-26.   For each situation make a quick sketch of the normal distribution with an appropriate scale and shading. Include appropriate random variable notation and units.

a.   Poison ivy is particularly sensitive to CO_2 levels in the atmosphere. While in New Jersey investigating the spread of poison ivy plants, Alexis collected data and determined the poison ivy plant heights are normally distributed with a mean of 87.96 cm and a standard deviation of 18.98 cm. 97% of poison ivy plant heights are less than _____ cm.

b.   Marsupial mice are solitary in nature. While in Australia observing threatened communities of marsupial mice, Hector collected data on that showed mice lengths are normally distributed with a mean of 19.43 cm and a standard deviation of 4.3 cm. 12% of marsupial mice lengths are **longer** than _____ cm.

5-27.   Rachna's physics class is going out to the football field to launch rockets today. The rocket that Rachna is launching has historically had a mean flight distance of 74 m with a standard deviation of 26 m. A rocket's flight distance is modeled with a normal distribution.

a.   Sketch a graph of the distribution of Rachna's rocket flight. Use what you know about standard deviation to scale the x-axis appropriately.

b.   From your graph, visually estimate the middle two flight distances between which the rocket will land 90% of the time. Shade this portion of your sketch.

c.   The middle 90% (or 95% or 99%) of the data is an important computation in statistics. It tells you what typical data might look like without considering the small or large extremes at either end. Use a calculator to check your estimate from part (b). How close to 90% did you come?

5-28.   Rachna and her sister, Rakhi, were both in the same physics class. They made a bet with each other on whose rocket would go farther relative to their classmates. The loser would have to wash the family dishes for a month! Unfortunately, Rakhi was assigned a very different style rocket from the one Rachna got, so it was difficult to make a fair comparison. They decided to compare the z-scores. Rakhi's style of rocket had a mean flight distance of 30 m with a standard deviation of 6 m.

Rachna's rocket went 66.74 m, while Rakhi's went 28.17 m. Use z-scores to determine who had to wash the dishes for a month.

5-29.   In response to a judging controversy during the 2002 Winter Olympics, a new scoring system for ice dancing was implemented in 2006. The new system uses a "grade of execution" (GOE) as part of the overall score. The GOE goes from –3 to 3, and can be modeled with a normal distribution with mean of 0 and standard deviation of 1. Isabella and Tony scored a 2.00 on the GOE. What percentile are they in? What percentage of ice dancers had higher scores?

5-30. Do you remember the students tardy to Mrs. Greene's class? The data Mrs. Greene gathered for 30 days is shown in the table below and histogram at right.

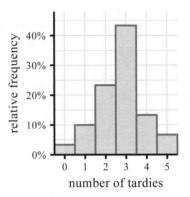

Number of tardy students per day

2	4	3	3	4	2
1	3	3	4	3	2
2	3	1	2	3	3
3	0	2	3	2	5
5	3	3	3	4	1

checksum: 82

a. Now that you have investigated how to create and use a normal distribution, does it seem appropriate to apply it to this situation? Explain

b. Find the mean and standard deviation of the number of tardy students.

c. Sketch a model of the data with a normal distribution. Use what you know about standard deviation to scale the *x*-axis appropriately.

d. According to your model, on what percentage of days were 4 people tardy? Shade this proportion on a new sketch of the model, and calculate the proportion using normalcdf(*lower, upper, mean, standard deviation*) on a calculator.

e. Assume that the last 30 days in Mrs. Greene's class were representative of the 180 days in the whole school year. According to your model, how many days this year can Mrs. Greene expect 4 or more tardy students? Sketch the area representing these days on a new graph of the model.

5-31. Concrete is loaded into trucks for a large construction project according to a normal distribution. The mean amount loaded is 230 cubic feet with a standard deviation of 7 cubic feet. Concrete trucks are rated by the number of cubic yards they can carry, and 9 cubic yards is a common maximum load. Hence the expression "the whole nine yards." Remember to include sketches with your answers and use proper $P(X)$ notation.

a. What proportion of the trucks will be loaded with between 220 and 240 cubic feet?

b. What proportion of trucks are loaded with more concrete than the 9 cubic yard maximum? (3 feet = 1 yard)

c. 235 cubic feet is what percentile load?

d. If a particular job requires at least 220 cubic yards of concrete, what is the probability there will not be enough concrete in a single truck?

Statistics

5-32.   Omar has a one year old little brother named Yusuf. Whenever Yusuf is finished eating cereal, he starts throwing cereal pieces on the floor. Omar starts keeping track of the number of cereal pieces on the floor after each time Yusuf eats cereal. He gathers the following sample: 13, 15, 13, 16, 14, 20, 15, 20, 21, 14, 17, 18, 19, 12, 14, 18, 13. Provide an appropriate graphical representation and describe the distribution of number of pieces of cereal on the floor.

5-33.   Mr. Knowlsen takes pride in his difficult chemistry tests, 60 multiple-choice questions with 4 possible answers for each question. He tells the students to study hard because the mean score is 15 correct, but just 20 correct is all you need to earn an A. Mr. Knowlsen admits that only about 10% of the students earn an A on the test. Jeff is wondering the value of Mr. Knowlsen's pep talk so he runs a simulation of 100 students taking Mr. Knowlsen's exam who blindly guess the answers for each question.

Questions correct in a simulation of 100 tests (the data is sorted)

8	11	14	16	18
8	11	14	16	19
8	11	14	16	19
9	12	14	16	19
9	12	14	16	19
10	12	14	16	19
10	12	14	16	19
10	12	15	16	19
10	13	15	16	19
10	13	15	17	19
11	13	15	17	20
11	13	15	17	20
11	13	15	17	20
11	13	16	17	20
11	13	16	18	20
11	13	16	18	21
11	13	16	18	22
11	13	16	18	22
11	13	16	18	22
11	14	16	18	24

checksum: 1489

a.   What is the mean number of questions answered correctly by the simulated students? As a percent?

b.   What percentage of the simulated students earned an A?

c.   Compare Jeff's simulated students to Mr. Knowlsen's claims about his actual students.

d.   What advice would you give Jeff about preparing for Mr. Knowlsen's famous chemistry tests?

5.2.2 How can I convert percentiles to z-scores?

The Standard Normal Distribution and z-Scores

In Chapters 1 and 2 you standardized data to create z-scores, which are measures of relative standing, describing relative distance from the mean. A z-score tells us how many standard deviations from the mean an observation, X_i, is located and in what direction relative to the mean (either below the mean or above the mean). A positive z-score represents an observation, X_i, that is greater than the mean. A negative z-score represents an observation, X_i, that is less than the mean.

The **standard normal distribution** is a special application of standardizing. The standard normal distribution provides a relationship between z-scores and percentiles for normally distributed data. In the standard normal distribution the mean $\mu = 0$, the standard deviation $\sigma = 1$ and the values of the random variable X have been transformed (standardized) to z-scores using the formula $z = \frac{X_i - \mu}{\sigma}$.

5-34.   GOING OLD-SCHOOL

Raymond asked his dad for help with this normal probability homework problem:

> Ponies require less food than a horse would if it was the same size. While in New Hampshire studying Shetland ponies, Iris found that pony masses are normally distributed with a mean of 213.24 kg and a standard deviation of 9.1 kg.

> What is the probability of selecting a Shetland pony with a mass greater than 204.14 kg?

Raymond's dad did not understand how to use the normal probability density functions on a calculator, so he made the following calculation and the sketch at right:

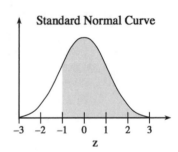
Standard Normal Curve

$$z = \frac{204.14 - 213.24}{9.1} = -1$$

After referencing a complex table, Raymond's dad then wrote:

$$P(-1 < z < 0) = 0.34$$
$$P(z > -1) = 0.34 + 0.50 = 0.84$$

Raymond realized that his dad's table was doing his calculator's job of returning probabilities so he entered normalcdf(–1, 10^99, 0, 1), because the mean and standard deviation are 0 and 1 respectively, and also got 0.8413.

For comparison Raymond performed the calculation without using the standard normal distribution: $P(X > 204.14) =$ normalcdf(204.14, 10^99, 213.24, 9.1) and again got 0.8413! Try the following problems "old-school," by using the standard normal distribution on a calculator normalcdf(z_{low}, z_{high}, 0, 1). Include a sketch of the standard normal curve. Then confirm the result using normalcdf(X_{low}, X_{high}, μ, σ).

5-35.   Most of the earth's atmosphere is made up of nitrogen. William is an engineering student at University of California Santa Barbara observing various levels of gases in air samples. William believes nitrogen percentages are normally distributed within air samples with a mean of 78.28% and a standard deviation of 2.13%.

What is the probability of selecting an air sample with a nitrogen percentage greater than 75.09%?

5-36.   Active or fidgety people produce more CO_2 and lactic acid, which is attractive to mosquitos. Miranda is in Missouri researching rich environments of salt marsh mosquitos. Miranda believes the distribution of mosquito wing speeds are normally distributed with a mean of 396.53 beats per second and a standard deviation of 105.84 beats per second.

What is the probability of selecting a salt marsh mosquito wing speed less than 343.61 beats per second?

5-37.   SOMETIMES OLD-SCHOOL IS THE ONLY SCHOOL

Raymond and his dad were getting more comfortable with each other's methods for solving normal distribution problems. They then tried this problem:

A relative of the familiar blue peafowl, the Congo peafowl is endemic to the Democratic Republic of the Congo. While collecting data on threatened communities of peafowls, Hannah observed that the distribution of peafowl weights is normally distributed.

If the 21st percentile is 2.5389 lbs, and the 83rd percentile is 3.2027 lbs, find the mean and standard deviation.

a.   This problem is solvable because two percentile measures are enough information to define any particular normal distribution. What about this problem prevents Raymond from using his method but is not a problem for his dad's z-score method? Discuss it with your team.

b.   Using Raymond's dad's method, find z-scores for both percentiles.

c.   Then, make sketches of the normal curves.

d.   Raymond remembers the normal distribution has two parameters: μ and σ. Two unknowns need two equations (or two independent pieces of information). His dad suggested, *"Let's try using the 'z' relationship."* He wrote the following down:

$$z = \frac{x_i - \mu}{\sigma}$$

Use this formula to write equations for each percentile. Solve the system of equations to find μ and σ.

5-38.   While working at his sister's gym observing the level of fitness of the members, Alejandro determined that the distribution of member resting heart rates is normally distributed.

If the 5th percentile heart rate is 54.685 bpm, and the 60th percentile is 61.234 bpm, find the mean and standard deviation.

5-39.   While in Missouri researching thriving communities of pheasants, Darius observed that pheasant lengths are normally distributed with a mean of 73.02 cm.

If the 85th percentile pheasant length is 80.431 cm, what is the standard deviation?

5-40.   While working at his mother's bakery studying customer satisfaction surveys, Julio observed that customer satisfaction ratings are normally distributed.

If the 33rd percentile is 6.775, and the 65th percentile is 7.394 on a scale from 0 to 10, find the mean and standard deviation.

5-41.   Assume the annual snowfall in the village of Thalhammer follows a normal distribution with a mean of 185 cm and standard deviation of 36 cm.

a.   Less than 100 cm of snow in a year is considered drought conditions in Thalhammer. What is the chance that a particular year will have drought conditions?

b.   The Rivera Valley lies below Thalhammer. Residents of Rivera Valley are placed on a flood warning due to snowmelt in the spring if annual snowfall in Thalhammer is greater than 250 cm. What is the probability the Rivera Valley residents will be placed on a flood warning this spring?

c.   What percentile corresponds to 160 cm of annual snowfall in Thalhammer?

5-42.   How many students at City High have met a friend online?

a.   Should an observational study or an experiment be carried out to answer the question? Explain.

b.   Research suggests that boys and girls differ in the way they use technology. Describe how you would carry out the study.

5.2.3 Where can I use the normal distribution?

Additional Practice Problems

This lesson offers additional problems for you to practice what you have learned this chapter.

Continue sketching every normal density function whether inverse or cdf. Remember to make sure you are also using correct random variable notation $P(X = k)$.

―――――――― Review & Preview ――――――――

5-43. Aurora is starting a fitness program at her school and needs to find an easy measure of fitness to assign workouts and gauge improvement. She decides that using resting heart rate would be helpful. Assume that the resting heart rate of young women is approximately normally distributed with a mean of 74 beats per minute (bpm) with a standard deviation of 5 bpm.

    a.   Aurora found a chart that said resting heart rates between 70 and 79 (inclusive) are considered average for women her age. What proportion of her classmates would she expect to find in the average range?

    b.   The chart also claims that resting heart rate of 66 or less indicates excellent fitness in otherwise healthy young women. What portion of her classmates would she expect to find in excellent shape?

    c.   If Aurora's fitness program lowers the mean heart rate of her female classmates by 4 bpm, what will be the *increase* in the proportion of women now classified as being in excellent shape?

5-44. David and Regina are competitive racers, and they both aim to break 2 minutes in their races. They are trying to figure out which who has the more difficult challenge, since they compete in different sports. David runs the 800-meter race and Regina swims the 200-meter freestyle. They agree to accept the following standards for high school boys and girls: boys' 800-meter mean time is 149 seconds with a standard deviation of 13.6 seconds, girls' 200-meter freestyle mean time is 145 seconds with a standard deviation of 8.2 seconds.

Currently, David's best time is 2:02 minutes and Regina's best time is 2:10 minutes. Assuming times in their respective events are normally distributed, find the percentile in which each David and Regina fall. Which athlete is relatively faster for their sport?

5-45.   According to the *National Health Statistics Report*, the average height of adult women in the U.S. is 63.8 inches with a standard deviation of 2.7 inches. Heights can be modeled with a normal probability density function.

a.   What percent of women are shorter than 4 ft 11 in tall?

b.   Most girls reach their adult height by their senior year in high school. In North City High School's class of 324 senior students, how many girls would you expect to be shorter than 4 ft 11 in? (Note: Assume half of the senior students are girls.)

c.   How many senior girls do you expect to be taller than 6 ft at North City High?

5-46.   Parking meters in a beach resort town cost 25¢ for 15 minutes. A normal distribution with a mean $10 and a standard deviation of $2 can be used to model the amount of money one parking meter makes on a busy summer day.

a.   Make a graph of the distribution of the money made by one meter. Scale the *x*-axis based on the standard deviation.

b.   From your graph, visually estimate where the middle 90% of meter earnings fall. Shade this portion of your sketch.

c.   Use a calculator to check your estimate. How close to 90% did you come?

5-47.   Nitrogen oxide, or NO_x, is a pollutant created by diesel engines that occurs when nitrogen and oxygen from the atmosphere are combined by the heat of the burning fuel. The EPA and many states limit the amount of NO_x a vehicle is permitted to produce. Assume that diesel cars and trucks on the road produce NO_x according to a normal distribution with a mean of 0.12 g/mile and a standard deviation of 0.04 g/mile. Imagine your state is lowering its limits of NO_x allowed over a 10-year time period.

a.   If the 2020 limit for NO_x is 0.100 g/mile, what proportion of diesel engines running today meet that standard?

b.   If the 2025 limit for NO_x is 0.065 g/mile, what proportion of diesel engines running today meet that standard?

c.   Now think of things the other way. If the 2030 limit for NO_x is 0.030 g/mile, what proportion of diesel engines running today *would not* meet that standard?

5-48.   In problem 5-14 Katelyn recorded the
number of cups of coffee sold at her
coffee shop each hour during a
48-hour time period.

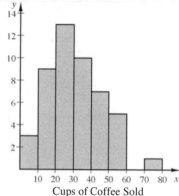

Katelyn then sorted the data and made
the following histogram:

Cups of Coffee Sold

a.   Katelyn decides to model her sales with a normal
distribution, but Duncan thinks that this is not a good
idea. What advice would you give Katelyn about
using a normal model?

b.   Katelyn needs to sell more than 15 cups per hour to
make a profit. What percentile is 15 cups per hour? Explain the percentile to Katelyn in
terms of profits.

c.   Duncan thinks Katelyn should expand her business. He estimates that if they hire another
server and add more tables and equipment, they will need to sell 48 cups per hour to
make a profit. What percentile does 48 cups sold represent? Use the percentile to explain
to Duncan whether or not expansion is a good idea.

5-49.   A narwhal's tusk can grow to be up to 10 feet long. While in Artic Sea studying
encroached upon habitats of narwhals, Chikae investigated that narwhal pod sizes
are normally distributed with a mean of 17.76 individuals and a standard
deviation of 2.44 individuals. Without using a calculator estimate the following:

a. $P(X > 22.64) \approx$ _____

b. $P(X < 15.32) \approx$ _____

c. $P(12.88 < X < 20.20) \approx$ _____

5-50. The term "curving" is often misused as it applies to test scores. Many believe it refers to adding points or otherwise adjusting test scores such that the highest paper is 100% or the average score is raised to some passing level. To curve is actually to model test scores with the normal distribution (normal "curve") and then use percentiles to assign letter grades.

a. A "curve" sometimes used is shown below:

Grade	D	C	B	A
Number of Standard Deviations Above or Below Mean	–2	–1	+1	+2
Minimum Percentile	2nd	16th	84th	98th

Using this curve, what percentage of students would earn each letter grade?

b. The following statistics are from the test scores on Mrs. Abraha's Chapter 11 test in Geometry. The mean was 76.5 points, and the standard deviation was 17.4 points.

If Mrs. Abraha used the curve in part (a), the minimum score for a B would be one standard deviation above the mean, or 93.9 points. What would be the minimum test scores for the other letter grades on Mrs. Abraha's test?

c. Shown at right is a histogram of the scores from this test. Is using the curve from part (a) reasonable to assign letter grades? What advice would you give students who want the test "curved"?

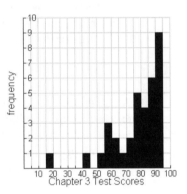

Statistics

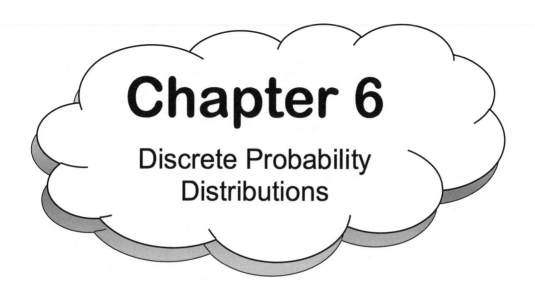

Chapter 6

Discrete Probability Distributions

CHAPTER 6   Discrete Probability Distributions

Chapter Goals

In Chapter 5 you studied the uniform and normal distributions. Each is an example of a continuous probability distribution. *What about discrete probability situations such as the number of passengers that show up for a flight of the number of cars going through an intersection?* This chapter focuses on discrete probability distributions, the binomial and geometric, and how can probability distributions be combined, added, subtracted, or transformed.

Discover the mean and variance of a discrete random variable

Explore combinations of independent random variables.

Understand the impact of false positives on in testing and detection systems.

Use the binomial and geometric probability distributions to determine complex probabilities.

Understand when a binomial situation can be estimated by a normal model.

Recognize probabilistic situations and apply the most appropriate probability model.

Chapter Outline

Section 6.1   You will discover how to calculate the mean and variance of a discrete random variable, a skill will be used throughout the chapter. You will then learn how make calculations involving linear combinations of independent random variables.

Section 6.2   You will begin with a binomial experiment that will lead into a discussion of the binomial setting then use the binomial probability density function to make basic calculations in a binomial setting. You will develop formulas for the mean and variance of the binomial distribution. The normal approximation to the binomial distribution will be explored, and calculations of probability will be compared.

Section 6.3   You will make a connection between a geometric sequence and the geometric distribution and make probability calculations using the geometric distribution, then practice identifying when each distribution is appropriate and making calculations of probability.

6.1.1 What can I expect from a random variable?

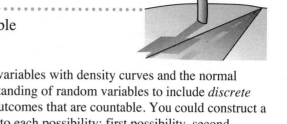

Mean and Variance of a Discrete Random Variable

In the previous chapter, you studied continuous random variables with density curves and the normal distribution. In this chapter, you will extend your understanding of random variables to include *discrete* random variables. **Discrete random variables** take on outcomes that are countable. You could construct a list of the possible outcomes and assign a whole number to each possibility: first possibility, second possibility, third possibility, etc. Often, discrete random variables represent a situation where the variable represents something that is being *counted* or *categorized*.

Have you ever had to guess on multiple choice questions? The number of questions answered correctly on a multiple choice test where you guessed on each question could be considered a discrete random variable. You might ask the following questions:

- How likely am I to answer a question correctly?

- What are my chances of passing the test?

- How many should I expect to get correct?

- How many do I typically have to answer before getting one correct?

- If I took the test again, how would my score typically change?

In this chapter, you will have the opportunity to explore all of these questions and many others. You will also learn some new statistical distributions in addition to an increased knowledge of the normal distribution.

6-1.   WHAT IS A DISCRETE RANDOM VARIABLE?

For each of the situations below, categorize the variable as discrete or continuous.

a.   The number of red cars in a parking lot at any given time.

b.   The mass of a randomly chosen bag of chips.

c.   The score of each team in a randomly chosen basketball game.

d.   The number of moves to complete a random game of chess.

e.   The outdoor temperature on a random day in June.

6-2. PROBABILITY MODEL AND EXPECTED VALUE

In order to investigate a discrete probability distribution, Mo and Lana use a spinner with three possible outcomes: 2, 4, and 5. The spinner has a 30% chance of spinning a 2, a 20% chance of a 4, and a 50% chance of a 5. They define a random variable X to represent the numerical outcome of a single random spin.

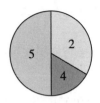

a. Explain why X would be considered a discrete random variable.

b. Lana wants to see the **probability model** representing this situation. She wants to list all possible outcomes with the associated probabilities, organizing it as a table. Explain why this is a valid probability model.

X	2	4	5
$P(X)$	0.3	0.2	0.5

c. Mo is interested in what the mean value for X would be after observing it many, many, many times. He suggests a thought experiment. *"Because the probabilities are all nicely given with one decimal place, let's pretend like we have a bag with 10 slips of paper in it. There are three 2s, two 4s, and five 5s. I think that if we find the mean of all of these slips of paper, we'll have the mean for X."* Reason through Mo's idea. What is the mean for X?

d. Lana takes Mo's idea one step further. She says, *"In your idea, we had to divide by 10 to find the average. What if we just left the probabilities as they are written in the table and did the same calculation? It'd be like having three tenths of a 2 in the bag rather than three. Then we'd divide by 1 in the end, rather than 10. Let's capitalize on the fact that the probabilities add to 1!"* Reason through Lana's idea. Do you get the same result?

e. The mean of a random variable X is also called the **expected value**, $E(X)$. Write a summary of how to find the expected value of a discrete random variable. Translate your thinking into mathematical symbols. Challenge your team to use summation notation.

6-3. WHAT DOES IT MEAN TO EXPECT?

Mo is unsure what to do with the expected value that they just calculated.

a. Mo is bothered by the fact that the expected value they calculated is not one of the possible outcomes. Help Mo to interpret why it might still make sense to have an expected value that is not a possible outcome.

b. Should Mo use $\bar{x}$ or μ to represent the expected value? Explain.

6-4.   DESCRIBING VARIABILITY

Lana notices that they can quantify what an "average" spin would be using the expected value, but there is definitely some variability. Using the concept of variance as a typical squared deviation from the mean, squared, she writes:

$W = (X - 3.9)^2$	$(2 - 3.9)^2$	$(4 - 3.9)^2$	$(5 - 3.9)^2$
$P(W)$	0.3	0.2	0.5

Use this table to calculate the variance and standard deviation of X. Write a few sentences describing how to calculate the variance of a discrete random variable. Try to translate your sentences into mathematical symbols.

6-5.   ANOTHER RANDOM VARIABLE

Lana suggests that they try an even simpler example. She proposes a coin where the value "4" is assigned to "heads" and the value "8" is assigned to "tails." Let Y be a random variable representing a random outcome of flipping this coin.

a.   Construct a table of probabilities for Lana's new random variable.

b.   Apply your techniques above to find the mean, variance, and standard deviation of Y.

MATH NOTES

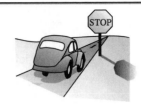

Discrete vs. Continuous

A **discrete random variable** can only take on certain outcomes. The set of all possible outcomes could be mapped to the natural numbers (1, 2, 3, …) and is considered to be **countable**. In statistics, discrete random variables are often the result of counting. For example, the number of hairs on a randomly chosen square centimeter of your head would be considered a discrete random variable. The set of all possible outcomes would be a subset of the natural numbers and be subject to probability as the number of hairs vary from location to location.

The mean or **expected value of a discrete random variable** is the sum of all possible values of X multiplied by their corresponding probabilities. $E(X)$ or $\mu_x = \sum X_i \cdot P(X_i)$.

The **variance of a discrete random variable** is the squared deviation from the mean for each value of X weighted by the probability $P(X)$ of each value of the random variable, then summed. $\sigma^2_x = \sum (X_i - \mu)^2 \cdot P(X_i)$.

A **continuous random variable** can take on all possible outcomes within its domain. The set of all possible outcomes is mapped to the real numbers. In Statistics, continuous random variables are often the result of measuring. For example, the thickness of a piece of paper at randomly chosen locations would be a continuous random variable. Relationships between ranges of X and their associated probabilities are found using cumulative probability density functions such as the normal and uniform distributions in Chapter 5.

Review & Preview

6-6.   The total leaf mass of a certain species of young plant saplings is approximately normally distributed with a mean of 14.2 grams and a standard deviation of 0.5 grams.

    a.   What is the probability of obtaining a randomly chosen plant sapling with a total leaf mass of more than 15 grams?

    b.   Identify the leaf mass that would represent the 99th percentile.

6-7. Consider the discrete random variable X with the following distribution.

X	5	6	8	12
$P(X)$	0.2	0.2	0.3	0.3

a. Explain why this represents a valid probability model.

b. Find the expected value and standard deviation of X.

c. What is the median for the distribution of X? Explain how you made your calculation.

6-8. Sports announcers frequently get excited when basketball players make several free throw shots in a row. They say things like *"He's on a hot streak tonight!"* or *"He's really in the zone—what an amazing performance!"*

Are these "hot" streaks really special, or are they just a natural run to be expected by probability? Assume a basketball player has a 50% free throw average, and a typical game has 20 free throw attempts. Use a calculator to set up a simulation for 20 free throws.

a. Run the simulation 25 times, and each time record the length of the longest streak.

b. How long would a streak have to be before you considered it unusual?

6-9. The state superintendent is interested in the opinion of elementary school students regarding a new policy affecting school lunch. Describe how each of the following sampling techniques could be carried out: simple random sample, stratified random sample, cluster sample. Which technique do you think is most appropriate in this setting? Why?

$6.1.2$ How can I combine random variables?

Linear Combinations of Independent Random Variables

In Chapter 1, you studied the effect of linear transformations of data on statistics such as the mean, median, standard deviation, and interquartile range. In this lesson, you will build upon your knowledge of linear transformations of data to linear combinations of random variables. Much of what you have previously discovered will directly apply, but there may be some surprises!

6-10. REVIEW OF LINEAR TRANSFORMATIONS

Consider a data set with $\bar{x} = 8$, median = 7.8, and $S = 2.2$.

a. If each number in the data set was increased by 2, what would be the new mean, median, and standard deviation?

b. If each number in the data set was tripled, what would be the new mean and variance?

c. If each number in the data set was first doubled and then decreased by 3, what would be the new mean and standard deviation?

6-11. LINEAR TRANSFORMATIONS OF RANDOM VARIABLES

Mo remembers his work on the effect of various linear transformations (adding the same number to each value or multiplying each number by some constant) on the various statistics such as mean, variance, and standard deviation.

a. He wonders what would happen if he took the same spinner and doubled each of the outcomes.

What effect does doubling each of the outcomes have on the expected value, the variance, and the standard deviation? Does this agree with what you learned previously about the effect of linear transformations?

b. Lana does the same thing, but she adds 5 to each of the outcomes.

What effect does adding 5 to each of the outcomes have on the expected value, the variance, and the standard deviation?

c. So far, Mo and Lana have not been surprised with applying previous knowledge to this new situation. They decide to combine the effects of (a) and (b). They first double X and then add five. Before making any calculations, predict how the mean, variance, and standard deviation will change. Then make your calculations!

X	2	4	5
$P(X)$	0.3	0.2	0.5

X'	4	8	10
$P(X')$	0.3	0.2	0.5

X	2	4	5
$P(X)$	0.3	0.2	0.5

X''	7	9	10
$P(X'')$	0.3	0.2	0.5

X	2	4	5
$P(X)$	0.3	0.2	0.5

X'''	9	13	15
$P(X''')$	0.3	0.2	0.5

6-12.   ADDING TWO RANDOM VARIABLES

Mo proposes a new experiment. He says, *"Rather than just spin it once and observe the outcome, what if we spin it twice? We could define a new random variable that represents the sum of two independent spins."* Lana likes the idea and proposes they organize the information like this two-way table.

Probability Distribution for $X + X$	First Spin		
	2 | 0.3	4 | 0.2	5 | 0.5
Second Spin 2 | 0.3	4 | 0.09	6 | 0.06	7 | 0.15
4 | 0.2	6 | 0.06		
5 | 0.5			

Mo sees where Lana is going. This allows them to systematically list all possibilities for the sum of two independent spins along with their associated probabilities.

a.   Explain why Lana was able to multiply probabilities in the margins to find the probabilities of each cell in the table.

b.   Finish the table. Use the table to find the mean, variance, and standard deviation of $X + X$. Compare these measures for X to the measures for $X + X$. What patterns do you notice?

6-13.   IS $X + X$ DIFFERENT THAN $2X$?

Mo and Lana are quite surprised now. They did not expect that $2X$ and $X + X$ would be different! Use the physical meaning of $2X$ and $X + X$ to help explain why there might be a difference. (What would you physically do to observe $2X$? What would you physically do to observe $X + X$?)

6-14.   TWO DIFFERENT RANDOM VARIABLES

Mo and Lana want to include their coin with heads = 4 and tails = 8 from problem 6-5. Let Y be a random variable representing one random flip of the coin.

a.   Recall the mean, variance, and standard deviation of Y. Write them down again here.

b.   Finish the two-way table for $X + Y$. Before making any calculations, predict what the mean, variance, and standard deviation will be for $X + Y$ (spinner plus coin).

Probability Distribution for $X + Y$	Spin		
	2 | 0.3	4 | 0.2	5 | 0.5
Flip 4 | 0.5	6 | 0.15	8 | 0.1	
8 | 0.5	10 | 0.15		

6-15.   APPLYING PATTERNS

Mo thinks that he has figured out some patterns. He says, *"I have a random variable A with* $\mu_A = 10$ *and* $\sigma_A = 3$ *and another random variable B with* $\mu_B = 8$ *and* $\sigma_B = 4$. *I think that as long as I know that A and B are independent, I can find* μ_C, σ_C^2, *and* σ_C *for each of these combinations without actually making the table of probabilities."* Find μ_C, σ_C^2, and σ_C for each of these below.

a.   Let $C = A + A$.

b.   Let $C = A + A + B$.

c.   Let $C = 2A + B$.

d.   Let $C = A + B + 2$.

6-16.   Consider the random variable X with the probability distribution given in the table at right. Find the mean, variance, and standard deviation of X.

X	1	5	11	12
$P(X)$	0.1	0.2	0.4	0.3

6-17.   Consider two independent random variables X and Y with $\mu_X = 16$, $\sigma_X = 3$, $\mu_Y = 12$, and $\sigma_Y = 2$. Let $Z = 2X - 2Y$. Find μ_Z and σ_Z.

6-18.   Consider a random variable X with $\mu_X = 40$ and $\sigma_X = 5$. Let $Z = X + X + X + X$.

a.   Find μ_Z and σ_Z.

b.   What does $X + X + X + X$ represent?

c.   What does $\frac{1}{4}(X + X + X + X)$ represent?

d.   Find $\mu_{\frac{1}{4}Z}$ and $\sigma_{\frac{1}{4}Z}$.

6-19.   The price of items at a large auction appear to be approximately normally distributed with a mean of $41 and a standard deviation of $10.

a.   What is the mean and standard deviation for the total cost of two items at this auction?

b.   What is the probability of finding two random items at this auction with a total price of less than $80?

6-20.   Imagine there is a rare but serious disease that is carried by three people per ten thousand. However, there is a reliable test that will identify infected individuals for treatment. Given that a person is infected or not, the test will correctly identify them 99.9% of the time. Now assume the test has just identified a randomly chosen person as having the disease (a "positive" result in testing terms). What is the probability this person actually has the disease?

6.1.3 Is $X - X$ really not zero?

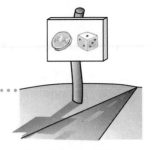

Exploring the Variability of $X - X$

Your training in algebra tells you that $X - X$ is zero. Why is this not true for random variables? In this lesson, you will explore the distribution of $X - X$.

6-21.   OBSERVING $X - X$

   a.   Let X be a random variable representing the number one if heads and two if tails when flipping a coin. Make a probability model for the distribution of X. (Make a table listing all possible outcomes and the associated probabilities.) Find the mean, variance, and standard deviation for X.

   b.   Physically, what would $X - X$ represent? How would you record $X - X$ using your one coin?

   c.   Record 20 observations of $X - X$. Make a dot plot for the 20 differences. Calculate the mean and standard deviation, and write a concise sentence describing the shape, center, and spread for the sample of differences.

   d.   Make a probability model for the distribution of $X - X$. (Make a table listing all possible outcomes and the associated probabilities.) Calculate the mean, variance, and standard deviation for $X - X$.

   e.   Compare your results from part (d) with your combined sample from part (c). How close were the observed sample statistics to the calculated values? What do you predict would happen if you had 400 observations of $X - X$ rather than 40?

   f.   Write an explanation to a friend, not in this class, why $X - X$ is not always zero. Discuss the expected value and standard deviation as part of your response.

6-22.   Continuing their work from Lesson 6.1.2, Mo and Lana recognize that there is no reason they have to simply add the two independent spins. What if they were to subtract them? One possible outcome is that the first spinner could read 5 and the second spinner could read 2. This would be a difference of 3. Or the first spinner could read 4, and the second spinner could read 5. This would be a difference of –1. There is some variability again. Finish the following two-way table for $X - X$, and find the mean, variance, and standard deviation. Were there any surprising results?

Probability Distribution for $X - X$		First Spin		
		2 | 0.3	4 | 0.2	5 | 0.5
Second Spin	2 | 0.3	0 | 0.09	2 | 0.06	3 | 0.15
	4 | 0.2	–2 | 0.06		
	5 | 0.5			

6-23.   THE DIFFERENCE AS A COMPARISON

Let Y represent the difference between two independent die rolls. Let C represent flipping a coin where heads is 1 and tails is 2.

   a.   Find the mean, variance, and standard deviation for C.

   b.   Suppose you are interested in the probability that C is greater than Y. One useful tool is to use the difference C – Y to make calculations like this. Explain why using C – Y could be useful to determine the probability that C is greater than Y.

   c.   Construct a table that allows you to investigate all possible outcomes of C – Y. (Hint: First make a list of all possible outcomes of Y along with the associated probabilities.) What is the expected value for C – Y?

   d.   Find the probability that C is greater than Y.

MATH NOTES

Combining Random Variables

Consider two random variables, X and Y. $E(X + Y) = E(X) + E(Y)$. Written using different symbols, $\mu_{X+Y} = \mu_X + \mu_Y$.

If a is a constant, then $E(aX) = aE(X)$. In the special case that $a = -1$, $E(-X) = -E(X)$ and therefore $E(X - Y) = E(X) - E(Y)$.

If X and Y are independent, then $\text{Var}(X + Y) = \text{Var}(X) + \text{Var}(Y)$. Written using different symbols, $\sigma^2_{X+Y} = \sigma^2_X + \sigma^2_Y$.

If a is a constant, then: $\sigma^2_{aX} = a^2\sigma^2_X$. In the special case that $a = -1$, $\sigma^2_{-X} = \sigma^2_X$ and therefore $\sigma^2_{X-Y} = \sigma^2_X + \sigma^2_Y$.

Note that when two independent variables are combined (even by subtraction), the result is always *more* variability.

Also, do <u>not</u> add standard deviations! When finding the standard deviation for a linear combination of independent random variables, first find the variance for the combination and then square root.

6-24.   A group of scientists is studying a certain insect species. A random sample of insects of various ages was gathered. They have determined that during the first week of life, the mass of the insect (in grams) can be predicted by the age in days according to the equation mass $= 0.35 + 0.06(\text{days})$ with $r^2 = 0.89$.

   a.   One scientist wants to change the unit of time from days to hours. What effect will this have on the correlation between mass and days?

   b.   Interpret the slope of the linear model.

   c.   Predict the mass of an insect after 10 days. Do you trust your prediction? Explain.

6-25.   Two people are working digging holes for the posts of a new fence. The first worker takes away a mean of 1.8 pounds of dirt with a standard deviation of 0.25 pounds with each shovelful. The second worker takes away a mean of 1.4 pounds of dirt with a standard deviation of 0.35 pounds with each shovelful. Both distributions are approximately normally distributed. Assuming the two workers work independent of one another, what is the probability that the second worker shovels more dirt than the first on the next shovelful?

6-26.   Three coins are shaken and dumped onto a table. Each coin has a side that represents heads and a side that represents tails.

   a.   List all possible arrangements of the three coins using H to represent heads and T to represent tails.

   b.   What is the probability that there is exactly two tails out of the three coins.

6-27.   Consider the random variables X and Y with the probability distributions given in the following tables.

X	3	5	8
$P(X)$	0.5	0.15	0.35

   a.   Find the mean and standard deviation for each random variable.

Y	4	5	6	7
$P(Y)$	0.4	0.3	0.18	0.12

   b.   Let $Z = X + X + 1$. Find the mean and standard deviation for Z.

   c.   Let $Z = 2X + 1$. Find the mean and standard deviation for Z. Remember that $X + X \neq 2X$.

   d.   What is the expected value for $X - Y$?

6-28.   Ben has been keeping track of the length of soccer games for a certain league. His data is displayed on the cumulative relative frequency chart (ogive) below.

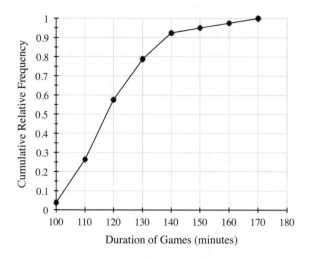

a.   Find the median value for the duration of games.

b.   The middle of the range of this data set is 140 minutes. What percentile does this correspond to?

c.   Use your answers above to estimate the shape of this distribution (skewed-right, skewed-left, or symmetric). Explain.

6.2.1 Can I pass the test?

. . . .

Introducing the Binomial Setting

You will take a four-question multiple choice pretest in preparation for this chapter. Each question has 5 possible choices. Please do not share any responses with other students or shout out answers. Your teacher will go over the answers with you, and you will score yourself.

6-29.   Mo and Lana felt like they had to guess on each of Mr. Knowlsen's questions. It made them wonder if the number of questions answered correctly followed some sort of predictable pattern. They imagined each of the four questions being represented with either "yes" or "no" depending on whether the question was answered correctly. Their goal was to figure out how likely they were to answer 0, 1, 2, 3, or 4 correct.

    a.   Mo is struggling to figure out how to approach this problem. He knows that organizing information is often a good way to start a problem involving probability, so he makes this table listing all possible outcomes on the quiz. Mo says, *"This table allows me to see that there is only 1 possible outcome in which all 4 are correct. There are 4 possible outcomes where exactly 3 are correct."* Help Mo finish his thinking. How many possible outcomes have exactly 2 correct? 1? 0? Have you ever seen a pattern like this before?

Y	Y	Y	Y
Y	Y	Y	N
Y	Y	N	Y
Y	Y	N	N
Y	N	Y	Y
Y	N	Y	N
Y	N	N	Y
Y	N	N	N
N	Y	Y	Y
N	Y	Y	N
N	Y	N	Y
N	Y	N	N
N	N	Y	Y
N	N	Y	N
N	N	N	Y
N	N	N	N

    b.   Mo wanted to say that since there are 16 possible outcomes and one of the sixteen had all four correct, the probability of getting all four correct was $\frac{1}{16}$. Lana disagreed, saying, *"That only works if Y and N are equally likely. Since each trial was independent, I think that to find the probability of each outcome in this table, we need to multiply $0.2 \cdot 0.2 \cdot 0.2 \cdot 0.2$ for the first row in the table, $0.2 \cdot 0.2 \cdot 0.2 \cdot 0.8$ for the second row, and so on."* Where did Lana get the 0.2 and 0.8?

    c.   Following Lana's idea, write down the probability associated with each row. Keep <u>all</u> of the decimals or use fractions!

6-30.   Mo noticed that since YYYY and YYYN could not both happen at the same time on the same quiz, they must be mutually exclusive events. He thinks that this allows him to add probabilities in this table. Try it out. What do all of the probabilities add to? Why did it have to work out this way?

6-31.   Lana suggests that they group the outcomes by how many Ys are in each outcome. For example, the first row has 4 Ys. The second row has 3 Ys. She wants to add up all of the probabilities within each group. Carry out Lana's idea, and fill out the following table.

Number of Ys	0	1	2	3	4
Probability					

6-32.   Mo is excited by Lana's idea. He says, *"That's it! I think we answered our question. This looks just like one of our discrete probability distributions that we've been working with. It lists all of the possible outcomes along with their probabilities. We already checked that the probabilities add to 1. I know how to find the expected value and the standard deviation!"* Help Mo carry out these calculations.

6-33.   Mo gets even more excited when he realizes that this also allows him to make a density histogram. He says, *"I can make a histogram with 5 bins. The 'Number of Ys' would be the midpoint of each bin, and the width of each bin would be 1. If I make the probability the height of each bar, I'll have a density histogram. The total area of all the rectangular bars combined will be 1. We must have some sort of density function here!"* Construct Mo's density histogram. Verify that the total area of the bars combined equals 1.

6-34.   Lana has a new idea. She says, *"If I list the number of ways to get each outcome, I see the list 1, 4, 6, 4, 1. I've seen this before! I tried a similar list if we had only 3 questions rather than 4. I get 1, 3, 3, 1. These are rows in Pascal's triangle! I think that they were also called binomial coefficients. They can be directly calculated. I think we can bypass needing to list out all of the outcomes!"*

a.   Help Lana out. Use the $_nC_r$ button on a calculator to calculate how many ways there are to arrange 2 "yes" answers out of 4 questions.

b.   Lana noticed that each of the outcomes that had 2 Ys in them all had the same probability. She thinks that if she takes $0.8 \cdot 0.8 \cdot 0.2 \cdot 0.2$ and multiplies it with her answer to part (a), she will get the probability of getting exactly 2 questions correct on this test. Carry out her idea. Do you agree with her?

6-35.   Mo wants to extend their idea to a 10 question test. He wants to calculate the probability of getting 4 questions correct on a 10 question multiple choice test (again with 5 possible outcomes for each question).

a.   Mo knows that if there are 10 questions, he will have $0.2 \cdot 0.2 \cdot 0.2 \cdot 0.2 \cdot 0.8 \cdot 0.8 \cdot 0.8 \cdot 0.8 \cdot 0.8 \cdot 0.8$ for each possible outcome with exactly 4 correct. Lana does not want to have to write all of this! Help Mo and Lana write this product in a more compact way using exponents.

b.   Use the $_nC_r$ button on a calculator to calculate how many ways there are to arrange the 10 questions so that there are exactly 4 correct.

c.   Combine your work with parts (a) and (b) to find the probability of getting exactly 4 questions correct on this 10 question test.

6-36.   Lana wants to generalize their work and construct a formula that uses 'n' instead of 10, 'p' instead of 0.2, and 'k' as the number correct. Help her to construct a formula that will tell them the probability of getting k correct out of n questions. That is, if X is a random variable that represents the number of correct answers, what is $P(X = k)$?

6-37.   Some customers of Shady Steve's Window Coverings have banded together. After talking with other customers, they have gathered a simple random sample of the sale price of Shady Steve's premium blinds. The customers are concerned that there may be outliers present. Perform appropriate calculations to determine if there are outliers present in the sale prices.

Sale price ($): 45.89, 47.98, 43.06, 48.20, 42.96, 42.57, 45.2, 43.34, 46.31, 42.39, 42.78, 52.70, 44.34, 42.29

6-38.   A certain type of bird has several different distinct color variations. One rare variation occurs in 7% of the population. If a bird watcher makes 40 independent observations of these birds in random locations, what is the probability that 5 will have the rare color variation?

6-39.   A certain cookie brand claims to have twice as many chocolate chips as the leading competitor. You want to test this claim and want to gather a representative sample of these cookies. You contact the company and find out that there are two factories that produce these cookies. The cookies are produced in "lots" with the lot number and date stamped on each package. Use your knowledge of sampling techniques to describe two different methods of obtaining a representative sample of 200 cookies.

6-40.   Tareq is playing a game where he rolls a 10-sided die. The faces are numbered from 1 to 10.

   a.   Let X represent the outcome of rolling this die once. Find the mean and standard deviation for X.

   b.   Find the mean and standard deviation for the sum of two dice rolls.

6-41.   A standardized test is designed to have scores that are normally distributed with a mean of 200 with a standard deviation of 25.

   a.   Find the probability of a randomly selected student scoring higher than 240.

   b.   What score on this test would represent the 99th percentile? Round to the nearest whole number.

   c.   If two students are randomly chosen, what is the probability that their scores differ by more than 50 points? (Hint: Use $X - X$.)

6.2.2 Is this a new distribution?

Binomial Probability Density Function

Mo and Lana have been reflecting on their work with probabilities on the multiple choice tests. They want to be able to apply their new understandings to other situations. They are hoping that if they can identify the important features of the multiple choice setting, they may be able to apply this in new situations. They come up with the following list:

- There were 4 questions on the test. No one had more or less questions.

- Each question had a 0.2 chance of being answered correctly.

- If they answered question 1 correctly, they were no more or less likely to answer question 2 correctly. The questions did not seem to depend on one another.

- Each question was recorded as either correct or incorrect.

6-42.   Help Mo and Lana write these important features into language that does not involve the specific situation of a multiple choice test.

6-43.   Mo finds an example in a completely different setting to see if these conditions can be met in other situations. He says, *"A park ranger is studying a disease that is found in trees in his forest. After studying many trees, he notices that 16% of the trees seem to be infected. There does not seem to be any pattern to the infections. If one tree is infected, neighboring trees do not seem any more or less likely to be infected. A colleague of his wants to investigate a sample of 30 trees, recording the number of trees that are infected."* Mo thinks that the colleague who investigates the 30 trees will experience the same setting as the multiple choice tests. Attempt to verify in context whether each of your conditions in the previous problem are present in Mo's new situation.

6-44.   Use your formula that you developed in the previous lesson to find the probability that exactly 5 trees out of the 30 are infected.

6-45.   Lana is pleased that they were able to extend their formula to other settings, but she still feels limited. She is concerned that they can only work with a small number of trials. For example, if there are 100 trials and she is interested in the probability of obtaining exactly 30 yes results, the number of ways to arrange 30 yes results out of 100 trials is HUGE. Make this calculation. Try calculating the number of ways to arrange 150 yes results out of 1000 trials. Does this seem to be a limitation?

6-46.   Mo, too, was bothered by the problem Lana identified. He remembers the term "binomial coefficient" earlier, and he also remembers that they were able to make a density histogram. He looks up the binomial distribution. He learns that they have already uncovered the four conditions of the binomial setting, and that many calculators and computers are able to make calculations involving the binomial probability density function. Mo says *"Eureka! This is exactly what we need. I found this feature in my calculator in the same place as the normal distribution! I can now take the situation with the infected trees and calculate the probability of obtaining 150 infected trees out of the 1000 trials."* Use the binomial probability density function to make this calculation. Write down all inputs that you needed to enter in addition to the answer.

6-47.   Lana noticed that in the same place she found the binomial probability density function, there was also something called a binomial cumulative density function. The word cumulative seemed to imply that something is being accumulated.

She applies it to their original setting with the 4 question multiple choice test. First, she recreates the original table using the binomial probability density function. Then she creates a similar table using the binomial cumulative density function.

Make a copy of each table and fill in the missing values. What does the cumulative density function seem to be doing? Explain.

Number of Ys	0	1	2	3	4
Binomial pdf					

Number of Ys	0	1	2	3	4
Binomial cdf					

6-48.   You have a bag of candy that comes in colors of red, yellow, pink, and orange. In the bag you happen to be eating, there are 7 red, 8 yellow, 8 pink, and 7 orange.

   a.   If you randomly choose candies from this bag to eat, what is the probability that the first three pieces of candy you eat will be pink?

   b.   Each time you eat 5 pieces of candy, you count the number of pink candies. Can this situation be modeled by the binomial distribution? Explain.

6-49.   You work for a grocery store unloading boxes. Some of your coworkers are very rough with the boxes, and they seem to independently damage about 5% of the boxes that are unloaded. If 70 boxes are unloaded, find the probability that:

a.   4 or less are damaged.

b.   3 are damaged.

6-50.   A company produces cases for a phone that is 5.8 inches tall. The case is designed to have a snug fit. The engineers designed the height of the case to be normally distributed with a mean of 5.85 inches and a standard deviation of 0.017 inches. Let X be a random variable representing the height of a randomly chosen case.

a.   Is X continuous or discrete? Explain.

b.   Find $P(X < 5.8)$.

c.   In a shipment of 1000 phones, let Y represent the number of cases that are smaller than 5.8 inches in height. Is Y continuous or discrete? Explain.

d.   In the shipment of 1000 phones, find the probability that $Y = 2$. Assume that the heights are all independent.

6-51.   You work for a local coffee shop. The owners require that you use 72 grams of coffee grounds for each 120 ounces of coffee. The mass of coffee grounds used for a random sample of fifty 72 ounce batches was gathered.

Mass of coffee (g): 70.9, 71.1, 71.3, 71.3, 71.3, 71.4, 71.4, 71.4, 71.5, 71.5, 71.6, 71.6, 71.6, 71.6, 71.6, 71.7, 71.7, 71.7, 71.9, 71.9, 71.9, 72, 72, 72, 72, 72.1, 72.1, 72.1, 72.1, 72.1, 72.1, 72.1, 72.2, 72.2, 72.2, 72.2, 72.3, 72.3, 72.3, 72.4, 72.4, 72.5, 72.6, 72.6, 72.7, 72.7, 72.8, 72.8, 73, 73.1

The data has a mean of 71.998 grams with a standard deviation of 0.503656 grams.

a.   Use the empirical rule to determine if there seems to be evidence that the sample is approximately normally distributed.

b.   Construct a boxplot of the data. Does this plot agree with your answer to part (a)?

6.2.3 What are pdf and cdf?

Exploring Binomial pdf and cdf

Mo and Lana's teacher, Mrs. Hoppenheimer, is pleased with their discoveries. She takes their setting of a forest with 16% of trees independently infected and creates a series of problems for Mo and Lana to solve using their newly found pdf and cdf functions for the binomial distribution.

6-52.　　　What is the probability that, out of 50 trees randomly chosen, 8 will be infected?

6-53.　　　Mo decides to practice using their original formula (not the pdf or cdf calculator command) to solve this problem. Apply the formula. Do you get the same answer?

6-54.　　　What is the probability that, out of 50 randomly chosen trees, 8 or less will be infected?

6-55.　　　What is the probability that, out of 50 randomly chosen trees, *more* than 8 will be infected? (Hint: Complement.)

6-56.　　　What is the probability that, out of 50 randomly chosen trees, less than 8 will be infected? (Hint: How is this different than problem 6-54?)

6-57.　　　What is the probability that, out of 50 randomly chosen trees, between 7 and 10 trees (including 7 and 10) will be infected?

　　　a.　　Solve this first using only the binomial probability density function (pdf). You may need to add up several calculations!

　　　b.　　Lana became bored repeatedly using the binomial probability density function. She makes the following list: 0, 1, 2, 3, ... , 5, 6, 7, 8, 9, 10, 11, 12, ..., 49, 50. She plans to use this with the cumulative density function to make the calculation much more efficient. How does her plan seem to work? Make the calculation!

6-58.　　　What is the probability that, out of 100 randomly chosen trees, between 10 and 20 (inclusive) will be infected?

6-59.   The chance of an EverCell AAA battery working properly is 65%. You test an "extra value pack" of 7 batteries in your calculator, what is the probability exactly 2 of the batteries are working?

6-60.   Jorge loves to bake banana bread, and his recipe calls for baking it at 350 degrees Fahrenheit for one hour. In reality, it seems as though it often takes longer than 80 minutes before it has reached the consistency that Jorge likes. If 55% of the loaves of bread take longer than 80 minutes, find the probability that out of a dozen loaves, 10 will take longer than 80 minutes.

6-61.   The distribution of scores on the 2014 AP Statistics exam is in the table below.

Score	1	2	3	4	5
% of students achieving this score	22.7%	17.9%	24.46%	20.91%	14%

Assume you will select a random sample of 15 test booklets from 2014:

a.   What is the probability 3 of the tests received a score of 5?

b.   How many of the 15 tests would you expect passed the exam with a score of at least 3?

c.   What is the probability that at least 10 of test will have a 3 or above?

MATH NOTES

The Binomial Setting

Many situations can be modeled with the binomial distribution. In general, the binomial distribution is used to model a situation in which a number of "yes" (or "success") are counted out of a set number of trials or attempts. The following four conditions define the binomial setting.

1. There are a fixed number of trials.
2. There are two possible outcomes for each trial: "yes" or "no."
3. The outcome of each trial is independent.
4. The probability of a "yes" remains constant for every trial.

If the conditions above are met and X represents the number of "yes" out of a fixed number of trials, the distribution of X is modeled by the binomial distribution.

Notation: We say that X is $B[n, p]$.

6-62.   Elizabeth and Scott are playing a game at the state fair that uses two spinners that are shown below. The player spins both wheels and if the colors match the player wins a prize.

Spinner #1   Spinner #2

a.   Make a probability diagram for this situation.

b.   What is the probability of winning a prize?

c.   If you won a prize, what is the probability that the matching colors were red?

6-63.   Min-seo has a little brother who is a happy baby. He smiles at Min-seo 85% of the time when she walks into the room. Assume that each smile is independent. If she walks into the room 25 times, what is the probability that her baby brother will smile at her

a.   more than 20 times?

b.   between 15 and 20 times? $(P(15 \le X \le 20))$

c.   18 times?

6-64.   University professors are complaining that the English Literature classes at community colleges are not demanding enough. Specifically, the university professors claim that community college literature courses are not assigning enough novels to read. A community college statistics student collected the following data from 42 universities and community college literature courses in the state. Compare the number of novels read in the two types of colleges.

Number of novels assigned in community college literature courses:
13, 10, 15, 12, 14, 9, 11, 15, 12, 14, 9, 10, 13, 15, 12, 9, 11, 15, 12, 10, 15, 14
checksum: 270

Number of novels assigned in university literature courses:
11, 8, 14, 13, 25, 11, 7, 13, 8, 16, 11, 10, 20, 7, 8, 13, 14, 16, 18, 10
checksum: 253

Be sure to include appropriate graphics, and discussion of center, shape, spread and outliers. Write a detailed conclusion <u>paragraph</u> based on the statistical evidence, which either supports or denies the university professors claim that their courses are more demanding because they assign more novels.

6.2.4 Can I describe the binomial distribution?

Shape, Center, and Spread of the Binomial Distribution

In Lesson 6.2.3, you used the binomial distribution in a variety of settings. You have explored the probability density function and the cumulative density function. Because it is called the binomial *distribution*, you might be wondering if you could describe this distribution. This triggers memories of describing shape, center, and spread!

6-65. Mo likes to think about shape, center, and spread when he sees the word "distribution." He thinks that he can quickly discover the mean as the center of the binomial distribution. He argues that he already recognized that he is working with a discrete random variable, and he knows that the mean is the expected value. As a thought experiment, he says, *"If I have 50 randomly chosen trees, and 16% of the population is infected, how many do I expect to be infected?"* Answer Mo's question, and extend his thinking to write a general formula for the mean of the binomial distribution using n for the number of trials, p for the probability of a "yes," and X representing the number of "yes" results out of the n trials.

6-66. Mo and Lana recognize that each time a sample is gathered, the number of "yes" results (represented by the random variable X) would naturally vary from sample to sample. They would like to find the standard deviation of X to help quantify how a sample would typically vary from the expected amount.

Lana knows that she can always list out every possible outcome and the associated probabilities, as in their four-question multiple choice test, in order to find the standard deviation, but she is hoping that she can uncover a general formula instead.

a. Lana has an idea. It would be simple to think about just one trial where the outcomes are either 0 or 1. She creates a random variable Y representing the outcome. She creates the table at right.

Y	0	1
$P(Y)$	$1-p$	p

Find the mean and *variance* of Y for this simplified case. Simplify your expressions as far as possible.

Problem continues on next page $\rightarrow$

6-66.   *Problem continued from previous page.*

b.   Next, Lana argues that she also knows how to find the mean and variance for combinations of random variables. She can define a new random variable X to be $X = Y + Y + Y + \ldots + Y$ where she adds Y a total of n times. Mo gets excited. *"I see what you are doing. This exactly models our situation! If any individual trial was a 'yes,' its value would be 1, and if it is a 'no,' its value would be 0, contributing nothing to the sum. We have n independent trials. X would exactly accumulate the number of 'yes' results out of the n independent trials by calculating the sum. And we know how to find the mean and standard deviation for this sum! This is it!"* Use your results in part (a) and your knowledge of combining random variables to find the mean, variance, and standard deviation of X.

6-67.   Mo and Lana move on to investigate the shape of the binomial distribution. They recognize that there are two *parameters* that define the distribution: n and p. They use technology to create the following graphs:

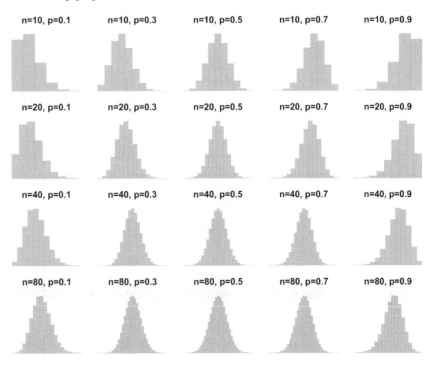

Summarize the effects of n and p on the shape of the binomial distribution. When will the distribution be skewed to the left? Symmetric? Skewed to the right? What happens as n gets larger? Explore other combinations of n and p using the Binomial Distribution eTool.

6-68. Lana thinks that some of the graphs for various combinations of n and p look a lot like the normal distribution. She is convinced there is something going on there! She cannot think of any formula to solve, but she has made some observations. She sees that the graphs on the far left and right are more skewed, but even that seems to be decreasing as n gets larger. She thinks that if n is large enough, nearly all of the graphs would look like a normal curve. Somehow n, p, and $1 - p$ (to account for both the left and right sides) must work together to create conditions for which the binomial distribution looks approximately normal. Brainstorm with your team. Can you come up with a rule for n, p, and $1 - p$ that can be applied to the graphic above that includes only the curves that look approximately normally distributed?

MATH NOTES

Bernoulli Trial

A **Bernoulli trial** is an experiment for which there are exactly two possible outcomes, repeated trials are independent, and the probability of success on any trial is always the same.

Let X be a random variable representing the outcomes of a Bernoulli trial with outcomes 1 (with probability p) and 0 (with probability $1 - p$). The mean and variance of the random variable X are $\mu_X = p$ and $\sigma_X^2 = p(1 - p)$.

The binomial distribution can be constructed out of n independent Bernoulli trials.

6-69. Moshe's younger cousins like to make creations out of play blocks. Many times, the creations are very elaborate, containing over 200 pieces. After keeping track of many creations, Moshe conclude that 72% of the creations contain over 200 pieces. Consider the next 10 creations. Let X represent the number of creations containing over 200 pieces.

a. Find the probability that exactly 8 of the creations contain over 200 pieces.

b. Find the mean and standard deviation of X. Interpret these values in this context.

6-70.   For each faux news story below, accept that the association is true and indicate a hidden confounding variable that may be the actual cause of the relationship.

   a.   BOOKS IN HOME ASSOCIATED WITH HIGHER TEST SCORES: Students buying truckloads of books before taking national exams.

   b.   CHESS CLUB BOASTS HIGHEST IVY LEAGUE MATRICULATION RATES: Club president now flooded with membership applications.

   c.   STUDENTS WHO LIVE OFF CAMPUS AT HIGHER RISK FOR AUTO ACCIDENTS: State police warn: play it safe, live on campus.

6-71.   Suppose in any given year for a certain California city, the probability of a major earthquake hitting is 0.04, the probability of a major fire is 0.351, and the probability of both a major earthquake and major fire is 0.008. What is the probability of a major fire given that a major earthquake hits?

6-72.   Consider the scatterplot at right comparing the amount of time a random selection of swimmers can hold their breath to their times in the 500-yard freestyle race.

   a.   Estimate and interpret the slope of the LSRL.

   b.   Estimate and interpret R^2 in context.

   c.   If a swimmer who holds their breath for 25 seconds and swims a 6 minute 500 free were added to the plot, what would be the effect on the slope of the LSRL and the correlation coefficient?

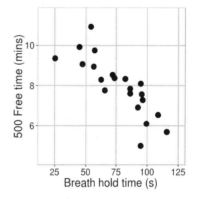

6-73.   Pigeons are used for racing because of their incredible speed and endurance. While in Pennsylvania describing communities of pigeons, Hugo discovered that the distribution of pigeon flight speeds are normally distributed with a mean of 55.6 mph and a standard deviation of 3.3 mph.

   Sketch the normal probability density function and determine the probability of selecting a pigeon flight speed less than 56.4 mph.

6.2.5 Does the binomial distribution normalize?

Normal Approximation to the Binomial Distribution

At this point you have studied both discrete and continuous probability distributions. Today you will consider how discrete and continuous probability distributions become more similar as the number of trials increases.

6-74.   Open the Binomial Distribution eTool.

   a.   Looking at the shape of the binomial distribution plotted, find several pairs of n and p that are obviously skewed. Find several pairs of n and p that produce a graph that looks quite normal. Find several pairs of n and p that produce a shape that is not quite skewed but questionably normally distributed.

   b.   Share these three tables with your class, plotting the various combinations of n and p on a scatterplot with p on the vertical axis. Use a different color to represent points from each category of points collected.

   c.   On the same scatterplot, add the lines representing the curves $xy = 10 \rightarrow y = \frac{10}{x}$ and $x(1 - y) = 10 \rightarrow y = 1 - \frac{10}{x}$. What do you notice?

6-75.   Mo and Lana consulted with other teams, and they agreed that if n is large enough that both np and $n(1 - p)$ are at least 10, then the binomial distribution will be approximately normal. They check a few more combinations of n and p to verify their conclusion.

n=20, p=0.5   n=50, p=0.25   n=50, p=0.75   n=500, p=0.03   n=1000, p=0.975

Do you agree with Mo and Lana's conclusion? Do these seem to be *approximately* normal? Why could they never be *exactly* normal, even if they were perfectly symmetrical?

6-76.   Lana has the idea that if some binomial distributions are approximately normally distributed, she should be able to calculate probabilities using the cdf function for the normal distribution, and it should closely approximate the cdf function for the binomial distribution. She wants to work with a binomial distribution with 80 trials and a 0.4 chance of success. She writes down "*X is B(80, 0.4)*" as notation for this setting.

   a.   Use the cdf function for the binomial distribution to find the probability that *X* is 30 or less.

   b.   Apply the formulas you discovered for the mean and standard deviation of the binomial distribution. Justify why the shape of this distribution is approximately normal.

   c.   Use the cdf function for the normal distribution to find the probability that *X* is 30 or less. Are you satisfied with the approximation?

6-77.   Mo is frustrated. He thought his answers from parts (a) and (c) of problem 6-76 would be closer. He makes the plot below.

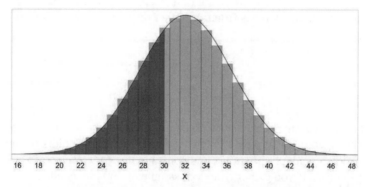

   He exclaims, "*I see what is happening here! If we shade 30 and less on the normal curve, we miss half of the '30-bar' for the binomial distribution. It is hard to model a discrete histogram with a smooth continuous normal distribution. Let's correct for this.*"

   Re-run the calculation in part (c) using 30.5 instead of 30 as a "continuity correction." Do you get a better approximation? Why was 30.5 chosen?

6-78.   Mo wonders if this continuity correction really works. He followed the steps below to test this new concept of continuity correction.

   a.   Use the cdf for the binomial distribution to calculate $P(26 \leq X \leq 30)$. This is the exact probability of *X* being between 26 and 30 for the binomial distribution.

   b.   Use the cdf for the normal distribution to calculate $P(26 \leq X \leq 30)$ *without* continuity correction. This calculation represents an approximation of part (a) using the normal distribution.

   c.   Use the cdf for the normal distribution to calculate $P(25.5 \leq X \leq 30.5)$ as a continuity correction. Was the approximation of part (a) better?

   d.   Make a quick sketch to show why 25.5 and 30.5 were chosen for the continuity correction in this example.

MATH NOTES

The Binomial Probability Density Function

If X is a random variable modeled by the binomial distribution with n trials and p probability of success (written "X is $B[n, p]$"), then the probability that k successes are observed out of the n trials is:

$$P(X = k) = \binom{n}{k} p^k (1 - p)^{(n-k)}$$

Additionally, the expected value for X is $\mu = np$, and the standard deviation for X is $\sigma = \sqrt{np(1 - p)}$.

Note that the probability density function of a discrete random variable is more accurately referred to as a **probability mass function** rather than a probability density function.

6-79. You are a marketing researcher, and you are studying the number of colors on various packages. Specifically, you are interested in the number of colors on generic brand packaging. After making many observations, you conclude that 65% of generic brands are packaged with 3 or less colors. If you gather a random sample of 300 independent generic products:

a. Find the probability that more than 200 are packaged with 3 or less colors.

b. Find the mean and standard deviation of X, the number observed with 3 or less colors.

c. Explain why the distribution of X is approximately normally distributed.

d. Use the normal distribution to find $P(X > 200)$.

6-80. Name, then write a one-sentence general interpretation of the following symbols in the context of bivariate quantitative data (regression).

a. r b. R^2 c. S

...within $\hat{y} = a + bx$...

d. a e. b f. $\hat{y}$

6-81.   While working at his neighborhood math tutoring center researching the comprehension level of the students, Dion investigated that the distribution of student test scores are normally distributed with a mean of 79.13% and a standard deviation of 6.34%.

Sketch the normal probability distribution and determine and complete the statement: 39% of the student test scores are less than _____%.

6-82.   You and your friend have just won a chance to collect a million dollars. You place the money in one room at right and then your friend has to randomly walk through the maze. In which room should you place the money so that your friend will have the best chance of finding the million dollars?

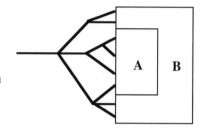

6-83.   Nina has been asked by the school librarian to conduct a survey of how many books students read during the year. She gets the following results: 12, 24, 10, 32, 12, 4, 35, 10, 8, 12, 15, 20, 18, 25, 21, and 9.

a.   Use the data to create a histogram. Use a bin width of 10 books.

b.   Is the mean or median a better measure of the center? Find the value of whichever is more appropriate.

c.   Make a boxplot of the data.

d.   Describe the center, shape, spread, and outliers of the distribution.

6.3.1 How long do I have to wait?

Introduction to the Geometric Distribution

Mo and Lana feel like they can model many situations with their new understanding of the binomial distribution. It feels even more powerful knowing that it can also be modeled by the normal distribution in many situations. Mrs. Hoppenheimer says that the binomial distribution has a "cousin" that they can also learn about, but first they need to remind themselves about sequences.

6-84.   Construct a geometric sequence with a first term of 0.16 and a multiplier of 0.84.

    a.   List the first 6 terms, keeping at least 4 decimals. As a way to organize your calculations, format it in a table like the one below.

n	1	2	3	4	5	6
$t(n)$	0.16					

    b.   Consider the geometric series resulting from this sequence. If the series continues indefinitely, find the sum of the infinite series.

6-85.   Mrs. Hoppenheimer returns to the setting of a large forest with 16% of the trees being independently infected with a certain disease. She asks Mo and Lana to calculate the probability that, as randomly chosen trees are inspected, the first diseased tree encountered would be the fifth tree.

    a.   Try to verify the conditions for the binomial distribution in this new context.

    b.   Hopefully you just determined that the situation almost matches the conditions of a binomial experiment, except one important condition was not met. Even though you cannot use the binomial distribution, you can still calculate the probability of seeing the first diseased tree on the fifth trial. Do it!

    c.   Find the probability that the first "yes" (seeing a diseased tree) will be on <u>or before</u> the fifth trial. For notation, let X represent the trial on which the first yes occurs. Find $P(X \leq 5)$. Hint: You may have a table that comes in handy…

    d.   You already found in problem 6-84 that
$0.16 + 0.16(0.84) + 0.16(0.84)^2 + 0.16(0.84)^3 + 0.16(0.84)^4 + \ldots$ (terms going on forever), is equal to 1. Use your knowledge of probability in this setting to explain why this must happen.

    e.   Find the probability that the first "yes" occurs some time *after* the 5th trial.

6-86.   Mo and Lana agree that they are working with a new probability density function. If they were to make a density histogram, it would have a total area of 1, even though it would have an infinite number of bars. Help Mo and Lana clarify some of the characteristics of the binomial and geometric settings.

   a.   In the binomial distribution, what does the random variable X represent?

   b.   The geometric distribution shares three of the four conditions with the binomial distribution. Which one is no longer present?

   c.   In the geometric distribution, what does the random variable X represent?

   d.   The binomial distribution has two parameters, n and p. How many parameters does the geometric distribution have?

6-87.   You have discovered a binomial probability density function (pdf) and a binomial cumulative density function (cdf) on the calculator. There is also a pdf and cdf for the geometric distribution!

   a.   Find the geometric pdf function on a calculator, and re-do part (b) of problem 6-85. Did you get the same result?

   b.   Find the geometric cdf function on a calculator and re-do part (c) of problem 6-85. Did you get the same result?

6-88.   Mo and Lana are interested in the shape, center, and spread of the geometric distribution. They recognize that it depends on the probability of a "yes."

   a.   Turn your table from problem 6-84 into a probability histogram. Indicate somehow on your chart that the bars should continue forever. Describe the shape of this specific geometric distribution.

   b.   Lana figured out what the expected value must be. She poses a related question in another situation. She asks Mo, *"If you are taking a multiple choice test with 5 choices for each question, you have 0.2 chance of success when guessing, right? How many questions would you expect to have to answer in order to see your first success?"* Can you generalize Lana's idea with p rather than 0.2?

   c.   Mo agreed with Lana's argument for the expected value of the geometric distribution. He had a hunch that because it represents a situation with an infinite series that it may be difficult to find a formula for the standard deviation. He looks it up and finds $\sigma_X = \sqrt{\frac{1-p}{p^2}}$.

        Use Mo and Lana's formulas for the mean and standard deviation of the geometric distribution to describe the shape, center, and spread of their random variable X in the situation with infected trees. Interpret each calculation in context. What information does it provide about the situation?

MATH NOTES

Normal Approximation to the Binomial Distribution

If X is a random variable modeled by the binomial distribution with n trials and p probability of success, X can be considered to be approximately normally distributed if n is large enough to expect at least 10 "yes" results and 10 "no" results.

If this is the case, then X is approximately normally distributed with a mean $\mu = np$, and a standard deviation $\sigma = \sqrt{np(1-p)}$.

6-89. A survey is being designed to determine whether or not people are in favor of legislation that would establish a seven day waiting period between the time a gun is purchased and when it is physically transferred to the owner. Write two poorly worded questions that would result in biased results, one in favor and the other not in favor.

6-90. Kseniya been buying box after box of Super Marshmallow Cereal trying to collect a specific action figure. There are ten different action figures, equally distributed so that any given box has a 0.1 chance of having a specific action figure.

   a. How likely is it that Kseniya will have to wait longer than 15 boxes before finding the single action figure she is interested in?

   b. Find the mean and standard deviation for the number of boxes before the first cereal box containing the action figure Kseniya is interested in. Interpret these values in context.

   c. Of the next 15 boxes, what is the probability that 2 of them contain the action figure Kseniya wants?

   d. Of the next 180 boxes, find the mean and standard deviation for the number of boxes that contain the action figure Kseniya is interested in.

   e. Use the normal approximation and the empirical rule to estimate the middle 95% for the number of boxes containing the action figure Kseniya is looking for.

6-91.   A random sample of 35 cars was taken from a car rental agency, and the highway mileage of each car was measured in miles per gallon (mpg).

33	37	40	40	36	37	34
42	36	36	35	40	27	43
29	41	35	40	26	37	41
39	41	32	33	28	36	37
37	38	37	37	25	38	41

checksum: 1264

a.   Use a calculator to determine the mean and standard deviation for this sample of cars.

b.   Create a relative frequency table and relative frequency histogram for the data. Begin your table at 24 mpg and use intervals of 3 mpg.

c.   The rental agency advertises that its fleet of compact cars gets at least 30 mpg. What percentage of the sample does not meet this standard?

d.   What interval would contain the median car?

e.   The State awards a "gold star" mileage rating to cars that get a minimum of 39 mpg. What percentage of cars in the sample attained this rating?

6.3.2 Can I recognize binomial and geometric?

Binomial and Geometric Practice

This section will give you the opportunity to hone your skills recognizing and using the binomial distribution (and the normal approximation) and the geometric distribution. For each problem below, first determine the appropriate distribution. Be able to justify your choice! Then find the requested probabilities.

6-92.   Takumi's favorite clothing store is a large store with a large inventory. Many items are on sale, but the store has a strange policy. You cannot find out if an item is on sale until you check out at the register. The store boasts that 60% of the items in the store are on sale. Takumi is curious and calls the company headquarters. They confirm that the items are all independently on sale.

     a.   As Takumi is checking out, what is the probability that the first item on sale is the third item checked out?

     b.   If he purchases 8 items of clothing, what is the probability that 5 of them will be on sale?

     c.   If Takumi plans to purchase a large number of items, what is the probability that he will have to wait longer than 4 items before seeing the first item on sale?

     d.   If he purchases 12 items of clothing, what is the probability that between 5 and 8 of them will be on sale?

6-93.   Alva works for a company that produces lumber. The company's standard boards are supposed to be 8 feet long. In reality, they are normally distributed with a mean of 8 feet and a standard deviation of 0.003 feet. The boards are all individually cut to length.

a.   Alva's company defines standard boards less than 7.995 feet in length to be too short. What is the probability of finding a randomly chosen board that is too short?

b.   If a customer purchases 120 standard length boards, what is the probability that more than 5 are too short?

c.   Alva has a picky customer that carefully inspects each board before purchasing. What is the probability that this customer inspects 4 boards or less before observing the first board that is too short?

d.   What is the probability that a randomly chosen board is longer than 8.002 feet?

e.   What is the probability of finding two randomly chosen boards with a total length longer than 16.01 feet?

6-94.   Sergei is a scientist studying the fish in a certain lake. His team is interested in estimating the size of the walleye population in the lake. He has tagged some of the fish and released them back into the lake. Although he does not know it, he has actually tagged 3.1% of the walleye in the lake. Assume that each fish is caught independently.

a.   What is the expected number of walleye that Sergei will need to catch until he finds his first tagged fish?

b.   If Sergei catches 80 walleyes, what is the expected value for the number of tagged fish? What is a typical deviation from this expected value?

c.   If Sergei catches 80 walleyes, does the normal approximation apply to the distribution of the number of tagged fish?

d.   If Sergei catches 80 walleyes, find the probability that 4 are tagged.

e.   If Sergei catches 80 walleyes, find the probability that more than 5 are tagged.

f.   If Sergei catches 80 walleyes, find the probability that 2.5% or less are tagged.

6-95.   Camila is playing a board game with some friends and rolls two dice during each turn.

   a.   What is the probability she rolls doubles (both dice have the same value showing) on any roll? Express your answer as a fraction.

   b.   What is the probability she rolls doubles 4 times out of 10 rolls?

   c.   What is the probability she rolls doubles between 4 and 8 times out of 20 rolls?

   d.   What is the probability she rolls doubles less than 3 times out of 10 rolls?

   e.   What is the probability that Camila have to wait more than 4 turns before rolling doubles?

   f.   If Camila rolls 300 times throughout the course of a game, justify that the normal approximation applies to the number of doubles observed. Use the normal approximation to find the probability that the number of doubles observed is less than 45.

MATH NOTES

The Geometric Setting

The geometric distribution arises in a binomial setting when there is no longer a fixed number of trials and the variable of interest becomes the number of trials until the first occurrence of a "yes." The geometric setting is very similar to the binomial setting and is defined by:

1. There are two possible outcomes for each trial: "yes" or "no."
2. The outcome of each trial is independent.
3. The probability of a "yes" remains constant for every trial.

If the conditions above are met and X represents the number of trials until a "yes" is observed, then the distribution of X is modeled by the geometric distribution.

The probability density function (or more accurately probability mass function) for the geometric distribution is given by $P(X = k) = (1 - p)^{k-1} \cdot p$.

The expected value in the geometric setting is $\mu = \frac{1}{p}$, and the standard deviation is $\sigma = \sqrt{\frac{1-p}{p^2}}$.

6-96.   Tiago works with electronics as a hobby. One supplier has very low cost circuit components but a relatively high defect rate. Suppose the defect rate from this supplier is 10%, and that each defect is independent.

   a.   If Tiago buys 320 items from this supplier, how many should he expect to be defective?

   b.   What is a typical deviation from the expected amount in part (a)?

   c.   Rounded to the nearest whole number, what number of items represents 1 standard deviation below the expected amount? What is the probability that fewer than 1 standard deviation below the expected amount are defective?

   d.   Use your knowledge of the relationship between the normal distribution and the binomial distribution to explain why your answer to part (c) is reasonable.

6-97.   The pet store sells a lot of pet food. On a particular day, three people buy cat food, two people buy dog food, and one person buys food for a pet snake. All of these were independent purchases. If half of the customers pay with cash and half pay with credit card, what is the probability that a customer buying pet food will buy dog food with cash? Set up a two-way joint probability table or tree diagram to help you find the probability.

6-98.   Wild boars are an invasive species in the United States. Matthew is in Texas studying the behavior of wild boars. Matthew believes the distribution of wild boar weights is normally distributed.

   If the 35th percentile of boar weights is 388.527 lbs, and the 94th percentile is 505.251 lbs, sketch the normal probability density function and find the mean and standard deviation.

6-99.   Does eating breakfast improve your ability to focus during school?

   a.   Should an observational study or an experiment be carried out to answer the question? Explain.

   b.   Describe how you would carry out the study. Be sure to describe how you would incorporate randomization into your design.

   c.   Are there other variables that may affect the outcome of your study? Explain.

6-100.   The scatterplots below have correlation coefficients of 0, 0.7, 0.9, and –0.7. Match each one to its graph. Then explain why the correlation coefficient itself does not tell you much about these associations.

a.

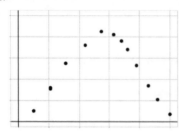

b.

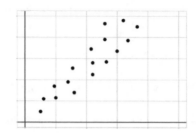

c.

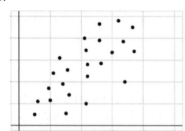

d.

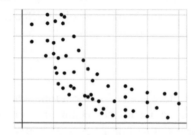

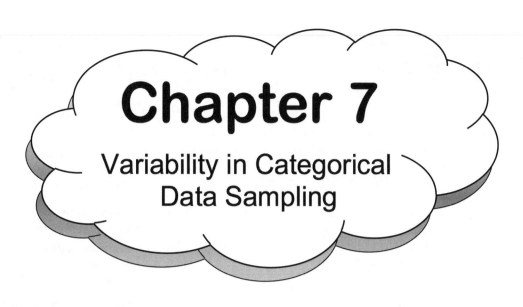

Chapter 7

Variability in Categorical Data Sampling

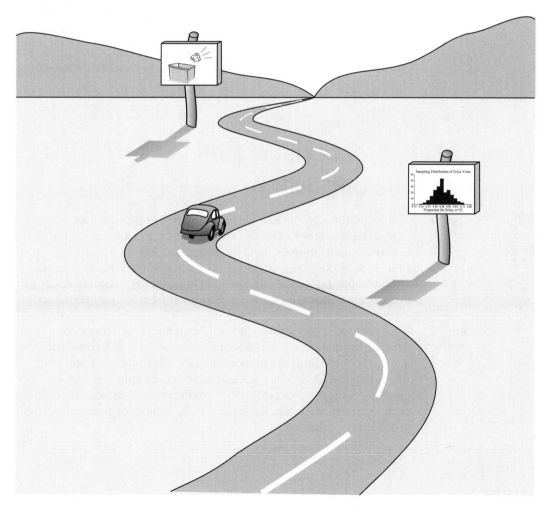

Sampling Distribution of Erica Votes

Proportion for Erica, *n*=25

CHAPTER 7

Statistical inference, making a statement about a population claim or parameter based on a sample statistic, is a large part of the field of Statistics. This chapter is the first of the remaining chapters in this text that will focus on some form of statistical inference. It begins by investigating variation in sample proportions drawn from a single population and ends with techniques for evaluating claims made about population proportions impossible to census.

Chapter Goals

Explore the amount of variation one can expect among sample proportions drawn from a single population.

Use a normal model to describe the variation of sample proportions.

Understand how the normal model can create a confidence interval where the population proportion may reside.

Determine approximate sample sizes required to attain a particular interval width at a specified level of confidence.

Evaluate claims about a population proportion using a confidence interval.

Chapter Outline

Section 7.1   You will informally explore the idea of sampling distributions and confidence intervals by creating many different random samples of size $n = 20$ and comparing proportions within the samples. Then using simulation to estimate a sampling distribution of a sample proportion, recognize that this creates a reasonable estimate of the variability of the true sampling distribution.

Section 7.2   You will extend your understanding of sampling distributions to develop a method of using one sample to come up with a confidence interval for the population proportion. You will formalize a procedure for finding confidence intervals and use z-critical values to calculate confidence intervals for any level of confidence and will use a confidence interval or proportion to test the validity of claims about the population parameter p.

7.1.1 How much do samples vary?

··

Introduction to Sampling Distributions

One of the most important questions in statistics arises when you only have a *sample* but are interested in information about a *population*. Using samples to draw information about populations is called **statistical inference** and is the single most important idea in an introductory statistics class.

The biggest concern when performing statistical inference is understanding **sampling variability**—that is, how much samples can differ from each other (and from the population) simply due to the random nature of choosing a sample. Sampling variability determines how "wrong" your sample might be, relative to the entire population. In this lesson you will explore the idea of a *sampling distribution*, the most commonly used method to visualize and explore sampling variability.

7-1.   WERE THERE ENOUGH BLUE ONES?

Abigail is eagerly looking forward to Friday, when each student in her fifth grade class has been promised a bag of candy-coated chocolates as a reward for figuring out the percentages of the different colors. Abigail's favorite color is blue. She is hoping her bag (which will contain 20 chocolates) is at least half blue! Explore the proportion of blue chocolates in the bags to see how likely Abigail's hope is to come true.

a.   Obtain one or more samples of 20 chocolates (or substitutes) from your teacher. For each sample, calculate the proportion of blue chocolates as a decimal proportion and share it with the class. Continue the sampling process until the class has between 80 and 120 samples, adding to the class dot plot or data sheet as you go.

b.   Sketch your class graph and describe the distribution.

c.   Generally, typical results are the ones that matter, not the extreme ones. For this problem, call the middle 90% "typical." Between what upper and lower bounds are the *middle 90%* of the blue proportions? That is, about 90% of the time, you can expect the proportion of blue candies in a sample of size 20 to be between ____ and ____.

d.   A way of describing this type of interval range, is using a point estimate and a **margin of error**, in the form "point estimate ± margin of error." In this case, the margin of error represents "the plausible variation of the statistic from sample to sample." In this case you have calculated a 90% interval for a sample proportion. How could you represent your answer from part (c) using margin of error form?

e.   Based on your class's samples, about how likely is it that Abigail's wish for "at least half blue" will be fulfilled?

The distribution you found in part (b) of problem 7-1 is a small part of the **sampling distribution** of the proportion of blue candy-coated chocolates with sample size 20. The sampling distribution of a statistic for a given size is a distribution made by calculating the value of the statistic from *every possible sample* of a given size. To build the complete sampling distribution of this statistic, you would need to sample every possible set of 20 candy-coated chocolates in the world! Obviously, this is not possible, so you generally must settle for smaller simulations of sampling distributions when it is important to explore them.

7-2.   Jack is trying to wrap his brain around the whole idea of sampling distributions. *"Every candy-covered chocolate in the world, or even a bag, would be a huge number of possible samples,"* he says, *"but what if we try to think about a much smaller one?"* Shari thinks this is a great idea. *"There are four people in our group,"* she says. *"What if we let our group the entire population of interest, and imagine picking samples of just 2 of us? Then there aren't as many samples to imagine."*

   a.   Assume that Jack, Shari, and Lilly are all right-handed, but Monica is left-handed. What is the true proportion, p, of left-handed people in their group?

   b.   Is "handedness" a categorical or quantitative variable?

   c.   Make a graphical display to represent the distribution of the variable "handedness" over this entire population. This is the *population distribution of your variable*.

   d.   Imagine you take a random sample of two people and get Jack and Shari. Make a graphical display to represent the distribution of the variable 'handedness' over this sample. This is a *sample distribution of your variable*.

   e.   List *every possible sample of size 2 from this population* and calculate $\hat{p}$ — the sample proportion of left-handed students — for each sample.

   f.   Make a graphical display of your values from part (e) to represent the *sampling distribution of $\hat{p}$ with $n = 2$*. What is its mean value?

   g.   Use the graph from part (f) to describe the *sampling variability* of this statistic with $n = 2$. That is, how much can you expect samples to vary from the true population value in this case?

MATH NOTES

Sampling Distributions

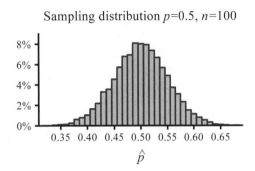

The **sampling distribution of a given statistic for a given sample size** is the distribution found by calculating that statistic using *every possible sample* of the given size. The sampling distribution is itself a quantitative distribution, even if the original population was concerned with categorical data. In most cases, there are too many possible samples to calculate the entire distribution directly, so simulations or theoretical explorations of the sampling distribution are performed instead.

Sampling distribution $p=0.5$, $n=100$

In Chapters 7 and 8 you will primarily explore the sampling distributions of *sample proportions* from samples of categorical data. However, sampling distributions can be created of any statistic, including means, medians, ranges, counts, IQRs, standard deviations, correlation coefficients, and so on; some of these will be explored more in Chapters 10 through 12.

The center of a statistic's sampling distribution shows the value of the statistic on average. If the mean of the distribution is the associated population parameter, then the statistic is an **unbiased estimate for the parameter.**

The spread of a statistic's sampling distribution shows the variability of the statistic across all samples. This can give an idea of how much one can expect a statistic to vary from sample to sample, so you know how "off" the sample statistic can reasonably be from the associated population parameter.

7-3.   Every year, seniors at Hallways School for Girls are randomly grouped together in teams of 6 for a school-wide trivia contest. Caitlin, a senior at Hallways, thinks that Statistics students have an advantage over other seniors and is wondering how likely it is that she will get at least three companions (out of five) that are in Statistics. Describe a way that Caitlin could explore this question. (Assume she does NOT know how many seniors are in Statistics, but that she can easily find out if a *specific* student is in Statistics.)

7-4.   Mary has a small bag of Sunbursts candies: two orange candies, one red candy, and two pink candies. She is going to randomly choose three of them.

    a.   Make a graphical display of the variable "color" across this entire population.

    b.   List every possible sample of three candies. It may help to name the orange candies O1 and O2 and the pink ones P1 and P2.

    c.   Make a graphical display of the variable "color" for *one* of the samples above.

    d.   Make a graphical display of the sampling distribution for the statistic "number of pink candies" with samples of size 3 from this population.

    e.   A statistic is an *unbiased estimate for a parameter* if the mean of its sampling distribution equals the value of its corresponding parameter. Is "number of pinks in sample" an unbiased estimate for "number of pinks"? Explain.

7-5.   The Bright Idea Lighting Company wants to determine what proportion of LED flashlights that come off of its assembly line are defective. It takes many samples of 100 flashlights over the week and determines the proportion that are defective in each sample. A dot plot of the results is shown at right.

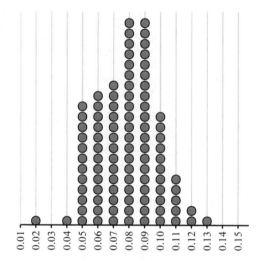

    a.   The mean of all of these values is 7.84%. What is the middle 90% interval?

    b.   Write the middle 90% interval in "Estimate ± Margin or Error" format.

7-6.   Due to natural variability in manufacturing, a 12 ounce can of soda does not usually hold exactly 12 ounces of soda. The quality control department at a soda factory allows cans to hold a little more or a little less. Assume that according to specifications, a soda-can filling machine must fill each can with a mean of 12 ounces of soda and a standard deviation of 0.33 ounces. Filling machines can often be modeled with a normal distribution.

   a.   Sketch a graph of a normal distribution. Use what you know about standard deviation to scale the x-axis appropriately.

   b.   How often do you actually get a 12 oz can of soda containing more than 12 oz?

   c.   What percent of cans contain between 11.5 and 12.5 ounces of soda? Shade your diagram from part (a) to represent these bottles.

   d.   Work backwards: what two weights of soda would the middle 92% of soda bottles fall between?

7-7.   In a certain town, 45% of the population has dimples and 70% has a widow's peak (a hairline above the forehead that makes a "V" shape). Assuming that these physical traits are independently distributed, what is the probability that a randomly selected person has both dimples and a widow's peak? What is the probability that he or she will have neither?

7.1.2 How can I simulate sampling distributions?

Simulating Sampling Distributions of Sample Proportions

Sampling distributions are powerful because they give you a sense of how much samples vary, so you can make predictions about the how future samples can be expected to naturally vary, as well as more reliable estimates of population parameters. Sampling distributions can be explored directly in cases where it is possible to take many samples, as in Lesson 7.1.1. In cases where that is not possible but information about the population is well known, you can estimate information about sampling distributions using simulations.

7-8.   Election Day is coming at Jefferson High. Students will be voting for one of two candidates for Student Council President: Erica or David.

   a.   You can think of a vote the same way you think of a survey. Is it a census or a sample? Identify the population, individuals, variable(s), and domain of the variable (that is, the possible values of the variable). For each variable identified, decide if it is categorical or quantitative.

   b.   What is the most important *parameter* or *statistic* you might look at in a vote?

7-9.   In an effort to learn about what proportion of students will vote for her, Erica plans to gather a random sample of 25 students from the senior class of 320 students. *Unknown to her,* 56% of the student body are planning to vote for Erica.

   a.   Each team in your class will simulate *one* possible sample Erica could get using a *table of random digits*. Since the population of 320 students is significantly greater than Erica's sample size, you can assume the probability of each student she draws voting for her is a constant 56%, even though she is drawing without replacement. Come up with a plan to use one row below (assigned by your teacher) to pick your version of Erica's sample and calculate the proportion of people that voted for Erica in your sample.

   [1] 74468 57656 61078 15719 21018 74900 79648 95360 48291 76878
   [2] 22001 47528 60397 94457 30786 49858 70072 27509 07640 49439
   [3] 65359 96713 48847 44712 85871 71193 13110 52757 63486 42875
   [4] 31647 86591 45086 70861 81795 61075 99442 28536 69095 87721
   [5] 63381 70187 83034 90439 20841 58215 97059 01381 65753 62541
   [6] 09421 38888 69310 71289 39722 50111 78461 36663 49393 91634
   [7] 86434 68972 74726 50215 22278 32158 69088 62792 15137 51117
   [8] 72130 14820 80629 61872 08150 67858 72105 95362 91507 64972

Problem continues on next page →

7-9.   *Problem continued from previous page.*

   b.   Collect responses from each team. What does each team's number represent? Describe the distribution of these responses. Is this a good representation of the total sampling distribution of Erica's $\hat{p}$?

   c.   Joe says, *"Wait a minute. Can't we just do what we did in the last lesson and list every possible sample to find the complete sampling distribution?"* What do you think, would that be possible in this case?

   d.   Random digits are a slow way to simulate. It is much faster to use calculators, and faster still to use computers. Your teacher will instruct you how to use the Proportions Sampling eTool to simulate 1000 different samples Erica might get and create a histogram. Sketch the histogram you created below and describe the distribution.

   e.   Use the histogram to estimate the probability that more than half of Erica's sample will say they are voting for her.

   f.   Find an approximate "middle 90% interval" for this sampling distribution. "I can be about 90% confident that Erica's sample will show a proportion voting for her between about _____ and _____."

7-10.   In the previous problem, you were able to simulate the sampling distribution for Erica's sample because you knew the true proportion! Erica, however, is not so lucky. Imagine she takes a sample and $\frac{12}{25}$ of the students *in her sample* vote for her.

   a.   Based on your answer from part (f), does this seem like a believable sample for Erica to get?

   b   After she takes her sample, what is *Erica's* best guess for the true proportion, p, of students who will vote for her?

7-11.   Because Erica is in AP Statistics, she knows that samples are variable and that her sample probably did not find the true proportion exactly. She is interested in exploring how *much* her sample might vary from others. From her study of sampling distributions, she knows that if she could just get an idea of the spread of a sampling distribution, she could answer that question.

         If Erica tries to use the proportion sample tool to simulate the sampling distribution, where will she run into a snag? What will be her best option to get past it? Discuss with your team and confirm with your teacher before moving on to the next question.

7-12.   Perform Erica's simulation to explore the sampling distribution with 1000 samples. Sketch the histogram of this new simulation. Does her simulated center match that of the true sampling distribution in problem 7-9? Does her simulated spread? Shape?

7-13.   Erica thinks, *"If my sample was in the middle 90% of the true sampling distribution, it seems that the reverse would also be true: the <u>true proportion</u> would likely be somewhere inside the middle 90% of my simulated distribution, since the spreads are about the same. So even though I don't know the true proportion, I can be pretty sure that it's inside the middle 90% of this distribution!"*

   a.   Find the middle 90% of Erica's distribution and use it to complete the sentence "Based on her sample and simulation, Erica can be about 90% confident that the true proportion of people who will vote for her is between _____ and _____."

   b.   Did Erica's simulated 90% confidence interval contain the true parameter in this case?

MATH NOTES

Estimating Sampling Distributions

When nothing is known about the sampling distribution of a statistic, one option is to use the information *from the sample itself* to make a simulated estimate for it. This process starts by assuming the entire population looks *exactly* like the distribution of the sample you started with, then simulates drawing many samples from such a population. For the sampling distribution of sample proportions, this simply means using the proportion from your sample as the "true" proportion in your simulation tool.

True Sampling Distribution

Sampling Distribution of Erica Votes

Proportion for Erica, $n=25$

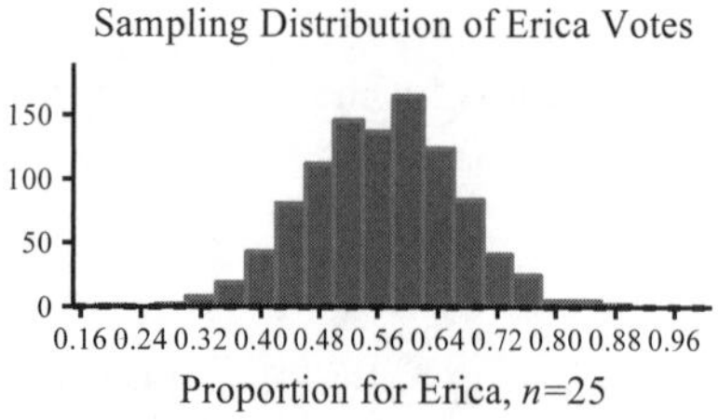

Created using true $p = 0.56$

Estimated Distribution

Estimated Sampling Distribution

Proportion for Erica, $n=25$

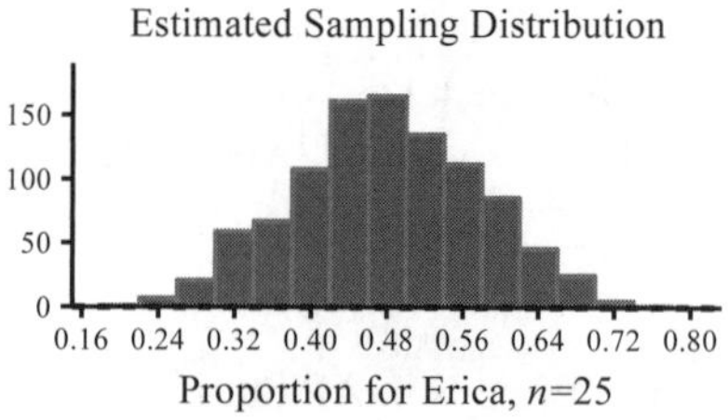

Created using sample $\hat{p} = 0.48$

This process works well to estimate the *shape* and *spread* of a sampling distribution of proportions. As you can see in the above diagrams, the shape and spread of the estimated distribution for a sample proportion are very similar to those in the simulation of the true sampling distribution.

7-14.   In problem 7-3, Caitlin from the Hallways School for Girls was trying to calculate the probability of her trivia team having at least 3 Statistics students. Imagine she knows that 43 out of the 100 other seniors are in Statistics. How could she use a simulation technology tool to estimate her chances of getting 3 or teammates who are studying Statistics? (Note: you do not actually have to do the simulation, just explain how you could.)

7-15.   A principal at a high school with 200 students in the senior class picks 100 of the seniors at random and finds that 80 of them play sports outside of school. She wants to create a 90% confidence interval for the proportion of all seniors at her school that play sports outside of school. The principal decides to *simulate an estimate* of the confidence interval for the proportion of all students in her high school that play sports outside the school. She uses the Proportions Sampling eTool to simulate 1000 possible samples *without replacement* using her information, and creates the following relative frequency histogram of her simulated samples.

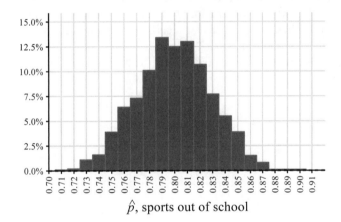

$\hat{p}$, sports out of school

Use the histogram to *estimate* the middle 95% interval for this estimated sampling distribution. Write your answer in margin of error form.

7-16.   You are playing a game of chance that you have a 43% chance of winning. If you play it five times in a row, what is the probability that you will win 3 or more times?

7-17.   Employee meetings at Patty Ann's Pancake Palace never seem to start on time. One employee calculated based on many observations that 65% of meetings start at least 5 minutes late.

   a.   What conditions need to be established before the binomial setting can be applied to this situation?

   b.   Find the probability that out of the next 6 meetings, 5 meetings will start at least 5 minutes late.

7-18.   Sure Shot Jane can hit the bull's eye with a bow and arrow 90% of the time. If she shoots five arrows, what is the probability that three or more arrows hit the bull's eye?

7-19.   The police chief of Madelinton is concerned about the number of false alarms from home security systems his officers respond to. The alarm manufacturers say that they are not to blame because during any given year their alarm systems correctly distinguish between criminal activity and other harmless events 99.5% of the time. Of the 319,200 residences in Madelinton only 200 were broken into last year, but the police chief says his officers responded to hundreds more false alarm calls. How many calls are the police likely to receive from home alarm systems in a year? If the Madelinton police department receives a call from a home alarm system, what is the probability it is the result of criminal activity?

7.1.3 Is there a sampling distribution shortcut?

Formulas for the Sampling Distributions of Sample Proportions

In the previous lessons you learned how to use simulation to explore the *sampling distributions* of sample proportions. This sampling distribution is so common and important, however, that it would be great to be able to skip the simulation. In this lesson you will explore one way to do that.

7-20. Think back to Erica's voting situation from problems 7-8 and 7-9. Recall that *unknown to her*, 56% of the population plan to vote for Erica. Let *V* be a random variable representing the *number* of students from a particular random sample of 25 students who will vote for Erica.

    a. Review: what are the properties of a binomial random variable? Which of the properties are satisfied by *V*? See the Math Notes box in Lesson 6.2.3 if necessary.

    b. Erica's class is very large compared to her sample size. Why is this necessary to ensure *V* follows the binomial distribution?

    c. Use the formula for the expected value of a binomial variable, $\mu_X = np$, to find the expected value of *V*.

    d. Use the formula for the standard deviation of a binomial variable, $\sigma_X = \sqrt{np(1-p)}$, to find the standard deviation of *V*.

    e. Are the conditions present to assume that *V* is approximately normally distributed? See the Math Notes box in Lesson 6.3.1 to remind yourself of those conditions if necessary.

7-21. Erica is not interested in the *number* of people that will vote for her in her sample. She wants to know something about the *proportion* of people who will vote for her.

    a. Erica's friend Ron wants to define a new random variable $P = \frac{V}{25}$. How might this be useful to Erica?

    b. Ron thinks that he can use the results of the previous problem to describe the distribution of *P*. Help Ron write a sentence that concisely describes the distribution (shape, center, spread) of *P* in context.

7-22.   To generalize: the sampling distribution for a sample proportion (given certain conditions as seen in problem 7-20) can be thought of as the distribution of a random variable $\hat{p} = \frac{X}{n}$, where X is a binomial random variable with parameters n and p and n is the constant sample size. Use the binomial formulas for binomial variables (seen in parts (c) and (d) of problem 7-18) to derive formulas for $\mu_{\hat{p}}$ and $\sigma_{\hat{p}}$, the mean and standard deviation of the sampling distribution for sample proportions. Simplify your formulas as far as you can and discuss with your teacher and class.

7-23.   Since the conditions for normal approximation were met in problem 7-20, you can use the normal approximation to calculate the probability that Erica's sample proportion $\hat{p}$ is higher than 50%. Show your work, sketching a shaded area under a normal curve as part of your response. Compare your result to your answer to part (e) of problem 7-9.

7-24.   Use the Empirical Rule to help Erica construct an interval, centered about $p = 0.56$, that would contain approximately 95% of the possible sample proportions from samples of 25 students.

7-25.   If Erica's sample of 25 students reported that 18 of the 25 students would vote for her, should this be considered an outlier? Explain.

7-26.   34% of Whigs believe that chocolate should be illegal. 53% of Tories believe that chocolate should be illegal. Use the formulas you derived (or see the following Math Notes box) and the normal approximation to answer the following questions.

   a.   If you take a sample of 300 Whigs, what is the probability that at least 40% of them will believe chocolate should be illegal?

   b.   From a sample of 200 Tories, what is the probability that between 95 and 105 of them will believe chocolate should be illegal?

   c.   If 100 Tories and 100 Whigs are sampled what is the probability that more than 40% of *both* samples are in favor of chocolate illegalization? (This will require two calculations and a probability rule.)

MATH NOTES

Sampling Distribution of Sample Proportions

Let there be a population with a true proportion p of some outcome of interest. If taking samples of size n, the sampling distribution of the sample proportion $\hat{p}$ will satisfy the following properties under the given conditions.

Desired Property	Condition Name: and how to meet it.	Explanation
$\mu_{\hat{p}} = p$	**Random:** the sample is randomly chosen from the population.	Ensures no bias and makes the binomial condition work.
$\sigma_{\hat{p}} = \sqrt{\frac{p(1-p)}{n}}$	**Independent trials:** Each sample is an independent event, drawn with replacement, OR drawn from a population at least 10 times the sample size.	The $\sigma_{\hat{p}}$ formula comes from the binomial setting, which requires every trial have the same p of success. If drawing without replacement, the population needs to be large enough to keep that *approximately* true.
Normal sampling distribution	**Large counts:** The *expected* number of successes, np, and the expected number of failures, $n(1-p)$, are both greater than 10.	This condition allows the binomial distribution to be approximated by the normal distribution (see Chapter 6). If p is not known, can use $\hat{p}$ to check this condition.

STOP your work if the sample is not random. Bias makes it useless!

CONTINUE BUT MENTION IT if the sample is less than 10 times the population without replacement. In these cases, your samples could actually be *less variable* than the formulas imply, but that is okay!

CONTINUE IF YOU DARE if the large counts condition is not met, but you will have to use a binomial distribution rather than the normal distribution for any calculations; this is tricky and outside the AP scope.

MATH NOTES

Example: Meeting the Conditions

A polling company surveys 897 randomly chosen citizens in Springdale, population 10,213. The company finds that 243 of the citizens have a college degree. Show that this scenario satisfies the conditions for a normal approximation of the sampling distribution for the proportion of students with college degrees in Springdale.

Sample Answer:
Only the bold pieces below would be expected in the actual answer. The italics are commentary and explanation.

Random, to avoid bias: the question says it is a random sample. *Write a few words to show the problem mentions it is random. If the sample is stratified, clustered or an SRS say so. The (avoid bias) shows you know the purpose of the condition.*

Independent trials, for an accurate σ: $10{,}213 > 10 \cdot 897$. *When drawing without replacement and the population is given, as in this problem, show the explicit comparison to show population $\geq 10 \cdot$ sample. If the population is not given but is obviously very large, like U.S. citizens, say so in words. If drawing with replacement or independent events, write that instead. The (accurate σ) shows the condition's purpose.*

Large counts, so the sampling distribution $\approx$ normal: $n\hat{p} = 243$ with a college degree, $n(1 - \hat{p}) = 654$ without, both > 10. *Note that since the true p is unknown here, the expected counts cannot be found. In such a situation use $n\hat{p}$ and $n(1 - \hat{p})$ instead, which give the sample counts! Show both are greater than 10 explicitly. The (so the sampling distribution $\approx$ normal) shows you know what correctly models the sampling distribution.*

7-27.   Read this lesson's Math Notes boxes then try to answer each of the following questions about the conditions for normal inference on the sampling distribution for proportions. Challenge yourself not to look back at the boxes!

a.   What condition ensures the formula $\sigma_{\hat{p}} = \sqrt{\frac{p(1-p)}{n}}$ is correct?

b.   Why do you check that the number of successes and failures in a sample are both greater than 10?

c.   When is it acceptable to continue and use the normal distribution to approximate the sampling distribution (with a note) even though the conditions are not perfectly met?

d.   Where does the independent trials condition come from?

7-28.   The Algiers High School booster club is planning a fund-raiser to collect money for a new synthetic turf field and stadium lights. The football field is $100 \times 53\frac{1}{3}$ yards. They cover it completely with playing cards (2.5×3.5 inches) face down. All the cards are aligned in the same direction as the football field (long side of the card along the long side of the field). There will be exactly one joker card placed at random among the face-down cards on the field.

Contestants pay five dollars for every card they wish to turn over. Whoever finds the joker wins one million dollars.

a.   What is the probability that the first contestant finds the joker?

b.   The playing cards used to cover the field cost $0.99 per pack (52 cards per pack). What is the largest amount of money the boosters could lose in this fundraiser?

c.   Assuming there is a winner, what is the maximum amount of money the boosters could make?

d.   Assuming there is a winner, what is a reasonable expected profit for the booster club? That is, if this fundraiser were done many, many times, what would be the average profit?

e.   A state Mega Millions lottery advertises odds of 176 million to one. If the state lottery were played like the booster club fundraiser, how many football fields covered with non-joker playing cards would be needed?

7-29.   Tisklets candies have five colors that are equally distributed, and bags represent a random
          sample of the entire population of Tisklets. A 14 oz bag of Tisklets generally has 220 candies
          in it.

          a.   Zsozso loves orange Tisklets and is interested in exploring how many orange Tisklets she
               can expect to get in a bag. Demonstrate that the sampling distribution of $\hat{p}$, the
               proportion of orange Tisklets in a bag, satisfies all three conditions for a normal
               approximation (see Math Notes box).

          b.   Find the mean and standard deviation of the sampling distribution of $\hat{p}$.

          c.   Sketch and label the sampling distribution curve using your values from part (b).
               Calculate the probability that Zsozso will get at least 50 Tisklets in her next bag, shading
               the appropriate portion of the distribution curve.

7-30.   Hydrangeas are sometimes mistaken for rhododendrons or viburnums. While in North
          Carolina studying native hydrangea species, Darius collected soil samples from the root
          systems of hydrangeas. Analysis discovered that the hydrangea soil pHs are normally
          distributed.

          Sketch the normal probability density functions. If the 13th percentile is 10.199 pH, and the
          79th percentile is 11.282 pH, find the mean and standard deviation.

7.2.1 What's your team's trashketball percentage?

Confidence Interval for a Population Proportion

In previous lessons, you have explored the variability of sample proportions that can arise from a single population proportion. Today you will learn how to reverse that process and use a single sample proportion to create a reasonable estimate for a population proportion.

7-31. One common statistic in basketball is the "free throw percentage"—the percentage of free shots taken by a player or team that go into the basket. Today your team is going to take 100 shots of trashketball and use that to *estimate* what your team's long-term free throw percentage would be. You will assume for this problem that your team's long-term percentage would not change if you played forever, that each shot is independent from all other shots, and that your team's first hundred shots represent a random sample of all shots.

a. What is the sample in this case, the individuals, the sample size, and the population of interest?

b. What statistic will you calculate? What parameter will you be estimating?

c. Will the sampling distribution of the sample proportion in this case satisfy the three conditions for the normal approximation? Explain.

7-32. Gather data. Each team member should take about the same number of shots, for a total of 100 shots. What do $\hat{p}$ and p represent in the context of this problem? Which can you calculate right now? Which can only be estimated? Calculate and estimate.

7-33.　To figure out reasonable values for your long term percentage p, you need to decide how far your $\hat{p}$ might vary from the true p. This is what the spread of the sampling distribution of $\hat{p}$ tells us! Recall the formula for the standard deviation of the sampling distribution of $\hat{p}$ was $\sigma_{\hat{p}} = \sqrt{\frac{p(1-p)}{n}}$.

a.　Since the value of p is unknown at this point, make an *estimate* of the standard deviation using $\hat{p}$ instead of the true p. (This is related to what you did with simulations in Lesson 7.1.2.)

b.　To confirm this is a *reasonable* (if not perfect) estimate, try calculating the standard deviation again under the assumption that your original $\hat{p}$ could have been wrong by as many as 10 percentage points in one direction or another. What effect does changing to the new $\hat{p}$ estimates have on the standard deviation?

c.　The **standard error of a sample proportion** is calculated as $SE_{\hat{p}} = \sqrt{\frac{\hat{p}(1-\hat{p})}{n}}$. Comment on the relationship between this calculation and the standard deviation of the sampling distribution of $\hat{p}$.

7-34.　Based on the previous problem, you should have a good sense for how far your sample free throw percentage will typically differ from the true population proportion. Use your standard error calculation to fill in the blanks on the following sentences.

a.　If you took many, many samples of size 100, about 68% of the time your *sample* free throw percentage would be within _____ percentage points of the true, long-term percentage.

b.　If you took many, many samples of size 100, about 95% of the time your *sample* free throw percentage would be within _____ percentage points of your team's true, long-term percentage.

c.　You can be 95% confident that your sample percentage (_____%) is within _____ percentage points of your team's true long-term percentage. Therefore, you can be 95% confident that your team's long-term percentage is within _____ percentage points of your sample proportion! In other words, you can be 95% confident that your team's long term trashketball percentage is between _____ % and _____%." This is called a **95% confidence interval for the population proportion**.

7-35.   At the moment of this writing (September 10, 2016), the latest ABC News/Washington Post election poll shows Republican U.S. Presidential candidate Donald Trump with 41% of the vote. The sample size of the poll was 642.

    a.   Use the process from earlier problems to estimate a 95% confidence interval for the *true* proportion of people like those in the poll that would have voted for Donald Trump on September 10, 2016. (Hint: start by finding the standard error, then add two standard errors above and below the sample proportion.)

    b.   What needs to be assumed to think this is a reasonable estimate for *all United States voters*?

    c.   Rewrite the confidence interval in the form *estimate ± margin of error*.

    d.   Does the margin of error from part (c) account for bias in the poll?

7-36.   The AP Statistics class at the Hallways School for Girls takes a random sample of 50 students (from the school population of 698) and asks them if they get enough sleep. 18 of the respondents say "yes."

    a.   Check that all conditions for using the normal approximation to the sampling distribution are met in this scenario.

    b.   Construct a 95% confidence interval for the proportion of students at the Hallways School for Girls that will say they get enough sleep.

    c.   Before doing this poll, Anna hypothesized that only 25% of all Hallways girls will say they get enough sleep. Based on your data and answer from part (a) do you think Anna's hypothesis should be rejected? Should it be accepted?

    d.   If 42% of all girls at Hallways School for Girls would actually say they get enough sleep, what is the probability of getting a sample with as few (or fewer) "yes" answers as the AP class got?

7-37.   In problem 7-15, you simulated an estimated proportion sampling distribution for a situation involving a principal choosing a sample from her student body without replacement. The principal took a sample of 100 seniors from a class of 200 and found that 80 of them play sports outside of school.

   a.   Which of the three conditions for the normal approximation are NOT met by this situation?

   b.   The standard deviation of the estimated sampling distribution the principal created was 0.0284 seniors. Show that the standard error formula does *not* provide an accurate estimate for that value.

   c.   If you used the value from part (b) and the steps from this lesson to create a 95% confidence interval, how would it compare to your estimated interval from part (a) of problem 7-13?

7-38.   Erika is tracking the depth of the water in her local creek. Her first twelve measurements are below, in inches:

   16 15 13 12 17 14 11 9 11 9 10 9

   a.   Find the median, first quartile (Q1), and third quartile (Q3).

   b.   Create a boxplot for the data.

   c.   What is the interquartile range (IQR) for Erika's data?

7-39.   While working at his mother's transportation engineering company studying peak hour traffic at congested intersections, Nicholas researched a cluster sample of 30 intersections which revealed the following information regarding the relationship between truck traffic and total number of vehicles.

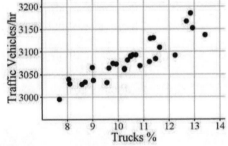

The mean truck traffic is 10.46 %/hour with a standard deviation of 1.50 %/hour. The mean total number of vehicle is 3082.00 vehicles/hour with a standard deviation of 43.72 vehicles/hour. The correlation coefficient is 0.9046.

   a.   Describe the association between the truck traffic and total number of vehicles of at congested intersections as seen in the sample.

   b.   Determine r^2 squared and its meaning in the context of this sample.

7.2.2 How can I change the confidence level?

Confidence Levels for Confidence Intervals

Today you will make and interpret confidence intervals for a population proportion.

7-40.　A random sample of 50 hydrangea bushes around Nashville, TN finds that 32 of them have blue flowers, 14 pink, 3 white, and 1 green.

　　a.　Show that conditions are satisfied to construct a confidence interval using the normal approximation for the proportion of blue hydrangea bushes in Nashville, TN.

　　b.　Could this data be used to construct a normal-based confidence interval for the proportion of pink hyndragea bushes? White bushes? Green bushes?

　　c.　Construct confidence 95% confidence intervals for every color that satisfies the conditions necessary to do so.

7-41.　Two students are arguing about the word "confident" versus the word "chance" when interpreting the confidence interval for blue hydrangeas above. One student says, *"There is a 95% chance that the proportion of blue hydrangeas in Nashville lies in this interval."* Another student says, *"We can only say that we are 95% confident that the population proportion lies in this interval."* Which student do you agree with? Why?

7-42.　To better understand what is meant by the phrase "95% confidence," use the Confidence Intervals for Proportions eTool to further explore how confidence intervals work. This eTool works by starting with a population parameter *p* and simulating samples from that population.

　　a.　Set the "Sample Size" to 50 and "Population Proportion" to 0.60. This is one possible *p* that could have resulted in the blue hydrangea sample from problem 7-40. Leave the other values at the defaults. Click the button "Draw Samples" and describe what happens. (You may need to make the "width of the x-axis" a bit wider to see everything.)

　　b.　How many red lines do you see? There are 100 lines total, so how many black lines are there?

　　c.　Each of the lines that you see represents a confidence interval constructed using a different simulated sample from the initial population. Click a line with your mouse or tap with your finger to see the confidence interval represented by the line. What do the red lines represent?

　　d.　Look at the "Proportion Captured" row in the "Latest Sample Set" column of the data table. What does that proportion represent?

Problem continues on next page →

7-42.   *Problem continued from previous page.*

   e.   Change the confidence level to a lower number, like 85. What changes about the lines? About the proportion captured?

   f.   Go back to a confidence level of 95 and push the "Draw Samples" at least 50 times, to gather several thousand samples. Look at the total "Proportion captured" row in the first column, "Normal with SE." What do you notice? Feel free to try other confidence levels to confirm your understanding.

   g.   Finish the following sentence to interpret the **confidence level**: "If we gather many, many samples and calculate a 95% confidence interval each time, then…"

   h.   What do you think is different if you use the option "Normal Model with Standard Deviation" calculation method?

7-43.   Kira points out to her partner Isabella that the interval simulator allows her to calculate intervals using other confidence levels, but she is not sure how to do that by hand. Isabelle says, *"Well, we can figure out how many standard deviations you'd have to use to enclose the middle 90% of the standard normal curve."* She sketches the picture at right.

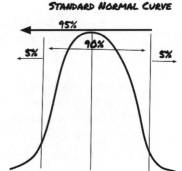

The number Isabelle is talking about is called a *critical value* for a confidence interval, often abbreviated z*.

   a.   Use Isabelle's picture and a calculator or normal probability table to find the critical value for a 90% confidence interval.

   b.   Use your value from part (a) to find a 90% confidence interval for the proportion of blue hydrangea bushes in Nashville.

7-44.   In problem 7-40 why was doubling the standard error a quick way to approximate the margin of error for a 95% confidence interval? With your team or class write down a procedure for finding the margin of error at any given confidence level.

7-45.   Find *and interpret* a 90% confidence interval for your team's trashketball shot percentage.

MATH NOTES

Interpreting Confidence Intervals

A **C% confidence interval** for a parameter is an interval of *reasonable* values for the parameter estimated from an estimating statistic or simulation. A confidence interval can be interpreted with the sentence below.

"I am [C]% confident that the interval from [minimum value] to [maximum value] contains the true value of [parameter in context]. This means if I were to repeat the sampling process many times, this method would capture the true [parameter in context] about [C]% of the time."

You should never say "probability" or "chance" when interpreting a confidence interval: once the interval is created, then it either *already* contains the true proportion (probability of containing the parameter = 1) or it does *not* (probability = 0). The word "confident" makes sense because you are C% confident in the *method itself*.

The value C in the confidence interval is called the **confidence level** and can be interpreted with the phrase

"If we were to repeat this method many times, with different samples, we would successfully capture the true [parameter in context] around [C]% of the time."

Here the word probability could be used, carefully: if *another interval is calculated in the future*, that interval will have a C% chance of capturing the true value of the parameter.

If written in the form "$a \pm M$", a is called the **point estimate of the parameter** while M is called the **margin of error.**

MATH NOTES

Confidence Intervals for Proportions
Procedures

To calculate a *C%* confidence interval for a population proportion p from a sample proportion $\hat{p}$, follow the four-step process: identify, check conditions, calculate, and conclude!

1. **Identify** the parameter you are trying to estimate, your confidence level, and any *claims* you will assess with your interval (see the Math Notes box in Lesson 7.2.4).

2. **Check** all three **conditions** for the normal approximation. You will have to use the *sample counts* $n\hat{p}$ and $n(1-\hat{p})$ for the large counts condition: use the correct notation!

3. **Calculate** the three necessary components to use the general form for a confidence interval, shown below:

    statistic ± (critical value)(standard error of statistic)

    a. **Statistic:** $\hat{p}$

    b. **Standard Error:** $SE_{\hat{p}} = \sqrt{\frac{\hat{p}(1-\hat{p})}{n}}$

    c. **Critical Value:** Use a calculator or table of normal probabilities to find the **critical value for the confidence level**, known as z*. This is the number of standard deviation needed to capture the middle *C%* of the standard normal curve.

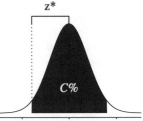

Standard normal curve

    To find z* for a given confidence level you will need to sketch the curve as shown at right and use a normal probability table or inverse normal function on a calculator to find the z-score that results in the appropriate tail. For example, to find the correct z* for a 90% confidence interval, you would recognize that each tail contains 5% of the data and find the z-score that results in a inverse normal function at either 0.05 OR 0.95 giving z* = 1.645.

4. **Conclude** by interpreting the confidence interval in context as described in the previous Math Notes box AND assessing claims (as seen in later section) if needed.

7-46.   The most commonly used confidence levels are 80%, 90%, 95%, 98%, and 99%. Find the critical value z* you would use for each one of these confidence levels, to the third decimal place.

7-47.   Assume an SRS of 305 U.S. citizens revealed 85 could correctly identify "Hoosier" as a nickname for a person from Indiana. Use the four step process from the preceding Math Notes box to construct and interpret a 90% confidence interval for the population of U.S. citizens who know what a "Hoosier" is.

7-48.   An SRS of 100 randomly chosen strawberries finds 11 ripe ones, from a patch of about 300 total strawberries.

a.   Which condition for calculating a confidence interval is not met?

b.   If you were to construct a confidence interval despite breaking this condition, would the interval be too wide, too narrow, or unpredictable?

c.   Go ahead and complete the process of calculating and interpreting a 94% confidence interval for the true proportion of strawberries in the entire patch that are ripe anyway.

7-49.   The English teachers at a certain high school want to know how many students read for pleasure during summer vacation.

a.   Should an observational study or an experiment be carried out to answer the question? Explain.

b.   Describe how you would carry out the study. Be sure to describe how you would incorporate randomization into your design.

7-50.   Different types of toads tend to lay different numbers of eggs. The following data was collected from two different species. Compare the number of eggs laid by American toads to the number laid by Fowler toads. Is it appropriate to summarize the distributions by using mean and standard deviation? Use a bin width of 250 eggs.

American toads: 7800, 8000, 8300, 8400, 8600, 8700, 8900, 8900, 8900, 9000, 9100, 9200, 9300, 9300, 9400, 9500, 9700, 9900, 10000, 10300 *checksum: 181,200.*

Fowler Toads: 8400, 8600, 8700, 8800, 8800, 8900, 9000, 9000, 9100, 9100, 9100, 9200, 9200, 9200, 9200, 9300, 9300, 9400, 9500, 9800 *checksum: 181,600.*

7.2.3 Can the margin of error be smaller?

Changing the Margin of Error in Confidence Intervals

In the prior lesson you learned to make confidence intervals for a population proportion and interpret the meaning of the interval. In this one, you will learn how you can manipulate the confidence intervals to provide more precise results.

7-51.   The general form for a confidence interval for ANY population parameter from a symmetric distribution is **statistic ± (critical value)(standard error of the statistic)**.

     a.   What is the statistic used to estimate population proportions?

     b.   How do you find the critical value for a particular confidence level?

     c.   What is the formula for the standard error of the statistic for proportion intervals?

7-52.   Olivia gathers 250 clovers and finds that 14 of them have four leaves. Assume her clovers represent a random sample of all clovers.

     a.   Confirm that the conditions for the normal approximation for confidence interval building are met.

     b.   Find and interpret an 80% confidence interval for the true proportion of cloves that have four leaves. Write your answer in margin of error form (estimate ± m.o.e.).

     c.   Find a 90% confidence interval for the true proportion of clovers that have four leaves. (No need to interpret.)

     d.   Find a 95% confidence interval for the true proportion of clovers that have four leaves. (Use the more precise z^*, not the approximation of 2, no need to interpret.)

     e.   Find a 99% confidence interval for the true proportion of clovers that have four leaves. (No need to interpret.)

     f.   What changes about the confidence intervals with increased confidence levels?

7-53.   Olivia decides to double down, and collects 750 more clovers, for a total of 1000. She finds that 56 of 1000 have four leaves.

a.   Find and interpret a 90% confidence interval for the true proportion of clovers with four leaves. Compare your margin of error to part (b) of problem 7-52. What is the relationship?

b.   Generalize: to cut a margin of error in half without changing confidence, what needs to be done with sample size? How does this connect to the equation for the standard error of the sample proportion?

7-54.   Discuss the questions below with your team. Be prepared to share with the class.

Discussion Points

What options are available for decreasing the margin of error in a proportion interval?

What are the advantages and disadvantages of each method?

What is the specific mathematical relationship between increasing sample size and decreasing the margin of error?

7-55.   Olivia is obsessed. She wants to know how many clovers she will need to collect in order to get her margin of error all the way down to 0.01 with a confidence level of 99%. With your team, figure it out!

7-56.   Most national polls use 95% confidence levels and want to ensure a margin of error of no more than 4 percentage points (0.04) each way. But they do not know in advance what the proportion of people responding to any question will be.

a.   Play with the numbers: what value of $\hat{p}$ yields the highest possible standard error for a given sample size? (Challenge: prove your answer using algebra or calculus!)

b.   Since the $\hat{p}$ you found in part (a) always yields the highest possible margin of error, national polls assume the answers to questions will be that value when calculating an ideal sample size, for safety. For a poll at the 95% confidence level to have a margin of error of no more than 4%, what sample size is needed?

c.   Some polls brag about how their large sample sizes increasing their accuracy. One prominent national poll uses sample sizes of around 1200 people. What is their margin of error? (You may be able to do this without calculating it from scratch if you think it through.)

d.   If a polling company decided to keep the same confidence but decrease their margin of error to 1%, what major inconvenience might they encounter?

7-57.   About how many trashketball shots would your team need to take in order to get your margin of error all the way down to 0.01 with a confidence level of 90%. With your team, figure it out!

7-58.   Assume an SRS of 588 U.S. citizens revealed 172 could correctly identify "Sooner" as a nickname for a person from Oklahoma. Use your five step process from problem 7-47 to construct and interpret a 98% confidence interval for the population of U.S. citizens who know what a "Sooner" is.

7-59.   The Mathamericaland Carnival Company wants to create a new game. It will consist of a tank filled with thousands of ping-pong balls of different colors. People will pay for the opportunity to crawl around in the tank blindfolded for 60 seconds, while they collect ping-pong balls. 93% of the ping-pong balls will be white, 4% will be red, 2% will be blue, and 1% will be green. The players will win $100 for each red, $200 for each blue, and $500 for each green ping-pong ball they carry out of the tank. At the end of the game, players pay $15 for each white ping-pong ball they bring out of the tank, and then get paid for each red, blue, and green ball they have.

a.   Makayla plans on collecting one ping-pong ball. What is her expected winnings?

b.   Anna was thinking about collecting 6 ping-pong balls. What is the probability she will win some money?

7-60.   Commercial cherry trees produce fruit according to a normal distribution with an average of 90 kg of cherries per tree and a standard deviation of 11 kg per tree.

Answer the following: (Include $P(X)$ notation and a sketch of the normal curve for each)

a.   What is the probability that a tree produces at least 95 kg of cherries?

b.   What is the probability that a tree yields between 85 and 105 kg of cherries?

c.   What percentile would a harvest of 80 kg be for a single tree?

7-61.   Summer is interested in exploring what percentage of her peers at the Hallways School for Girls are vegetarian. She polls 25 of her 100 fellow seniors and finds that 4 of the 25 responses to her poll are vegetarian. She plans to calculate a confidence interval for the true proportion of seniors who are vegetarian.

   a.   Which of the conditions for the normal approximation to the proportion sampling distribution are not met by Summer's situation?

   b.   Summer decides to use a simulation to help her come up with her confidence interval. She simulates 5000 different samples of 25 students using her $\hat{p}$ as the true p and creates the histogram below. Use the histogram to make a reasonable estimate of a 90% confidence interval for the true proportion of vegetarian seniors at the Hallways School for Girls.

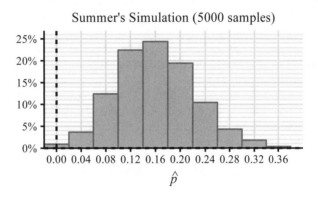

7.2.4 Is the claim believable?

....

Evaluating Claims with Confidence Intervals

In the last lesson, you learned how to *estimate* the value of a population proportion by using a confidence interval built from a sample proportion; one type of statistical inference. In this lesson, you will learn how to extend that to testing specific hypotheses about a population proportion.

7-62.   Grace is reading a book that claims 40% of American families own dogs. She is not sure if she believes that claim, and decides to look up some data. She finds that in a recent poll conducted by Giddyup, 348 out of 994 surveyed families owned at least one dog.

      a.   Before Grace can trust this poll to help her think about the book's claim, what conditions must she assume or confirm are true?

      b.   Grace decides to create a confidence interval for the proportion of families who own dogs. Help her by creating *and interpreting* a 95% confidence interval for the proportion of families with dogs, given the poll's data.

      c.   Based on the confidence interval, does it seem reasonable that the true proportion of dog owning families could be 40%? Why or why not?

      d.   Grace says, *"There's only a small probability that the book is right!"* What common mistake did Grace make with this interpretation of probability? Fix her mistake.

7-63.   A **claim** is a general statement made about any statistical parameter that you might subject to statistical testing. The book's claim in the previous problem could be written using symbols like "claim: $p = 0.4$." For each newspaper headline below, write the claim in symbolic form.

      a.   37% of Americans believe that the number 13 is unlucky.

      b.   Students at OSU study a mean of 1.2 hours a night.

      c.   Less than half of breakfast cereals contain enough fiber to help in heart health.

      d.   At least 15% of traffic lights in Sleepyville are broken.

      e.   The mean time spent waiting for a traffic light in Quickville is no more than 45 seconds.

      f.   The standard deviation of time spent waiting for at traffic light in Quickville is 18 seconds.

7-64.   Consider the claim in part (a) of problem 7-63 above: "37% of Americans believe that the number 13 is unlucky."

a.   Imagine a high-quality national poll shows 325 out of 925 people agreeing with the statement "13 is an unlucky number." Assume all conditions for inference are met and calculate *and interpret* a 95% confidence interval for the true proportion of Americans who think 13 is unlucky.

b.   Only one of the statements below is reasonable, based on the evidence from part (a). With your team, decide which statement is the correct one, and for each incorrect one explain why it is an incorrect conclusion in this case.

   i.   *We can be 95% confident that the claim is correct; 37% of Americans believe 13 is unlucky.* (accept the claim)

   ii.   *We can be 95% confident that the claim is incorrect; 37% is not the true proportion of Americans who believe 13 is unlucky.* (reject the claim)

   iii. *We do not have evidence at the 95% confidence level to reject the claim that 37% of Americans believe 13 is unlucky; it could be the true amount.* (fail to reject the claim)

c.   If the poll from part (a) had instead shown $\frac{305}{925}$ supporting the statement, which conclusion from the above list would you be able to draw?

d.   If the poll from part (a) had instead shown $\frac{395}{925}$ supporting the statement, what conclusion would you be able to draw?

7-65.   Consider the previous claim that "at least 15% of traffic lights in Sleepyville are broken."

a.   What is different about this claim compared to the claim from problem 7-64?

b.   Imagine a random sampling of 200 traffic lights in Sleepyville finds 18 of them are broken. At a 95% confidence level: should you reject the claim, accept the claim, or fail to reject the claim?

c.   Imagine a random sampling of 200 traffic lights finds 34 of them are broken. At a 95% confidence level: should you reject the claim, accept the claim, or fail to reject the claim?

d.   Imagine a random sampling of 200 traffic lights finds 45 of them are broken. At the 95% confidence level: should you reject the claim, accept the claim, or fail to reject the claim?

e.   You will call a claim like this an **inequality claim** and a claim like the one in problem 7-60 an **equality claim**. Based on these problems, what are the differences in the conclusions you can draw for these claim types?

7-66.   Statistics teacher Mr. C is talking trashketball trash-talk and claims as a team, Harper, Jamison, and Cory cannot do better than a long-term 50% completion rate. If they made 59 out of 100 shots, what do you think? Back it up with a statistical analysis.

MATH NOTES

Evaluating Claims with Confidence Intervals

A **parameter claim** is a numeric statement made about a population parameter, such as population proportion, mean, median, or standard deviation, that can be statistically evaluated. Example claims about proportions might include "24% of AP Statistics students also take calculus" ($p = 0.24$) or "less than 7% of people know what a confidence interval is." ($p < 0.07$). These can be statements of equality or inequality.

To evaluate the believability of a parameter claim, one option is to construct a confidence interval for the parameter at a high confidence level, and compare the confidence interval to the claim. One of the following conclusions can be drawn:

Reject the claim if no piece of the claim is inside the confidence interval, since nothing about the claim is "reasonable." Both equality and inequality claims can be rejected.

Fail to reject the claim (a.k.a. no conclusion) if some portion of the confidence interval matches the claim, but some other portion does not. Both equality and inequality claims can result in this. It is possible to say the claim is "reasonable" at this point, but not to accept it as definitely, or even most likely, true.

Accept the claim only if the entire confidence interval falls within the claim. This can never happen for equality claims, since some values in the confidence interval will always be different from the claim! NEVER accept an equality claim as true!

7-67.   In 2016, a city homeless organization wanted to estimate with 95% confidence the proportion of adults who have struggled to afford food in the last 12 months in a major U.S. city.

    a.   Interpret the 95% confidence level in this context.

The organization selected a random sample of adults residing in the city and used the sample to estimate the percent of adults aged 18 and older that have struggled to afford food in the last 12 months. The resulting 95% confidence interval was 0.182 ± 0.039.

    b.   A national polling organization claims that their data shows that 15% of all U.S. adults have struggled to afford food in the last 12 months and that this rate is at its lowest level since 2008. Does the city homeless organization's interval estimate provide evidence that the proportion of adults who have struggled to afford food in its city is different from the claimed national proportion? Explain.

    c.   How many adults were selected in the organizations city sample? Show how you obtained your answer.

7-68.   A grocery store surveys a group of randomly selected customers about their shopping habits and finds that 45% of their sample shop primarily on weekends. The company statistician constructs a confidence interval for the portion of shoppers who shop primarily on weekends and gets 0.45 ± 0.08

    a.   Does this interval provide convincing statistical evidence that less than 50% of all shoppers shop primarily on the weekends?

    b.   Does the interval provide convincing statistical evidence that more than 50% of all shoppers shop primarily on the weekends?

    c.   The grocery store manager does another survey, this time surveying four times as many customers. Again, 45% of those surveyed shop primarily on weekends. What is the new confidence interval for the proportion of all shoppers who shop primarily on weekends?

    d.   Does your new confidence interval provide convincing statistical evidence for either of the questions in part (a) or (b)?

7-69.   Explain how you would design both an observational study and an experiment to answer the following question: "Does eating carrots lead to better vision health?"

7-70.   You own your own grapevine, and you are gathering information about your grapes. You would like to be able to estimate the mass of a grape by quickly measuring its minor diameter (if the grape is elliptical, measure the distance across the smaller dimension). You gather the following measurements for 9 grapes:

Minor Diameter (cm)	1.61	1.49	1.64	1.38	1.43	1.65	1.41	1.51	1.74
Mass (g)	9.62	8.83	9.36	8.49	9.00	10.41	8.44	9.43	10.75

a.   Standardize each row in the table.

b.   For each grape in the table, write down the product of the standardized diameter and mass.

c.   What is a typical product? (Average the products in part (b), with a "funny average," dividing by $n-1$.)

d.   What is the term for the answer in part (c)? (Hint: See the Math Notes box from Lesson 2.2.1.) What does it tell you about the relationship between the minor diameter and the mass for your sample of grapes? (Interpret this value in context.)

e.   In this setting, which variable (diameter or mass) is the explanatory variable? Which is the response variable?

f.   For your final result in part (c), would it have mattered if you reversed the explanatory and response variables? (Does it matter which one is x and which one is y?) Briefly explain, making an argument about how the calculation was actually constructed.

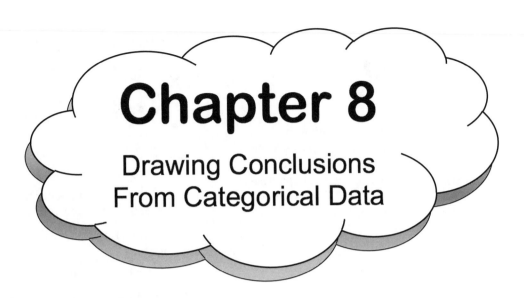

Chapter 8

Drawing Conclusions From Categorical Data

CHAPTER 8

Drawing Conclusions From Categorical Data

In Chapter 7 you studied sampling distributions of sample proportions. This chapter extends those concepts to hypothesis testing of proportions including *p*-values, Type I and Type II errors, and the power of a hypothesis test. In later chapters these same ideas will transferred to tests involving quantitative variables.

Chapter Goals

Simulate sampling distributions to determine *p*-values.

Understand how to formulate and state a null and alternative hypothesis.

Perform a full hypothesis test.

Investigate the concepts of Type I and Type II errors.

Create simulations to estimate the power of a test.

Derive the sampling distribution for the difference between two sample proportions.

Compare two population proportions using hypothesis testing.

Chapter Outline

Section 8.1   You will get an intuitive feel of the structure of a hypothesis test using simulation to calculate a *p*-value then work through a full example of a hypothesis test for a population proportion. You will understand the thought process for choosing an alternative hypothesis to match a situation.

Section 8.2   You will evaluate the meaning and probabilities of Type I and Type II errors, as well as the idea of power of a test. You will walk through a calculation of power under a specific suspected hypothesis, then use a simulation to explore how to change power by tweaking variables in the test.

Section 8.3   You will derive the sampling distribution for the difference between two sample proportions and apply it to an inference test comparing two population proportions. You will apply a hypothesis test for the difference of two proportions to decide if two variables are independent. Finally you will identify whether scenarios are one-sample or two-sample proportion inference and run tests based on the scenarios.

8.1.1 Can I test that theory?

. . . .

Introduction to Hypothesis Testing

For this section, a brief break will be taken from proportions, in order to introduce a new type of statistical structure—the hypothesis test. The entire lesson will use the following setup.

A company decides to take a group of employees and give them management training, with the goal of identifying some for promotion. They originally train 28 employees: 18 men and 10 women. At the end of the training period, every single one of the employees is declared worthy of promotion! Unfortunately, there are only 8 managements slots available. The CEO decides to randomly choose 8 employees from the 28. When she reports the result of her random drawing, 5 of the new managers are women and 3 of them are men.

8-1.   Some of the men who did not get promoted are upset—they think the CEO cheated the system in order to promote more women.

    a.   **Gut check:** do you think they have a fair case?

    b.   One of the men, Gerald, remembers his AP Statistics class from high school. *"The CEO is claiming that she randomly chose,"* he says. *"We don't believe that. I remember in stats we talked about ways to test whether a claim is believable or not."* He writes the following statements on a napkin.

        H_0: The CEO really did choose randomly.

    *"The H_0 line is something called a **null hypothesis**. I remember that term! I also remember that we always start a testing process by temporarily assuming the null hypothesis is true. But after that I'm a little fuzzy."*

    His friend Edwin says, *"I don't want to assume it's true! It's clearly impossible! There's no chance of getting this split if she chose randomly."* Explain why Edwin is incorrect in his hotheaded assertion.

    c.   *"I don't want to assume it's true either, Edwin,"* replied Gerald, *"but the fact is that she has to get the benefit of the doubt; it's up to us to gather evidence."* The specific claim weighed against the null hypothesis is called the **alternative hypothesis**. In words, write the men's alternative claim—what do they believe really happened?

8-2.   Edwin says, *"Okay, so maybe it's not impossible that she could be telling the truth, but I still don't believe it! It must be a tiny chance. Can't we calculate the probability of getting this split if she's telling the truth? Isn't it just that binomial distribution thing?"*

   a.   Explain to Edwin why the binomial distribution will not work here.

   b.   Stymied, Gerald starts to sulk in the corner and pulls out a deck of cards to play solitaire. Edwin sees the cards and says *"Gerald! You're a genius! We can simulate the probability of this split, under the assumption that the CEO really chose randomly!"*

   With your team, obtain a deck of cards and come up with a plan to *simulate* one round of the CEO's drawing, assuming she actually drew randomly. Make sure you can record the numbers of men and women drawn. Describe how many cards you will use, which cards will stand for which outcomes, and how you will run the test. Be ready to present your plan to the team.

8-3.   Once your plan has been approved, obtain a deck of cards (or more than one!). Conduct at least 10 trials with your team, (though your teacher may tell you to conduct more). For each trial, record the number of men and women in your sample, then answer the questions below.

   a.   What percentage of your trials had exactly 3 men?

   b.   What percentage of your trials had 3 or fewer men?

8-4.   With your class, build a dot plot showing the number of men in every trial conducted by every member of your class.

   a.   What percentage of the class trials had exactly 3 men?

   b.   What percentage of the class trials had 3 or fewer men?

8-5.   You have almost finished your hypothesis test! The final step requires estimating or calculating a special probability called a *p*-**value**. It is defined as the probability of observing a statistic as *extreme or more extreme* than the one actually obtained, assuming the null hypothesis is true.

   a.   Which of the values from problem 8-4 is your best estimate for the *p*-value in this situation?

   b.   Conclude: do you believe, based on your answers above, that you have enough information to show the CEO cheated in favor of women?

8-6.   In Lesson 7.2.4, you learned to evaluate statistical claims using confidence intervals. Hypothesis tests evaluate statistical claims as well; the null hypothesis of this hypothesis test, "H_0: The CEO really did choose randomly" is a statistical claim. Explain why this statistical claim cannot be evaluated by a confidence interval using the methods from Chapter 7.

MATH NOTES

Hypothesis Test Procedure

A **hypothesis test** is a statistical structure used to assess the believability of a claim, given specific evidence. It consists of four steps:

First, <u>identify</u> the null hypothesis and the alternative hypothesis. It is best to start with the alternative hypothesis, which is the claim you are trying to *show is true*. You should already have or plan to gather some specific evidence that backs up the alternative hypothesis. The *null hypothesis* is a statement that represents the "status quo" position; the test will assume it is true then decide whether your evidence for the alternative is compelling enough to make the assumption unbelievable. The null hypothesis is often a statement of equality, or "no difference," or "sameness."

Second, <u>check</u> that the data used to support your alternative is reasonable to use for calculating statistics with your chosen technique. This may require certain conditions (such as random sampling) to be satisfied.

Third, assume (temporarily) the null hypothesis is true, and <u>calculate</u> or simulate the probability of getting data *as or more extreme by random chance* than the supporting data you actually have. This conditional probability, P(data as or more extreme | null hypothesis is true), is called the *p*-value. A lower *p*-value means your data is more unlikely under the null, meaning you have a less believable null hypothesis!

Finally, <u>conclude</u> something in context based on the *p*-value. If the *p*-value is low enough (below a threshold you will set in advance called the **significance level**) then it is reasonable to **reject the null hypothesis and accept the alternative**. Otherwise, you will **fail to reject the null hypothesis and fail to accept the alternative**. *You will never officially accept the null hypothesis*, as your evidence is only considered as an attempt to "validate" the alternative, not the null!

8-7.   A certain soccer player has made 80% of her penalty shots over her professional career. She is injured, but recovers. On her return, she only makes 5 of her first 10 penalty shots.

   a.   Assuming she is actually just as good at penalty shots as she was before her injury and each shot is independent of each other shot, calculate the probability of her making exactly 5 out of 10 penalty shots.

Problem continues on next page →

8-7.   *Problem continued from previous page.*

    b.   Calculate the probability of her making 5 or fewer penalty shots out of 10, assuming she is still an 80% shooter.

    c.   The previously calculated value could be thought of as the *p*-value for a hypothesis test. The null hypothesis for this test is H_0: $p = 0.8$. Define p in context and write the alternative hypothesis for this test.

    d.   What conclusion would you draw about the soccer player's penalty shot ratio?

8-8.   Evelyn loves to eat tacos, but she is frustrated whenever the box of hard taco shells has cracked shells. She notes that about 1 in 8 boxes she purchases has cracked shells. Assume that the proportion of boxes with cracked shells is in fact $\frac{1}{8}$ and that boxes have cracked shells independent of other boxes.

    a.   Of the next 10 boxes Evelyn buys, what is the probability that more than 2 of the boxes will contain shells that are cracked?

    b.   How many boxes should Evelyn expect to purchase until purchasing a box with cracked shells?

    c.   What is the probability that the first box with cracked shells occurs on the 12th box she purchases?

8-9.   A National Association of Professional Organizers survey of random U.S. residents found that 54% of those surveyed are overwhelmed by their clutter, and 78% find it too complicated to deal with.

    a.   Assuming 150 people were surveyed with an SRS, establish and interpret a 0.95 confidence interval estimate of the proportion of U.S. residents that are overwhelmed with their clutter.

    b.   Assuming that 300 people were surveyed, what would be the margin of error in estimating the true proportion of U.S. residents who find clutter too complicated to deal with at 99% confidence?

    c.   Assuming that 600 people were surveyed, with what degree of confidence can they assert that the proportion of persons who are overwhelmed by their clutter is between 51% and 57%?

    d.   How many people should they sample to estimate the proportion of U.S. residents who find clutter too complicated to deal with if they want a maximum 3% margin of error using a 90% confidence interval?

8.1.2 How can I test proportions?

· ·

Hypothesis Tests for Proportions

In Lesson 8.1.1, you learned about a procedure called hypothesis testing. Review the Math Notes from that lesson to recall vocabulary concerned with this process. In this lesson, you will learn how to apply the hypothesis testing procedure to the specific case of population proportions.

8-10. Aliah and Tobiah decide to play another round of trashketball. Aliah claims that she is "at least" a long-run 80% shooter, but Tobiah thinks she is worse than that. When it is Aliah's turn, she makes 90 out of 120 shots. Tobiah laughs and says, *"See! I told you!"* but Aliah responds, *"Nonsense, this doesn't disprove my hypothesis."*

    a.   Summarize the thinking behind each of their arguments.

    b.   In symbols, what is Aliah's claim? What is Tobiah's?

8-11. Their friend Jermaine comes over and says *"Guys! This is a perfect opportunity for a hypothesis test. Tobiah doesn't believe Aliah's claim, so let's test it!"* He stands at the whiteboard and writes:

$$H_0: p \geq 0.8 \qquad H_A: p < 0.8$$

    a.   Aliah looks at his statements and says, *"Those are the right claims, but I don't think we can use that null hypothesis. In the next step, we have to assume the null hypothesis is true and plug it into some formulas. That won't really work here."* Finish Aliah's thought— what is wrong with this null hypothesis that makes it impossible to assume it is exactly true as written?

Problem continues on next page →

8-11.   *Problem continued from previous page.*

b.   To satisfy Aliah's qualms, Jermaine modifies his statements to look like this:

Aliah's claim: $p \geq 0.8$ $H_0: p = 0.8$ $H_A: p < 0.8$ (T's claim)

"That feels a little weird," he says, *"But I guess it make sense if you think of the alternative hypothesis as the thing you are trying to show is true and the null hypothesis as just the thing we need to assume for the test to make sense."*

At this point Ms. Hoppenheimer walks by and says, *"I like the idea that you are looking for evidence to support or refute the alternative hypothesis."* She adds a line underneath the hypotheses:

Sample evidence for H_A: _____

Finish her statement. What evidence do they have that the alternative hypothesis might be true? Use symbols.

c.   Ms. Hoppenheimer prompts, *"There are two possible reasons for this evidence that are related to your hypotheses. Can you tell me what they are?"*

d.   *"Okay,"* says Tobiah, *"so to show that Aliah is less than a 80% shooter we need to figure out whether her $\hat{p}$ of $\frac{90}{120}$ shots could reasonably occur by chance if the null is true. That sounds like a z-score question to me."* Tobiah is right. You need to figure out where Aliah's $\hat{p}$ lies relative to all the other possible $\hat{p}$s in the sampling distribution. *If the null hypothesis is true*, what are the mean and the standard deviation of the sampling distribution of $\hat{p}$ for sample size $n = 120$?

e.   Use your values from part (d) to find the z-score of Aliah's $\hat{p}$ relative to all the other possible $\hat{p}$ values.

f.   Interpret this z-score in context.

g.   Use your gut: is this a significantly unusual z-score?

h.   This z-score is called the **standardized test statistic for proportions** and is found in one step using the formula $z_{\hat{p}} = \dfrac{\hat{p} - p}{\sqrt{\dfrac{p(1-p)}{n}}}$. Explain why this formula is simply a special case of the general z-score formula $z = \dfrac{\text{value} - \text{mean}}{\text{standard deviation}}$.

8-12.   Aliah sees the z-score from the previous problem and realizes they are almost ready to calculate a *p*-value. *"A p-value,"* she reminds her teammates, *"is the probability of that we could get a statistic as or more extreme than the statistic we actually got by chance alone, assuming the null hypothesis is true."*

a.   With these hypotheses, what $\hat{p}$ z-scores would be as or more extreme than the z-score Aliah actually earned, given this alternative? That is, what z-scores would provide at least as much evidence for the alternative hypothesis?

b.   Finish the *p*-value calculation: use the normal approximation for the sampling distribution to calculate the probability of getting a score as or more extreme than the one Aliah earned if the null hypothesis is true. Sketch and shade the standard normal distribution you use to make the calculation.

8-13.   After calculating a *p*-value, the final step is to decide if you believe the null hypothesis could be true.

a.   **Gut Check:** does the *p*-value you found seem low enough to confidently reject the null hypothesis that Aliah shoots 80% in the long run?

b.   For consistency, you should decide *in advance* what probabilities will be low enough to reject the null and accept the alternative hypothesis. Before starting a hypothesis test, you should decide on the **significance level**, represented by α (the Greek letter alpha) that will serve as the "too weird to believe the null" border value. The most common significance level is $\alpha = 0.05$, but any low value can be used. Any *p*-values lower than α are considered low enough to reject the null hypothesis and accept the alternative.

Using $\alpha = 0.05$, should you reject the null hypothesis that Aliah is an 80% shooter?

8-14.   Tobiah realizes his claim (and Aliah's claim) from the first problem could also have been tested using a confidence interval. Create a 90% confidence interval for Aliah's true shot percentage and use it to evaluate their claims. Do you get the same result as the hypothesis test?

8-15.   MekDee's restaurant claims that at least 75% of Americans have eaten one of their hamburgers in the last year. A simple random sample of 528 Americans finds that 375 of them have eaten a MekDee's burger in the last year. You think they are wrong and want to show that less than 75% of Americans have eaten a MekDee's burger. Follow the guided steps to test this hypothesis at the $\alpha = 0.05$ significance level; the process should be very similar to the previous one.

    a.   State the restaurant's claim, the null and alternative hypotheses, and your sample evidence for the hypothesis, defining any symbols you use.

    b.   Check the conditions for using the normal approximation for the sampling distribution of the sample proportion. One important note: in hypothesis tests, the large counts condition should be checked by using the *expected counts under the null hypothesis*, calculated using np and $n(1 - p)$ with the proportion from the null hypothesis, rather than the actual sample counts.

    c.   Calculate the standardized test statistic. Sketch the test statistic on a standard normal curve, shade as appropriate, and calculate and interpret the *p*-value.

    d.   Draw a conclusion in context.

8-16.   A school board in a large district is investigating whether parents would be willing to extend the school year by 5 days. They will only do it if they are quite confident that more than 50% of parents will support the decision. They conduct a random phone survey of 200 parents and find that 112 of them would be willing to support the decision to extend the school year.

    a.   Using the hypotheses H_0: $p = 0.5$; H_A: $p > 0.5$ and $\alpha = 0.05$, conduct a hypothesis test to see if the school board should extend the school year. Make sure to check conditions and use the p from the null hypothesis when appropriate to do so!

    b.   Use a 90% confidence interval to evaluate the alternative hypothesis (no need to check conditions again). Do you get the same result?

8-17.   Cody is a quality control engineer at a major laptop manufacturer. He uses the following rule to decide if he should reject or accept a shipment of 10,000 keyboard keys every week by the key supplier: Select a sample of 400 keys from each shipment. If 3% or more of the keys are defective, reject the entire shipment; if less than 3% are defective than accept the lot. Suppose the percent of defective keys of one of the shipments is actually 4%. Use the normal approximation for the sampling distribution of sample proportions to estimate the probability that Cody will reject the shipment based on his rule.

8-18.   An entomologist has been researching a certain species of ant. As a result of the research, the following graph has been constructed.

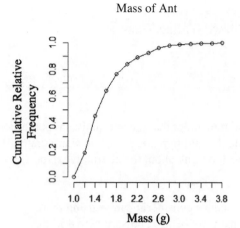

Mass of Ant

a.   Identify the median mass for this type of ant.

b.   If an ant has a mass of 2.2 grams, approximately what percentile does this mass correspond to?

c.   This data has a shape that is skewed to the right. Describe how this graph communicates a right skew.

8.1.3 How can tests differ?

· ·

Alternative Hypotheses and Two-Tailed Tests

In this lesson you will continue to solidify all the types of hypothesis tests you can use to test population proportions from a single sample.

For these problems, it can help to remember that the alternative hypothesis is "the claim you are trying to show is true with evidence" while the null hypothesis is "the claim that will be assumed to be true for the purpose of the test." It is often best to think about the alternative hypothesis *first*.

8-19.   A company that sells nails is considering advertising that "less than 1% of our nails are bent." They know that if they are caught lying, they will get fined lots of money, so they want to make sure the claim is true.

a.   One quality control engineer suggests they perform a hypothesis test at the $\alpha = 0.01$ level with the hypotheses $H_0: p = 0.01$, $H_A: p > 0.01$. What are the two possible outcomes of this hypothesis test, and what effect will that have on the advertising?

b.   Another quality control engineer suggests a different set of hypotheses: $H_0: p = 0.01$, $H_A: p < 0.01$. What are the two possible outcomes of this hypothesis and advertisement?

c.   The quality control engineers take it to the PR manager, who says, *"We really don't want to run the ad unless we have strong evidence that it is true."* Based on this argument and the possible outcomes, which of the hypothesis options is the better choice?

8-20.   The same company tells its employees, "less than 2% of employees are unhappy here!" A disgruntled employee decides to sue the company over that claim.

a.   The court is also considering two different hypothesis test options. The first one has the hypotheses $H_0: p = 0.02$, $H_A: p > 0.02$. If this test is used, what are the two possible outcomes, and what will be the results for the company?

b.   The second hypothesis option is $H_0: p = 0.02$, $H_A: p < 0.02$. If this test is used, what will be the possible outcomes and results for the company?

c.   The rule of law in the United States is that a civil defendant (the company, in this case) should be presumed innocent unless shown to be guilty by "clear and convincing evidence." This is called the "burden of proof," though it does not really require *proving* in the mathematical sense, only convincing. Given this law, which of the two hypothesis options is the better choice?

The last two problems are both examples of **one-tailed tests**, since the alternative only considers one side of the null hypothesis. With one-tailed tests, deciding which side of the claim should get the "benefit of the doubt" helps determine what alternative hypothesis to use. Remember: the alternative hypothesis is what you need to SHOW is true while the null is given the benefit of the doubt.

If the claim you wish to test is actually a test of equality, then a **two-tailed test** is needed.

8-21.   Barack Obama received 51% of all votes in the U.S. Presidential election of 2012. One county in Indiana likes to brag that it voted "exactly like the country"—which implies a claim that their proportion of votes for Obama should also have been 51%. Kiran is interested in testing this claim.

   a.   Write the county's claim in symbols and define them.

   b.   Explain why the appropriate hypotheses for this test are $H_0: p = 0.51$ and $H_A: p \neq 0.51$.

   c.   Kiran performed a random sample of voters from the county and found that 308 of the 652 sampled voted for President Obama. The county has around 12,000 residents. Check that all the conditions for the normal approximation to the sampling distribution are met, assuming the null hypothesis is true.

   d.   What evidence does Kiran have for the alternative hypothesis (use symbols)?
   [$\hat{p} = 0.472$]

   e.   Calculate the standard deviation of the sampling distribution assuming the null hypothesis is true. Then calculate the test statistic (z-score of the sample). Sketch the standard normal curve and shade the entire region that represents statistics as or more extreme than the one calculated, based on the new alternative hypothesis. (Hint: remember this is called a two-tailed test.)

   f.   Use a calculator to calculate the area of the shaded region (the p-value). You can use the symmetry of the situation to help.

   g.   Conclude: at $\alpha = 0.05$, does Kiran have have sufficient evidence to reject the county's claim?

8-22.   For each of the scenarios below, write the null and alternative hypotheses you would use in a hypothesis test. Be sure to consider which side should be given the benefit of the doubt in one-tailed tests!

   a.   The Highways Flight School has a dress code that requires all instructor pilots wear scarves while flying with students. The chief inspector pilot, Ms. Spotdale, claims that at least 50% of instructor pilots break this rule every day! Anna is convinced that Ms. Spotdale is overstating the proportion and decides to test her claim.

   b.   Jane reads in a magazine that more than 75% of teenagers sleep less than the recommended 8 hours a night. She decides to test that theory in her population by doing an SRS of students from her large high school and asking how long they sleep.

   c.   The candy company states that the true proportion of blue candy-coated chocolates is 24%. Abigail wants to check this number by assuming the bag she has is equivalent to a random sample and measuring the blue M&Ms in her bag.

   d.   Assume a certain hospital prescribes a certain generic drug that causes severe side effects in 5% of patients. A new drug is being tested for approval.

MATH NOTES

One-Sample Hypothesis Tests for Population Proportions: Four-Step Process

Step 1: <u>Identify</u> the type of test, the null and alternative hypotheses and the significance level. Define population variables and give sample evidence for H$_A$. These tests are "one-sample z-tests for proportion" or "one-sample proportion tests." Choices for hypotheses are two-tailed tests such as "H$_0$: $p = 0.3$, H$_A$: $p \neq 0.3$" or one-tailed tests such as "H$_0$: $p = 0.3$, H$_A$: $p < 0.3$." The alternative hypothesis should be the claim that needs to be *convincingly shown* for action to occur. The null hypothesis is *always* an equality. Unless specified, a significance level of $\alpha = 0.05$ is usually appropriate. The sample evidence for H$_A$ is generally the value of $\hat{p}$. If $\hat{p}$ does not support the alternative hypothesis, there is no point in performing an inference test.

Step 2: <u>Check conditions</u> for inference. In a one-sample proportion test, these are the same as the conditions for using the normal approximation to the sampling distribution: random sample for no bias, independent trials for an accurate $\sigma_{\hat{p}}$, and large counts for an approximately normal sampling distribution. However, because you have an assumed value of p in the null, you should calculate the *expected* counts of successes and failures (np and $n(1 - p)$) for large counts, rather than using the sample values.

Step 3: <u>Calculate</u> the mean and standard deviations of the sampling distribution (assuming the null hypothesis), the test statistic (z-score of the sample), and the

***p*-value.** The test statistic can be calculated directly from the formula $z_{\hat{p}} = \dfrac{\hat{p} - p}{\sqrt{\dfrac{p(1-p)}{n}}}$ or in

stages. Always sketch the standard normal curve, mark the z-score on the sketch, and shade the "more extreme" region—either one tailed or two-tailed to help calculate the *p*-value. Most calculators can calculate the z-score and *p*-value for you; if using them, make sure to report both values and the sketch!

Step 4: <u>Conclude</u> whether to reject the null hypothesis or fail to reject it by comparing the *p*-value to α. Write conclusion *in context*. If *p*-value $< \alpha$, conclude "there is sufficient evidence to reject the null hypothesis and accept the alternative." Otherwise, "there is insufficient evidence to reject the null and accept the alternative." Use the context of the problem to explain what your conclusion means.

MATH NOTES

One-Proportion Hypothesis Test: Sample Solution

In 2010, 24.5% of the citizens of Springdale, population 10,213, had a college degree. In 2016, a polling company surveys 897 randomly chosen citizens in Springdale and finds that 243 of the citizens have a college degree. Is there sufficient evidence to conclude that the proportion of Springdale residents with a college degree changed between 2010 and 2017?

Sample solution: Not all of the information below would be expected in the actual answer. The italicized text is commentary and explanation.

Identify: This is a one-sample z-test for a population proportion. H_0: $p = 0.245$; H_A: $p \neq 0.245$. Sample evidence for H_A: $\hat{p} = 0.271$. $\alpha = 0.05$. p is the proportion of Springdale residents with a college degree in 2017. *This is a two-tailed test because the question stem says "changed" rather than "increased" or "decreased."*

Check conditions: "randomly chosen citizens" satisfies random condition, no bias. Population of 10,213 is > 10 · sample size of 897, satisfies independent trials so formula for $\sigma_{\hat{p}}$ is correct. Expected counts are $0.245(897) \approx 220$ and $0.755(897) \approx 677$, both >10 satisfying large counts so sampling distribution is approximately normal.

Calculate: $\sigma_{\hat{p}} = \sqrt{\frac{0.245(0.755)}{897}} \approx 0.01436$,
$z \approx \frac{0.271 - 0.245}{0.1436} \approx 1.804$. p-value = $2 \cdot$ normalcdf(min = 1.804, max = 1E99, mean = 0, sd = 1) ≈ 0.071. *If you use a calculator to perform the test, the z-score, p-value, and sketch need to be included here.*

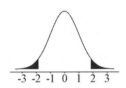

Conclude: Since the p-value of $0.071 > \alpha$ of 0.05, there is insufficient evidence to accept the alternative hypothesis. I am unable to conclude that the proportion of Springdale residents with a college degree changed between 2010 and 2017.

8-23. Refer back to part (a) of problem 8-22. If Anna checks the scarves of 104 randomly chosen instructor pilots (choosing *with* replacement to avoid large population concerns) and finds that 42 of them flying without scarves, does she have enough evidence to reject Ms. Spotdale's claim? Use the four-step process to conduct a complete hypothesis test.

8-24. In the previous problem, what would have happened if Anna's sample had found 57 out of 104 instructor pilots without scarves?

8-25.   A clothing sales company takes a random sample of 500 customers who have visited their website in the past week. From this sample of 500, 260 have actually completed a purchase on the website. Their website usually has between 2500 and 3000 unique visitors per day.

   a.   Find a 95% confidence interval for the actual percent of visitors in the last week that made a purchase on their website.

   b.   What are two ways the clothing company could achieve a smaller interval?

   c.   Is it reasonable to assume that there is a 95% probability that the true percent of customers who make a purchase is between 47.62% and 56.38%? Justify your reasoning.

   d.   What relevance does the following statement have with regards to the interval you calculated: "Their website usually has between 2500 and 3000 unique visitors per day."

8-26.   Deadly swarms of locusts are mentioned in the Bible as the eighth plague. Kacey is in Sub-Saharan Africa studying locusts. A stratified sample of 22 locusts yielded the following information regarding the relationship between swarm size and insect mass.

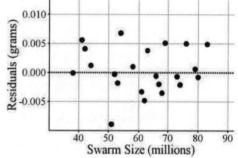

The mean swarm size is 61.55 million individuals with a standard deviation of 12.43 million. The mean mass is 2.00 g with a standard deviation of 0.02 g. The correlation coefficient is 0.9752.

   a.   Describe the association between the swarm size and mass of locusts as seen in the sample.

   b.   Determine R^2 and explain what it tells you about the relationship between swarm size and mass.

8.2.1 What if my hypothesis test doesn't work?

Types of Error in Hypothesis Testing

Like everything in Statistics, hypothesis tests are not perfect; it is impossible to use data to completely *prove* a claim true or false. Therefore, it is always possible (even probable in some cases!) that a hypothesis test will result in some sort of error.

8-27.   Imagine a man has been charged with murder in a Texas court, and the DA is pursuing the death penalty. A court case in the U.S. is like a hypothesis test: the defendant is assumed innocent until there is enough evidence presented to "disprove" that hypothesis.

    a.   Write sentences representing the null and alternative hypothesis tests for the "hypothesis test" of a court case.

    b.   What are the two errors that could be made in this case? What are the *consequences* of these types of errors?

    c.   A **Type I error** occurs when the null hypothesis is *rejected* even though it is actually true. A **Type II error** occurs when the null hypothesis is *not rejected* even though it is actually false. Identify the Type I error and Type II error in this context.

    d.   In this situation, at least, which has worse consequences: the Type I error or the Type II error?

8-28.   In the U.S., it is required for conviction in a criminal case that a defendant is proven guilty "beyond a reasonable doubt." In a civil case, however (a suit for money only), the only requirement is there be "clear and convincing evidence."

    a.   Why do you think these levels are different?

    b.   In a hypothesis test, what would be the mathematical equivalent of easing the requirement for conviction like this? (If you are not sure, move on the next problem then come back.)

8-29.   Imagine you are on a jury, hearing the evidence in a case. One of the other jurors is a trained statistician, and when it comes time to decide whether to convict, she brings some math to the table! *"I have calculated the p-value!"* she exclaims. *"If the defendant were really innocent, there would only be a 9% chance that the evidence we've seen could exist."*

   a.   For now, assume this is a *criminal case*, for murder. Do you think this 9% *p*-value qualifies as "beyond a reasonable doubt"?

   b.   Jermaine thinks that you should convict. *"After all, he says, a 9% chance isn't that much. If there's only a 9% chance of this evidence with an innocent defendant, we should convict and send him to jail! Anything under 10% should be enough to convict, since it would be really bad to let a murderer go."* In the language of hypothesis tests, what is Jermaine's number, 10%?

   c.   Aliah disagrees, *"If we convicted with any p-value under 10%, then that means that over the course of many trials, our courts would convict an innocent defendant about 10% of the time! $\frac{1}{10}$ of all convictions would be wrong!"* Use her realization to make a general statement: what is the probability of a Type I error in any significance test?

   d.   What significance level do you think might be reasonable for criminal cases? If using that significance level, about how often will innocent people be convicted?

8-30.   Jermaine comes back. *"Okay, but if we make the significance level something really low, like 1%, won't that mean it will be difficult to gather enough evidence ton convict and we will let lots of guilty criminals go? Is there any way we can figure out the probability that we will let a murderer go free in this scenario?"*

   a.   Discuss this with your team. Do you agree that lowering α will make P(Type II error) higher?

   b.   Can you calculate P(Type II error) with $\alpha = 0.01$? Remember, in this case a Type II error would happen when you have a guilty man but do not get enough evidence to convict at $\alpha = 0.01$. Check with your teacher or class before moving on after this problem.

8-31.   Aliah says, *"I'm a little confused about connecting these metaphors to our statistics problems. Let's make up a test scenario with some numbers and talk about it in context."* Jermaine replies, *"Sounds good! How about this: Mrs. Hoppenheimer claims that 75% of all AP Stats students in the country understand Type II errors."*

   "Good!" says Aliah, *"and we think she's wrong about that number. We are going to conduct a test at the 0.10 significance level."*

   a.   Write the null and alternative hypotheses for this test.

   b.   What is a Type I error in this case?

   c.   What is a Type II error?

   d.   What is P(Type I error) before conducting your test?

8-32.   Aliah remembers from earlier that *P*(Type II error) is tricky to calculate. She looks up the formal definition of a Type II error: "A Type II error occurs any time the alternative hypothesis is true, but the test fails to reject the null hypothesis."

   a.   In the previous question, what if the true proportion of AP Stats students who understand Type II errors is 74.8%? The alternative hypothesis is, therefore, technically true! In this case the **effect size**, or the difference between the null hypothesis and the truth, is only 0.2%. Would a Type II error be rare or common?

   b.   Consider a different scenario: what if, in reality, only 30% of AP Stats students understand Type II errors, so the effect size is a whopping 45%? Would the Type II error be rare or common?

   c.   Summarize: why are Type II error calculations for a hypothesis test always a conjecture?

MATH NOTES

Types of Errors in Hypothesis Tests

A Type I error occurs when the null hypothesis of the test is rejected but should not be. Since the null is rejected when "the probability of getting a sample this or more extreme when the null is true is less than α" the probability of making a Type I error is simply α; it is made when the sample actually *is* extreme solely by random chance.

A Type II error occurs when a null hypothesis is *not* rejected by a test, even though the alternative hypothesis is true. The probability of a Type II error depends on the effect size of the situation, or how far off from truth the null hypothesis is; this means it cannot be calculated without additional information. The probability of a Type II error in a particular test is often denoted with β, the Greek letter beta.

Type II errors are usually both more common and less damaging than a Type I errors. There may be rare exceptions where a Type II error causes more damage than a Type I error, but usually those situations can be avoided by good choice of hypotheses.

8-33. Refer back to part (c) of problem 8-22, in which Abigail uses her bag of candy-coated chocolates to check the company's claim that 24% of the chocolates are blue. She uses the hypotheses "$H_0: p = 0.24$, $H_A: p \neq 0.24$."

    a. Describe what a Type I error and a Type II error would mean in this context.

    b. Abigail gets a bag of 250 candies and finds that 40 of them are blue. Assuming the conditions for inference are met, show that Abigail has sufficient evidence to reject the company's claim at the $\alpha = 0.01$ significance level.

    c. Abigail sends a message to the company and they respond, *"The advertised proportion of 24% is correct. However, the machines that mix the chocolates together is not designed to mix perfectly, so individual bags may differ significantly from the population."* In statistics terms, which condition does this mean was not met in Abigail's original test?

    d. Does the calculation you came up with in this chapter that $P(\text{Type I Error}) = \alpha$ apply when the conditions are not met? Explain.

8-34. Eliza likes throwing paper airplanes into her friend Grace's locker. When she flies paper airplanes made out of card stock, she hits Grace's locker 38% of the time. When she throws airplanes made out of tracing paper, she hits Grace's graces locker 17% of the time. For this problem, assume all airplane tosses are independent.

    a. Eliza throws one of each kind of airplane. Create a Venn diagram or two-way table showing every combination of outcomes and its probability, including marginal distributions.

    b. Eliza throws 5 card stock airplanes. What is the probability she hits Grace's locker with at least three of them?

    c. Eliza throws 40 tracing paper airplanes. What is the probability that she will have at least a 20% hit rate? (Use a normal approximation for the proportion if conditions are satisfied, the binomial distribution otherwise!)

    d. Eliza throws 120 card stock airplanes. What is the probability she has a hit rate of 45% or better? (Use a normal approximation for the proportion if conditions are satisfied, the binomial distribution otherwise!)

8-35.   The superintendent of your school district would like to know how students react when they are bullied.

   a.   Should an observational study or an experiment be carried out to answer the question? Explain.

   b.   The superintendent suspects that students of different ages respond differently to bullying. Is there a way to design the study to account for this variability? Explain.

   c.   Describe how you would carry out the study. Be sure to describe how you would incorporate randomization into your design.

8-36.   It is inventory time at the Mathletes Shoe Super Store. To speed up the process, Iris, the storeowner, decided to find the value of the inventory by counting the number of pairs of shoes that belong in $30 intervals. She made the following table:

Value ($)	# of pairs
0 up to 30	47
30 up to 60	67
60 up to 90	60
90 up to 120	46
120 up to 150	18
150 up to 180	6
180 up to 210	4
210 up to 240	2

   a.   Make a relative frequency histogram of the distribution of shoes in the store.

   b.   Which intervals contain the median, the first quartile and third quartile?

   c.   Describe the distribution of shoe values in terms of center, shape, spread, and outliers.

   d.   What proportion of shoes are valued at least $150?

$8.2.2$ How strong is my test?

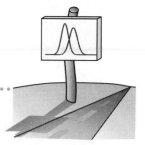

Power of a Test

You have learned that you can determine your chance of making a Type I error by using an appropriate significance level, but a truly useful test will also minimize the chance of a Type II error. Today you will discover ways to ways to reduce Type II errors in hypothesis tests.

8-37.　TrustUs Pharmaceuticals is planning to test a new heartburn relief drug for side effects. Because heartburn is not a life-threatening condition, many medical practices require that new drugs cause side effects in less than 20% of patients in order to prescribe them. TrustUs is trying to design a hypothesis test that will allow them to show that less than 20% of patients have side effects under the drug. For this problem you can assume all conditions for inference are met.

　　a.　Assume the burden of evidence is on the pharmaceutical company: <u>identify</u> the null hypothesis and alternative hypothesis for this test.

　　b.　What would a Type I error and a Type II error be in this context, including consequences?

　　c.　Assume the company decides to do a clinical trial, giving the drug to 200 heartburn-sufferers and measuring their side effects. α will be 0.05. Assuming H_0 is true, the sampling distribution has $\mu_{\hat{p}} = 0.20$, $\sigma_{\hat{p}} = \sqrt{\frac{0.2(0.8)}{200}}$. Sketch the sampling distribution for $\hat{p}$ and label it "Hypothesis $\hat{p}$ sampling distribution" Note that this is NOT the standard normal distribution—this curve should still be in terms of proportions.

　　d.　TrustUs wants to know: what is the *maximum* proportion of patients that can develop side effects in their test and still allow the test to reject H_0 so they can get approved? You can figure this out without using trial and error by working backwards: find the value of $\hat{p}$ that would give a p-value of exactly α, and anything below that value will reject the null. Find this critical value and shade your sketch from part (c) where the drug will be approved (H_0 is rejected).

　　e.　TrustUs suspects their medication is so good that only 14% of the subjects will experience side-effects. Assume they are right. Sketch this suspected $\hat{p}$ sampling distribution. Using the critical value from part (d) shade the area under the curve where the drug is approved and H_0 is rejected.

　　f.　Use your sketch and answer this question: assuming the company is correct about the suspected $p = 0.14$, what is the probability that the sample proportion they get will be less than the critical value for the hypothesis test? This value is called the power of this hypothesis test at $p = 0.14$.

　　g.　Use your answer to part (h) to calculate the probability of a Type II error under this alternative. This is written $P(\text{Type II error} \mid p = 0.14)$.

8-38. The idea of power of a test is complicated. This problem uses the Errors and Power eTool to explore the concept further. Open the eTool then follow the instructions below.

   a. Modify the values on the left sidebar to match the scenario from problem 8-35: $p_0 = 0.2$, $H_A: p < p_0$, $n = 200$, $\alpha = 0.05$, and suspected $p_A = 0.14$. Sketch the curves you see at right. Do the calculations at the top match your calculations from problem 8-35?

   b. Click the shade options for "Type II Error" and "Power" above the graph. What is the relationship between those two shaded regions?

   c. The company wants to *increase* the power of the test; they are not satisfied with only a 70% chance of getting approved! For each of the following options, describe what you modify on the eTool to represent the change and state the new power. After each exploration, reset the eTool back to the initial state of the problem before trying the next change!

      i. The company modifies an inactive ingredient of the drug slightly and reduces the suspected proportion of side effects to 12% (this is called increasing the *effect size*, or the amount the null is wrong).

      ii. The company believes they can convince medical practices to approve the drug if they can confidently show less than 22% of patients have side effects (this is another version of increasing the effect size).

      iii. The company decides to try using $\alpha = 0.10$ instead of 0.05.

      iv. The company increases the sample size of the study to 300 people.

   d. In most cases, modifying the null hypothesis or the true value of a parameter is impossible, and modifying α increases P(Type I error), which is an obvious downside. What therefore seems to be the best way to increase power in most situations?

8-39. The main reason increasing sample size works to increase power of a test to detect a specific result is because it lowers the variability of samples. Use this idea to evaluate whether you think the following changes to the design of a study or experiment will increase or decrease power of tests based on the study. For any that increase power, discuss any drawbacks. For any that decrease power, discuss any other advantages.

   a. Conducting a stratified sample rather than a simple random sample.

   b. Blocking an experiment by an important variable, considering a hypothesis test that is trying to detect a difference between two groups.

   c. Cluster sampling rather than sampling randomly.

   d. Controlling for more potentially confounding variables in an experiment.

   e. Change the scope of a study or experiment to draw from a larger, more varied population.

   f. Change the scope of the study or an experiment to draw from a smaller, more homogeneous population.

MATH NOTES

Power of a Test

The **power of a hypothesis test** under a specific alternative hypothesis is the probability that the test will *correctly* reject the null hypothesis under the given specific value of the alternative hypothesis.

$$\text{Power} = 1 - P(\text{Type II error}) \text{ for a specific alternative.}$$

In the one-tailed proportion test depicted below, the line down the middle of the "true p" curve represents the critical value p^*. Sample proportions $> p^*$ will result in rejecting the null hypothesis. Thus, the dark shaded region represents the power of the test, while the light shaded region represents the probability of a Type II error.

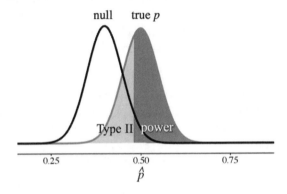

Power increases when:

i.   The null hypothesis is made "more incorrect." This is also known as increasing the *effect size*.

ii. α is increased

iii.   Sample size or treatment group size is increased

iv.   Sample or treatment group variability is decreased by stratification, blocking, or other techniques

It is a good idea to test power under several possible alternatives before running an expensive or time-consuming experiment or study, as a low-powered test may not be worth the time and money devoted to it.

8-40.   494 emperor penguins were randomly sampled, and it was discovered that 146 of them were juveniles (less than 2 years old). Assume conditions for inference are met.

    a.   Construct a 95% confidence interval for the proportion of all emperor penguins that are juveniles (use technology if available to save time).

    b.   Use this confidence interval to evaluate the claim "more than a third of emperor penguins are juveniles."

    c.   Construct a 90% confidence interval for the proportion of all emperor penguins that are juveniles and use the new interval to evaluate the claim.

    d.   Finally, conduct a one-tailed hypothesis test testing the claim against the alternative "H_A: $p < \frac{1}{3}$" at $\alpha = 0.05$. Which confidence interval matches the conclusion from the test?

    e.   If you changed the test in part (d) to a two-tailed test, what would change? What confidence interval would then be matched?

8-41.   Jeralyn has decided to raffle off her 2010 Fonda Concord EX and give the money to the school's running club. She estimates the car has a value of $17000. She plans on selling 200 tickets at $100 each. For someone with a single ticket, what is the expected value and standard deviation of the raffle?

8-42.   Evidence suggests the mixture of gases in the atmosphere has taken over 4.5 billion years to evolve. Andrew is an engineering student at Washington State University investigating levels of greenhouse gases in air samples. An SRS of 24 samples revealed the following summary regarding the relationship between carbon dioxide levels and oxygen percentage.

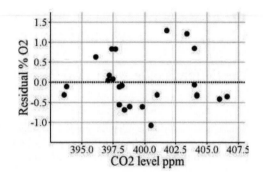

Regression Output for Oxygen Percentage vs. Carbon Dioxide Levels

Predictor	Coef	SE Coef	T	P
Constant	84.07	3.06	27.52	0.00
CO_2 Levels	-0.16	0.01	-20.33	0.00

S = 0.642   R-Sq = 0.4496   R-Sq(Adj)= 0.4246

a.   Determine the correlation coefficient, then describe the association between the carbon dioxide levels and oxygen percentage in the air samples.

b.   Determine r^2 and its meaning in the context of this sample.

c.   Discuss the standard deviation of the residuals and what it tells you about the relationship between carbon dioxide levels and oxygen percentage.

8.3.1 How can I compare two proportions?

The Difference Between Two Proportions

In previous proportion inference questions, you have explored proportions that come from a single sample. It is extremely common, perhaps more common, to want to compare two sample proportions in order to make an inference about their population proportions; in this lesson you will explore one way to do that.

8-43. Jermaine and Aliah are competing for the title of "Best Trashketball Player." They compete head-to-head, each shooting 200 shots. Jermaine makes 160 shots and Aliah makes 168 shots, so Aliah begins celebrating her win.

a. *"Not so fast,"* Jermaine says. *"Just because you won this round doesn't mean you are the best overall. If we played another round, I might win!"* How does Jermaine's argument connect to the ideas of population and samples?

b. Assuming conditions are met, calculate the standard error for each sample proportion.

c. Aliah is confident that her overall skill level (population proportion p_{Aliah}) is higher than Jermaine's overall skill level (p_{Jermaine}). Write her *claim* using symbols.

8-44. Aliah realizes that she can re-write her claim as $p_{\text{Aliah}} - p_{\text{Jermaine}} > 0$. *"It seems like a number might make things easier…,"* she muses.

a. In symbols, what *statistic* will serve as the best approximation for the parameter $p_{\text{Aliah}} - p_{\text{Jermaine}}$?

b. Given the sample data from problem 8-43, what is the current *point estimate* for $p_{\text{Aliah}} - p_{\text{Jermaine}}$?

c. In Chapter 6 you learned how to add or subtract random variables to create a new one. Use your results from part (b) of problem 8-43 (and refer to the Math Notes box in Lesson 6.1.3 if need be) to find the standard error of $\hat{p}_{\text{Aliah}} - \hat{p}_{\text{Jermaine}}$.

8-45.   In earlier lessons you decided that the sampling distribution for a Trashketball proportion should qualify as approximately normal. Therefore, the shape of the difference between two such proportions should be normal as well!

   a.   Sketch the estimated sampling distribution of $\hat{p}_{Aliah} - \hat{p}_{Jermaine}$, given the values from parts (b) and (c) of problem 8-42.

   b.   Construct a 95% confidence interval for the value of $p_{Aliah} - p_{Jermaine}$ and interpret the meaning in context.

   c.   Does the interval give compelling evidence to accept or reject Aliah's claim that she is better than Jermaine?

8-46.   A poll of 1000 random U.S. voters yields the following two-way table comparing gender to political party.

	Male	Female	
Republican	223	202	425
Democrat	194	251	445
Independent	65	65	130
	482	518	1000

   a.   Find the proportion of men who are Republicans and the proportion of women who are Republicans in this sample.

   b.   A Republican strategist claims that Republicanism is gender-neutral: that is, being a Republican is independent from gender. Using the symbols p_m to represent the proportion of men that are Republicans and p_w to represent the proportion of women who are Republicans, write his claim using a difference statement, as in problem 8-44.

   c.   Check all conditions for normal inference for **both** proportions, p_m and p_w. This is necessary to insure it is acceptable to perform inference on the difference. Important note: even though only one sample was done, in this situation it is reasonable to consider it equivalent to two smaller independent samples, one of men and one of women.

   d.   Use the sample data to find the estimated values and standard errors for $\hat{p}_m$, $\hat{p}_w$, and then $\hat{p}_m - \hat{p}_w$.

   e.   Calculate a 95% confidence interval for the difference between the proportions, interpret it in context, and use it to evaluate the strategist's claim.

MATH NOTES

Difference of Two Proportions:
The Sampling Distribution

The sampling distribution for the difference of two sample proportions, written $\hat{p}_1 - \hat{p}_2$, can be approximated using a normal distribution as long as the conditions for normal inference below are met. All but the last one should be familiar from earlier inference.

i. **Random selection or assignment,** to avoid bias: *both* sample proportions must come from random samples (or one large random sample).

ii. **Independent trials,** of draws for an accurate standard error: the populations for *both* samples should be larger than 10 times the sample size OR the values must be drawn with replacement.

iii. **Large counts,** so the sampling distribution ≈ normal condition: *both* samples need at least 10 successes and 10 failures.

iv. **Independent sample proportions,** also for an accurate standard error: the two samples must be independent of one another; this means that one of them should be able to change (at least in theory) *without* affecting the other one.

Important note: It is possible for this (and other) conditions to be met with one large sample that is later broken into smaller samples. For example, a large poll could satisfy these conditions to compare the proportion of men who are Republicans $P(R \mid M)$ to the proportion of women who are Republicans $P(R \mid F)$. However, the proportion of men who are Republicans $P(R \mid M)$ could *not* be compared to the proportion of men who are Democrats $P(D \mid M)$ because of condition *iv*, since one person changing their answer could affect both of these proportions at the same time.

The mean of the sampling distribution is the difference between the population proportions, $\mu_{\hat{p}_1 - \hat{p}_2} = p_1 - p_2$, and the standard deviation of the sampling distribution is

$\sigma_{\hat{p}_1 - \hat{p}_2} = \sqrt{\sigma_{\hat{p}_1}^2 + \sigma_{\hat{p}_2}^2} = \sqrt{\frac{p_1(1-p_1)}{n_1} + \frac{p_2(1-p_2)}{n_2}}$. As with single proportions, you can calculate

the standard *error* by using the sample proportions $\hat{p}_1$ and $\hat{p}_2$ in the above formula when the population proportions are not known.

8-47.   In problem 8-40, it was discussed that 146 out of 494 randomly sampled emperor penguins were juveniles. In another survey, 92 out of 278 randomly sampled chinstrap penguins were juveniles. Check that the conditions for inference are met and conduct a 95% confidence interval for the difference in the proportion of juveniles between the two penguin types.

8-48.   Two six-sided dice are thrown. The number of points is the sum of the values displayed by the two dice.

   a.   How many ways are there to get 7 points?

   b.   What is the probability of getting 7 points?

   c.   If you got 7 points, what is the probability that the result on one of the dice was a 5?

8-49.   Coastal redwoods are considered the tallest land organisms in the world. While in California studying valuable supplies of mature coastal redwoods, assume Jamal investigated a random sample of 22 redwoods which showed the following results regarding the relationship between leaf length and seed cone length.

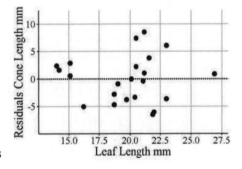

The mean leaf length is 19.73 mm with a standard deviation of 3.20 mm. The mean seed cone length is 24.73 mm with a standard deviation of 6.12 mm. The correlation coefficient is 0.7220.

   a.   Determine the LSRL equation and label the variables in context.

   b.   Describe the slope and its meaning in the context of this sample.

   c.   Use the LSRL to predict the seed cone length of a mature coastal redwood whose leaf length is 16.33 mm.

   d.   Calculate the residual for the point (21.60, 31.10).

   e.   Is a linear model the most appropriate? How do you know?

8.3.2 How can I compare two proportions?

Two-Sample Proportion Hypothesis Tests

Today, you will look for a significant difference between two independent sample proportions.

8-50.   A grocery store surveys 250 randomly chosen customers and finds that 160 of the customers have bought apples in the last month and 120 have bought oranges. 80 people bought both. The store decides to go ahead and compare apples and oranges.

a.   Create a two-way table to represent this situation.

b.   Create a conditional relative frequency table that allows you to see the proportion of apple-buyers who bought oranges and the proportion of non-apple buyers who bought oranges.

c.   **Gut check:** Does it appear as if the buying of apples and oranges are associated variables in the larger population of customers?

8-51.   One way to check if variables are associated in this sort of situation is to frame it as a *hypothesis test for the difference of proportions*. In words, the null hypothesis *means* "these variables are independent." Let p_A represent the population proportion of apple-buyers who buy oranges and let p_N represent the proportion of non-apple-buyers who buy oranges.

a.   If you were to choose a random shopper from this grocery store, p_A and p_N could be expressed as probabilities in probability notation. Do it, then explain why these values being equal would mean apple-buying and orange-buying are independent.

b.   In symbols, write a null hypothesis for the hypothesis test. Put the null hypothesis in terms of the *difference* in these proportions.

c.   In this situation the alternative hypothesis, in words, is "the variables are associated." In symbols, write the alternative hypothesis as a difference in proportions.

d.   Check conditions: is it reasonable to approximate the sampling distribution of this proportion difference using the normal distribution? Note: you *are* allowed to use the sample counts for the large counts condition in this case.

e.   The next task is to find the standard deviation or error of the difference *assuming the null hypothesis is true*. Recall that the formula for the standard deviation of the difference of proportions is $\sigma_{\hat{p}_1 - \hat{p}_2} = \sqrt{\frac{p_1(1-p_1)}{n_1} + \frac{p_2(1-p_2)}{n_2}}$. Explain why you do not have enough information to calculate this value, even assuming the null hypothesis of $p_A - p_N = 0$ is true.

8-52.   Aliah runs into the same problem you ran into and says idly to Jermaine, *"Our null hypothesis says the two different p's are the same. So the proportion of apple eaters who buy oranges should equal the proportion of non-apple eaters who bought oranges, which should be equal to simply the proportion of shoppers who bought oranges..."* Jermaine says, *"Hey, we can calculate that!"*

   a.   Calculate the proportion of all shoppers who bought oranges in the original sample.

   b.   Aliah says, *"Wow, thanks! I think it makes a lot of sense to use this value for BOTH proportions in our standard deviation formula."* Mrs. Hoppenheimer happens to be walking by and says, *"We call that number the **pooled sampled proportion** and you're right! It's the best estimate for the equal proportions under the null hypothesis. Since the pooled proportion is an estimate, this will be a standard error."* Help Aliah calculate the standard error of the difference of proportions using the pooled proportion for *both* proportions.

   c.   Tobiah says, *"Let's finish this! The difference in the sample proportions was 0.5 – 0.444 = 0.056."* What was its z-score under the null hypothesis and its *p*-value? Make sure to sketch and shade the standard normal distribution as well.

   d.   Should the grocery store conclude apple-buying and orange-buying are associated variables?

8-53.   Cable-finity, a cable TV provider, runs ads saying they have better customer service ratings than their rival, Comcable. A random sample of 1000 Comcable cable customers found that 235 of them are satisfied with Comcable's customer service. A random sample of 500 Cable-finity customers found that 138 of them are satisfied with Cable-finity's service. Both cable companies have millions of subscribers.

   a.   Based solely on these samples, is Cable-finity correct that they have a higher proportion of satisfied customers?

   b.   Comcable sues Cable-finity, saying they should only be allowed to make this claim if they can show significant evidence that the claim is true *across the entire population*. What null and alternative hypotheses should be used? What evidence is there in favor of H_A? Make sure to define any symbols you use.

   c.   Confirm that the conditions for inference are met.

   d.   Calculate the standard error of the sampling distribution of the difference in proportions under the null hypothesis, using the pooled proportion method.

   e.   Find the z-score of the sample difference under the null hypothesis and find the *p*-value for this situation, sketching the distribution.

   f.   Write a conclusion: does Cable-finity have sufficient evidence at $\alpha = 0.05$ to conclude they truly have more satisfied customers?

MATH NOTES

Two-Sample Hypothesis Tests for Proportions

The process for a two-sample hypothesis test for proportions is much the same as a one-sample, with a few calculation differences.

Step 1: Identify the test and the null and alternative hypotheses, identify the sample evidence for the alternative, and decide on a significance level. This test can be called a "two-proportion z-test" or "two-sample z-test for proportions." The null hypothesis is almost always written H_0: $p_1 = p_2$ or H_0: $p_1 - p_2 = 0$. The alternative is an inequality: less than, greater than, or not equal. The sample evidence for H_A is that the difference between the sample proportions matches the inequality.

Step 2: Check conditions for inference. See the Math Notes box from the previous lesson. Unlike one-proportion tests, it is acceptable in two-proportion tests to use the sample counts for the Large Counts condition, *or* you can calculate np and $n(1 - p)$ using the pooled proportion described below for *both* samples, which finds the estimated counts.

Step 3: Calculate standard error of the difference $p_1 - p_2$, the z-score of the sample difference, and the p-value, sketching and shading the standard normal curve. To calculate the standard error it is necessary to first find the *pooled sample proportion* $\hat{p}_p$ by treating the two samples as one combined sample. This value is then used as to estimate both proportions in the formula for the standard deviation of differences, yielding the standard error $SE_{\hat{p}_1 - \hat{p}_2} = \sqrt{\frac{\hat{p}_p(1-\hat{p}_p)}{n_1} + \frac{\hat{p}_p(1-\hat{p}_p)}{n_2}} = \sqrt{\hat{p}_p(1-\hat{p}_p)\left(\frac{1}{n_1} + \frac{1}{n_2}\right)}$. This can then be used to find the test statistic and p-value. In practice, it is generally best to use a calculator for these calculations if possible, in which case you must identify the z-score and p-value at least, and ideally also the pooled proportion and a shaded sketch.

Step 4: Conclude whether to reject the null hypothesis and accept the alternative by comparing the p-value to α. Write a sentence in context that begins with "Because the p-value is greater than α, I do not have sufficient evidence to conclude the proportions of ____ and ____ are different" or "Because the p-value is less than α, I have sufficient evidence to…"

MATH NOTES

Two-Proportion Hypothesis Test
Sample Solution

A polling company surveys 897 randomly chosen citizens in Springdale, population 10,213 and finds that 243 of the citizens have a college degree. They poll 773 random citizens of Cookeville, population 11,312, and find that 245 of them have a college degree. Is there sufficient evidence to conclude that the proportions of Springdale and Cookeville residents with college degrees differ?

Sample solution: Not all of this information would be expected in the actual answer. The italics are commentary and explanation.

Identify: This is a two-sample z-test for proportions. H_0: $p_S - p_c = 0$; H_A: $p_S - p_c \neq 0$. Sample evidence for H_A: $\hat{p}_s - \hat{p}_c \approx 0.271 - 0.317 = -0.046$, which is $\neq 0$. p_s is the proportion of Springdale residents with a college degree, p_c the proportion of Cookeville residents with a college degree. $\alpha = 0.05$.

Check conditions: "Randomly chosen citizens" satisfies random condition, so no bias. Population of 10,213 is > 10 times sample size of 897 and 11,312 > 10 times 773, satisfying independent trials for accurate standard error formula. Sample counts are 243 and 654 for Springdale, 245 and 528 for Cookeville, all > 10, satisfying large counts so sampling distribution of differences is approximately normal. The two samples are independent of each other since there is no overlap in the populations.

Calculate: $\hat{p}_{pooled} = \frac{243+245}{897+773} \approx 0.292$.

$SE_{diff} = \sqrt{0.292(0.708)\left(\frac{1}{897} + \frac{1}{773}\right)} \approx 0.022$, z $\approx \frac{-0.046}{0.022} \approx -2.06$, p-value ≈ 0.039. *If using a calculator to perform the test, report the pooled proportion, the z-score, and the p-value, and include a shaded sketch.*

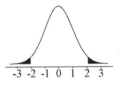

Conclude: Since the p-value of 0.039 < α of 0.05, there is sufficient evidence to reject the null hypothesis and conclude that the proportions of Springdale residents and Cookeville residents with a college degree differ.

8-54.   A survey of 440 randomly selected persons in Claire's city found 326 people who have a hybrid car. Anna is also collecting data on the proportion of people who have a hybrid car. A survey of 254 randomly selected persons in Anna's city found a 0.6693 proportion of people who have a hybrid car. Use an appropriate hypothesis test to determine if a larger proportion of people earn a hybrid car in Claire's city than in Anna's city at a 0.03 significance level.

8-55.   Are cereals marketed to children actually placed lower on the grocery store shelf than cereals marketed to adults?

   a.   Should an observational study or an experiment be carried out to answer the question? Explain.

   b.   Describe how you would carry out the study. Be sure to describe how you would incorporate randomization into your design.

8-56.   Corbin is concerned about the amount of sodium in breakfast cereal. After examining labels from a random sample of cereal brands, he discovers that the amount of sodium in breakfast cereal is approximately normally distributed with a mean of 6.5 milligrams sodium per gram of cereal and a standard deviation of 1.6 mg/g. Corbin has listed his three favorite cereals and their sodium content below and wants to know how they compare to the population of breakfast cereals as a whole. For each cereal listed below, find its sodium content percentile and provide Corbin an explanation of what each percentile means.

   a.   Tweeties cereal has 7.4 milligrams sodium per gram of cereal.

   b.   Apple Flakes cereal has 4.5 mg/g.

   c.   Korn Crispies cereal has 3.9 mg/g.

8.3.3 How can I put it together?

More Proportion Inference

In this lesson you will identify and work through a variety of proportion hypothesis tests and confidence intervals. Your teacher may show you how to use your technology to speed up the calculation process at some point in the lesson as well. If you use technology to conduct a hypothesis test, it is sufficient to report the test statistic (z-score), shaded curve sketch, and *p*-value in the calculation step. Confidence intervals require a report of the critical value and the standard error/deviation.

8-57. Coach Griswold and Coach Faulder decide to see if one of them is a better field goal kicker. They each kick 120 field goals from the 20-yard line. Coach Griswold scores on 100 of the goals, and Coach Faulder scores on 105 of his. Assume each kick is independent of every other kick and neither coach is getting better or worse with practice.

By now you should know that the four-step process below can be used to guide *any* hypothesis test; this problem guides you through it as a reminder, but you should always follow it!

   a. Identify a test you could do to analyze whether there is any difference between the coaches long-run field goal skill, write hypotheses, define your population variables, give sample evidence for the alternative and choose α if not given.

   b. Check conditions for inference with the normal approximation. Make sure to include the *purpose* of each condition when applicable.

   c. Calculate the appropriate standard deviation or standard error of the statistic, the test statistic, and the *p*-value. Include a sketch.

   d. Conclude whether to reject or fail to reject the null hypothesis (making sure to explicitly compare the *p*-value to α) and write a conclusion statement in context.

8-58. Construct a confidence interval for the difference in the coaches' skill above and confirm that it leads to the same conclusion. You will want to show a calculation for the standard error. Remember: confidence intervals and hypothesis tests have slightly different estimates for the standard error!

8-59. A sample of 250 African elephants found that 173 of them were over 10 feet tall. A sample of 200 Asian elephants found that 112 of them were over 10 feet tall. Conduct a hypothesis test at $\alpha = 0.10$ to decide if the proportion of African elephants over 10 feet tall is different from the proportion of all Asian elephants over 10 feet tall, assuming these samples are random.

8-60.   TrustUs Pharmaceuticals is trying to come up with an even better heartburn medication. Their last one has been used for years and has consistently helped 74% of patients. A clinical trial of the new medication with 200 randomly selected heartburn patients found that it helped 159 of them. Use a 95% confidence interval to decide if the new medication is a statistically significant improvement over the old one.

8-61.   Test the same scenario as above, using a hypothesis test with $\alpha = 0.05$. Do not check the conditions again.

8-62.   Joshua is bothered by the fact that the two previous problems had disagreeing results. Emily tells him, *"Well, it's because confidence intervals always consider both directions; they are always two-tailed! If this has been a two-tailed test instead of a one-tailed test, the results would have agreed."*

   a.   Look back at your work for problem 8-61 and confirm Emily's insight. Would a two-tailed test have given the same result as the confidence interval?

   b.   Discuss with your team: if you wanted to adjust problem 8-60 a bit to make a confidence interval that would give the same conclusion as problem 8-61, how could you do that?

   c.   Quickly find the confidence interval you discussed in (b) (technology is fine if you have it, no need to show all work) and confirm that the results are the same.

   d.   Discuss with your team: what α could you have used in problem 8-61 to be equivalent to the original 95% confidence interval? Would the results have matched?

MATH NOTES

Confidence Intervals and Hypothesis Tests

Confidence intervals and hypothesis tests can both be used to evaluate claims. Using confidence intervals instead of hypothesis tests can be powerful, but requires some care.

A two-tailed hypothesis test at a significance level α is approximately equivalent to a confidence interval at a confidence level of $1 - \alpha$ for evaluating claims. The most common example is that a two-tailed test at $\alpha = 0.05$ is approximately equivalent to a confidence interval with 95% confidence.

A one-tailed hypothesis test at a significance level α is approximately equivalent to a confidence interval with $C = 1 - 2\alpha$ for evaluating claims. For example, a one-tailed test with $\alpha = 0.05$ is approximately equivalent to a CI with 90% confidence.

These equivalencies are not perfect when working with proportions. Since a confidence interval uses a standard error calculated *entirely* from samples while a hypothesis test uses one calculated using information from the null hypothesis, they do not always match perfectly. This is especially true if the proportions involved are very high (> 0.8) or low (< 0.2), and in two-sample situations.

Review & Preview

8-63. For each confidence interval or test, name the confidence interval or test(s) that would allow you to test claims equivalently. For example, for "two-tailed test with $\alpha = 0.05$" the correct answer would be "95% confidence level."

  a.   one-tailed test, $\alpha = 0.10$

  b.   one-tailed test, $\alpha = 0.01$

  c.   two-tailed test, $\alpha = 0.01$

  d.   85% confidence interval

  e.   99.9% confidence interval

8-64. Malik is looking for the proportion of people who have blue eye coloring. Imani claims that "the proportion of people having blue eye coloring is not equal to 0.58." Malik found a published survey of 453 randomly selected persons which found 235 people who have blue eye coloring. Use the results of the survey Malik found to evaluate Imani's claim with a hypothesis test at a 0.04 significance level.

8-65.   Jack is planning flights to Fort Lauderdale to catch a cruise ship. The least expensive route will require three separate flights to arrive in Miami and then a shuttle bus connection to Fort Lauderdale. Jack believes that if more than one of the legs is delayed he will miss his ship. Jack researches and finds the airline and bus company both have an 80% on-time rating. If Jack buys the least expensive ticket, what is the probability that Jack misses his ship? Describe how you would carry out a simulation using random digits to assess this probability. Run your simulation enough times to get a reasonable estimate of the probability.

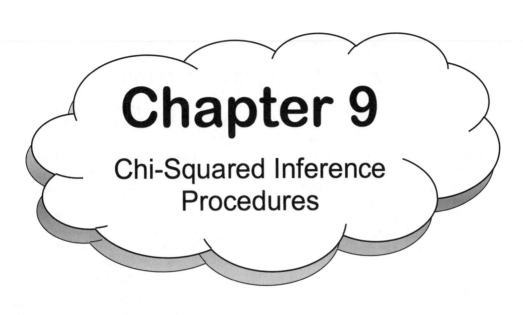

Chapter 9

Chi-Squared Inference Procedures

CHAPTER 9   Chi-Squared Inference Procedures

In Chapter 3 you studied associations between two categorical variables by comparing conditional probabilities looking for near equality. Beyond intuition a test is needed to answer more questions such as: *Is there enough inequality to reject a claim of independence? If I reject independence, how certain can I be?* The chi-squared distribution is categorical inference test designed to answer these questions.

Chapter Goals

Compare multiple proportions from independent samples to look for a significant difference.

Compare multiple proportions among multiple categorical variables from a single sample to look for an association or compliance to a particular distribution.

Recognize and correctly apply the appropriate chi-squared technique, goodness of fit, homogeneity, or independence, in the proper situation.

Chapter Outline

Section 9.1   You will be introduced to the chi-squared distribution out of the need for a method of comparing three proportions. A single procedure that summarizes the difference across multiple samples is more efficient and powerful than running multiple two-sample tests. You will then learn the chi-squared goodness of fit test and have an opportunity to practice applying the procedure in multiple contexts.

Section 9.2   You will extend your use of chi-squared procedures to tests of independence. When the comparison is extended to include two categorical variables with multiple possible categories, the same need arises for a test that summarizes differences across multiple comparisons. The same procedure is then applied to a setting where multiple samples have been gathered, and the question of homogeneity of proportions is considered. The section ends with an opportunity to identify and practice all of the chi-squared procedures.

9.1.1 What if I have more than two samples?

Introduction to the Chi-Squared Distribution

So far, you have been able to model the distribution of sample proportions with the normal distribution. You know that the center (the mean) of this distribution is the actual population proportion ($\mu_{\hat{p}} = p$). Using the standard deviation as a measure of the sample-to-sample variability, you observed that

$$\sigma_{\hat{p}} = \sqrt{\frac{p(1-p)}{n}} \ .$$

You also learned that the normal distribution can be used to model differences in sample proportions. If you have two samples and you are finding the proportion of observations within each sample that have some feature, the difference in proportions for the two samples are centered about the difference in the true population proportions. ($\mu_{\hat{p}_2 - \hat{p}_1} = p_2 - p_1$). Again using the standard deviation as a measure of the sample-to-sample variability, you observed that $\sigma_{\hat{p}_2 - \hat{p}_1} = \sqrt{\frac{p_1(1-p_1)}{n_1} + \frac{p_2(1-p_2)}{n_2}}$.

In this chapter, you begin to ask the question, "What if there are more than two samples?" What if you are looking for differences across many categories? Can you develop a procedure that will allow you to test for significant differences across many categories?

To begin to answer these questions, let's return to Mrs. Hoppenheimer's class with Trashketball competitions. The class is really getting into the game. This time, three students (Jermaine, Aliah, and Tobiah) want to have a three-way competition. They want to see if at least one of their proportions will stand out as significantly different from the rest of the group.

9-1.   Gathering a new sample for each student, Jermaine made 162 out of 200, Aliah made 170 out of 200, and Tobiah made 174 out of 200. Their gut reaction is that these are all pretty close. Jermaine says, *"I can't figure out how to run one test that answers our question. What if we calculated a pooled proportion for all three of us and ran three separate 1-sample z-tests for proportions with this pooled proportion as our null hypothesis. If any of us differ from this pooled proportion significantly, we'd have evidence that at least one of our proportions stands out from the rest."* Do it! Divide up the work among your team members. Refer to the Math Notes box in Lesson 8.1.3, skipping the "Identify, Check, and Conclusion" steps, performing only the "Calculate" step. Carefully write down the z-score for each group member for each test.

9-2.   The group is not sure what to do with the results of the three separate tests from problem 9-1. Discuss with your teammates what conclusions you might try to make from the results of the three tests.

9-3.   Jermaine, Aliah, and Tobiah are not satisfied with attempting to combine the results of three separate hypothesis tests simultaneously. They ask Mrs. Hoppenheimer for help. She tells them, *"The **chi-squared distribution** (also written as χ^2 distribution) with k degrees of freedom are the sum of the squares of k independent standard normal random variables. This might be a way to combine the information from all three tests into one. You'll have a little bit of research to do about this new chi-squared distribution."*

   a.   Aliah says, *"I think that might be helpful here! We have three standard normal random variables with our three z-scores. It kind of makes sense. We have been squaring and adding things a lot in this class."* Take the three z-scores that they have calculated, and find the value of the "chi-squared test statistic" by squaring and adding them.

   b.   However, Tobiah is critical of this calculation. He says that the definition from Mrs. Hoppenheimer requires that the standard normal random variables would have to all be independent. Tobiah thinks that if he had any two of the three z-scores, he could have worked backward through the calculations to figure out what the third one had to be because they were all calculated based on a common pooled proportion. Mrs. Hoppenheimer smiles and says, *"Tobiah, you just uncovered the concept of a degree of freedom for this chi-squared distribution. The degrees of freedom are the number of values in a calculation that are free to vary. That is, they can't be calculated using other values."* What are the degrees of freedom in this setting?

   c.   Aliah says, *"So we have a single number that summarizes the differences in our three proportions compared to a common pooled proportion. It is supposed to follow this new chi-squared distribution that results from adding squared standard normal. Because we have $\chi^2 = 2.8257$ and $df = 2$, I think we can calculate a p-value based on the region as or more extreme than $\chi^2 = 2.8257$. We already know how to use the cdf function of the normal distribution. I found a cdf function for χ^2!"* Use this cdf function to calculate a p-value as the "tail probability."

9-4.   Tobiah really likes what his group accomplished today, especially discovering that they can square and add standard normal random variables to work with a new known distribution. He feels as though he would be fully convinced if he could see the same method work with a test comparing two proportions.

   a.   Quickly run the "Calculate" step of a two-tailed significance test for the difference of two proportions as detailed in the Math Notes box in Lesson 8.2.3, comparing Jermaine (162 out of 200) and Aliah (170 out of 200) only. Write down the z-score and p-value.

   b.   Calculate a "pooled" proportion representing the combination of both samples.

   c.   Carry out the "Calculate" step for two separate one-proportion significance tests shown in the Math Notes box in Lesson 8.1.3, comparing Jermaine and Aliah to the pooled proportion as the null hypothesis. Write down each z-score and calculate the chi-squared statistic from the two z-scores.

   d.   Use the cdf function of the chi-squared distribution to find the p-value. How many degrees of freedom will you use?

   e.   How did the two procedures compare? Just for fun, also square your z-score in part (a). What do you notice?

9-5.   Tobiah has been thinking about why he needed to run a two-*tailed* significance test for the difference in proportions in order for the *p*-values to match. He thinks that it might have something to do with squaring the negative z-scores. Discuss among your team why squaring might automatically make the chi-squared procedure the equivalent of a two-tailed procedure involving proportions.

9-6.   Demonstrate that the chi-squared methods can also be used in place of a two-tailed significance test of one proportion. Try testing H_A: $p \neq 0.4$ with a sample proportion of $\frac{110}{250}$. Calculate a *p*-value both using a standard significance test for one proportion and again using this chi-squared procedure (with one degree of freedom).

MATH NOTES

Chi-Squared (χ^2) Distribution

The chi-squared distribution with k degrees of freedom is derived from the sum of k independent standard normal random variables.

The general shape of the chi-squared distribution is skewed to the right, and it is centered about its degrees of freedom. (The mean for the distribution is equal to the degrees of freedom.) Notice how the example at the right for df = 8 is centered about 8 for the chi-squared statistic.

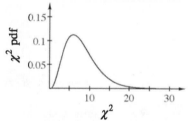

The variance (the square of the standard deviation) for the chi-squared distribution is twice the degrees of freedom. So for the distribution displayed, the variance is $2 \cdot 8 = 16$. The standard deviation would then be 4.

Knowing the mean and standard deviation help you know whether a value of χ^2 should be considered "typical" or "unusual." For this distribution, $\chi^2 = 10$ would be considered relatively typical because it is within one standard deviation of the expected value (the mean). $\chi^2 = 18$ would be more unusual because it is more than 2 standard deviations from the mean.

9-7.   A certain state has a requirement that only one largemouth bass greater than 16 inches in length can be kept per day while fishing. A random sample of largemouth bass is collected at three popular lakes. The proportions of largemouth bass longer than 16 inches for each of these samples are: $\frac{7}{54}$, $\frac{9}{58}$, and $\frac{17}{56}$.

   a.   Find the "pooled proportion."

   b.   Run three separate one-proportion tests ("calculate" step only), comparing each sample proportion to this pooled proportion as the value of the parameter. Write down each z-score.

   c.   Square each z-score, and add them to calculate the chi-squared test statistic. What are the degrees of freedom?

   d.   Calculate a *p*-value based on the chi-squared test statistic.

9-8.   The marketing manager of a leading photography company claims that no more than 80% of all U.S. adults rate their photography skills as good to excellent. The manager commissions a polling agency to take a random sample of 1000 U.S. adults. The agency finds that 77% of the adults they sampled claim to rate their photography skills as good to excellent. Based on these results, should you accept or reject the manager's claim at the 0.05 significance level?

   a.   State the null and alternative hypothesis.

   b.   What type of test should be done?

   c.   Assume conditions are satisfied, complete the test and interpret the results.

   d.   Based on your conclusion in part (c), what type of error (Type I or Type II) could have been made? Clearly explain this error in the context of the problem.

9-9.   Do low birth weight babies start crawling at a later age than babies born at an average weight? A psychologist collected and then sorted the following data for the age at which children started crawling:

low weight: 7, 10, 10, 10, 10, 11, 11, 11, 11, 11, 12, 12, 13, 13, 14, 15 months
checksum: 181

average weight: 5, 6, 6, 6, 7, 7, 7, 7, 7, 7, 7, 8, 8, 8, 8, 8, 9, 9, 10, 10, 11, 12, 13 months
checksum: 186

Refer to the Math Notes box in Lesson 1.2.4 and compare the distributions of crawling ages in detail. Include appropriate graphics.

9.1.2 Do these counts match what I expected?

Chi-Squared Goodness of Fit

There are mathematical models of real-life scenarios that predict observations to occur in certain proportions. This could be the distribution of lottery winnings, the physical characteristics of a species of plant, or the frequency of outcomes on a fair die, or the frequencies of first-digits in audited numerical records for a large company.

In these scenarios, a set of observed frequencies are compared, using the expected proportions, to a set of expected frequencies. The question is then posed: *"Do my observed frequencies seem to fit the same distribution as the expected frequencies?"*

Benford's Law

Benford's law predicts that in naturally occurring sets of numbers (like the price of an automobile, the population of a country, the heights of oak trees, the volume of freshwater lakes, the distances to observable stars) the leading significant digit (the first digit) is likely to be small and follow a known distribution. Specifically, the first digit d (from the set of integers 1 to 9) has the following probability: $p(d) = \log(d + 1) - \log(d)$. The following table of probabilities can be constructed for the leading significant digit:

d	1	2	3	4	5	6	7	8	9
$P(d)$	0.301	0.1761	0.1249	0.0969	0.0792	0.0669	0.058	0.0512	0.0458

Application of Benford's Law

Assume researchers investigating the heights of white oak trees in a large forest obtained the following data (units are feet) for a random sample of white oak trees. Anything from a short sapling to a full-grown tree was included in the sample.

48.39	2.58	2.77	25.36	23.00	45.94	15.45	81.55	19.60	4.75	5.53	3.56
100.87	1.45	33.83	3.17	84.73	106.92	2.54	28.18	4.91	3.57	21.24	2.09
20.20	117.84	10.21	43.31	4.35	1.32	3.75	69.81	51.29	93.4	49.05	8.67
1.77	2.51	11.58	1.79	31.69	61.25	45.36	93.65	2.55	1.63	1.71	1.03
20.51	3.04	17.08	27.59	17.13	7.87	48.83	26.62	13.54	11.97	7.10	38.2
3.62	23.81	99.34	16.62	74.20	135.44	105.33	6.55	19.42	8.68	18.56	59.56
30.23	57.20	40.25	31.30	5.92	2.10	2.11	22.4	10.69	11.27	7.02	1.31
23.94	8.04	89.72	4.10	81.78	10.81	6.18	32.44	32.15	15.18	1.56	117.29
1.91	3.15	8.11	24.86	123.45	13.60	7.80	137.18	9.72	3.35	3.01	93.99
5.53	10.23	1.25	12.72	1.13	140.25	1.15	28.56	1.17	17.15	3.59	77.41

9-10.   Make a copy of the blank table below. Assign the first digits 1 to 9 to members of your team and have each person make a count of their first digits of tree heights. Share your counts and double check that all counts add to 120!

1st digit	1	2	3	4	5	6	7	8	9
count									

9-11.   Based on the table of expected frequencies for Benford's law, make another table of expected frequencies if Benford's law holds true. (Hint: You will need to use the fact that there are 120 trees in the sample.) Note that expected frequencies need not be integers. An **expected count** of 6.2, for example, simply means that you expect to observe something close to 6 for that category. Keep at least a few decimals of accuracy in your expected counts! (Double-check that your expected counts also add to 120 *within reasonable rounding error*. You should not expect more or fewer trees than you observed!)

9-12.   In a statistical test of significance, the null hypothesis usually says something similar to "nothing is going on, everything is as expected," and the alternative hypothesis says, "something is going on, at least one category differs from expected." Ask the question, "Do the white oak tree heights seem to follow Benford's law?" Write out a carefully constructed null and alternative hypothesis in this context. Due to the number of parameters involved, these will often be written as complete English sentences rather than symbolic statements.

9-13.   Before any statistical inference procedure is carried out, a series of questions should be asked. In general, these questions are: Was this data randomly gathered? Is each "trial" independent? Is the sample size large enough? (Note: For procedures involving counts (or proportions) and multiple categories, it is common to reduce the requirement for 10 "yes" to 5 for each.) Answer each of these three questions in context.

9-14.   In Lesson 9.1.1, the chi-squared distribution was introduced as: "The chi-squared distribution with k degrees of freedom are the sum of the squares of k independent standard normal random variables." When considering individual counts (such as one category today), each count can be "standardized" like this: $\frac{\text{observed} - \text{expected}}{\sqrt{\text{expected}}}$. These each roughly follow a standard normal curve after the appropriate conditions have been met above. Since the chi-squared statistic is the sum of squared independent standard normal random variables, you simply add $\frac{(\text{observed} - \text{expected})^2}{\text{expected}}$ for each count in the table. Each observed/expected pair creates a "contribution" to the overall chi-squared statistic. Find each "contribution", and then report the chi-squared statistic as the sum.

9-15.   The expected counts always have the same sum as the
         observed counts. If you were to be missing one of the
         expected counts, it could easily be calculated. The
         degrees of freedom, then, are one less than the number of
         categories. At right is the sketch of the chi-squared
         distribution with 8 degrees of freedom (notice that the
         distribution is centered about its own degrees of freedom).
         Make a sketch of the distribution. Label your chi-squared
         statistic from problem 9-14, and shade the area to the
         right of your statistic. Find this area. This is the p-value.

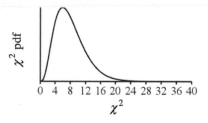

9-16.   Write a conclusion for this statistical test in context. Use the p-value as part of your response.

9-17.   While in Cameroon studying endangered populations of giraffes, Eric collected height data on
         a random sample of 116 giraffes and calculated the following expected frequencies for each
         quartile assuming giraffe heights are normally distributed:

	Sample Quartile			
	Q1	Q2	Q3	Q4
Observed Frequencies	29	29	29	29
Expected Frequencies	31.3	38.5	29.5	16.7

Are giraffe weights normally distributed at a 0.01 significance? Conduct a chi-squared
goodness of fit test.

9-18.   A large candy company claims that a certain type of candy is produced, by color, at the
         following relative frequencies: Blue: 18%, Green: 24%, Red: 24%, Purple: 18%, and Yellow:
         16%. You gather a random sample of this candy, and you observe: Blue: 23, Green: 45, Red:
         47, Purple: 28, and Yellow: 22.

Carry out a chi-squared goodness of fit test, at a 5% level of significance, to test whether the
observed candy in your sample agrees with the stated proportions from the company.

a.   Write a null and alternative hypothesis.

b.   What evidence in favor of H_A does the sample provide?

c.   Verify that the conditions necessary for inference have been met.

d.   Find the chi-squared test-statistic and p-value. Record the degrees of freedom used in
      your calculation.

e.   Based on your p-value and the level of significance, write a conclusion in context.

9-19. Zach is doing an experiment on whether or not playing different modes of a video game can raise your blood pressure. He randomly assigns 120 students from his school to two treatments. 60 students will play Call of Battle: Limit to Infinite in the online mode, while the other 60 will play offline. He then measures their blood pressure after 20 minutes of playing. Zach found that 42 of the online players raised their systolic figure to over 131, while 34 of the offline players had a systolic figure over 131.

A test of significance ($\alpha = 0.05$) was conducted on the following hypotheses: the percent of high blood pressure players is the same for both treatments (H_0), and a larger percentage of people playing the game online will have high blood pressure (H_A).

This test resulted in a p-value of 0.0648.

a. Interpret the results of the test. Specifically, interpret the p-value and what conclusions can be drawn from this experiment.

b. Based on your explanation from part (a), what type of error (Type I or Type II) could have been made? Clearly explain this error in the context of the problem.

9-20. While working at his father's law office observing billing categories of clients, Nicholas researched a random sample of 27 clients which yielded the following summary regarding the relationship between costs billed to clients and litigation time.

Cost to Client (1000s of $) vs. Litigation Time (hours)

Regression Output for Cost to Client vs. Litigation Time

Predictor	Coef	SE Coef	T	P
Constant	-2.92	0.20	-14.31	0.00
Litigation Time	0.90	0.01	112.71	0.00

S = 0.491   R-Sq = 0.9513   R-Sq(Adj)= 0.9513

a. Describe the association between costs billed to clients and litigation time as seen in the sample.

b. Determine R-squared and its meaning in the context of this sample.

c. Discuss the standard deviation of the residuals and what it tells you about the relationship between negotiation time and litigation time.

9.1.3 Is this a reasonable assumption given these counts?

χ^2

More Applications of Chi-Squared Goodness of Fit

In Lesson 9.1.2, the question was posed, *"Do my observed frequencies seem to fit the same distribution as the expected frequencies?"* You will further explore this question in a variety of settings. The expected frequencies can come from many possible sources.

For problems 9-21 through 9-24, conduct a full procedure for each. Write out an appropriate null and alternative hypothesis, verify that the conditions have been met for the underlying assumptions, calculate a chi-squared test statistic and *p*-value, and write a conclusion in context. A 5% level of significance can be assumed for each of these settings.

9-21. *IS THIS A FAIR DIE?*

A die is rolled 600 times, and the outcomes are displayed below. Does the die appear to be fair? Conduct an appropriate test.

X	1	2	3	4	5	6
Freq	97	107	101	96	108	91

9-22. In Mendelian genetics, a dihybrid cross is a cross between two parents that are both heterozygous ("hybrid") for two ("di") observed traits, each with two possible observable expressions. A classic example is of a type of seed that is either yellow or green and either wrinkled or smooth. The following Punnett square can be constructed displaying all possible outcomes.

	AB	Ab	aB	ab
AB	AABB Yellow, Round	AABb Yellow, Round	AaBB Yellow, Round	AaBb Yellow, Round
Ab	AABb Yellow, Round	AAbb Yellow, Wrinkled	AaBb Yellow, Round	Aabb Yellow, Wrinkled
aB	AaBB Yellow, Round	AaBb Yellow, Round	aaBB Green, Round	aaBb Green, Round
ab	AaBb Yellow, Round	Aabb Yellow, Wrinkled	aaBb Green, Round	aabb Green, Wrinkled

The observed characteristics happen in the ratio 9:3:3:1. (For example, you can count 9 of the above boxes that contain "Yellow, Round.")

Problem continues on next page →

A group of scientists conducts an experiment to determine if this model does in fact account for the differences in observed traits. They mate an SRS of 256 plants and obtain the following data:

154	51	39	12
Yellow, Round	Yellow, Wrinkled	Green, Round	Green, Wrinkled

Do the observed traits appear to follow this model of Mendelian genetics? Conduct an appropriate statistical test.

9-23.   Years ago, a census was taken in a large U.S. city to determine the ethnic origin of its residence. Data was recorded regarding the continent for which the city resident considered most significant in his or her ethnic heritage. The following relative frequencies resulted.

Asia	Africa	North America	South America	Europe	Australia
0.13	0.12	0.28	0.09	0.35	0.03

The city planners suspect that there has been a shift in the population of the city. They obtain a SRS of 500 city residents, and the following are observed:

Asia	Africa	North America	South America	Europe	Australia
93	57	132	46	159	13

a.   Does the data suggest that there has been a shift in the ethnic background of the population of this city? Conduct an appropriate test.

b.   With a chi-squared goodness of fit test, the test itself does not reveal *which* category is responsible for any statistically significant difference. It only concludes that at least one category differs significantly from what was expected. Even so, an analysis of the contributions to the overall chi-squared statistic can help provide an indicator for future research. Which category had the largest contribution to the test-statistic? What was the contribution?

9-24.   The square root of 2 is a famous number, dating at least as far as the ancient Babylonians. The existence of irrational numbers was a topic of debate among the Pythagoreans. It was, as thought by some, considered outrageous that a square's sides would be "incommensurable" with its diagonal. Today, it is assumed that the decimal representation of $\sqrt{2}$ never repeats and goes on indefinitely forever. An analysis was done on the first 10,000 digits of the decimal representation of $\sqrt{2}$. The frequency of each digit is reported in the table below.

Digit	0	1	2	3	4	5	6	7	8	9
Freq	952	1005	1004	980	1016	1001	1032	964	1027	1019

Do the digits of $\sqrt{2}$ seem to be uniformly distributed? Conduct an appropriate statistical test.

MATH NOTES

Chi-Squared Goodness of Fit Test

The chi-squared goodness of fit test is used to test whether a set of observed counts "fits" an expected distribution of counts. The expected counts are calculated based on some external ideal (such as uniformity) or set of assumed proportions or ratios.

Step 1: Identify the appropriate test, null and alternative hypotheses and sample evidence in favor of the alternative hypothesis and decide on a significance level. Usually the null and alternative hypothesis is written in the form of a sentence in context rather than using symbols. An example out of context might be:

H_0: The distribution of the variable is as described.
H_A: The distribution differs from the description in at least one category

Step 2: Check conditions for inference. The conditions are very similar as those for proportion tests. Random sampling is needed to avoid bias. Independent trials and large counts are both needed to insure the sampling distribution is approximately chi-squared. For the large counts condition, at least 80% (preferably all) of the expected counts should be *at least 5* Make sure to check the *expected* counts, not the observed ones.

Step 3: Calculate the expected counts and the "chi-squared contributions" for each observed/expected count pair. As a "quality control" check, verify that the observed and expected counts have the same sum. They should!

The chi-squared statistic is calculated as: $\chi^2 = \sum \frac{(O-E)^2}{E}$ with "categories – 1" degrees of freedom.

Calculate a *p*-value by using the cdf function of the chi-squared distribution. The *p*-value is the area to the right of the chi-squared statistic. Make sure to report the test statistic, p-value, and degrees of freedom.

Step 4: Write a conclusion in context. Compare the *p*-value to α. If the *p*-value is less than α, accept the alternative hypothesis that the true distribution of the variable differs from the described distribution. Otherwise, fail to accept that alternative.

9-25.   A state lottery produces a scratch-off game with the following prizes: No prize ($0), $1, $5, $10, and $50. The tickets are reported to be produce according to the ratio (in the same order): 10:60:30:20:1

   a.   Calculate the expected value (the expected prize) and the standard deviation for this scratch-off game.

   b.   If the state sells these scratch-off tickets for $5 each, how much profit should the state expect to make on the sale of 500,000 tickets?

   c.   An independent group was hired to test the state's prize frequencies by gathering a large, independent sample. 500 tickets were purchased, and the counts for each prize (in the same order) were: 67, 226, 130, 75, 2. Is there evidence, at a 5% level of significance, that the state is not producing the tickets at the advertised ratios? Conduct an appropriate test, carrying out all relevant steps.

9-26.   A fish biologist tags 150 fish and releases them into a lake. Two months later he takes a sample of fish by applying a mild electrical current to the middle of the lake and netting the stunned fish that float to the top. The fish were then counted and returned to the lake. Of the 297 in the sample, 14 were tagged.

   a.   Find and interpret a 95% confidence interval for the actual percent of tagged fish in the lake.

   b.   Based on your results from part (a), what is a reasonable interval estimate for the total number of fish in the lake. Comment on its usefulness.

   c.   What could be done to make the intervals more precise?

9-27.   People of Madelinton are security-conscious and have sophisticated car alarms installed on their cars. Over the course of a year these alarms correctly distinguish between a break-in attempt and other harmless events at a 99% rate. Of the 820,600 cars in Madelinton about 100 are broken into each year. If a citizen of Madelinton hears a car alarm, what is the probability the car is being broken into?

9.2.1 Are these two characteristics independent?

Chi-Squared Test for Independence

Back in Mrs. Hoppenheimer's class, Aliah and Tobiah continue their study of Trashketball.

After Tobiah's analysis of the distribution of types of paper being thrown, Aliah wonders if the different types of paper influence how often it goes in. Her hypothesis is that some may be more "sturdy" or have more mass and therefore be easier to throw. She sets up an experiment where one student throws each type of paper in Tobiah's experiment. She randomly chose paper from each type. To ensure that each toss represents an independent toss, it was randomly decided what type of paper each toss would be before the toss was made. Aliah hoped that this would help account for a possible confounding variable of skill growth over time. Her data is displayed in the table below.

	Lined paper	Graph paper	Copy paper	Cardstock	
Make Basket	71	78	89	65	303
Miss Basket	29	22	31	15	97
	100	100	120	80	400

Aliah says, *"Look, my hypothesis is correct! The lined paper was the thinnest and lightest, and it had the lowest proportion of shots made. The cardstock was the heaviest paper, and it had the highest proportion of shots made."* Jermaine is nervous about making such a quick conclusion. He wants to be convinced that the differences observed are actually significant.

9-28. The structure of this two-way table reminds Tobiah of his study of probability and asking whether two events are independent. He recognizes that one categorical variable is the success of the shot made, and the other categorical variable is the type of paper. He says, *"I think I can figure out what the first cell in the table (the 71) would have to be if the events 'a randomly chosen piece of paper was lined' and 'a randomly chosen basket was made' are independent."* He writes down the following:

$$P(\text{make basket}) = \tfrac{303}{400} = 0.7575 \text{ and } P(\text{make basket} \mid \text{lined paper}) = \tfrac{71}{100} = 0.71$$

These are close, but not exactly the same.

a. What if Tobiah applies the marginal proportions ($\frac{303}{400}$ and $\frac{97}{400}$) to the column representing the 100 pieces of lined paper in the sample. Do it! Do the counts you just calculated represent what would be expected if the two events "a randomly chosen piece of paper was lined" and "a randomly chosen basket was made" are <u>perfectly independent</u>? Briefly explain.

b. Extend Tobiah's reasoning to "re-proportion" each type of paper to match the proportions observed in the marginal distribution. Label this table your expected counts. Also, fill out the margins of the table of expected counts. What do you notice about the margins of the expected count table?

9-29.   Aliah thinks that she can now write a well-worded null hypothesis. She says, *"Rather than focusing on one specific pair of events in this table such as 'the paper was lined' and 'the basket was made,' we can focus on the two categorical variables themselves. I bet we can use our chi-squared procedures to test all of these pairs between observed and expected in one test. This would allow us to test whether the two categorical variables themselves are independent or whether there is evidence that there is some significant evidence of a dependence or association between the two."*

Extend Aliah's thinking by constructing a well-written null and alternative hypothesis in this context. These will be written as sentences again (rather than trying to use symbols).

9-30.   Tobiah continues his thinking with expected counts. He says, *"We learned earlier that, in a context like this, repeated observations of $\frac{\text{observed} - \text{expected}}{\sqrt{\text{expected}}}$ for a single count roughly followed a standard normal distribution. When we squared it to get $\frac{(\text{observed} - \text{expected})^2}{\text{expected}}$, we were able to add each of these together to build a chi-squared statistic. I think we can do this here as well for each of the 8 counts in the table. Each observed/expected paring will make a contribution to the overall chi-squared statistic, and we will have a single number that communicates the overall difference between observed and expected if the variables are independent."*

Do it! Organize each contribution to the chi-squared statistic into a table. Add the 8 contributions up to form the chi-squared statistic.

9-31.   The group wants to make sure that the appropriate conditions for inference have been met. They ask themselves the same questions: Does the data represent a random sample? Were individual observations independent? Was the sample size large enough? Investigate these questions in context.

9-32. Aliah and Jermaine disagree at what the degrees of freedom should be. Aliah thinks it should be 3, and Jermaine thinks it should be 7. Jermaine says, *"There are 8 contributions. The degrees of freedom are usually one less, so it should be 7."* Aliah says, *"Yes, but each of the numbers in the margin was used in our calculations for expected values. I think there is some dependence going on there. If I hide an entire row and an entire column, I can reconstruct the missing values."*

	Lined paper	Graph paper	Copy paper	Cardstock	
Make Basket					
Miss Basket		22	31	15	97
		100	120	80	400

Test out Aliah's idea. Could the hidden values in the table be reconstructed based on the <u>three</u> counts displayed? What do you think the degrees of freedom are for this setting?

9-33. Now that you have a chi-squared statistic and a degrees of freedom, Tobiah suggests that his group calculate a *p*-value. Sketch a picture of the chi-squared distribution. Label your degrees of freedom as the center (it is a skewed-right distribution, so make your best attempt at labeling "center"), and label your chi-squared statistic as well. Shade the area that represents the *p*-value. Then find it!

9-34. Aliah says, *"I see now that we do not have sufficient evidence to reject our null hypothesis."* How did Aliah come to this conclusion? What conclusion, in context, does her group make?

MATH NOTES

Chi-Squared Independence Test

The chi-squared independence test is used to test whether an association (dependence) exists between two categorical variables. An example might be, "Is there an association between ethnicity and political party affiliation?" A single sample would be collected, and each person's ethnicity and political affiliation would be recorded.

The procedure is carried out in the following steps:

Step 1: Identify the appropriate test, null and alternative hypotheses, and sample evidence in favor of the alternative hypothesis and decide on a significance level.

The null and alternative hypothesis is written in the form of a sentence again. The null hypothesis always assumes that the two categorical variables are independent. Using the same context with ethnicity and political affiliation, you would write:

H_0: Ethnicity and political affiliation are independent.

H_A: Ethnicity and political affiliation are not independent.

An equivalent pair of hypotheses would be:

H_0: Ethnicity and political affiliation are not associated.

H_A: Ethnicity and political affiliation are associated.

In either case, the null hypothesis is the equivalent of saying, "nothing is going on," and the alternative hypothesis is the equivalent of saying, "something is going on."

Step 2: Check conditions for inference. The conditions are the same as for the chi-squared goodness of fit test. All expected counts must be at least 5 (in addition to randomly gathered data and independent observations).

Step 3: Calculate the expected counts and the "chi-squared contributions" for each observed/expected count pair. Create a table (a matrix) of expected counts with the same dimensions as the observed counts. Each individual expected count can be found by calculating $\frac{(\text{row total}) \cdot (\text{column total})}{\text{overall total}}$. All "chi-squared contributions" can be found by pairing observed and expected values in the tables and calculating $\chi^2 = \sum \frac{(O-E)^2}{E}$.

Finally, calculate a *p*-value by using the cdf function of the chi-squared distribution. The degrees of freedom are found by "covering up" a row and column in one of the tables and counting the number of values that remain or calculating (# of rows − 1) · (# of columns − 1). The *p*-value is the area to the right of the chi-squared statistic.

Step 4: Write a conclusion in context. Compare the *p*-value to α. If the *p*-value is less than α, accept the alternative hypothesis that the variables are associated. Otherwise, fail to accept that hypothesis.

9-35.   Eliza is collecting data on potential relationships between one having an urban residential demographic and an optimistic outlook on the economy. Assume a survey of 200 randomly selected persons revealed:

	Residential Demographic		
	Rural	Suburban	Urban
Positive Opinion	20	21	51
Negative Opinion	15	24	69

Are the variables residential demographic and outlook on the economy independent? Conduct an appropriate statistical test.

9-36.   A scientist is studying a certain type of insect, and the scientist is wondering if the size of the insect is related to the loudness of chirp. The scientist counts each insect as either large, medium, or small. The chirps are rated at volume levels 1, 2, or 3.

	V. Level 1	V. Level 2	V. Level 3	
Large	35	32	38	105
Medium	32	35	31	98
Small	33	34	30	97
	100	101	99	300

Conduct an appropriate test, reporting all relevant steps.

9-37.   Jada lives in an apartment building that has posted quiet hours from 11 p.m. to 7 a.m. However, her neighbor has a parrot that squawks loudly whenever it wakes up in the morning. Annoyed, Jada has begun keeping track of the times that the parrot squawks during quiet hours in in terms of minutes before 7 a.m. Her data suggests that the times are approximately normally distributed with a mean of 18 minutes and a standard deviation of 15 minutes.

a.   Find the probability that the parrot wakes up before 6:30 a.m.

b.   Assuming that each day is independent, what is the probability that over the next week Jada will hear a noisy parrot before 6:30 a.m. on three or more of the days?

9-38. A school has just finished building a new athletic stadium. The results of a survey claim that 93% of all people are satisfied with the new stadium. For each example below, identify the type of sample taken and who is included in the population.

    a. The survey was conducted by interviewing every 10th person to enter the stadium for a soccer game.

    b. The survey was emailed to all households with students enrolled in the school district.

    c. The school district was divided into neighborhoods and then five of those neighborhoods were randomly selected. Interviewers went door-to-door with the survey in each of those neighborhoods. Two additional attempts were made to contact households where no one was home.

9.2.2 Are these populations proportioned the same?

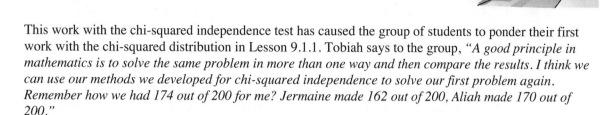

Chi-Squared Test for Homogeneity of Proportions

This work with the chi-squared independence test has caused the group of students to ponder their first work with the chi-squared distribution in Lesson 9.1.1. Tobiah says to the group, *"A good principle in mathematics is to solve the same problem in more than one way and then compare the results. I think we can use our methods we developed for chi-squared independence to solve our first problem again. Remember how we had 174 out of 200 for me? Jermaine made 162 out of 200, Aliah made 170 out of 200."*

Tobiah suggests that the group structure their data in a table like this:

	Jermaine	Aliah	Tobiah	
Make Basket	162	170	174	506
Miss Basket	38	30	26	94
	200	200	200	600

Tobiah continues his thoughts and says, *"See how this looks just like our data with the chi-squared independence test? We have two categorical variables: The person shooting the basket and the status of whether the shot went in. Could we approach the test for significance in the same way?"*

Aliah says, *"I agree that we could approach it in the same way, but there is a key difference. In this test, one of the categorical variables actually represents three independent samples from three independent populations. In our chi-squared independence test, there was only one actual sample."*

Jermaine adds his thoughts, saying, *"In our original problem, we wanted to know if our three proportions were essentially the same or if there was evidence that at least one was difference. I think that we can try to solve this problem again using the same technique as our chi-squared independence test, but we should call it something different. Something related to proportions being the same."* Mrs. Hoppenheimer smiled as she overheard the conversation. She suggested that the students use the name "chi-squared test for homogeneity of proportions."

9-39.   Tobiah suggests to the group that if they are going to use the same calculation methods as with chi-squared independence, they should be able to use the same method for calculating expected counts. The only problem was that these were calculated based on a concept of independence. Help convince Tobiah that the same technique could be applied to this data if the assumption is made that the proportions of success are the same for each of the three students. Then construct a table of expected counts.

9-40.　The team of students wants to phrase the null and alternative hypothesis in terms of homogeneity of proportions. Help them to carefully word a null and alternative hypothesis.

9-41.　The team wonders if the conditions for inference have been met. They list the same conditions but add a condition that since there were multiple independent samples, they wanted to make it clear that the samples themselves are also independent. Verify for this group that their conditions for inference have been satisfied.

9-42.　Finish the chi-squared test for homogeneity of proportions. Calculate each of the contributions to the chi-squared statistic as well as the chi-squared statistic itself, calculate a p-value, and write a conclusion in context. Did the analysis agree with the group's original analysis in Lesson 9.1.1?

9-43.　The school district that Jermaine, Aliah, and Tobiah are part of is trying to pass a referendum with local voters to build a new school. The city is broken into four districts, and the school board has asked Mrs. Hoppenheimer's class to conduct a study in each of the four districts to estimate the proportion of voters who will vote "yes" for the referendum. The class obtains a SRS from each of the four districts and records the following data. Is there evidence, at a 5% level of significance, that the voter status categories are proportioned the same in each of the districts?

	District 1	District 2	District 3	District 4	
Vote Yes	152	136	151	164	603
Vote No	28	42	38	32	140
Undecided	40	22	31	14	107
	220	200	220	210	850

a.　What wording in the question statement indicates that this problem will be represented with a chi-squared test for homogeneity of proportions?

b.　How might the problem be reworded to indicate that a chi-squared independence test would be more appropriate? Would this change the calculations of the test statistic and p-value?

c.　Carry out the full chi-squared test for homogeneity of proportions. Interpret the results in context.

d.　Which combination of district and response had the largest contribution to the chi-squared test statistic?

MATH NOTES

Chi-Squared Test for Homogeneity of Proportions

The chi-squared test for homogeneity of proportions used to test whether the proportion of categories of counts across multiple populations are the same ("homogeneous"). An example might be, "Are the proportions of students who eat hot-lunch at school the same for each ethnic subgroup in these four large districts?"

The procedure is carried out in the following steps:

Step 1: Identify the appropriate test, null and alternative hypotheses and sample evidence in favor of the alternative hypothesis and decide on a significance level.

The null and alternative hypothesis is written in the form of a sentence again. The null hypothesis always assumes that the proportions are in fact homogenous across the multiple populations. Using the same context with eating hot-lunch at school, you would write:

H_0: The proportions of students who eat hot-lunch, for each subgroup, are the same at all four districts

H_A: At least one district has a subgroup whose proportion of students who eat hot-lunch differs significantly from the other districts.

Sample evidence for the alternative would be that the observed and expected frequencies do not match. Use a significance level of 0.05 unless stated otherwise in the problem.

Step 2: Check conditions for inference. The conditions are the same as for the chi-squared goodness of fit test. All expected counts must be at least 5 (in addition to randomly gathered data and independent observations). Because multiple samples are taken from multiple populations, there is the added condition that all samples themselves are independent from one another.

Step 3: Calculate the expected counts and the "chi-squared contributions" for each observed/expected count pair. The calculation procedure is identical to the calculations involved in the chi-squared independence test.

Step 4: Write a conclusion in context. Compare the p-value to α. If the p-value is less than α, accept the alternative hypothesis that the variables differ in at least one subgroup. Otherwise, fail to accept that hypothesis.

9-44.   A researcher is interested in determining whether environmental conditions (based on geographic location) may be linked with fidgeting and seat-time. An experiment is designed where random samples of 5 year old children are gathered from three different cities. The child was instructed to sit in a chair and is given a toy to play with. The researcher observed the child and recorded the amount of time the child remained in the chair before getting up.

	City 1	City 2	City 3
Less than 1 minute	24	18	22
Between 1 and 3 minutes	18	25	19
More than 3 minutes	8	7	9

Is there evidence, at a 5% level of significance, that the proportion of seat times differs in at least one of the cities? Conduct an appropriate test, reporting all relevant steps.

9-45.   Meg is at volleyball tryouts. On squad A there are 6 juniors and 4 seniors. On squad B there are 3 juniors and 7 seniors. Two practice captains are to be selected randomly, one from squad A and one from squad B.

a.   If Meg is a junior on Squad A, what is the probability she will be a captain with one of her classmates?

b.   What is the probability that both captains are from the same class?

c.   The coach announces that one of the captains is a junior and the other is a senior, what is the probability that Meg is a captain?

9-46.   Grace is working at her brother's coffee shop observing the production of donuts. Grace believes donut calorie counts are normally distributed.

Sketch the normal probability density functions. If the 18th percentile is 256.65 Cal, and the 91st percentile is 324.56 Cal, find the mean and standard deviation.

9.2.3 How do I choose which chi-squared procedure to use?

Practicing and Recognizing Chi-Squared Inference Procedures

Aliah, Jermaine, and Tobiah realize that they have learned a powerful procedure with their chi-squared methods. It can apply to many situations involving categorical data and counts. In order to help each other grasp the methods, they create a variety problem for each other to solve. Their strategy is to categorize each problem as chi-squared goodness of fit, independence, or homogeneity of proportions *before* solving it. They agree to do a full write-up (identify the procedure, write out null/alternative hypothesis, verify conditions, make calculations, conclusion in context) for each problem for practice.

Solve each of these problems below using the group's ideas above.

9-47. Mrs. Hoppenheimer loves to tell jokes during class. She wonders if the age (or grade level) of a student influences whether or not the student laughs at her jokes. She gathers a random sample of observations from her students and records the following data.

	9th grade	10th grade	11th grade	12th grade
Laughs	50	48	36	38
Does not laugh	12	12	24	20

a. Is there evidence, at a 5% level of significance, that students' grade levels influence whether a student laughs at Mrs. Hoppenheimer's jokes?

b. Which category (cell in the table) had the largest contribution to the chi-squared statistic?

9-48. Mr. Knolsen is notorious for giving very difficult short multiple choice chemistry quizzes. Each of his questions has 4 possible choices. He likes to give short quizzes that have 3 questions on them, and the students study very hard. The students band together and gather a random sample of results on these 3-question quizzes to investigate the distribution of scores. They obtain the following results:

Score	0	1	2	3
Number of students	140	140	56	6

Is there evidence, at a 5% level of significance, that studying did not help and the students were essentially just guessing on Mr. Knolsen's quizzes? (Hint: If they were guessing on each question, these counts would follow a binomial model for expected counts.)

9-49. Crafty, a large food company, is introducing a new product called "SMac" (Simple Macaroni and Cheese). It hires an outside company to distribute the new product to a random sample of adults from each of three large cities. The subjects were requested to test the product and indicate whether they would purchase it at a grocery store if available. The company wants to know if there is a strategy to which city they distribute the new product to first.

	City A	City B	City C
Would purchase	418	390	422
Would not purchase	182	220	188

Is there evidence, at a 5% level of significance, that one (or more) of these cities differ in proportion of people who would purchase the product?

9-50. Write a summary of how each chi-squared test can be recognized. When is a chi-squared goodness of fit test used? When is a chi-squared independence test used? When is a chi-squared test for homogeneity of proportions used?

Review & Preview

9-51. Burger 'N Bounce, a local fast-food restaurant with an indoor playground, makes a significant amount of profit off the sales of soft-drinks. The owner has been training the employees at the registers to ask customers whether they would like to purchase a drink. The owner has come up with two different ways of asking and has asked the employees to take part in the gathering of a random sample of data.

	No question	Wording #1	Wording #2
Buys drink	56	82	91
Does not buy drink	24	18	9

Is there evidence, at a 5% level of significance, that the employees' customer prompts are associated with the customers' purchasing choices? Conduct an appropriate test, reporting all relevant steps.

9-52.   Kayla is working at her sister's pizzeria studying the making of combination pizzas. A cluster sample of 30 pizzas yielded the following statistical information regarding the relationship between baking time and cost to make.

The mean baking time is 26.77 minutes with a standard deviation of 1.36 minutes. The mean cost to make is 13.87 dollars/lb with a standard deviation of 2.88 dollars/lb. The correlation coefficient is 0.7674.

a.   Determine the LSRL equation and label the variables in context.

b.   Describe the slope and explain what it tells you about the relationship between baking time and cost to make.

c.   Use the LSRL to predict the cost to make of a combination pizza whose baking time is 21.83 minutes.

d.   Calculate the residual for the point (28.10, 19.14).

e.   Is a linear model the most appropriate? How do you know?

f.   Kayla's sister is thinking of offering a personal size pizza for the lunch hour that bakes in just 10 minutes, would the LSRL make a reasonable estimate of the cost of this pizza? Explain

9-53.   Jack's shooting percentage last season in basketball was 62%. His goal this season is to make at least 70 of his first 100 shots.

a.   Assuming Jack shoots as well as he did last season, what is the probability he meets his goal?

b.   What is the probability that Jack makes less than half of his first 100 shots?

c.   What is the probability that Jack makes his first 5 shots before he misses?

Chapter 10

Drawing Conclusions From Quantitative Data

CHAPTER 10

Drawing Conclusions From Quantitative Data

Chapter Goals

Explore sampling distributions from a variety of quantitative statistics.

Create and interpret sampling distributions of means and medians through the use of simulation.

Use simulations to explore the Central Limit Theorem and generate rules for its use.

See the necessity of the t-distribution when performing quantitative inference using the sample standard deviation.

Use the t-distribution to make confidence intervals and perform tests of means.

In Chapters 7, 8, and 9 you performed statistical inference with categorical variables using samples to make statements about population differences and relationships. *But what can be inferred about populations using quantitative statistics like the mean and standard deviation?* The remaining chapters of this course are devoted to answering that question.

Chapter Outline

Section 10.1 Unlike categorical information which is typically limited to counts and proportions, quantitative samples provide an opportunity to explore a variety of different sampling distributions like median, variance, IQR, and mean. Using technology you will be looking for patterns and determining which sample statistics will be the most unbiased and consistent. You will then increase the your understanding of sampling distributions and confidence intervals by creating and interpreting them through the use of simulation.

Section 10.2 You will use simulations to explore the Central Limit Theorem and generate rules for its use. You will derive a general formula for the standard deviation of the sampling distribution of means.

$$S_n = \frac{X_1 + ... + X_n}{n}$$

Section 10.3 You will encounter the t-distribution and learn of its advantages and disadvantages by comparison with the standard normal or z-distribution. You will gain confidence with the t-distribution and use it to make confidence intervals of means.

10.1.1 What about quantitative data?

Quantitative Sampling Distributions

In the previous chapters, you have been exploring statistics from *categorical* data. Today you will begin to investigate what happens with *quantitative* data. Specifically, you will start with a realistic discrete data set.

There is an entire branch of study called forensic linguistics that uses statistics to try to answer questions such as "Did William Shakespeare really write all of his plays?" and "Did J.K. Rowling, author of *Harry Potter*, also write the mystery novel *The Cuckoo's Calling* under a pseudonym?"

One simple variable that is used as part of the statistical analysis for such question is the average word length. You will do some explorations with the average word length of some famous novels to explore the idea of sampling distributions with quantitative data.

10-1.   You will use an eTool to explore the average word length of *Alice's Adventures in Wonderland*, by Lewis Carroll.

   a.   Open the eTool and use the dropdown box under "Population" to select the "10-1 Alice in Wonderland word count" data set. (You do not need to change any other settings). Press "Update" and a graph should appear of the entire dataset. Sketch and briefly describe the distribution. Use the summary statistics provided next to the graph to support your description.

   b.   Would a normal distribution be an appropriate model for this data? Explain.

In Chapter 7, you explored the *sampling distribution of a sample proportion* using categorical data. With quantitative data, there is a sampling distribution for every statistic. Now look at a couple of them with this small population.

10-2.   To understand how this works, start by setting "Number of samples to draw" at 1 and set the sample size to 5. Click the "Draw!" button. The computer will simulate drawing 1 sample of 5 words from the original population. You should see three separate graphs now: the original population data, a histogram of the *most recent sample*, and a histogram of *all the means you have chosen so far*. Use the information on the screen to answer the following questions:

   a.   Find the mean and standard deviation of your most recent sample. What are they?

   b.   Find the mean and sample standard deviation of the actual population. Does the sample appear to be a reasonable estimate for those respective values?

Problem continues on next page →

10-2.   *Problem continued from previous page.*

c.   Why is the variance of the "Sample Means" distribution "NA"? (If it is not, you did something wrong—click the "delete all samples" button and try again!)

d.   By default, this tool scales each histogram to fit, but it can be easier to compare all distributions if they all have the same scale. Click the "Change scale?" checkbox next to each of the three graphs and set the scale for all three to go from 0 to 15. Where does the one bar you should have in the "Sample means" graph fall relative to the original population?

10-3.   Click the "Draw!" button about 10 more times, slowly. Describe what happens to the "Sample Means" graph for each click.

10-4.   Now speed it up! Change "Number of samples to draw" to 5000, then click the "Draw!" button. With so many samples, your "Sample Means" graph should now be a good approximation of the true *sampling distribution for the sample mean of size 5* from this population.

a.   Why is this not the entire sampling distribution?

b.   For the rest of this question, assume your simulated "Sample Means" distribution is a good approximation of the true sampling distribution.

Describe the sampling distribution of the sample means for this population and sample size and compare it to the distribution of the original population.

c.   An extremely important idea in statistical inference is *sampling variability*—that is, a measure of how much you can expect a statistic to typically vary from sample to sample. What aspect of the sampling distribution of the mean—shape, center, or spread—addresses the sampling variability of these sample means?

d.   Recall from Chapter 7 that a statistic (such as the sample means measured here) is called an *unbiased estimator of a parameter* if the statistic correctly estimates the parameter "on average"—if the mean of its sampling distribution equals the parameter. Based on your data, what is the mean value the sampling distribution for means for samples of size 5? Does the sample mean appear to be an unbiased estimator of the population mean?

e.   Would a normal model be appropriate to model the sampling distribution of the sample mean for samples of size 5 from this population, or is the distribution skewed?

10-5.   You will now explore another sampling distribution. Use the pull-down menus labeled "Graph" to change the "Most Recent Sample" graph to a "Median."

   a.   You will now see a graph that says "Sample Medians." This is the *simulated sampling distribution of the sample medians*—that is, a histogram of the median for every sample you have drawn so far. Describe the distribution, comparing it to both the sampling distribution of the mean and the original population distribution.

   b.   Does the sample median of size 5 appear to be an unbiased estimator of the population median, based on the definition in part (d) of problem 10-4?

   c.   Do sample medians appear to be *more variable*, *less variable*, or *approximately as variable* as sample means in this case? Use data about standard deviations to answer this question.

   d.   Would a normal distribution be an appropriate model for the sampling distribution of the median?

10-6.   If you click any bin on any of the histograms, it brings up a box that shows you the min and max of the bin, the count of elements in the bin, the relative frequency (pdf) of the bin, and the cumulative frequency (cdf) of the bin up to and including the bin.

   a.   Use this tool—specifically the cdf values—to roughly estimate the interval of the middle 90% of means for a random sample of size 5 from this population (do not worry about finding the perfect values, just get pretty close).

   b.   Do the same thing with the medians—between what two values do the middle 90% of sample medians lie?

10-7.   All of this exploration so far has been done with relatively small samples of size 5.

   a.   If you increase the sample size, what should happen to the variability of the sample means and medians?

   b.   Confirm your result. Change the sample size to 35 and collect 5000 new samples. Describe the sampling distributions of the mean and median and express how they changed with the larger sample size.

   c.   Does a normal distribution appear to be an appropriate model for either sampling distribution with sample size of 35?

10-8.   The images below represent a classic metaphor for bias vs. variability of a statistic. The arrows represent the statistic from various samples, while the bull's eye represents the parameter. Choose "high" or "low" for the bias and variability in each illustration as appropriate.

a.

b.

c.

d.

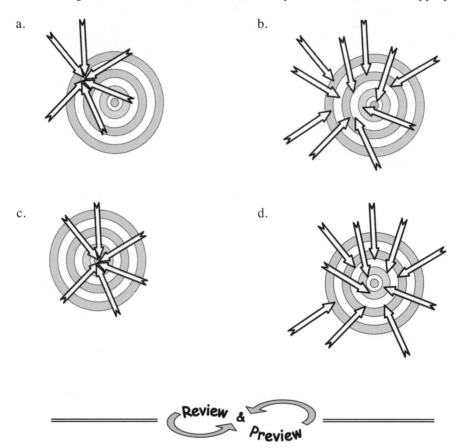

———————— Review & Preview ————————

10-9.   A classic Statistics estimation problem stems from WWII, when the Allies wanted to estimate the number of German tanks manufactured each month by using serial numbers.

Imagine the Germans had a simple serial number scheme where the first tank produced in a month was marked "1," the second "2," and so on. If the Allies captured 5 tanks from the same month—e.g. numbers 3, 17, 39, 64, and 98—they could use the numbers to try to estimate the number of the *last* tank produced that month. That would tell them how many tanks were made that month! In Statistics terms, they are trying to estimate the *population maximum* (a parameter!) using a statistic based on a sample of size 5.

Problem continues on next page →

Problem continued from previous page.

The pictures below shows simulated sampling distributions for four different statistics calculated from samples of size 5. The true maximum in the simulation, which they are trying to estimate, is 172 (represented by the arrow).

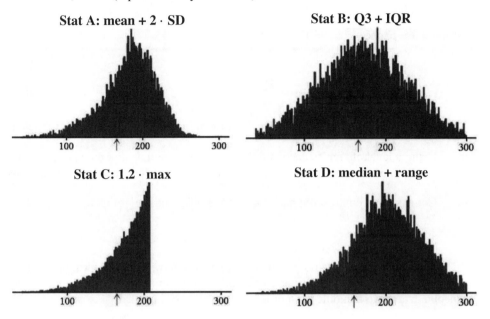

a.   Discuss each statistic in terms of its bias. (It is sometimes hard to tell if an estimate is *perfectly* unbiased based from only its graph, but it is usually possible to tell if it at least *could* be unbiased).

b.   Order the estimators from least variable to most variable.

c.   For this application, the best statistic is the one that is closest to the true value the most often. Which of the statistics seems to have the highest proportion of estimates within 25 tanks of the true value?

10-10.   Anna set up the following study at a local intersection. She sat at a stoplight intersection and recorded the number of people that used their cell phones during a red light. She also recorded their approximate age as teenager, adult, older adult. Her results are in the table below.

	Teenager	Young Adult	Older Adult	
Used phone	62		54	226
Did not use phone	141			
		325		1027

a.   Complete the table.

b.   Find the expected value of each cell and write it next to the cell count in the table.

c.   Using a level of significance of 0.05, can Anna conclude that the phone use at the stoplight is independent of age group? Perform the calculate and conclude steps only.

d.   Compare and contrast the phone use of the different age groups.

10-11.   Davis is investigating the proportion of people who have a middle birth order among one's siblings. Davis found a published survey of 891 randomly selected persons, which found 157 people who have a middle birth order among one's siblings.

a.   Find and interpret a 93% confidence interval for the population proportion of people who have a middle birth order among one's siblings.

b.   If Davis wanted to increase his margin of error to just 1.5% without changing his confidence level, what sample size would he need to use?

10-12.   Compare the amount of time the flavor lasted for people chewing brand 10 chewing gum to the amount of time the flavor lasted in Strident chewing gum. See the graph at right. Estimate the mean for each type of gum. Remember: center, shape, spread and outliers!

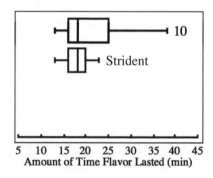

10.1.2 What about other statistics?

More Sampling Distributions

In the previous lesson, you explored the concepts of sampling bias and sampling variability through the lens of sampling distributions of medians and means. In this lesson you will extend these ideas to other statistics, particularly measures of position and spread.

10-13   Before diving into the eTool, consider a simple example. Consider the very simple population: $1, 2, 3, 4, 5$.

   a.   What is the range of the population?

   b.   The table below shows a few possible samples of size 2 from this population and the sample range for each one. Complete the table with all other possible samples (there are 10 total).

Sample	1, 2	1, 3	1, 4	
Range	1	2	3	

   c.   What is the mean of the sample ranges in this case?

   d.   Is the sample range an unbiased estimator for the population range? Explain.

10-14.   Recall pet rock ownership on Planet Claire from Lesson 1.2.3, where you first worked with two different variance formulas: the population variance $\sigma_x^2 = \frac{\sum(x_i - \mu)^2}{n}$ and the sample variance $s_x^2 = \frac{\sum(x_i - \bar{x})^2}{n-1}$, as well as the corresponding standard deviations.

That lesson was your first instance of creating a sampling distribution! Now consider another much larger sampling distribution of variances and standard deviations. Open the Simulation Sampling Distributions eTool and load the "Alice in Wonderland" population. Then set sample size to 5 and draw 5000 samples. Then use the "Graph" drop-down boxes to make the sampling distributions for the population variances (marked "Pop. variance (n)" and sample variances ("Samp. Variance (n-1)") appear. Make sure to uncheck the "Change scale" boxes.

   a.   Compare the shape, center, and spreads of the two distributions.

   b.   The "Sample Pop Variances" distribution shows the value of the variance for *each sample* you simulated IF calculated using n in the denominator. What is the average variance calculated using this method? What is the true population variance? Is this method of calculating variances an unbiased estimator for the true population variance?

Problem continues on next page →

10-14. *Problem continued from previous page.*

    c.   The "Sample samp variances" distribution instead calculates the variance for each sample by dividing by $n - 1$. Does this statistic appear to be an unbiased estimator for the true population variance?

    d.   Use your results from (b) and (c) to explain why divide by $(n - 1)$ to find the variance of a sample.

10-15.   If the sample variance is an unbiased estimate of the population variance, does that necessarily mean the sample standard deviation is an unbiased estimate of the population standard deviation?

    a.   Use the eTool to create sampling distributions for both the population standard deviation (calculated with n in denominator) and the sample standard deviation $(n - 1)$ and decide whether each one is unbiased.

    b.   To better understand why variances and standard deviations behave differently here, consider a simple example: imagine some very simple distribution with a population variance of 56 and a simple sampling distribution with only three sample variances: 4, 64, and 100. Verify the sample variances are an unbiased estimator in this case.

    c.   Continuing from part (b), what is the true standard deviation of the population?

    d.   Use the three sample variances to find the three sample standard deviations. What is their mean? Does it correctly estimate the true SD?

10-16.   Use the eTool to decide if the sample IQR is an unbiased estimate for the population IQR. Explain how you did so.

10-17.   For this population with samples of size 5, what has more variability—the sample IQR or the sample standard deviation? Explain how you know.

10-18.   Does increasing the sample size reduce the variability of the sample IQR and sample standard deviations? Try it by increasing sample size to 31 and drawing 5000 new samples.

MATH NOTES

Bias and Variability of a Statistic

A statistic is considered to be an **unbiased estimator of a parameter** if the mean of the sampling distribution of the statistic is equal to the value of the parameter.

For example, the sample mean $\bar{x}$ is an unbiased estimator of the population mean μ because the mean of the sampling distribution of the sample mean, denoted $\mu_{\bar{x}}$ (the **mean of all sample means**), is equal to μ. Similarly, you saw in Chapter 7 that the sample proportion $\hat{p}$ is an unbiased estimator for the population proportion p.

The sample variance is an unbiased estimator for the population variance.

The sample median and sample standard deviation are each *slightly* biased estimators for the corresponding parameters.

Most other common statistics, including IQR and range, are more severely biased estimators and should not be used as such.

The **variability** of a statistic can be measured by examining the standard deviation of the sampling distribution for the statistic. For example, the variability of sample means is usually measured using $\sigma_{\bar{x}}$ (the **standard deviation of the sample mean**), just as you measured the variability of proportions using $\sigma_{\hat{p}}$, the standard deviation of the sample proportion.

Many techniques you have explored in this course, including stratifying samples and using large sample sizes, are used to reduce the variability of statistics such as the mean.

10-19.   Consider the population shown in the graph below.

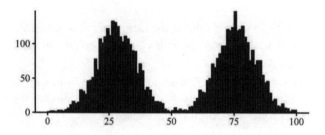

a.   Describe the shape and center of this distribution.

b.   You could think of this distribution has having two parts: "high" values (centered around 75) and "low" values (centered around 25).

   If you were to take samples of size 2, what is the approximate probability they will both be high? The approximate probability they will both be low? The approximate probability they will be one of each?

c.   What would be the approximate mean value of samples with two highs? Two lows? One of each?

d.   Based on your answers from parts (a) through (c), explain why the graph below could represent the sampling distribution for means of sample size 2 from this population.

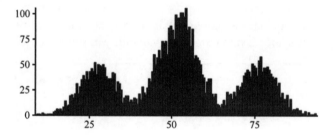

e.   Expand this idea—if you made a sampling distribution of the means for samples of size 3, sketch what the sampling distribution might look like.

10-20.   Meg took a simple random sample of students from three different local high schools. She wanted to make sure she had a representative amount from each high school, so she sampled 30 from Three Puddles High School, 80 from Riverland High School, 50 from Eagle Lakes High School. Meg asked the question, *"Which sport do you like better, hockey or basketball?"* Her results are in the following table:

	Puddles	Riverland	Eagle Lakes
Basketball	18	45	19
Hockey	12	35	31

a.   What type of sampling did Meg use?

b.   Construct a graphical display on your paper that represents the association between school and which sport they prefer.

c.   Write a few sentences about what the graphical display reveals about the students in the sample.

d.   Which test should be used to see if there is an association between school and sport preference. State the null and alternative hypothesis but do not run the test.

10-21.   Poison ivy is particularly sensitive to CO_2 levels in the atmosphere. While in Maine studying garden infestations of poison ivies, Julio investigated a random sample of 29 ivies which revealed the following information regarding the relationship between plant height and soil pH reading.

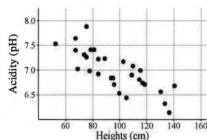

Regression Output for Soil pH vs. Plant Height

Predictor	Coef	SE Coef	T	P
Constant	8.32	0.04	218.50	0.00
Plant Height	-0.0138	0.00	-35.94	0.00

S = 0.252   R-Sq = 0.6308   R-Sq(Adj)= 0.6171

a.   Determine the LSRL equation and label the variables in context.

b.   Describe the slope and its meaning in the context of this sample.

c.   Use the LSRL to predict the soil pH reading of a poison ivy whose plant height is 120.72 cm.

d.   Calculate the residual for the point (136.70, 6.14).

e.   Is a linear model the most appropriate? How do you know?

10.2.1 Can I use a normal distribution?

The Central Limit Theorem

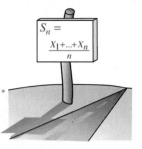

In Chapter 7, you calculated confidence intervals for the population proportion first by simulating the sampling distribution of the sample proportion but then you realized you could use a *normal approximation* for the sampling distribution under certain conditions, which saves a lot of time and effort.

There are similar methods for simulating confidence intervals with quantitative data—the most well-known is a technique called *bootstrapping*—but they take more time than is available in this introductory course. In this lesson you will explore how the normal distribution helps with quantitative data. Specifically, can the normal distribution help with estimating the mean of a population?

10-22.   By now, your teacher should have asked you to take "just a few" of some object.

    a.   Copy the class data in a place you will be able to find later (you will need to refer back to it several times over the next few lessons), make a sketch of the distribution, and describe the distribution.

    b.   Based on this sample, what would be your **gut check** *confidence interval* for the true average meaning of "just a few" of your object for all students like those in your class?

10-23.   Before you can answer this question more mathematically, you will need to start by exploring conditions under which the normal distribution is an appropriate model for sampling distributions of sample means. The Simulation Sampling Distributions eTool will continue to be useful for this exploration.

    a.   Open the eTool. The default data that loads in is random data based on the *uniform* distribution. Generate 2000 samples of size $n = 30$ and examine the sampling distribution of the sample means. Does it appear to be reasonably normal? (You can click the "overlay normal" checkbox to help you decide.)

    b.   Obtain a resource page that has a table for guided exploration. You will explore the sampling distribution for means using several different combinations of *populations* and *sample sizes* and evaluate normality in each case. Each time you make a change to the population, remember to click the "Update" button. Be on the lookout especially for *skew*—the normal distribution is symmetric! Use the eTool to fill out the table.

    c.   Discuss with your team and class, looking for patterns. Under what circumstances is the distribution of the sample means approximately normal in shape?

Statistics

MATH NOTES

The Central Limit Theorem

The **Central Limit Theorem** is one of the most important (and amazing!) theorems in all of Statistics—some people even call it the "fundamental theorem of Statistics." The theorem states that if you repeatedly take the mean of n independent observations of a random variable (with a well-defined mean and variance), the shape of the distribution of these *means* approaches a normal distribution as n approaches infinity.

In other words: as you increase sample size, the sampling distribution of the sample means looks less and less like the population and more and more like a normal curve.

Practically, this means it is reasonable to assume the sampling distribution of the sample means is *close* to normal if either or both of the following conditions are satisfied:

- The original population distribution is mostly symmetric with few outliers, in which case only a small n is needed to normalize the sampling distribution. (This is usually checked by graphing the sample and looking for outliers or *extreme* skew.) The closer the population is to normal, the smaller the n you need. In the special case of an almost perfectly normal population, even $n = 2$ is acceptable!

- The sample size is "big enough" that enough averaging has taken place for the curve to normalize. How big is "big enough?" There is no perfect answer to this, but many statisticians agree that 30 is a reasonable rule of thumb. In most realistic situations, if the sample size is at least 30, the sampling distribution of the sample mean is pretty close to normal.

It is important to note that this theorem applies **only to sample means**. There is no guarantee that sampling distributions of other statistics, such as the median, will approach normal distributions for every population.

10-24. Look back at your data from problem 10-22 to see of you can use this info to calculate a confidence interval!

    a. Calculate the mean, sample standard deviation, and sample size of that data.

    b. Tony is excited. *"This means we already have everything we need to make a confidence interval!"* he says. *"Our sample size was pretty big given the shape of the distribution, so we can trust that the sampling distribution is approximately normal. All we have to do is the same thing we did with proportions: use the formula 'statistic ± (critical value)(standard deviation of the statistic).' The sample mean is our statistic, and we know the critical value for a 95% interval is just 1.96."*

        Discuss with your team. Is Tony correct? Do you have all the information you need to find a confidence interval for the population mean? If so, sketch the model of the sampling distribution and calculate a 90% confidence interval for the population mean.

10-25.   To correctly find the standard deviation of the sampling distribution of the sample mean ($\sigma_{\bar{x}}$) you need to find a formula, just as you found a formula for $\sigma_{\hat{p}}$ in Lesson 7.1.3: using random variables. Let X be a random variable that represents the value one person chooses for "a few." Let μ be the true mean value of X. Let σ be the standard deviation of the original population, so σ^2 is the variance of X. (Assume that each observation of X is independent, which requires fulfillment of the same "Independent Trials" condition used for proportions!)

   a.   **Review:** What is the difference between $2X$ and $X + X$ in this context?

   b.   Use your knowledge of combining random variables to find the mean and standard deviation of $X + X$ in terms if μ and σ.

   c.   Use your knowledge of transforming random variables and your answer from part (b) to find the value of $\frac{X+X}{2}$ in terms of σ and μ. This is equivalent to $\mu_{\bar{x}}$ for $n = 2$.

   d.   Find the mean and standard deviation for $\frac{X+X+X}{3}$ in terms of σ and μ.

   e.   Extend the pattern: what is the mean and standard deviation of $\frac{X+X+X+...+X}{n}$ for n independent trials? These are the values of $\mu_{\bar{x}}$ and, the mean and standard deviation of the sampling distribution for a sample mean.

10-26.   Tony decides to try again. *"Okay,"* he says, *"we <u>definitely</u> have all of the information we need now. We just take the sample standard deviation of our sample; plug it into the formula we just came up with for $\sigma_{\bar{x}}$; and use that value to find the confidence interval. Right?"*

   There is still a small mistake in Tony's logic. Can you find it?

The problem Tony encountered cannot be surmounted just yet, so you will have to finish working with this data in a future lesson. But his flaw does not always exist.

10-27.   A manufacturer of nails is worried that one of its machines has lost calibration and is making nails slightly too small. In the past, the nails have always had a mass of about 1.25 g with a standard deviation of 0.05 g caused by tiny errors in the machine.

   Concerned the mean size has changed; the company takes a random sample of 100 new nails and finds the average mass of these nails to be 1.22 g. *Assuming the error in the machine has not changed* and the masses are normally distributed, construct a 95% confidence interval for the new population mean and evaluate the claim: are the company's fears of miscalibration reasonable?

10-28.   The ACT college entrance exam is approximately normally distributed with a mean score of a 21 and a standard deviation of 4.7.

   a.   You plan to take a random sample of three students and average their score. Explain why the sampling distribution of this *mean* can be approximated using the normal distribution.

   b.   What is the probability that the average of these three scores will be greater than 23? To figure this out, first sketch and shade the sampling distribution for the sample means. Use the formulas $\mu_{\bar{x}} = \mu$ and $\sigma_{\bar{x}} = \frac{\sigma}{\sqrt{n}}$ you derived in problem 10-24.

   c.   You take a sample of 10 random students. What is the probability that the average score for these 10 students will be greater than a 23? Again, sketch and shade the curve.

   d.   How many students would you need to sample for the probability of the average score being greater than 23 to fall all the way to 2%? (Hint: start by figuring out the critical value—what z-score would 23 need to be in order for $P(\text{average} > 23)$ to be 0.02 or less?)

10-29.   Jacob is looking at his Friday morning basketball statistics. He has taken 155 free throw shots this season and made 105. He believes that his percentage today is better than 75% so he decides to test his hypothesis by doing a one-proportion test.

$$H_0: p \geq 0.75$$
$$H_A: p \leq 0.75$$

Find as many flaws in Jacob's reasoning as you can.

10-30.   The Madelinton fire chief is concerned about false alarms for fires. Not just because they require a response from his fire units, but because as people grow tired of false alarms they do unwise things like disabling their required smoke detectors or ignoring them. If the required smoke detectors in Madelinton are accurate to 99% during a year, and typically 0.2% of residences catch fire each year, what is the chance of a false alarm when a residential smoke alarm sounds in Madelinton? Even with a high probability of a false alarm, why does the chief insist citizens continue paying attention to home smoke alarms?

10.2.2 How do I use this?

• •

Using the Normal Distribution with Means

In this lesson you will explore how to decide if the normal approximation for the sampling distribution of means is appropriate, then use it to conduct hypothesis tests and create confidence intervals.

10-31.　For each of the scenarios below, decide if you could use the normal approximation for the sampling distribution of the sample mean for the measured variable. Feel free to look at the Math Notes box at the end of this section for a refresher on the conditions if need be. If a condition is not met, explain what could be changed or what additional information you would need to be able to use the normal approximation.

　　a.　Summer asks a random sample of 30 of her fellow seniors (out of her class of 104 seniors) how many hours of sleep they got the night before.

　　b.　Latavia selects a random sample of 14 navel oranges from a huge display at Fresh Foods Market, takes them home, and weighs them.

　　c.　Anna pulls 100 pennies out of a very large, mixed up bag and writes down the year of each one.

　　d.　Emily takes one of Anna's pennies that looks remarkably worn out and wonders if it is still a fair coin. She flips it 100 times, recording if it comes up heads or not each time.

10-32.　Consider the example from the previous problem, in part (b). The sizes (in grams) of Latavia's 14 oranges are 124, 126, 129, 130, 134, 136, 139, 142, 146, 149, 152, 154, 155, and 157 g.

　　a.　Find the sample mean of Latavia's data.

　　b.　Make a boxplot or a histogram of Latavia's data with a bin size of 10.

　　c.　If even a small sample is graphed and has no major skew or outliers, it is generally reasonable to assume that the population "could reasonably be normal," and therefore that the sampling distribution of the mean is approximately normal. This is the "normal population" condition. Does this sample appear to satisfy this condition?

　　d.　Latavia reads online that medium-sized navel oranges have a mean mass of 131 g with a standard deviation of 18 g. She is interested to test if the Fresh Foods oranges match those parameters. State a null and alternative hypothesis for this situation using symbols. Note that Latavia is making *two* assumptions in her test.

Problem continues on next page →

Statistics

10-32.   *Problem continued from previous page.*

   e.   Calculate a test statistic: what is the z-score of Latavia's mean within the sampling distribution if the provided values hold? Use the formulas for the mean and standard deviation of the sampling distribution found last class (see Math Notes box in this lesson).

   f.   Calculate her *p*-value, the probability of Latavia getting a sample mean as extreme as the one she got if the online data is correct. Sketch and shade a standard normal curve to represent the p-value. Can Latavia reject the hypothesis at $\alpha = 0.05$?

   g.   What can Latavia conclude about the oranges at Fresh Foods?

   h.   What kind of error, Type I or Type II, might Latavia have made? Describe the effects of such an error in context.

10-33.   Latavia is willing to keep operating under the assumption that the standard deviation of the Fresh Foods orange sizes are, in fact, 18 g. Use this fact and the data from problem 10-32 to create a 95% confidence interval for the true mean size of all of the Fresh Foods oranges. This type of confidence interval is called a **one-sample z-interval for the population mean**.

10-34.   Anna selects 100 pennies from a very large, mixed up bag of pennies her teacher has collected over the years, and records the year of each (as described in problem 10-31.) The median year of her sample is 1995, the mean year is 1992.32 and the standard deviation is 16.2 years.

   a.   Do you think this population is likely to be left-skewed, right-skewed, or symmetric? Explain, using both evidence from the data and intuition from the context.

   b.   Explain why the sampling distribution of the sample mean is still normal in shape, despite the skewed distribution of the population.

   c.   For large sample sizes, the standard deviation of a sample is generally very close to the standard deviation of the population. Assume the standard deviation of the population is very close to the 16.2 years from Anna's sample and create a 95% confidence interval for the mean year of all of the pennies in the bag.

10-35.   Kalani is a civil engineer working at the Ventura County waste water treatment plant. Each day she examines a random sample of 12 water samples from the plant's treated discharge pipes to determine if the concentration of *E. coli* bacteria and other contaminates are within acceptable limits. She knows from long term sampling that the distribution of *E. coli* bacteria from the plant is normally distributed with a long-term standard deviation of 32 colony forming units per 100 milliliters (cfu/100 mL). Today's samples had a mean of 147 cfu/100 mL.

   a.   Determine a 95% confidence interval for the concentration of *E. coli* bacteria using the four-step approach: <u>identify</u>, <u>check conditions</u>, <u>calculate</u>, and <u>conclude</u>.

   b.   Assume an environmental regulatory agency has made the claim that the day's discharge of *E. coli* bacteria exceeded 175 cfu/100 mL. How should Kalani respond to the claim?

MATH NOTES

Sampling Distribution of Sample Means

Let there be a population with a true mean μ of some variable of interest. If taking samples of size n, the sampling distribution of the sample mean $\bar{x}$ will satisfy the following properties, under the given conditions.

Property	Condition	Explanation
$\mu_{\bar{x}} = \mu$	**Random:** the sample is randomly chosen from the population.	Random choosing of the sample ensures there is no bias in the mean.
$\sigma_{\bar{x}} = \frac{\sigma}{\sqrt{n}}$	**Independent trials:** Each sample is an independent event, drawn with replacement, OR drawn from a population at least 10 times the sample size.	The $\sigma_{\bar{x}}$ formula derives from the rules for combining random variables, which require independence of each variable. If drawing without replacement, the population needs to be large enough to keep that *approximately* true.
Normal sampling distribution	**Large sample *or* normal population:** the sample size $n \geq 30$ *or* the population is "approximately normal" (limited skew/outliers).	This follows from the Central Limit Theorem. To check for an "approximately normal" population, graph the *sample* and look for outliers or major skew.

STOP your work if the sample is not random. Bias makes it useless!

CONTINUE BUT MENTION IT if the sample is less than 10 times the population without replacement. In these cases, your samples could actually be *less variable* than the formulas imply, but that is okay!

CONTINUE IF YOU DARE If the third condition is not met, probabilities cannot be calculated using the techniques presented in this course.

10-36.   A farmer is interested in calculating the average size (in grams) of the apples in her orchard this year. From detailed historical data she is pretty confident that her apples likely vary with a standard deviation of about 50 g. She plans to take a random sample of apples from her orchard to create a confidence interval.

    a.   If she takes a sample of size 100, what will be the standard deviation of the distribution of sample means? What will be the margin of error for a 95% confidence interval?

    b.   She decides she wants to create a 95% confidence interval for the average size with a margin of error of 5 grams or less. How large of a sample will she need in order to guarantee such a margin of error?

    c.   The farmer decides to round her sample quantity up from your calculation in part (a) to the next hundred apples. She takes the sample and finds the apples in the sample have a mean size of 185.2 g. Check conditions and construct her 95% confidence interval for the mean size of apples in her orchard.

    d.   Last year, the average size of the apples in the orchard was 190 g. Does the farmer have sufficient evidence to conclude her apples are smaller this year than last year?

10-37.   Mo believes that students who are asked to take an arithmetic test will perform better when they are allowed to use a calculator.

    a.   Should an observational study or an experiment be carried out to answer the question? Explain.

    b.   What are the explanatory and response variables?

    c.   Describe how you would carry out the study. Be sure to describe how you would incorporate randomization into your design.

10-38.   Mary Kate is describing the proportion of people who have the ability to curl their tongue. Mary Kate found a published survey of 684 randomly selected people that found 497 of them had the ability to curl their tongue.

    Determine a 93% confidence interval for the population proportion of people who have the ability to curl their tongue. Follow the complete four-step process.

10.3.1 What if I don't know σ?

Introducing the t-Distribution

Refer back to Lesson 10.2.1 and the data your class gathered about "just a few" objects.

10-39.   In problems 10-24 and 10-26, Tony attempted to come up with a plan to calculate a 95% confidence interval for the mean of the population. His plan was to take the following steps after checking conditions:

- Find the mean and deviation of your *individual sample* ($\bar{x}$ and s).

- Use the sample standard deviation, s, INSTEAD of the population standard deviation σ in the formula $\sigma_{\bar{x}} = \frac{\sigma}{\sqrt{n}}$ to estimate the standard deviation of the mean.

- Find the critical value of 1.96 from the normal curve and use the confidence interval formula CI = estimator ± (critical value)(standard deviation of statistic) to find the confidence interval.

Jenny thinks this is a good technique. She says, *"It's okay that we're just estimating σ in the second step, because s will be too big about as often as it will be too small. This will mean some confidence intervals are narrower and others are wider, but things should cancel out overall."*

Maria disagrees. *"We learned in Lesson 10.2.1 that s is actually a biased estimator for σ. I'm worried that confidence intervals created in this way won't capture the true value 95% of the time."*

How could you decide whether Jenny or Maria is right?

10-40.   The Confidence Interval of Means eTool will allow you to explore how often confidence intervals capture the true mean in various situation. It allows you to simulate drawing samples from a standard normal distribution with different confidence levels and calculation techniques.

a.   Open the eTool and examine the settings. By default, the eTool draws 100 samples of size 20 and calculates confidence intervals with a 95% confidence level for each one, using the true σ of 1 each time. This is like the problems in Lesson 10.2.2.

What do the red lines and black lines in the output represent?

b.   Press the "Draw Samples" button several times, until you have drawn at least two thousand samples. Examine the data table at the right, looking at the "Normal with σ" column. Does this method of generating confidence intervals seem to match your set confidence level *over the long run?*

Problem continues on next page →

10-40.   *Problem continued from previous page.*

    c.   Under this method, are all of the confidence intervals the same width or different widths? Use the formula for a confidence interval to decide why this is so. If you click one of the lines you will see the estimate and margin of error for the associated interval if that will help understand.

    d.   **Predict:** if you make sample size higher, what should happen to the width of these confidence intervals? If you make the confidence level higher, what should happen to the width? After discussing and answering, use the tool to confirm your prediction.

10-41.   The simulations in the previous problem used the true standard deviation σ to calculate each confidence interval, but in practice a confidence interval would normally need to use s, the standard deviation of the individual sample.

    a.   Set sample size to $n = 10$ and the confidence level to 95. Choose the second option for calculating samples "Normal model with the sample standard deviation"; this is the technique proposed by Tony in the first part of this lesson. Draw several thousand samples and observe: does this capture the true mean at the correct rate?

    b.   Are all of the confidence intervals the same width or different widths using s and the normal model? Explain.

    c.   Try several different sample sizes to see how that changes the results. Do some sample sizes result in more "correct" capture proportions? (Make sure to try some very small samples like $n = 3$ and very large samples like $n = 100$).

    d.   Summarize your conclusions: in what cases is it reliable to use a normal model to estimate confidence intervals for the population mean?

10-42.   Jenny is thinking about the previous problem and says, *"For cases where the normal model isn't good enough, I wonder if we could still use our confidence interval formula and just increase our critical values to make intervals wider?"* Maria does not understand why this would work. Write an explanation for Maria explaining why larger critical values could potentially lead to more accurate confidence levels.

10-43.   Click the final option on the eTool, "T-distribution with sample SDs."

    a.   Without getting new samples, click back and forth between that option and the "Normal model with sample SD" option. How do the confidence intervals change when you switch models?

    b.   Click "Draw samples" at least 10 times and look under the "T-dist with s" column to see the proportion this new model is capturing. Is it closer to your requested confidence level?

To understand how these confidence intervals were created you need to examine another sampling distribution.

10-44. The Central Limit Theorem says that the sampling distribution of the sample means will be approximately normal under certain conditions. Thus, the sampling distribution of the **normal test statistic**, $z = \dfrac{\bar{x}-\mu}{\frac{\sigma}{\sqrt{n}}}$, is the *standard* normal distribution. As long as the conditions are met, the sampling distribution of that test statistic is always normal, so the standard normal critical value of 1.96 is always appropriate for 95% confidence intervals if σ is known and conditions are met.

However, you cannot use that test statistic when you do not know σ. How do you find a critical value in that case? Since you cannot calculate the true value of z, you have to use a different statistic, called the **t-test statistic**. It is represented by $t = \dfrac{\bar{x}-\mu}{\frac{s_x}{\sqrt{n}}}$ where $\dfrac{s_x}{\sqrt{n}}$ is called the

standard error of the sample mean. The sampling distribution of this test statistic is called a **t-distribution**.

a. The picture and data tables below were made with the Simulation Sampling Distribution eTool after drawing 20,000 samples of size 3 from a large, normal population. The curves overlaid are the standard normal curves in both cases. Describe the similarities and the differences between the sampling distributions of the normal test statistic and the t-test statistic.

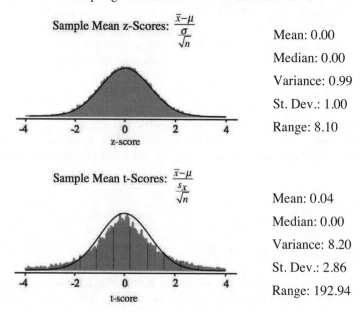

Sampling distributions for test statistics: $n = 3$

Sample Mean z-Scores: $\dfrac{\bar{x}-\mu}{\frac{\sigma}{\sqrt{n}}}$

Mean: 0.00

Median: 0.00

Variance: 0.99

St. Dev.: 1.00

Range: 8.10

Sample Mean t-Scores: $\dfrac{\bar{x}-\mu}{\frac{s_x}{\sqrt{n}}}$

Mean: 0.04

Median: 0.00

Variance: 8.20

St. Dev.: 2.86

Range: 192.94

Problem continues on next page →

10-44.   *Problem continued from previous page.*

b.   The same sampling distributions are shown for samples of size $n = 9$ below. Again, compare and contrast the distributions.

Sampling distributions for test statistics: $n = 9$

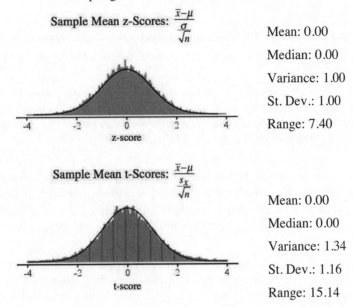

Sample Mean z-Scores: $\dfrac{\bar{x} - \mu}{\frac{\sigma}{\sqrt{n}}}$

Mean: 0.00

Median: 0.00

Variance: 1.00

St. Dev.: 1.00

Range: 7.40

Sample Mean t-Scores: $\dfrac{\bar{x} - \mu}{\frac{s_x}{\sqrt{n}}}$

Mean: 0.00

Median: 0.00

Variance: 1.34

St. Dev.: 1.16

Range: 15.14

c.   If a distribution is normal, the critical value for a 95% confidence interval is 1.96. Based on the pictures above, would you expect critical values for these t-distributions to be higher, lower, or equal to 1.96?

d.   If possible, watch the t-distribution animation. It should make the relationship between the normal distribution and the various t-distributions more obvious. Then read the Math Notes box at the end of this lesson and decide how many *degrees of freedom* you would need to model your class data ("Just a Few") from Lesson 10.2.1 with a t-distribution.

Math Notes

Student's t-Distribution

The **Student's t-distributions** (or simply t-distributions) are a *family* of distributions that represent the sampling distributions of the t-test statistics for the sample mean, $t_x = \frac{\bar{x} - \mu}{\frac{s_x}{\sqrt{n}}}$,

when conditions are satisfied. These t-distributions have a similar shape to the normal curve but wider spreads and thicker tails, so more of the probability is contained in the tails. This leads to higher critical values than those of the normal curve thus creating wider confidence intervals and higher *p*-values than normal distributions.

The exact shape of a t-distribution is determined by its **degrees of freedom**. The more degrees of freedom, the more similar the t-distribution is to the normal distribution; in fact, you can interpret the normal distribution as a t-distribution with ∞ degrees of freedom! Sample means from samples of size *n* will create a t-distribution with *n* – 1 degrees of freedom.

An amateur mathematician named William Sealy Gosset, a brewmaster by trade, first published information about these distributions under the pseudonym "Student," hence their official name. He used the distributions to run experiments on the various components of beer for the Guinness Brewery!

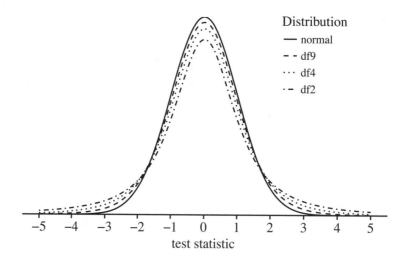

10-45.   Three different t-distributions (for three different sample means) have 95% critical values of 3.18, 2.03, and 2.57.

    a.   Rank these distributions from lowest sample size to highest sample size.

    b.   What is the lowest possible 95% critical value for a t-distribution?

    c.   Try to figure out how to use a calculator (or a t-distribution probability table such as Table B provided on the AP exam) to find the 95% critical value for a confidence interval made using a sample of size $n = 20$ (assume conditions are met). Hint: the process is quite similar to normal curves on most calculators.

    d.   Try to figure out how to you use a calculator to find the probability of a sample of size 15 having a t-test statistic greater than 1.7 (assuming conditions are met). Tables can only estimate this value. The t-Distribution eTool can also do this.

10-46.   Oysters have a three-chambered heart, colorless blood, and a pair of kidneys. While in the Southern Ocean describing vulnerable preserves of oysters, Joshua described that oyster lengths are normally distributed. Sketch the normal probability density function. If the 1st percentile is 7.439 cm, and the 83rd percentile is 13.278 cm find the mean and standard deviation.

10-47.   A national survey of consumers found that 68% of consumers say they are more likely to visit a restaurant serving locally sourced items than one that does not. A random sample of 100 consumers in your area found that 75 answered "yes" when asked, "Do you prefer to visit a restaurant that serves food grown locally?" Is this a good reason to think that the proportion of consumers that would say "yes" in your area differs from the national proportion? Demonstrate all four inference steps.

10.3.2 How do I use the t-distribution?

Calculating Confidence Intervals for μ

In Chapter 7 you learned to make confidence intervals with proportions. In this lesson, you will use the t-distribution and quantitative data samples to make confidence intervals of means.

10-48.   Mo and Lana are discussing the new t-distributions. Lana says, *"Since the tails are a little thicker than the normal distribution, critical values, and p-values will be higher when using s instead of σ to estimate, so we'll need a new way to find them."* Mo says, *"I found commands on my calculator for the probability density function, cumulative density function, and inverse cumulative density function!"*

Use the commands Mo found to find the following values. For each, sketch and shade a curve to match the question. When sketching, t-curves and normal curves look basically the same, but you should write "df =" and the degrees of freedom next to or above the sketch.

a. $P(t < -1.80)$ on a t-distribution with 25 degrees of freedom.

b. $P(t > 1.42)$ on a t-distribution that models the mean of samples of size 13.

c.   Find the value of t for which 5% of the area is to the right of t in a t-distribution with 39 degrees of freedoms.

d.   For a t-distribution for modeling samples of size 9, find the 2.5[th] percentile.

e.   Find the critical value for estimating a 90% confidence interval using samples of size 15.

10-49.   A simple random sample of 35 residents of Smallville, WI (population 6792) finds that they eat an average of 3.2 servings of cheese each week, with a sample standard deviation of 1.1 servings. A histogram of the sample data shows heavy right skew.

a.   To what population could conclusions from this sample be generalized?

b.   Which of the three conditions assures a lack of bias in samples? Does this situation satisfy that condition?

c.   Which of the three conditions assures the formula for the standard deviation of the sampling distribution $\sigma_{\bar{x}} = \frac{\sigma}{\sqrt{n}}$ is correct? Does this situation satisfy that conditions?

d.   Which of the three conditions allows for the normality of the sampling distribution? Does this situation satisfy that condition?

e.   Find the standard error for the sampling distribution.

f.   Use the t-distribution with appropriate degrees of freedom to find the critical value for a 90% confidence interval for the population mean.

g.   Use the information found above to calculate and interpret a 90% confidence interval for the population mean in this context.

10-50.   The time has come! Refer back to your data from Lesson 10.2.1, the "just a few" data. Assuming your data follows the conditions for inference, calculate a 95% confidence interval for the population mean and interpret it in context.

10-51.   Quick practice! Without checking conditions, quickly calculate confidence intervals for each of the following situations. Note that these could be z-intervals, t-intervals, or proportion-intervals; name which one you are using. If you have technology that can calculate confidence intervals, such as most graphing calculators, try to use those to check your work.

a.   A random sample of 17 adult foxes finds they have an average weight of 12.1 lbs with a standard deviation of 4.3 lbs. Create a 92% confidence interval for the mean weight of all adult foxes.

b.   A random sample of 325 sheep in New Zealand finds that 72 of them are black. Create an 88% confidence interval for the proportion of New Zealand sheep that are black.

c.   A random sample of 25 glass bottles from a particular production line on a particular day finds they hold an average of 343 g of liquid. This particular production line has historically created bottles with a standard deviation holding capacity of 5 g. Use this information to create a 98% confidence interval for the average capacity for the bottles on the sampled day.

MATH NOTES

Confidence Intervals for the Population Mean

To calculate a C% confidence interval for a population mean μ from a sample mean $\bar{x}$, you will first check for all conditions for inference, then use the general confidence interval formula

statistic ± (critical value)(standard error of statistic).

The statistic used in this formula is $\bar{x}$. The values of the critical value and the standard error depend on whether the population standard deviation is known.

Known Info	Critical value	Standard Deviation/ Error of statistic
σ (or both)	z^*, taken from the normal distribution	$\sigma_{\bar{x}} = \frac{\sigma}{\sqrt{n}}$
s only	t^*, taken from the t-distribution with $n - 1$ degrees of freedom	$SE_{\bar{x}} = \frac{s}{\sqrt{n}}$

When constructing the confidence interval, make sure to state whether you are using a normal distribution (sometimes called a *z-interval*) *or* a t-distribution (sometimes called a *t-interval*), and the degrees of freedom used if appropriate.

10-52. The temperature in a refrigerator is not the same throughout its interior because of distance from the compressor and the way air flows throughout. The refrigerator's "power" setting determines the *mean* temperature in the refrigerator, but temperatures throughout the refrigerator vary by an approximately normal distribution with a standard deviation of 1 degree Fahrenheit. David wants to estimate the average temperature in his refrigerator when it is set at power setting 4, so he carefully measures the temperature at four randomly chosen spots in his fridge, finding an average temperature of 35.1 degrees Fahrenheit in his measurements.

    a. Is the standard deviation mentioned in this problem a population standard deviation or a sample standard deviation?

    b. Does this satisfy all of the conditions for inference on means?

    c. <u>Calculate</u> and <u>conclude</u> a 95% confidence interval for the average temperature in David's fridge.

    d. Interpret the term "95% confidence" from the previous question in context.

10-53.   Summer wants to estimate the average height of a
          sunflower in her huge sunflower patch with a 95%
          confidence interval. She would like the margin of error to
          be no more than 3 inches and is trying to figure out her
          ideal sample size. She knows she has done problems like
          this in AP Statistics before (see, for example, problem
          10-36). Unfortunately, Summer quickly realizes she has a
          problem. What problem(s) does Summer face in
          estimating the sample size she needs?

10-54.   Jack is designing a game for the school fundraiser. Players will be paying $5 for each game.
          There will be three prizes. The smallest prize has a value of $5.50; the second prize has a value
          of $8. Jack has not yet determined the first place prize value. The probability of winning the
          smallest prize is 0.15, the probability of winning the second prize is 0.05, and the probability
          of winning the first prize is 0.01. The probability of not winning any prize is 0.79. If the school
          wants make an expected value of $1 per ticket, what should Jack choose as the value of the
          first prize?

10-55.   The number of cellphone apps has been recorded for a large cellphone company in the past few
          weeks. There are eight types of apps the company is interested in. The table below shows how
          sales of the apps is distributed.

Games	Business	Education	Lifestyle	Entertainment	Utilities	Travel	Books	Total
120000	70350	55700	40600	30800	17500	13300	1750	350000

The company plans to randomly sample 2500 application sales in the next two months and ask
the buyer some information about their purchase.

a.   For a simple random sample of 2500 application sales in the next two months, what is the
      expected value and standard deviation of the number of book apps sampled.

b.   When selecting a simple random sample of 2500 application sales, how likely is it that
      fewer than 10 of the sales in the sample would be book app sales? Justify your answer.

c.   The company is concerned that a simple random sample of 2500 owners would include
      fewer than 10 buyers of book apps. Describe a sampling method that would ensure at
      least 10 buyers for each type of application in the sample.

10.3.3 How can I test claims with means?

z-Tests and t-Tests for Population Means

One measure of the difficulty of a book's reading level is the length of its words. In this lesson, you will gather data about the length of words in various books and use tests and confidence intervals to explore the word length in the books.

10-56. Your team will be working with one book. Each member of your team will start with a different randomly chosen page in your book—either a page will be printed for you or you will use a calculator to choose a random page. After choosing your page, record the lengths of the first 25 words.

   a. Enter your data in some technology tool (such as a calculator, a spreadsheet, or the Univariate Data Comparison eTool) and calculate the mean and standard deviation of your dataset.

   b. You are hoping to use your sample to estimate the average word length in this entire book. Is your sample most similar to a simple random sample, cluster sample, stratified sample, or systematic sample?

   c. Assuming the conditions for inference are all met, use your sample to construct and interpret a 95% confidence interval for the true average length of words in your sample.

   d. Combine your team's data into one larger sample and construct a new confidence interval. If combining data will take too much time using your technology, you can estimate: average the means to get your combined mean and average your *variances* to get your combined variance then square root it for the standard deviation in your estimate.

   e. Share your results out with the class and have a discussion—which book appears to have the shortest words? The longest words?

10-57.   Theodor Geisel, also known as Dr. Seuss, is famous for writing children's books such as *The Cat in the Hat* and *Green Eggs and Ham*. His first book, *The Cat in the Hat*, is famous for its intricate rhyming and word play using only 236 words with an average length of 3.8 letters.

a.   Your book is likely more difficult to read than *The Cat in the Hat*, and it is reasonable therefore to claim that your book has an average word length higher than that of *The Cat in the Hat*. Identify a null and alternative hypothesis you could use to statistically confirm your claim and provide sample evidence for the alternative hypothesis.

b.   Using your *personal* data from part (a) above, what is the t-statistic for your actual mean under the null hypothesis?

c.   Sketch and shade a curve that represents the probability of being *as or more extreme* than your t-statistic under these hypotheses. Remember to report the degrees of freedom you are using next to the curve!

d.   Use a calculator to calculate the *p*-value and draw a conclusion at the $\alpha = 0.05$ level.

10-58.   One common example of a *one-sample t-test* is to check if the mean of some quantitative variable appears to have changed since the last time a census was completed. In 2010, the average household size in Boone County, KY (population 125,000) was 2.78 people. A recent randomized telephone poll of 100 Boone County residents found an average household size of 2.69 people with a standard deviation of 0.54 people. Conduct a t-test to decide if there is sufficient evidence that the mean household size in Boone County has changed. Make sure to follow all four steps for hypothesis tests: <u>identify</u>, <u>check conditions</u>, <u>calculate</u>, and <u>conclude</u>. See the Math Notes box in this lesson if you need a refresher.

10-59.   In the previous section, you may have calculated a confidence interval for the average value of "a few." When Lana's class of 18 students were asked to take "a few" jellybeans from a bowl, they plotted the number of jellybeans each person took as shown on the dot plot at right. The mean of this data is 5.3889 jellybeans with a sample standard deviation of 1.9445 jellybeans.

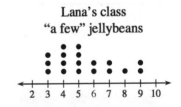
Lana's class
"a few" jellybeans

Lana says, *"'A few' is definitely 4 or fewer! And on average, I'm sure students like us agree with me."* Mo disagrees. Conduct a hypothesis test at $\alpha = 0.01$ to see if Mo has convincing evidence that Lana is wrong. Make sure to <u>identify</u> the test and hypotheses, <u>check</u> all conditions, <u>calculate</u> the correct statistics and *p*-value, and <u>conclude</u> whether Mo has strong evidence in context. You may assume Lana's class is equivalent to a random sample of students like them.

MATH NOTES

Hypothesis Test Procedures for Sample Means

Step 1: <u>Identify</u> the type of test and parameter, the null and alternative hypotheses, sample evidence in favor of the alternative hypothesis, and the significance level. These tests are "one-sample z-tests for the population mean" OR "one-sample t-tests for the population mean" depending on whether σ is known. Choices for hypotheses are two-tailed tests such as "H_0: $\mu = 74$ mm, H_A: $\mu \neq 74$ mm" or one-tailed tests such as "H_0: $\mu = 12$ volts, H_A: $\mu < 12$ volts." The sample statistic "$\bar{x} = 10.6$ volts" must provide some evidence for the alternative hypothesis or there is no point in performing an inference test. Unless specified, a significance level of $\alpha = 0.05$ is usually appropriate.

Step 2: <u>Check</u> conditions for inference. See the Math Notes box in Lesson 10.2.2.

Step 3: <u>Calculate</u> the mean and standard deviations of the sampling distribution (assuming the null hypothesis), the test statistic (z-score or t-score of the sample), and the *p*-value. This should always involve a sketch of the standard normal curve or t-curve, marking the test statistic on the sketch, and shading the "more extreme" region, based on the alternative hypothesis.

Step 4: <u>Conclude</u> whether to reject the null hypothesis or fail to reject it by comparing the *p*-value to α. Write a conclusion *in context*. If *p*-value $< \alpha$, reject the null hypothesis and accept the alternative. Otherwise, "fail to reject the null"—no conclusion is drawn (though in practice this usually means the null hypothesis is given the benefit of the doubt). In either case, explain in context what this means.

10-60.   A sample survey of 500 families in Milwaukee, Wisconsin shows an average of $475 were spent on shoes each year with a standard deviation of $240.

    a.   <u>Calculate</u> and <u>conclude</u> a 95% confidence interval estimate of the average annual amount spent on shoes in Milwaukee, Wisconsin.

    b.   Find and interpret the margin of error at 99% confidence.

    c.   With what degree of confidence can you say that the average annual expenditure is between $460 and $490?

10-61.   Megyear tires have a mean life of 45,000 miles with a standard
          deviation of 700 miles.

          a.   Assuming tire lives are normally distributed, what is the
                probability that any one Megyear tire would last less than
                44900 miles?

          b.   What is the probability that the mean life of 64 Megyear
                tires is less than 44900 miles?

          c.   What is the probability that the mean life of 256 Megyear
                tires is less than 44900 miles?

10-62.   Write a hypothesis statement and test the following situations. Include all four steps in the
          process and be sure to provide the test statistics, critical values, and p-values and conclusions
          in context for $\alpha = 0.05$.

          a.   In a recent study of 427 randomly selected people between the ages of 18 and 60, of the
                252 men, 62% said they respond to text messages while driving, while 67% of the 175
                women reported the same. Is the percentage of women who respond to text messages
                while driving significantly larger than the percentage of men who do so?

          b.   In the same survey, 47% of men and 53% of women agreed with the statement that using
                your phone is the most dangerous thing to do while driving (compared to eating,
                smoking, or a combination of all three). In this case, is the percent of women who agreed
                with the statement significantly different than the percent of men who did?

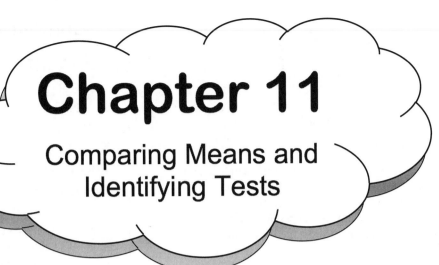

Chapter 11

Comparing Means and Identifying Tests

CHAPTER 11

Chapter Goals

Identify matched pairs situations.

Learn matched pairs procedures.

Perform complete matched pairs hypothesis tests.

Investigate tests and confidence intervals using two independent samples.

Identify situations and perform the appropriate inference techniques for all the tests and intervals presented thus far in this course.

In Chapter 4 you studied the benefits of blocking variables to reduce variation. In Chapter 8 you found that less variation in sample data makes a test more able to reject a false null hypothesis (more power!) This chapter details the procedures for the most powerful blocking tool of all, *matched pairs*. You will also identify situations where samples are drawn from independent populations and perform t-tests for the difference of two independent means.

Chapter Outline

Section 11.1   You will review matched pairs vs. completely randomized designs for detecting a difference in treatments and apply your knowledge to compare the ideas of paired t-tests and two-sample t-tests. You will complete hypothesis tests with matched pairs data and test for the difference in two independent means.

Section 11.2   You will identify and implementing the appropriate inference test from a variety of problems from Chapters 7 through 11.

11.1.1 How can I determine differences?

Paired and Independent Data from Surveys and Experiments

Today you will revisit experiments from Lesson 4.2.3, this time associating the results of the experiments with the details of their design.

11-1. Your teacher will help you conduct an experiment to the reaction time of left and right hands. Each member of the class will be asked to collect one or two data points in this experiment.

    a. What are explanatory and response variables in this experiment?

    b. What are the treatments?

    c. Describe the design—is it completely randomized, blocked, matched pairs, or other?

    d. Sketch comparative histograms or boxplots of the "left hand" and "right hand" data sets. Record the mean/standard deviation of each one.

    e. Use your gut: does it appear that these data sets are different enough to conclude that left hand and right hand necessarily have different reaction times in this experiment?

    f. There are two common situations that involve means and comparing two datasets. One of them arises when comparing two different measurements from the same or paired individuals—such as in matched pairs experiments or before/after experiments. The other arises when comparing the means of two unconnected (independent) samples. Which of these situations does this experiment fit?

    g. You do not know how to calculate a t-test for a difference yet. You will learn more in Lesson 11.1.4, but for now, know that the hypotheses for this test are "H_0: the true means of the two groups are equal. H_A: The true means for the two groups differ." Using the p-value provided by your teacher and $\alpha = 0.05$, draw whatever conclusion you can (assume any necessary conditions for this test are met).

11-2. Your teacher will now guide you through a modified version of this experiment.

    a. Identify as many differences as you can between this experiment and the experiment from problem 11-1, and why they may improve on the results from the first experiment.

    b. Because this data is *paired data*, it is possible to calculate the difference for each individual: non-dominant time minus dominant time. This gives a third data column, the "difference" column. Call that difference D. With your team, conduct a t-test for the hypotheses "H_0: $\mu_D = 0$, H_A: $\mu_D \neq 0$". Since you are only using one column (the difference column) this is exactly like tests conducted in the previous chapter! Assume all conditions for inference are met.

11-3. For each situation below, decide if the situation will result in comparisons of *paired data* or *independent samples*.

    a.   A survey of 500 people measures the length of their left leg and their right leg, the compares the left legs to right legs.

    b.   A survey measures the length of the left leg of 250 women and 250 men then compares the lengths.

    c.   An experiment randomly assigns 200 people to drink decaffeinated coffee and another 200 people caffeinated coffee and compares the average typing speed of the two groups.

    d.   An experiment randomly assigns 200 people to drink decaffeinated coffee and 200 people caffeinated coffee, measures their typing speed, then repeats the measurement again a week later, switching which type of coffee they get.

11-4. Recall, the notation $N(\mu, \sigma)$ means "normal with a mean of μ and a standard deviation of σ." Consider two random variables A and B, where A is $N(-4, 2)$ and B is $N(4, 1)$.

    a.   Find the mean and standard deviation of $2A$.

    b.   Find the mean and standard deviation if $A + 3$.

    c.   Find the mean and standard deviation of $3B$.

    d.   Find the mean and standard deviation of $3B - 12$.

    e.   Find the mean and standard deviation of $A + B$.

    f.   Find the mean and standard deviation of $3B - 2A - 4$.

11-5. Coach Faulder wants to conduct an experiment to measure whether drinking CrocodileAde helps players run the 100 m dash faster than water.

    a.   Describe how he could use a *completely randomized design* to test this relationship. Explain what values you will calculate and what values you will compare.

    b.   Describe how he could use a *matched pairs design* to test the relationship. State what you will calculate and compare.

    c.   Assume CrocodileAde ingestion does cause a slight improvement on running speed. Explain why the matched pairs design is more likely to make that difference visible than the completely randomized design.

11-6.   Park rangers study the pellets of hawks to determine their eating habits. Hawks regurgitate the indigestible portion of their diet in a pellet. Pellets are about one or two inches long, and can contain the bones, fur, feathers, and claws of their prey.

In order to determine if hawks were changing their diet to cope with a particularly harsh winter, rangers collected a random sample of ten pellets. The rodent bones in the pellets had masses of: 7.3, 12.1, 3.1, 11.9, 6.3, 3.9, 9.7, 6.3, 0.0, 7.0 grams.

From the sample park rangers will make predictions for the population using a normal model. Construct and interpret a 98% confidence interval.

11-7.   **Multiple Choice:** 85 randomly selected students were asked what their favorite class was. The results are listed in the table below. What kind of graphical representation would best represent this data?

	Math	Science	Social Studies	English
Male	11	14	3	7
Female	17	15	7	11

A.   Side-by-side boxplots

B.   Side-by-side stem-and-leaf plot

C.   Two circle graphs

D.   Two histograms

E.   All of these graphical representations would be appropriate.

11.1.2 How do I perform paired inference?

Paired Inference Procedures

Situations that result in *paired data* will often require you to perform tests or calculate confidence intervals for the difference in the paired data. The process is mostly the same as performing one-sample inference on means, as in Chapter 10. The most difficult part of these procedures is often analyzing the design and interpreting the results.

11-8. The GunShow protein shake company claims that their protein shake helps builds bicep circumference by "up to 10% in just six months!" When asked to provide evidence for this claim, they provide documentation of a study performed on eight randomly chosen mid-tier body builders. In the study, the 8 body builders had their biceps measured to the nearest half-centimeter, then were asked to drink GunShow daily before their normal workout routine for six months. At the end of that period, their biceps were measured again. The study resulted in the data below.

Circ. before (cm)	45	39.5	42.0	46.0	41.5	40.0	42.0	49.5
Circ. after (cm)	44	43.5	44.0	44.0	44.5	41.0	42.0	48.5

a. Add a new row to the dataset called "change." The values should be positive if the biceps increased in size.

b. Sketch dot plots or histograms with a bin width of 1 for *each* of the three rows: before, after, and difference. Which ones appear to have outliers?

c. Looking at this data, where does it seem the company got their "up to 10%" claim?

d. The GunShow company would like to be able to claim that "GunShow increases bicep diameter within six months, on average!" for their mid-tier body building customers. Explain why their study, as designed, could never truly allow them to draw that conclusion.

e. The GunShow company *could* theoretically make the claim "GunShow is associated with a statistically significant average increase in bicep circumference!" based on this study, if an appropriate hypothesis test on the differences confirms their statement. Check that the *differences* satisfy the conditions for inference using a t-test. (Note that it does not matter if the *original* rows satisfy the conditions, only the difference row.)

f. Perform a complete t-test on the difference data to see if the company has sufficient evidence for their claim in part (e). You do not need to check conditions again. Hint: if their claim is incorrect, what will the average difference be?

11-9. Lilly is interested in the relationship between caffeine and typing speed. She gets 200 volunteers to participate in an experiment and decides to perform a matched-pairs experiment to measure the relationship. She decides to give her participants a placebo, wait 20 minutes, and then measure how long it takes them to type a 200 word paragraph accurately. She will then repeat the process the next day, using a caffeine pill. Finally, she plans to calculate a 95% confidence interval for the difference between the two times.

a. Lilly's plan does not include any randomization. Why is this a problem and how can she fix it?

b. Will Lilly be able to extend the results of this experiment to the entire population of humans? Why or why not?

c. After performing the experiment, Lilly gets the following summary statistics for the caffeine time, the placebo time, and the paired differences

	Time with caffeine pill (s)	Time with placebo (s)	Difference in time (placebo – caffeine) (s)
Mean	332.7	336.1	3.4
Standard deviation	62.2	54.5	15.9

d. At first glance, Lilly thinks she made a calculation mistake. *"But 15.9 isn't equal to 54.5 minus 62.2!"* she says. Explain why that does not matter and her calculations above could still be correct.

e. Calculate a 95% confidence interval for the difference between caffeine times and placebo times and interpret it. Do you have evidence that caffeine increases or decreases typing speed? If so, is it a large or small difference?

11-10. Mark loves the carnival game where participants guess the number of jellybeans in a jar, and has decided to spend some time practicing so he can win next time. He has come up with two different methods for estimating the number of beans. To test his methods, he goes to the thrift store and buys eight random jars of different shapes, fills them with jellybeans, then tests his methods. His estimates are shown below:

	Jar							
	1	2	3	4	5	6	7	8
Method A	437	519	743	88	217	1032	612	333
Method B	453	515	741	108	222	1041	618	343

Is there a significant difference in the number of jellybeans estimated by Mark's two different methods for jars like those he used? Provide a statistical justification to support your answer.

MATH NOTES

Inference on Paired Data:
The Mean Difference

When interested in comparing two quantitative variables (with the same unit) that were collected in a *paired manner*, it might be possible to use **paired t-procedures** on the mean difference. These data are often gathered from matched-pairs experiments, but can also be gathered from stratified studies or studies of two different variables from the same or closely connected individuals.

To do a paired t-test or create a paired t-interval, find the difference between the values for *each pair* (making sure to carefully define which way you are subtracting) then perform a one-sample t-test or calculate a one-sample t-interval on *just the differences*, ignoring all other data. The "mean difference" is often represented with the symbol μ_D but it can also be written μ_{A-B}, where A and B represent the two variables or groups being subtracted.

The null hypothesis in such a test is almost always: H_0: $\mu_D = 0$ ("the two variables are the same on average") though the procedures can evaluate other claims. For example, such a test could be used to test the claim "our product increases test scores by an average of 10 points" with the hypothesis H_0: $\mu_D = 10$.

11-11.   One day, John and Scott were discussing how some problems in their math book are harder than others. *"It seems like homework problems with people's names in them always take longer than problems without names,"* exclaimed Scott. John decided to test Scott's hypothesis. John went through his AP Statistics book and randomly circled 10 "non-name" problems and 10 "name" problems in each chapter. The next school year when he encountered a circled problem, he timed how long it took to do the problem in minutes. Below are his results for the average minutes spent on circled problems in each chapter. Complete the test for John: do the named problems seem to take more time on average than the non-named problems? (Note: the 10% condition is complicated in this situation, but you can assume it is met since the population of homework problems is very large!)

	Chapter										
	1	2	3	4	5	6	7	8	9	10	11
Names	7.8	8.1	6.6	8.6	7.1	7.3	5.6	8.4	6.2	6.8	7.6
No Name	4.8	7.0	6.9	7.2	5.3	6.4	7.8	7.4	6.1	4.8	6.2

11-12.   Anna has more friends than she can count and unlike her, they always seem to have money! She decided to do a study to determine how much money her friends carried in their bags on a daily basis. She decided that friends that had more than 40 dollars were likely to have jobs. She collected a random sample of 23 friends in her school and counted how much money they had. Anna then organized the data in the stem-and-leaf plot at right.

0	
0	8
1	0
1	5 8 8
2	0 1 2
2	6 7 8
3	0 1 2 2 3 4
3	9 9
4	3 4
4	7 8

Key 2 | 1 = $21

a.   What percent of Anna's friends would she consider likely to have a job?

b.   The mean amount of money in the sample was $28.91, with a standard deviation of $11.32. Construct and interpret a 95% confidence interval for the mean amount of money that Anna's friends have.

11-13.   The king cobra is one of the world's most venomous snakes. Olivia is in Vietnam researching thriving ranges of king cobras. Assume a SRS of 30 cobras yielded the following information regarding the relationship between king cobra mass and length.

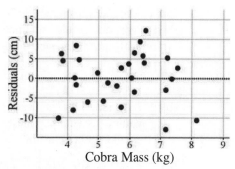

Regression Output for Length (cm) vs. Mass (kg)

Predictor	Coef	SE Coef	T	P
Constant	1.88	0.01	184.54	0.00
Mass	38.0	0.00	216.48	0.00

S = 6.50   R-Sq = 0.9830   R-Sq(Adj) = 0.9824

a.   Describe the association between the mass and length of king cobras as seen in the sample.

b.   Determine R^2 and its meaning in the context of this sample.

c.   Discuss the standard deviation of the residuals and its meaning in the context of this sample.

11.1.3 What if my data aren't paired?

Tests for the Difference of Two Means

As you saw in Lesson 11.1.1, many situations in which you want to compare two quantitative variables using an average do not come from paired data, so the paired techniques will not work. In this lesson you will begin exploration of how to conduct tests and create confidence intervals to compare the means of two *independent* samples.

11-14.   Latavia (from problem 10-32) is at Fresh Foods again, looking at the oranges. This time she notices that the Fresh Foods has both organic and traditionally grown oranges. She buys an organic orange and notices that it is not as juicy as traditionally grown oranges she has had before, and she decides she needs to investigate. She buys a random sample of 30 traditionally grown oranges and 30 organic oranges from the Fresh Foods display, takes them home, gets out her electric juicer, and measures the volume of juice from each orange, in milliliters (mL).

a.   Is this an observational study or an experiment?

b.   Assuming Latavia discovers a difference in the juice volume to what population can she reasonably extend her conclusion?

c.   Latavia wants to see if the organic oranges have less juice, on average, than the traditionally grown oranges. Explain why it would not make sense to conduct a t-test using paired values in this case.

d.   The comparative boxplot and summary data for Latavia's investigation are shown below. Use your gut: do you think that Latavia has statistically significant evidence that the average volume of juice from organic oranges is less than the average volume from traditionally grown ones?

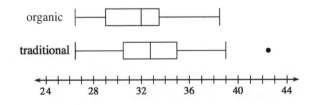

n_O	30
$\bar{O}$	31.6167
s_O	2.9673

n_T	30
$\bar{T}$	33.1333
s_T	3.3885

Problem continues on next page →

11-14.   *Problem continued from previous page.*

   e.   Latavia wants to perform a hypothesis test with the null hypothesis "the mean volume of juice from organic oranges is the same as the mean volume of juice from traditional oranges" and the alternative hypothesis "the mean volume of juice from traditional oranges is higher than the mean volume from organic oranges." How could she write these null hypotheses in symbols? See if you can come up with two different ways. Hint: one of them will involve a difference.

   f.   Does Latavia's data satisfy all of the conditions for inference if she considers each sample separately?

   g.   Latavia remembers from proportion tests that there is one more condition she needs to consider before doing a difference test—are the two samples independent *of each other?*

11-15.   Unfortunately, Latavia is stuck. In order to calculate a *p*-value for her test, she needs to know what the sampling distribution for the difference in her means looks like so she can correctly shade and calculate.

   a.   Let μ_O and σ_O represent the mean and standard deviation of distribution of the volume of juice in the appropriate population of organic oranges. Let μ_T and σ_T represent the same for the traditionally grown oranges. Finally, let n_T and n_O represent the sample sizes for the two. What are the formulas for $\sigma_{\bar{O}}$ and $\sigma_{\bar{T}}$, the standard deviations of the sampling distributions of the means for the two populations?

   b.   Use your knowledge of combining random variables to find a formula the standard deviation of the sampling distribution of the difference between these means. That is, what is $\sigma_{\bar{T}-\bar{O}}$?

   c.   Of course, Latavia does not know the values of σ_T and σ_O. Use s_T and s_O values Latavia found in her sample to instead calculate the standard error of the difference in the means, $SE_{\bar{T}-\bar{O}}$.

11-16.   Latavia is ready to calculate a test statistic! The "recipe" for test statistics is test statistic $= \frac{\text{statistic} - \text{parameter}}{\text{SD of statistic}}$.

   a.   For Latavia's test, the parameter of interest is $\mu_T - \mu_O$, the difference in population means. What does the null hypothesis say you should *assume* is the value of $\mu_T - \mu_O$?

   b.   What is the value of the *estimating statistic* for the parameter—that is, what is Latavia's best guess for the difference in the means based on her sample?

   c.   You now have all of the ingredients necessary to calculate Latavia's test statistic. This statistic will follow a t-distribution, so go ahead and use the variable *t* to represent it, and calculate the statistic.

11-17.   Latavia is *almost* ready to calculate her *p*-value, but she hits a snag—degrees of freedom! She does not know how many to use. Should use 29, since *n* was 30 for both samples? Or should she combine for a sample size of 60, and use 59 degrees of freedom? Maybe she should use 58?

a.   Latavia does some research and learns there are two common approaches. The first "conservative" approach uses the degrees of freedom for the *smaller* of the two samples. If Latavia uses this approach, how many degrees of freedom will she use?

b.   The more precise formula for the degrees of freedom in this situation is found using the complex formula $df = \dfrac{(SE_1{}^2 + SE_2{}^2)^2}{\frac{SE_1{}^4}{df_1} + \frac{SE_2{}^4}{df_2}}$. Latavia runs this calculation and gets a df of 57.05 (note this can be and is a decimal!). What advantage does this method offer over the value from part (a)? What is its disadvantage?

11-18.   Use the degrees of freedom from part (b) above to complete Latavia's test. Calculate the *p*-value (with a sketch!) and draw a conclusion in context.

MATH NOTES

Hypothesis Test for the Difference in Two Independent Means (Two-Sample z-Test/t-Test)

This very common hypothesis test can be used to decide if two variables have different average values in two different populations OR under two different treatments in an experiment.

Identify the test by name (two-sample t-test, or z-test in the rare case that both population standard deviations are known) and state hypotheses. The null hypothesis is almost always in the form $\mu_1 = \mu_2$ or $\mu_1 - \mu_2 = 0$, though in theory the difference could be compared to another number. Define any symbols in context. Provide sample evidence in favor of the alternative hypothesis. State the value of α being used.

Check the conditions. First, make sure (and state) that the samples are independent *of each other*—no matched pairs! Then check each sample for the one-sample conditions from Chapter 10. For two-sample tests, the random condition can be met either through random *sampling* or through random *assignment to treatments* in an experiment; make sure to state explicitly which is met. If random assignment is used, the independent trials condition can be skipped. See the Math Notes box in the next lesson for more details.

Calculate. If calculating by hand, find your test statistic using the formula for standard error of the sampling distribution $SE = \sqrt{\dfrac{s_1^2}{n_1} + \dfrac{s_2^2}{n_2}}$, or use the population standard deviations if known. For t-test degrees of freedom, use $n - 1$ where n is the size of the smaller sample. It is often easier to calculate the test statistic and p-value using technology. Report the test statistic, the degrees of freedom, the p-value, and a shaded sketch of the curve.

Conclude. Make sure to state in the conclusion sentence whether the p-value is less than or greater than α, and mention the value of α again. Do not forget the context!

Note that a confidence interval for the difference in the means can be found using a very similar four-step process.

11-19.   To compare the average life of two cell phone batteries, a random sample of 100 πPhone 7s are compared to a random sample of 100 Noid Universe 6s. The sample of πPhones have an average life of 15 hours and 30 minutes with a standard deviation of 1 hour and 15 minutes. The mean life of the Noids is 14 hours and 15 minutes with a standard deviation of 2 hours and 45 minutes. Is the observed difference between the means of two samples significant at the 0.05 level?

11-20.   A national survey by Pew Research Center was conducted from June 15 to June 26 among 2245 U.S. adults, prior to the 2016 presidential election. The results showing highest education level and party affiliation are listed below.

	Post Grad	College Grad	Some College	High School or Less
Democrat Candidate	60%	54%	47%	50%
Republican Candidate	33%	38%	46%	43%
Other				
	268	460	629	888

http://www.people-press.org/files/2016/07/07-07-16-Voter-attitudes-release.pdf *counts assumed

a.   Redraw the table in your notebook and find observed frequencies based on the number of people surveyed. Add row totals.

b.   Find the expected value of each cell and write it next to the cell count in the table.

c.   Run and interpret a chi-square significance test at a 0.05 alpha-level.

d.   Interpret your results and explain what you think the data in the table means.

11-21.   Nurse Nina is working in the emergency room over the weekend. From past data, she knows that there is a 60% chance that the patient will be from out of town and a 50% chance the patient will be over the age of 60. She also knows that there is a 30% chance the patient will be over 60 years old and from out of town. What is the probability that the patient will be either from out of town or over 60 or both?

11.1.4   How else can I use these procedures?

· ·

Two-Sample Mean Inference with Experiments and
Two-Sample Confidence Intervals

11-22. Independent random samples of marriage certificates were taken in 1950 and 2000 and the age
of the male participant on each certificate was taken (certificates with two men had one chosen
randomly, while those with two women were discarded for this study). The graphs and
summary statistics below show information about these samples.

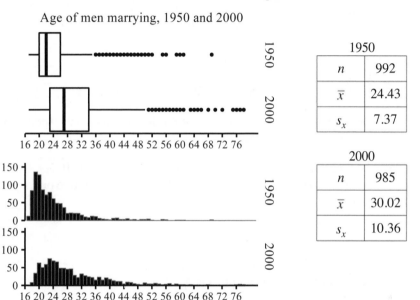

Age of men marrying, 1950 and 2000

	1950
n	992
$\bar{x}$	24.43
s_x	7.37

	2000
n	985
$\bar{x}$	30.02
s_x	10.36

a.   Compare these two distributions.

b.   It is obvious from this data that the mean marriage age of men has increased from 1950
to 2000, but a researcher wants to get an estimate range for *how much* the mean has
increased in the entire population of American marrying men. She plans to make a
confidence interval for the difference in the means, $\mu_{2000} - \mu_{1950}$. Does this study satisfy
all of the conditions for a confidence interval?

c.   The researcher lost their graphing calculator and is not near a computer, and does not
have a table of t-values. However, the researcher remembers that the 95% critical value
for a NORMAL distribution is 1.96. Could the researcher safely use 1.96 as her critical
value in this calculation? Explain.

d.   Use the conservative method to estimate degrees of freedom for this situation, and find
the critical value for a 95% confidence interval using a calculator. Check your answer to
part (c): how close is it to the normal critical value?

e.   Calculate the standard error of the difference between the means using the formula
$SE = \sqrt{\dfrac{s_1^2}{n_1} + \dfrac{s_2^2}{n_2}}$, then use it to create and interpret a confidence interval for increase in
the average age of men getting married from 1950 to 2000.

11-23.   A certain very large high school is planning to start an enrichment program to prepare students for standardized tests such as the SAT. They are considering an expensive online test prep program called "Get Prepped!" The principal, who also teaches Statistics, decides to run an experiment to see whether the program is worth the money. She gathers 20 volunteer students from the sophomore and junior classes and gives all of them the same pretest. She then randomly assigns 10 students to a prep class using "Get Prepped!" and 10 students to a class that simply encourages them to prepare and provides free online resources. After 30 days in the class, she gives all of the students a post-test, and measures the change for each student. The tables below give the increase in test scores for both groups. Note that the SAT is scored out of 1600 points in units of 10 points.

Group A (free online resources)

Score increase	20	10	80	40	190	180	70	120	80	170

Mean increase: 96   Standard deviation of increase: 66.2

Group B ("Get Prepped!")

Score increase	280	190	180	170	200	−30	130	100	90	170

Mean increase: 148   Standard deviation of increase: 82.7

a.   Read the Math Notes at the end of this lesson. Does this experiment satisfy the "random" condition for inference?

b.   Do the data provide convincing evidence, at the $\alpha = 0.10$ level, that the "Get Prepped!" class caused a larger increase in SAT scores than the free online resources? Conduct a complete hypothesis test.

11-24.   Fitness trackers are electronic devices that can be worn to measure the activity of a person, including the number of steps they take in a day. Some fitness trackers offer an option to alert the user when an hour has passed without the user engaging in activity. One fitness tracker company is interested in testing whether the activity alert feature actually increases step count in users. They recruit 200 volunteers for a fitness study. 100 of the volunteers are randomly chosen to receive a tracker with the fitness alert feature available and enabled, while the other 100 receive a tracker with no fitness alert available. Neither group is told which feature of the tracker is being tested. Each group reports their daily step count for 30 days and their median step count is found.

The average of the median counts for the group with the activity alert feature is 8324 steps with a standard deviation of 4312 steps. The average of the median counts for the group with no activity alert feature is 7113 steps with a standard deviation of 3912 steps. Both distributions show a distinct right skew.

Does the activity alert feature appear to increase step count on average? Give appropriate statistical evidence to support your conclusion at $\alpha = 0.05$.

MATH NOTES

Inference with Experiments:
Differences in Conditions

Experiments and samples are related, but their underlying math and purpose is actually quite different. It is not necessarily obvious that the same procedures used to decide if *two populations are different* can be used to decide if *a treatment caused a change in two treatment groups*, but amazingly they generally can be—however, the conditions for inference are a bit different for experiments.

Random condition. Experiments are often done on volunteers or convenience samples, so no random sampling is done! Instead, it is necessary that experiments have *random assignment to treatments* so as to avoid confounding variables. If no sample was done, do not use the phrase "random sample"—there was none! On the rare occasion that both random sampling *and* random assignment are used, mention both.

Independent trials condition. Skip it in problems! Since participants are not a random sample from a population, the *large population* requirement is unnecessary. If it is important that experimental units within a treatment do not affect one another, random assignment and good experimental design assure this additional checking.

Large sample/normal population condition (means) or large counts condition (proportions or chi-squared) For this condition, simply check the condition as normal for the *treatment groups* rather than samples; these conditions are still necessary for the theoretical distributions to correctly model the statistics. In proportion tests, sample counts (rather than expected counts) are acceptable.

Independent samples condition. Skip it in problems! If it is important that participants from one treatment group to not affect participants in the other group, again random sampling and good experimental design assure this without an additional check.

Conclusion. Rather than concluding, "the population mean is …" you can instead conclude "those receiving treatment A differ from those receiving treatment B" or "the treatment caused the groups to differ." If the treatment groups can be justified as a representative sample of some population, often the conclusion is extended to the population.

11-25. The Dallas University Health Center is conducting a study comparing two existing medicines to treat fibromyalgia. They need to compare the ages of the two groups receiving the medicines. A random sample of medical records for patients known to be taking one of the medicines produced the following data:

Group A: 48, 48, 49, 53, 57, 57, 59, 60, 62, 68, 68, 70, 71, 72, 72 *checksum: 914*

Group B: 28, 29, 32, 34, 45, 49, 51, 55, 64, 68, 74, 75, 79, 80, 85, 94 *checksum: 942*

Is there a significant difference in the populations mean ages of those taking treatments A and B? Use a 5% significance level.

11-26. Does eating dark chocolate reduce cholesterol?

   a. Should an observational study or an experiment be carried out to answer the question? Explain.

   b. Describe how you would carry out the study. Be sure to describe how you would incorporate randomization into your design.

11-27. Steve the fisherman has been testing the strength of 20 lb fishing lines for several years. He has found that 20 lb fishing line strength is approximately normal, with a mean break strength of 24.2 lbs and a standard deviation of 3.733 lbs.

   a. Find the 30th percentile of the distribution of break strengths.

   b. What is the chance that if 10 randomly selected 20 lb fishing lines were selected, 4 or more of them would have a breaking strength less than the 30th percentile calculated in part (a).

   c. To label your fishing line "20 lbs" you must have a mean break strength more than 22.2 lbs. What is the probability of 10 randomly selected fishing lines have a mean strength greater than 22.2 lbs.

11.2.1 Which technique do I use?

Inference in Different Situations

Join Mo and Lana as they investigate variables associated with paper.

11-28.   There are many, many reams of copy paper in the copy room at Mo and Lana's school. Lana has always wondered how thick a piece of paper actually is. The reams of paper all labeled "20 lb." She contacted the paper company, and they told her that the paper is manufactured in large sheets, and a ream (500 large sheets) of 20 lb paper, before cutting them to size, would weigh 20 pounds. They also told her that the mean thickness for their 20 lb paper should be 0.1 mm.

Lana decided to check the company's claim. She gathered a random sample of paper marked "20 lb" and measured the thickness of each sheet of paper in random locations. Her results (in mm) are displayed below:

0.101, 0.104, 0.102, 0.106, 0.101, 0.104, 0.108, 0.096, 0.106, 0.103, 0.107, 0.100, 0.104, 0.097, 0.100

a.   Lana made the combined boxplot and dot plot below and found the summary statistics shown. Does Lana have evidence that the company's reported average of 0.1 mm is incorrect? Back up your conclusion with statistical evidence. (You may assume that Lana's sample is equivalent to an SRS from the population of all 20 lb paper from this company).

Paper thickness (mm), 20 lb

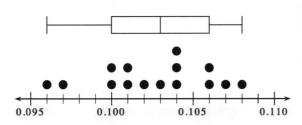

n	15
$\bar{x}$	0.1026
s_x	0.0035

b.   It turns out the company rounds all values to the nearest tenth millimeter when reporting their average thicknesses. Does this affect your conclusion?

11-29.   Mo notices an enormous pile of multi-colored index cards next to the copy paper. He grabs a big pile of index cards randomly and counts the number of cards of each color, creating the following table:

Blue	Red	Green	Purple	Yellow
12	23	19	27	21

Does Mo have evidence that the colors are *not* equally distributed in the entire pile?

11-30.   While Mo was distracted by index cards, Lana was still playing with the digital caliper. She found a big pile of blue paper in another corner, also labeled "20 lb," and wonders if it is the same thickness as the white paper labeled "20 lb." She uses the same technique she used in problem 11-28 to pick a random sample of pages, measures the thicknesses of the blue paper, and then creates the combined boxplots and histograms below.

Blue Paper Thickness (mm), 20 lb

Blue Paper	
n	15
$\bar{x}$	0.099
s_x	0.0049

White Paper Thickness (mm), 20 lb

White paper	
n	15
$\bar{x}$	0.1026
s_x	0.0035

Does Lana have evidence that the blue paper and white paper have different thicknesses on average? Back up your answer with statistical evidence at $\alpha = 0.05$.

11-31. Lana and Mo are both surprised by the results from the blue paper, and they wonder if the blue paper is simply lower quality overall. Mo decides they should conduct an experiment to see if the paper is uniform in thickness. He takes another random sample of 12 pieces of blue paper and measures them in two locations—1 cm from the edge and 10 cm from the edge of one long side. The data from the measurements are shown at right. All measurements are in mm.

1 cm	10 cm
0.092	0.096
0.096	0.101
0.096	0.099
0.103	0.112
0.093	0.097
0.085	0.087
0.085	0.094
0.092	0.093
0.097	0.107
0.089	0.094
0.099	0.105
0.091	0.096

Do Lana and Mo have sufficient evidence to conclude the paper is of different thicknesses at the 10 cm than the 1 cm spot, on average?

11-32. The difference between life and death is often just minutes when it comes to stopping bleeding. Two emergency procedures are being compared for their speed in stopping bleeding at the scene of accidents. The time from when 911 was called to the time that paramedics reported the bleeding stopped was recorded and sorted for a random sample of accidents. The data is shown below (in minutes).

Procedure C-2: 3, 4, 4, 5, 6, 6, 7, 7, 7, 8, 8, 8, 10, 14, 14, 15, 16, 17, 19, 19
checksum: 197

Procedure C-7: 8, 9, 10, 11, 11, 12, 12, 12, 13, 13, 13, 14, 14, 15, 16
checksum: 183

a. Determine if there is a difference between the population mean times it takes to stop the bleeding between the two procedures.

b. What error (Type I or Type II) is possible from your analysis in part (a)? Is it likely and what would be the potential consequences or that error?

c. Obviously a shorter average time would be an asset to either method. Name two other parameters that might be useful in evaluating these procedures and explain why they are useful.

11-33.   The American bison is the national mammal of the United States. Julio is in Nebraska studying endangered habitats of American bison. Julio believes the distribution of individual bison daily roaming movements are normally distributed with a mean of 3.32 km/day and a standard deviation of 0.75 km/day.

    a.   Sketch the normal probability density function. 6% of individual American bison daily roam <u>less</u> than how many km/day?

    b.   If a random sample of 50 bison is observed, what is the probability that fewer than 46 will roam more than the distance you found in part (a)?

    c.   How likely is it that a sample of 50 bison would roam an <u>average</u> of more than 3.20 km/day?

11-34.   **Multiple Choice:** Which of the following is not a condition needed to do a hypothesis test on a proportion?

    A.   Each sample point can only have two outcomes: success and failure.

    B.   The population size is at least 20 times bigger than the sample size.

    C.   The sample was collected randomly.

    D.   The sample has a minimum of 10 successes and 10 failures.

    E.   If sample data are displayed in a contingency table, the expected frequency count for each cell of the table is at least 5.

11-35.   **Multiple Choice:** Which of the following is not a condition needed to test a hypothesis with a χ^2 test?

    A.   The two variables are independent.

    B.   The data was sampled using a random sample.

    C.   The variables are categorical.

    D.   If sample data are displayed in a contingency table, the expected frequency count for each cell of the table is at least 5.

    E.   All of these are conditions.

11.2.2 How do you connect all inference?

Identifying and Implementing an Appropriate Test

This lesson combines all of the material from Chapters 7 to 11 with shorter questions to probe understanding. Think of it as a review of nearly all of inference.

11-36.   A researcher is conducting a study on how adults volunteer their time. She wants to determine if there is convincing statistical evidence that more than 20% of adults in the city volunteered at least on hour a month last year. Let p represent the proportion of all adults in the city that volunteered at least an hour a month last year. What kind of test can the research do, and what are the hypotheses?

11-37.   A mathematician calculates a confidence interval for a sample mean at a confidence level of 95%. What does the 95% mean in this context?

11-38.   The mathematician from the prior problem originally used a sample size of 200. What would happen to the confidence interval if she increased her sample size to 400 and changed nothing else? (Use numbers in your answer.)

11-39.   Mariah takes a sample of students at her school to see if they get the average amount of sleep for people their age. She does some research and finds that the average amount of sleep for high school teenagers is 7 hours and runs a test with these hypotheses:

$$H_0: \mu = 7$$
$$H_A: \mu \neq 7$$

where μ is the mean number of hours slept by students at Mariah's school. The results of the test are shown in the table below.

Sample mean	Std. Error	df	T	p-value
7.4	0.246	24	1.626	0.117

Confirm the t-statistic makes sense given the standard error and sample mean, then calculate a 95% confidence interval for the mean.

11-40.   In the previous question, what was the standard deviation of the hours of sleep in the original sample? Interpret the value in context.

11-41.   For each of the following scenarios, identify the appropriate hypothesis test to analyze the data, assuming all conditions are met in each case.

   a.   A scientist splits a group of 60 volunteers into two groups. One group takes a test while listening to classical music. The other takes the same test in silence. Each participant's score out of 20 is measured.

   b.   A teacher gives his entire class a pre-test for a topic. Two weeks later, after conducting several investigative activities with the class, he gives them the same test again.

   c.   A pollster polls 1248 people including 612 men and 636 women. One question asked is *"Do you listen to country music?"* The pollster wants to identify if there is a difference between men and women in this questions.

   d.   A surplus hardware store sells large boxes full of screws of *"assorted sizes"* for low prices. A contractor wants to evaluate whether there are about the same number of each size screw in a box.

   e.   A commercial claims that replacing one meal a week with SlimQuick shakes helps overweight people lose *"at least 10 lbs in a month!"* on average. A doctor decides to conduct a study to test whether this claim applies to his patients.

   f.   The pollster from part (c) had another question in her survey that asked, *"What is your favorite kind of music?"* with twelve different choices. She is interested to see if the answer to this question differs based on gender.

11-42.   A simple random sample 101 high school students are asked what their favorite type of movie is. The table lists the actual and expected frequencies for their responses. Which of the χ^2 conditions are not met?

	Drama	Comedy	Horror	Romance
Actual Frequency	26	45	3	27
Expected Frequency	30	52	2	17

11-43.   In 2003, the U.S. Census Bureau began collecting data for the ATUS (American Time Use Survey) which surveys individuals over 15 years of age about how they spend their time. In 2015, approximately 10,900 people were interviewed.

   a.   Approximate how many men were surveyed in 2015.

   b.   The survey reported, *"On an average day, 85% of women and 67% of men spent some time doing household activities such as housework, cooking, lawn care, or financial and other household management."* Assume conditions are met and calculate and interpret a 95% confidence interval for the percent of men that spent some time doing household activities.

   c.   Suppose the approximate number of men in the survey that you calculated in part (a) was an underestimate by exactly 550 men, giving 6000 men in the sample. Recalculate the confidence interval for the correct number of men.

   d.   Compare the two intervals.

11-44.   3000 different simple random samples of 100 students each are selected from a very large school district where the average age of the students is 15 years and the standard deviation is 2 years.

   a.   How will the 3000 sample means be distributed? (Attend to precision in your answer.)

   b.   Using the Empirical Rule from Chapter 5, between what two values will approximately 68% of the sample means fall?

   c.   Using the Empirical Rule, between what two values will 95% of the sample means fall?

   d.   What will the distribution of ages look like for any 1 sample of 100 students?

11-45.   For each situation below explain what it would mean to have a Type I error.

   a.   It is hypothesized that a certain medical procedure (procedure A) has a faster recovery rate than the standard procedure (procedure B). An experiment is run to compare the average recovery time for the procedures at $\alpha = 0.05$ level.

   b.   A container of milk from a bottling plant is supposed to contain 3.78 L of milk. It is suspected that one of the bottling machines is not correctly filling the bottles. A random sample of 100 bottles is measured to see if the average fill amount is significantly different than 3.78 L.

11-46.   For each situation below explain what it would mean to have a Type II error.

a.   It is hypothesized that a certain medical procedure (procedure A) has a faster recovery rate than the standard procedure (procedure B). An experiment is run to compare the average recovery time for the procedures at $\alpha = 0.05$ level.

b.   A container of milk from a bottling plant is supposed to contain 3.78 L of milk. It is suspected that one of the bottling machines is under-filling the bottles. A random sample of 100 bottles is measured to see if the average fill amount is significantly different than 3.78 L.

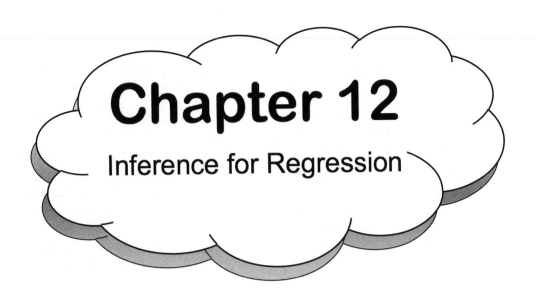

Chapter 12

Inference for Regression

CHAPTER 12 Inference for Regression

Chapter Goals

Explore sampling distributions of slopes.

Learn inference techniques for determining linear relationships in populations of paired data.

Investigate curved relationships between quantitative variables.

Use technology to create and analyze nonlinear models.

Use nonlinear models to make predictions.

In Chapter 2 you learned ways to show relationships between two quantitative variables. At that time you had very little knowledge of sample variation. Now knowing that the data pairs represent samples that vary, you will explore the distribution of sample slopes to make statements about populations of data pairs. In Chapter 2 you also learned to identify when a relationship was nonlinear, but made no effort to determine it. In this chapter you will examine techniques to determine curves of best fit.

Chapter Outline

Section 12.1 You will explore the sampling distribution of the slope, and the conditions for inference are developed. The connection between the slope and the correlation coefficient is further explored. Finally, students carry out a confidence interval and hypothesis test for the slope.

Section 12.2 There are many situations where a curved model between two variables is most appropriate. Using technology you will explore the models $y = (a + bx)^2$ and $y = a + bx^2$, then use logarithms to linearize exponential ($y = ab^x$) and power ($y = ax^p$) models.

12.1.1 Does the slope have a distribution?

Sampling Distribution of the Slope of the Regression Line

Two researchers working for different companies are studying a certain type of coffee plant. They each independently conduct the same large study on the same population of plants. The study is designed to describe the effect of rainfall on the amount of coffee produced per plant. In each of the studies, 10 coffee plants are randomly assigned to receive a controlled amount of rainfall (measured in inches) for the duration of its season. The amounts range from 35 to 80 inches, in increments of 5 inches.

12-1.   The first research group, Sunbucks, obtained the following equation: $y = 0.0606x + 1.4624$ where y is the predicted weight of coffee produced (pounds) and x is the amount of rainfall (inches). The coefficient of determination was $r^2 = 0.9157$, and a residual plot appears completely scattered.

   a.   Interpret the slope of the regression equation in context.

   b.   Find the correlation coefficient, and interpret it in context. Explain how you know that it should be positive and not negative.

12-2.   The second research group, Folvers, obtained the following equation: $y = 0.0580x + 1.5921$ where y is the predicted weight of coffee produced (pounds) and x is the amount of rainfall (inches). The coefficient of determination was $r^2 = 0.8934$, and a residual plot appears completely scattered.

   a.   Both research groups conducted identical studies on the same population of coffee plants. Explain how they could have obtained different results.

   b.   If ten more identical studies were to be conducted, make a guess for a possible range of values that the slope might be found in for each of the regression equations.

   c.   Explain what it means for the slope of the regression equation to have a sampling distribution.

12-3.   Because the slope of the regression equation has a sampling distribution, you could carry out inference procedures such as a confidence interval or hypothesis test if you could describe the sampling distribution of the slope. Suppose 12 identical studies were conducted resulting in the following equations:

$y = 0.0592x + 1.6151, y = 0.0593x + 1.5258, y = 0.0604x + 1.4829, y = 0.0575x + 1.6715,$
$y = 0.0616x + 1.4210, y = 0.0595x + 1.5539, y = 0.0598x + 1.5032, y = 0.0615x + 1.4317,$
$y = 0.0616x + 1.4214, y = 0.0597x + 1.4946, y = 0.0588x + 1.5694, y = 0.0591x + 1.5404$

a.   Based on the twelve equations above, describe the sampling distribution of the slope. Use the mean and standard deviation in your response to describe center and spread.

b.   When we discussed the sampling distribution of the sample mean, we observed that there is a population mean μ, and sample means ($\bar{x}$) are centered about the population mean μ. We said that the sample mean is an *unbiased estimator* of the population mean. Similarly, slopes based on a random sample (we will use the symbol b to match the form $y = a + bx$) are centered about a slope β based on the population. Use your work from part (a) to estimate how a typical sample slope would differ from the "true" slope β.

c.   The Sunbucks research group from problem 12-1 was studying its regression output, shown below.

Regression Output for Yield/Plant (lbs) vs. Rainfall (in)

Predictor	Coef	SE Coef	T	P
Constant	1.4624	0.1101	13.2883	0.0000
Rainfall (in)	0.0606	0.0012	20.6088	0.0000

S = 0.2667   R-Sq = 0.9157   R-Sq(Adj) = 0.9149

The "Coef" column displays the coefficients in the linear model (the y-intercept and slope). The "SE Coef" column displays the standard error for each statistic, based on the sample data. How does the standard error of the slope reported compare to the standard deviation you found in part (a)? Interpret the standard error of the slope from this printout.

12-4.   Certain assumptions need to be clarified before any inference (confidence interval or hypothesis test) regarding the slope can be carried out. In general, the same types of inference conditions still apply. Answer the following questions below based on the description of the study at the beginning of this lesson.

   a.   *Randomness:* Does the data represent a random sample from the population?

   b.   *Independence/large population:* Are the data independent and/or sampled from a large population?

   c.   The *x*-values are considered to be the *independent* or *explanatory* variable. The *y*-values are the *dependent* or *response* variable. The theory behind inference in a regression setting is based on assuming that the response variable has a known distribution for each fixed value of the explanatory variable. Assume that each value of the explanatory variable produces a normally distributed response variable with the same spread (standard deviation). Does this seem like a reasonable assumption in this setting?

   d.   If inference is carried out in a *linear* regression setting, it should be established that the data does indeed have a linear form! Is there anything to suggest that the data has a linear form?

12-5.   It can be shown that the distribution of the sample slopes follows the t-distribution. Consider a bivariate (*x* and *y* paired data) set with *n* points.

   a.   What clue is provided in the regression output in part (c) of problem 12-3 that the slope follows the t-distribution?

   b.   How many points define a line? Use this fact to make an educated guess to the degrees of freedom for the slope.

MATH NOTES

Inference for Slope and Regression Line
Assumptions and Conditions

Assumptions	Conditions to check
Individuals are chosen as a simple random sample from the population.	Was it stated, or can it be inferred, that the individuals were randomly chosen?
Individual paired observations (and residuals) are independent.	The same large population condition exists. Also, check that there is no pattern in the residual plot.
For each fixed value of the explanatory variable, the response variable is normally distributed with the same standard deviation.	The residual plot should have no pattern of increasing/decreasing spread. If the response variable is normally distributed for each explanatory variable value, a histogram of residuals should have a symmetric shape.
There is a linear relationship between the explanatory and response variables in the population.	The form of the sample scatterplot should be linear with a randomly distributed residual plot.

Review & Preview

12-6.   Greg and his sister Jenn share a computer at home for doing their homework and gaming. Jenn claims that Greg is "hogging" the computer so she checks the login times for both usernames in separate random samples of 14 days each. Their usage in minutes follows:

Gregory: 49 48 51 52 68 40 73 68 61 60 69 55 51 59

His sister: 49 45 37 63 56 57 62 50 42 48 55 64 40 42

a.   What type of data did Jenn collect, quantitative or categorical, and how do you know?

b.   Is Greg a "computer hog" or could his higher use be attributed to random variation? Run an appropriate test to determine this.

12-7.   All octopuses are venomous, but only the
         small blue-ringed octopuses are known to be
         deadly to humans. Nicole is in the Pacific
         Ocean researching encroached upon ranges of
         octopuses. Assume a cluster sample of
         21 octopuses gave the following summary
         regarding the relationship between octopus
         mass in grams and venom amount in
         microliters.

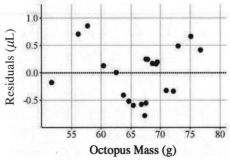

Octopus Mass (g)

Regression Output for Venom Amount vs. Octopus Mass

Predictor	Coef	SE Coef	T	P
Constant	-10.23	0.26	-38.64	0.00
Mass	0.3444	0.00	86.79	0.00

S = 0.492   R-Sq = 0.9520   R-Sq(Adj) = 0.9494

a.   Determine the LSRL equation and label the variables in context.

b.   Describe the slope and its meaning in the context of this sample.

c.   Use the LSRL to predict the venom amount of an octopus whose mass is 66.65 grams.

d.   Calculate the residual for the point (67.60, 12.50).

e.   Is a linear model the most appropriate? How do you know?

12-8.   Suppose a test for a certain rare condition claims to be 99% accurate.

a.   If you scan 10,000 people and only 2% actually have the condition, how many of the
      10,000 people have the condition? How many do not have the condition?

b.   Of the people who have the condition from part (a), how many of them will be given
      accurate results from the test?

c.   Of the people who have the condition from part (a), how many of them will be given
      inaccurate results from the test? This is known as a false negative.

d.   A 99% accurate test will also produce *false positives* at a rate of 1%. Of the people who
      do not have the condition (see part (a)), how many will be told that they have it?

e.   How many total positive tests were indicated among the 10,000 people?

f.   What percent of total positive tests are genuine?

g.   What would happen to the percent of total positive test that are genuine if only 1% of the
      10000 actually have the condition?

12.1.2   Can I make an inference about the slope?

Inference for the Slope of the Regression Line

The research group for Sunbucks wanted to conduct another smaller study on the effects of a new organic fertilizer on the total mass of coffee beans produced per plant. The company obtains a random sample of 33 coffee plants and grows them in a controlled environment similar to the actual growth environment. The company uses a completely randomized design, randomly assigning 3 plants to receive a level of organic fertilizer between 0 and 40 g in increments of 4 g. The mass (kg) of coffee produced by each plant during its growing season is recorded.

Ironically, the supervisor for Sunbucks spilled coffee on the computer in the research lab, destroying the computer. It was not a complete loss since there had been a paper report created. The following graphs and calculations survived, although there is a significant coffee stain on the regression output table.

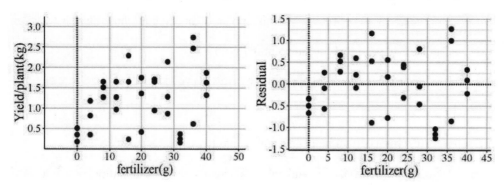

Regression Output for Yield/Plant (kg) vs. Fertilizer (g)

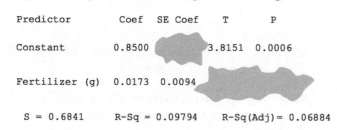

Predictor	Coef	SE Coef	T	P
Constant	0.8500		3.8151	0.0006
Fertilizer (g)	0.0173	0.0094		

S = 0.6841   R-Sq = 0.09794   R-Sq(Adj) = 0.06884

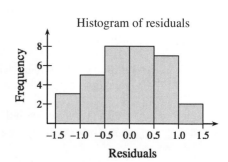

Histogram of residuals

12-9.   In Lesson 2.2.2, you discovered that the slope can be calculated as $b = r\dfrac{s_y}{s_x}$.

    a.   Use the regression output to identify the slope of the regression line.

    b.   Use the regression output to identify the correlation coefficient r.

    c.   One of the Sunbucks researchers remembered that the standard deviation for the fertilizer amounts was 12.845 because these amounts were controlled by the design of the study. Use these values to solve for the s_y, the standard deviation of the yield/plant. Include units in your response.

12-10.   The Sunbucks team would like to construct a 95% confidence interval for the slope of the regression line.

    a.   Do the conditions for inference appear to be met in order to carry out this inference procedure? Explain in detail.

    b.   There were 33 plants included in the study. What degree of freedom should be used for the t-distribution?

    c.   Find the critical value t^*.

    d.   Using the value for the standard error of the slope from the printout, construct a 95% confidence interval for the slope. Clearly identify the margin of error, and include units.

    e.   Interpret your confidence interval in context.

12-11.   The Sunbucks team wants to know if the confidence interval in problem 12-10 provides evidence that the new organic fertilizer had a positive impact on the coffee produced.

    a.   Is it possible that the organic fertilizer actually had a negative impact? Explain.

    b.   Does the confidence interval allow for the possibility that the slope is zero? Explain.

    c.   Just like there is a slope from the sample (b) and a slope for the population (β), there is also a correlation coefficient from the sample (r) and a correlation coefficient for the population (ρ). Use the equation $b = r\dfrac{s_y}{s_x}$ to explain why if the slope is zero, the correlation coefficient must also be zero.

    d.   Can the Sunbucks team conclude that the organic fertilizer had any effect on the mass of coffee beans produced? Explain.

12-12.   The Sunbucks supervisor (who spilled the coffee) is demanding that the missing values on the regression output be found, or the study will need to be replicated. The research team sets up a two-tailed hypothesis test for the slope in order to find the missing values. They already have established that the conditions for inference have been met, so they jump straight to the null/alternative hypotheses and the calculations.

    a.   The null hypothesis always says something similar to, "There is nothing going on. There is no significant relationship." In this context, what value for the overall slope β would indicate no relationship between the explanatory and response variables? Write your null and alternative hypotheses.

    b.   Because the slope is modeled by the t-distribution, you can use the formula $t = \frac{b-\beta}{SE_b}$ to calculate the standardized test-statistic. Make the calculation using the information from the regression output and your value for β from the null hypothesis in part (a).

    c.   Use your standardized test-statistic and the degree of freedom from problem 12-10 to find the p-value. Remember that it is a two-tailed test!

    d.   Write a conclusion in context for the hypothesis test based on your p-value. Use a 5% level of significance. Does this conclusion agree with your confidence interval?

12-13.   The Sunbucks supervisor (who spilled the coffee) is very pleased with the research team's recovery of the information hidden behind the coffee stain. While the standard error for the intercept for this linear model is not important to the research group, the supervisor still would like to recover this value.

    a.   Identify and interpret the y-intercept in this context.

    b.   The team uses the equation $y = a + bx$ and therefore the symbol a to represent the y-intercept. Using the convention of Greek letters, they use α for the population parameter. They make a similar calculation, setting up the equation: $t = \frac{a-\alpha}{SE_a}$ where a is the y-intercept. Using 0 for α (no fertilizer predicts no coffee produced), solve for SE_a using the other values provided on the regression output.

MATH NOTES

Interpreting Regression Computer Output

The output below was created by computer software comparing pinky length to thumb length in 14 randomly chosen adults.

Regression Output for Thumb length (cm) vs. Pinky length (cm)

Predictor	Coef	SE Coef	T	P
Constant	0.3926	0.9685	0.4053	0.6924
Pinky length (cm)	0.9563	0.2659	3.5958	0.0037

S = 0.3676   R-Sq = 0.5187   R-Sq(Adj) = 0.4785   r = 0.7202

The "Coef" column shows the values of the y-intercept (constant coefficient) and the slope (coefficient of the explanatory variable). In this case the LSRL equation would be:

$$\overline{\text{thumb length}} = 0.3926 + 0.9563(\text{pinky length})$$

Underneath the output are values for S, the standard deviation of the residuals, R^2, the coefficient of determination, and r, the correlation coefficient. Some computer output does not include r, as it can be calculated using R^2 and the sign of the slope. "Adj R-Sq" can be ignored.

The "SE Coef" column shows the **standard error of the coefficients**; these estimate variability in the calculations of both the y-intercept and the slope. These values can be used to create *confidence intervals* for the slope or y-intercept with the formula "statistic $\pm$ (critical value)(standard error of statistic)." Critical values come from a t-distribution with $n - 2$ degrees of freedom. In this example, a 95% confidence interval for the slope would be $0.9563 \pm (2.179)(0.2659)$.

The "T" column represents the t-test statistic and the "P" column the p-value for a hypothesis test with the null hypothesis "coefficient $= 0$" and alternative "coefficient $\neq 0$." Note that the t-statistic is simply the coefficient divided by the standard error. If the p-value is greater than your chosen α then that means the null hypothesis that the coefficients is 0 cannot be rejected. In the case of y-intercepts this would mean that it is possible these variables *vary directly in the population*. In the case of the slope, this would mean that it is possible the variables have *no association in the population*. The slope test is the more common of the two in AP exam questions.

12-14.   A Statistics professor was bothered by students being tardy to class. The professor decided to conduct a study. A random sample of students was gathered. The cumulative number of minutes tardy and the overall grade (as a percent) was recorded for each student. The following computer output was produced:

Regression Output for Course Grade vs. Minutes Tardy

Predictor	Coef	SE Coef	T	P(>|t|)
(Intercept)	94.0555	6.4603	14.56	0.0000
Minutes Tardy	-0.6369	0.2412	-2.64	0.0138

Residual standard error: 19.23 on 26 degrees of freedom
Multiple R-squared: 0.2114, Adjusted R-squared: 0.1811

Conduct an appropriate test to determine if there is significant evidence of an overall correlation between a student's cumulative number of minutes tardy and a student's overall course grade. Use a 5% level of significance. Assume that the conditions for inference have been satisfied.

a.   The null hypothesis would assume that there is no relationship between these two variables. Use the symbol ρ to represent the overall population correlation. Write out an appropriate null and alternative hypothesis.

b.   Use the computer output to identify the p-value for the test. (Remember that $\beta = 0$ implies $\rho = 0$!)

c.   Write a conclusion in context.

d.   Suppose the professor wanted to test whether there is evidence of an overall *negative* correlation? Write a new null and alternative hypothesis. How would the p-value change?

e.   You have not yet learned a formula for the standard error of the sample correlation coefficient. However, this test has the same standardized test statistic as the comparable test for the slope. Solve $t = \frac{r-\rho}{SE_r}$ (with $\rho = 0$) to find the standard error. Note that you will first need to locate t and r!

12-15.   Mr. Rhode, the fitness and conditioning teacher, wants to test the impact of heart rate monitors on student fitness. He would like to divide his 42 students into two groups. One group would use heart rate monitors every day in class, while the others would not. Then he would compare the fitness of the two groups at the end of the semester.

a.   Design a well thought-out experiment that Mr. Rhode could run to determine if heart rate monitors are more effective at increasing student fitness.

b.   One problem that Mr. Rhode has is that certain students love the heart rate monitors. 28 of his students want to be in the heart rate monitor group. If he allows these 28 student to be in the heart rate monitor group and puts the remaining 14 students in the non-monitor group how could this effect his experiment? Be specific with your justification and use examples.

c.   If you used your design from part (a), what type of hypothesis test would you run at the completion of your experiment? State the test and provide the null and alternative hypotheses.

12-16.   Sleep apnea is a potentially dangerous sleep disorder. A new surgical implant has been developed that is less invasive than the existing surgical treatment. The researchers have expressed an interest in conducting trials comparing the new treatment to a control group.

a.   Would you recommend the researchers conduct an experiment comparing the new implant to the existing surgical treatment? Explain.

b.   Would you recommend the use of a placebo with the control group? Explain.

12-17.   The litter size of the Japanese hare varies from 1 to 6. Joshua is in Japan researching vulnerable environments of Japanese hares. Joshua believes the distribution of hare body lengths are normally distributed with a mean of 48.45 cm and a standard deviation of 2.08 cm.

a.   Sketch the normal probability density function. 33% of Japanese hare body lengths are less than what amount?

b.   If a random sample of 15 Japanese hares are measured, what is the probability that more than 6 hares will be below the measure you found in part (a)?

c.   If a random sample of 15 Japanese hares are measured, what is the probability that their average length will be less than the measure you found in part (a)?

12.2.1 What if a line does not fit the data?

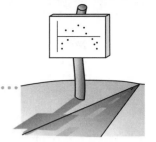

••

Transforming Data to Achieve Linearity

So far you have looked at a variety of linear models, but what happens when the best model is not linear?

12-18.   Top-It-Off Incorporated makes numerous lids for a variety of containers. Some of the most popular lids they produce are circular lids for oil drums and other cylindrical containers. Although the lids are ordered by the diameter of the circle, the price is set by the amount of metal used. Top-It-Off needs to set up a price structure that relates the weight of a lid to its diameter. Below is a list of weights for the standard size lids currently produced and a scatterplot displaying the data.

Diameter of lid (in)	Weight of metal (lbs)
10	4.0
12	4.9
16	7.1
20	10.0
24	13.5
30	20.0
36	27.9
40	34

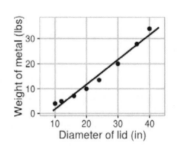

a.   The company analyst needs to find a good model for the weight as a function of the diameter. She creates a linear model displayed in the graph above. Use a calculator to find the line of best-fit.

b.   What is the coefficient of determination? Write a sentence about R^2 in context.

c.   The company analyst creates a residual plot, shown below. What does this residual plot reveal about her linear model?

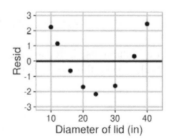

The residual plot in the previous problem suggested that you should consider a nonlinear model to represent the data. There are two choices that can be used to model data with a nonlinear model: the first option is to try to fit the data to a curved model, for example using built-in functions for "quadratic regression" or "exponential regression." You may have done this in an earlier course. In this course, however, you follow the path of most statisticians and transform the *data* instead to try to make the data linear.

a. Thinking about the relationship between the weight and the area, why is it reasonable to assume that a quadratic equation will model this relationship better?

b. A general quadratic of the form $y = a + bx + cx^2$ has three *coefficients*. For statistical reasons, we generally prefer to stick with only two coefficients, if possible. Thus, we would rather try to model our data using one of two special type of quadratics. In the first option, we will rewrite this as a single square: $y = (a + bx)^2$.

What could you do to this expression to *transform it* so the right side of the equation is a typical linear model?

c. The company analyst made the following scatterplot and residual plot. To find the equation for this model, you need to calculate the square root of each y-value. If your original lists are stored in lists called L1 and L2, you can do this on many calculators using a command such as $\sqrt{L2} \rightarrow L3$ to put the square root y-values into L3, then using L3 for your y-values in all normal scatterplot and residual plot making.

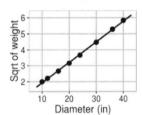
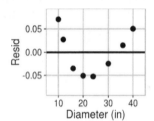

Make this transformation. Use a calculator to find the new line of best fit. Write your regression equation in terms of $\sqrt{y}$.

d. Does this new model seem to "fix" our data?

12-20. The quadratic model in the previous problem works well for many data sets with a quadratic relationship, but it did not seem quite right for this one. Another option is use the slightly different quadratic expression, $y = a + bx^2$ to model our data.

    a. The first equation, $y = (a + bx)^2$ gave us a linear relationship between $\sqrt{y}$ and x. What two values have a linear relationship in our new equation, $y = a + bx^2$?

    b. The company analyst made another scatterplot and residual plot for this new model. Assuming, again, that your original data was stored in lists labeled L1 and L2, you can transform the x-values by storing $(L1)^2 \rightarrow L3$. Then use L3 for the x-values and L2 for the y-values. Find the equation for this model. Does this model work better for the data?

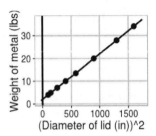

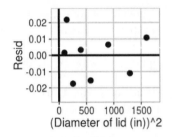

    c. Use the new model to predict the weight of a lid with a diameter of 32 inches.

12-21. With your team, write a short summary of this process to transform variables when you have reason to believe they are related by a polynomial of degree k (for example, a quadratic relationship of degree 2 or a cubic relationship of degree 3).

12-22.   Every year on September 8th at 1:00 a.m., the infamous chemistry teacher Mr. Knowlsen attempts to measure the acceleration due to gravity on earth by dropping various coins from windows on different floors of the science building and recording the time until they land. His most recent attempts are shown below:

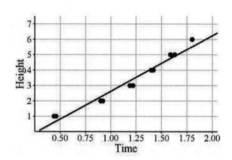

Time (s)	Height (floor)
0.46	1
0.44	1
0.92	2
0.90	2
1.19	3
1.22	3
1.40	4
1.42	4
1.63	5
1.59	5
1.80	6

Regression Output for Height vs. Time

```
Predictor    Coef      SE Coef       T           P

Constant    -0.9912    0.2979     -3.3272      0.0088

Time         3.6163    0.2371     15.2527      0.0000


S = 0.3415      R-Sq = 0.9628     R-Sq(Adj)= 0.9586     r = 0.9812
```

Mr. Knowlsen is feeling confident that he has finally found a strong positive linear relationship between the initial height of a free-falling object and the time it take to hit the ground. He estimates that a coin falling for 5 seconds would have been dropped from the 17th floor of a building. Use the techniques of problem 12-21 to build Mr. Knowlsen better model. Include your residual plot and a better height estimate for the coin falling 5 seconds.

12-23.   Each team in Ms. Zaleski's class cut a circular disks from cardboard file folders. They could cut the disks any size they chose. The mass and radius were recorded. The information is shown in the table below. Since students chose the radius, consider radius the independent variable.

Radius (cm)	9.6	9.0	7.7	6.3	5.3	4.7	3.7	2.4	1.3
Mass (g)	5.4	4.6	3.4	2.3	1.6	1.2	0.8	0.3	0.1

a.   Make a scatterplot for the data and sketch it onto your paper. Describe the association between mass and radius.

b.   The mass of the cardboard disk depends on its area. What kind of equation do you suggest to model this data?

c.   Use a transformation to model the data. Does this model appear to be superior?

d.   Predict the mass of a 7 cm disk. Use appropriate precision in your answer.

12-24.   A t-test is performed on the slope of a regression line and the following statement is made: "Since the p-value $= 0.0028 < 0.05 = \alpha$ (or $|t| = 3.67 > 2.16 = t_{crit}$), we reject the null hypothesis. The 95% confidence interval for the population slope is $b \pm t_{crit} \cdot s_b = -628 \pm 2.16(0.171) = (-0.998, -0.259)$."

a.   What was the slope of the regression line?

b.   What is the null hypothesis for this test?

c.   Since we reject the null hypothesis, what can you conclude about this regression line?

12-25.   Steve likes to play Friday morning basketball with his friends at the school. The players keep careful statistics of how well they are shooting during their games. Steve knows that he makes about 63% of the shots that he takes. One Friday morning, it seems like Steve is having a terrible time making his shots.

   a.   What is the probability that it takes Steve 7 shots until he makes his first?

   b.   What is the expected number of shots that Steve will take until he makes his first basket?

   c.   After Steve finally makes his first basket, his friend Jacob says, *"Steve, I bet you $10 that you can't make at least 3 out of the next 5 shots."* Assuming Steve takes at least 5 more shots, decide if Steve should take the bet or not.

12-26.   Mitesh is collecting data on the proportion of U.S. adults who have not served in the military. Kacey says, *"The proportion of U.S. adults who have not served in the military is less than 0.91."* Mitesh found a published survey of 698 randomly selected persons that found 652 people who have not served in the military.

   Use the results of the survey Mitesh found to construct a 90% confidence interval for the proportion of U.S. adults who have not served in the military. Does Casey's claim seem reasonable?

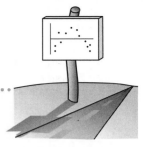

12.2.2 Is there another way to linearize data?

Using Logarithms to Achieve Linearity

In Lesson 2.2.3, Giulia's father was researching how much to charge for additional toppings for his new pizza restaurant. For the pizza restaurant, her father uses dry ice to keep the glasses in the restaurant very cold. In problem 2-67, Giulia investigated how long a piece of dry ice would last, and she concluded that the relationship between time and the weight of dry ice remaining was not a linear relationship. In this lesson, you will begin by helping Giulia determine an appropriate nonlinear model for her data.

12-27.   Recall Giulia's data from problem 2-67. The dry ice evaporates in the restaurant cooler as shown in the table at right.

Hours after noon	Weight of dry ice (oz)
0	15.3
1	14.7
2	14.3
3	13.6
4	13.1
5	12.5
6	11.9
7	11.5
8	11.0
9	10.6
10	10.2

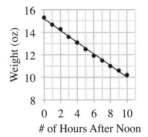

a.   When Giulia tried to construct a linear model for this data she obtained the following scatterplot (above) and residual plot (at the right). Her linear equation was $y = 15.21 - 0.52x$. At first glance, the linear model was promising because the best-fit line appeared to fit the data well. What indicated to her that a linear model was not appropriate?

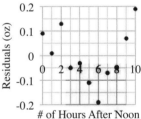

b.   Cooling and heating over time are often exponential functions. The standard *exponential* equation is $y = ab^x$. Because x is in the exponent, it is in a very "nonlinear place." What mathematical technique could you apply to bring that x out of the exponent? Apply the technique to both sides and see what you get. Simplify your equation as much as possible.

c.   In the new equation you found in part (b), what *transformations* of x and/or y are in a linear relationship? (Hint: if you used a logarithm, remember that if C is a constant (just a number), then $\log(C)$ is also a constant.)

d.   Use a similar calculator technique to that used for your quadratic relationship to make a scatterplot, residual plot, and model equation comparing the transformed variables from part (c). Does this appear to be a better model than the linear one?

Problem continues on next page →

Statistics

12-27.   *Problem continued from previous page.*

    e.   Algebra time! Using your new model equation, work backward and find the expected dry ice weight 24 hours after noon. Then use the original LSRL from part (a) to estimate the weight 24 hours after noon. Which do you think is a more reliable estimate?

    f.   Summarize: when you have a data set you have reason to believe might have an exponential relationship of the form $y = ab^x$, how can you model the data?

12-28.   The final type of situation you see often in nature is called a *power relationship*. This is a relationship of the form $y = ax^p$ where p could be any constant, which you might not know in advance. If you can make a reasonable guess for p, you can use the technique from problem 12-21, but if you cannot, you have to try another technique.

    a.   Take the equation $y = ax^p$ and apply a logarithm to both sides and show that in this situation there is a linear relationship between $\log(x)$ and $\log(y)$ (or, alternatively, $\ln(x)$ and $\ln(y)$). What does the *slope* of this linear relationship tell us?

    b.   We call a graph that uses logarithms of both sides a log-log graph. Below you have a log-log graph comparing the body mass to the brain mass of many different animal species, as well as the computer output from its regression. Explain why this is a good fit for the model and write an equation for the model in two forms: first, in terms of the logarithms, then as an actual power model.

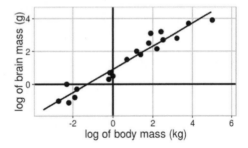

Regression Output for log(brain mass) vs. log(body mass)

Predictor	Coef	SE Coef	T	P
Constant	0.90	0.10	8.70	0.00
log of body mass (kg)	0.71	0.04	15.78	0.00

S = 0.4247   R-Sq = 0.9361   R-Sq(Adj) = 0.9323

    c.   Use your new model to predict the brain size of a unicorn with a body mass of 135 kg.

    d.   Summarize: if you have reason to believe data may be modeled by a power model $y = ax^p$ but are unsure of the exponent, what should you do?

12-29.   At the right is a list of amounts of oil produced from 1905 to
         1972. MMbbl stands for millions of barrels and is the standard
         abbreviation used by the oil industry.

         Obtain a copy of the Lesson 12.2.2 Resource Page. On the
         resource page are four different scatterplots, and computer
         regression outputs based on this data. Decide based on this
         information what your best choice for model is and write an
         equation for the model in terms of y. Justify your decision,
         then use your model to predict how many MMbbl were
         produced in 1938.

Year	MMbbl
1905	215
1910	328
1915	432
1920	689
1925	1069
1930	1412
1935	1655
1940	2150
1945	2595
1950	3803
1955	5626
1960	7674
1962	8882
1964	10,310
1966	12,016
1968	14,104
1970	16,690
1972	18,584

checksum:
108,234

MATH NOTES

Nonlinear Models

Sometimes a nonlinear model best fits the data, and therefore makes better predictions, than a linear model. This is usually made apparent by comparing the residual plots of various models.

A good model should also be representative of the physical situation. In problem 12-27 an exponential model made physical sense because you were measuring decay over time. On the other hand, if you were making predictions about the path of a rocket, a quadratic model of the data would make a lot of sense because gravity has a quadratic relationship with height. If you were modeling a relationship between volume and length, a power model would be appropriate, because volume is related to length by a power of 3.

In AP Statistics, when faced with a nonlinear model you attempt to transform one or both variables to *create* a linear model from the transformed data.

The most common two-variable nonlinear models are:

- Known power (e.g. quadratic): $y = (a + bx)^k$ or $y = a + bx^k$. To model a known power scenario, look for a linear relationship between y and x^k or between $\sqrt[k]{y}$ and x (or try both!)

- Exponential: $y = ab^x$. To model an exponential scenario, look for a linear relationship between $\log(y)$ and x. A logarithm of any base (such as a natural log) will work.

- Unknown power: $y = ax^b$. To model an unknown power scenario, look for a linear relationship between $\log(y)$ and $\log(x)$.

If it is not clear which model is the best for a situation, it is acceptable to try some or all of these options and compare them, paying particularly close attention to any patterns in the residuals, to decide which model is the best fit for the data.

12-30.   An analyst is trying to construct a model of a bivariate data set. The following outputs are produced.

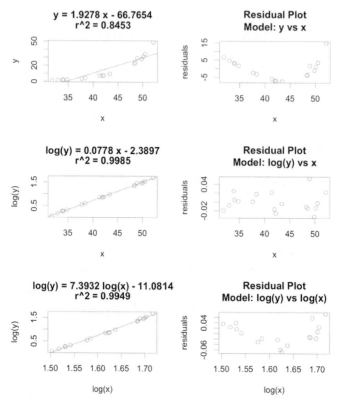

a.   Which model seems to be the most appropriate fit for the data? Explain how you made your choice.

b.   Based on the model you chose, describe the relationship between x and y.

c.   Use your chosen model to predict the value of y when x is 40.

d.   Even though the scatterplot of y vs. x does not have a linear form, it still accurately displays the curved trend of the untransformed data. Does your prediction for y when x is 40 from part (c) seem reasonable, given the scatterplot for y vs. x?

12-31. Assume *Car Consumer* magazine collected data for the fuel efficiency of
        cars (miles per gallon) compared to weight (thousands of pounds). The
        regression model at right was created.

        $y = 49 - 8.4x$

        $r = -0.903$

        a. Interpret R^2 in context.   b. Interpret the slope in context.

12-32. Here are some more news headlines from observational studies. Determine at least one
        plausible confounding variable that could explain the cause and effect. Remember, do not
        argue about the link expressed in the headline. Accept the association as true. Your task is to
        find the other variable(s) that could be the actual cause(s).

        a. The graveyard shift may be aptly named. Working nights will soon be listed as a likely
            cancer cause.

        b. Daily meat diet tied to higher chance of early death.

12-33. Do freshmen really have the largest backpacks, or is that just a high school legend? Delenn
        was able to weigh a random sample of student backpacks throughout the school year. She also
        recorded the number of quarters of high school completed by the student who owns the bag.
        Using spreadsheet software, Delenn found the following plots and regression information:

        LSRL $y = 13.84 - 0.55x$ $r = -0.66$

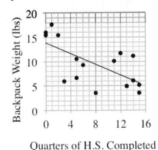 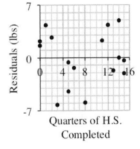

        a. Interpret the slope of the least squares regression line in the context of this study.

        b. Calculate and interpret R^2 in context.

        c. What is the residual with the greatest magnitude and what point does it belong to?

        d. Using the LSRL model, estimate the weight of a backpack for a student who has
            completed 10 quarters of high school. Use appropriate precision in your answer.

        e. Is a linear model the best choice for predicting backpack weight in this study? Support
            your answer.

12-34.   Isaiah is in the Southern Ocean investigating endangered porpoises. Assume a stratified sample of 15 porpoises gave the following weight summary:

121, 129.4, 135.7, 138.9, 154.7, 156.2, 159.3, 159.4, 162.4, 168.2, 173.5, 178.7, 183.7, 185.5, 186 pounds

Determine the mean, sample standard deviation, and five number summary. Which would be best to describe this data, mean and standard deviation or median and IQR? Why?

Chapter 13

ANOVA and Beyond!

CHAPTER 13

You have studied sampling distributions and learned inference techniques using sample proportions, means, and slopes. *What about measures of spread?* The sample variance is an unbiased statistic that can be used to make comparisons between the spread of different populations. You used the chi-squared technique to compare several proportions in a single test. *Can more than two means be compared in a single test?* You will learn a new and powerful technique called ANOVA to accomplish this. *What do you do when your data does not seem to follow the distribution you need it to? What if your sample shows strong skewing and outliers?* Discover another world of inference procedures called nonparametric inference that typically have fewer conditions for implementation.

Chapter Goals

Use the chi-squared distribution to make confidence intervals of population variance.

Perform hypothesis test for the difference of two population variances using the F-distribution.

Use a one-way ANOVA hypothesis test for the difference of multiple population means.

Understand the need for and the reasoning behind nonparametric test.

Conduct a variety of nonparametric techniques for differences in population medians.

Chapter Outline

Section 13.1 The chi-squared distribution is established as a way to model confidence intervals for population variances. This is expanded to comparing two sample variances using the F-distribution.

Section 13.2 You will take the newly developed F-distribution and use the variance between samples compared to the variance within samples to carry out a one-way analysis of variance for a difference of population means.

Section 13.3 Faced with a sample that contains outliers and is too skewed to use previous methods, nonparametric inference is introduced with a simple sign test for the median. This is expanded to Mood's median test with two (or more) samples.

13.1.1 What if I square a standardized observation?

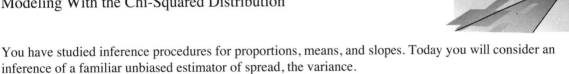

Modeling With the Chi-Squared Distribution

You have studied inference procedures for proportions, means, and slopes. Today you will consider an inference of a familiar unbiased estimator of spread, the variance.

13-1.   Because it has probably been a while since you have calculated a sample variance "by hand" (without a graphing calculator or computer), discuss with your team, and write down a set of instructions to calculate the sample variance without technology.

13-2.   Recall the Quantitative Sampling Distributions eTool that you used to investigate sampling distributions in Lesson 10.1.1. Use this tool to investigate the sampling distribution of the sample variance for samples with $n = 9$. Check the "sampling with replacement" box. In the "number of samples" box, enter 5000. Each member of your team should use a different population shape. Make sure that one team member uses the normal distribution for the population shape.

   a.   For each population shape, write down the population variance. Click "draw" several times. How does the mean of the sample variance distribution compare to the population variance?

   b.   For each population shape, write down the population variance. Click "draw" several times. Make a quick sketch of the *shape* of the sample variance distribution.

13-3.   The data below represents the mass (grams) of a random sample of a certain species of worm.

   10.26, 9.87, 9.88, 10.62, 10.15, 10.4, 10.23, 10.45, 10.12 $\bar{x} = 10.22$ g

   a.   Find the sample variance for this sample "by-hand" using your team's ideas in problem 13-1.

   b.   Suppose a scientist was interested in using this data to construct a 95% confidence interval for the population variance for the worms. Do the conditions for inference seem to be present?

   c.   Use the eTool to construct a 95% confidence interval for the population variance using the "repeated sampling" method. Choose "manual" for the population data, and enter this small data set. Because the sample is acting as a small population set $n = 9$ and check the box "Sample with replacement" to meet the independent samples condition.

13-4.   Consider, for the moment, that you know the mean μ and standard deviation σ for the entire population of this species of worm. Assume, also, that the population is normally distributed.

   a.   Suppose you have a random observation, x_i. Write down an equation for a standardized value z_i.

   b.   If for every value of x_i you find and square z_i, then sum them, you would have the sum of the squares of n independent standard normal random variables. What distribution does this follow? (Hint: see problem 9-3.)

13-5.   Since you do not actually know the population mean, you could take $\sum_{i=1}^{n}\left(\frac{x_i-\mu}{\sigma}\right)^2$ and replace μ with $\bar{x}$. This replacement has the effect that $\sum_{i=1}^{n}\left(\frac{x_i-\bar{x}}{\sigma}\right)^2$ still follows the chi-squared distribution but with one less degree of freedom. Note that this formula can be written as $\frac{\sum_{i=1}^{n}(x_i-\bar{x})^2}{\sigma^2}$ because σ can be considered to be a constant. The numerator looks like part of the calculation for the sample variance. Use the formula $s^2 = \frac{1}{(n-1)}\sum_{i=1}^{n}(x_i-\bar{x})^2$ to simplify this expression without any summation notation.

13-6.   Knowing the distribution of $\frac{(n-1)s^2}{\sigma^2}$ allows you to calculate a confidence interval for σ^2 (and therefore for σ if needed). A table of chi-squared critical values has been printed below. Use the table to help construct a 95% confidence interval for the population variance, σ^2, based on the sample data in problem 13-3. Follow the steps below.

Table of χ^2 values

Table entry for p is the probability of lying below χ^2

		0.01	0.025	0.05	0.1	0.9	0.95	0.975	0.99
	1	0.0002	0.0010	0.0039	0.0158	2.7055	3.8415	5.0239	6.6349
	2	0.0201	0.0506	0.1026	0.2107	4.6052	5.9915	7.3778	9.2103
	3	0.1148	0.2158	0.3518	0.5844	6.2514	7.8147	9.3484	11.3449
	4	0.2971	0.4844	0.7107	1.0636	7.7794	9.4877	11.1433	13.2767
df	5	0.5543	0.8312	1.1455	1.6103	9.2364	11.0705	12.8325	15.0863
	6	0.8721	1.2373	1.6354	2.2041	10.6446	12.5916	14.4494	16.8119
	7	1.2390	1.6899	2.1673	2.8331	12.0170	14.0671	16.0128	18.4753
	8	1.6465	2.1797	2.7326	3.4895	13.3616	15.5073	17.5345	20.0902
	9	2.0879	2.7004	3.3251	4.1682	14.6837	16.9190	19.0228	21.6660

   a.   Use the table to identify the appropriate critical values for a 95% confidence interval for this sample. Remember that the degree of freedom is $n - 1$. Note that *two* critical values are needed because the chi-squared distribution is not symmetric and centered at zero!

Problem continues on next page →

Statistics

13-6.   *Problem is continued from previous page.*

    b.   Set $\frac{(n-1)s^2}{\sigma^2}$ equal to each of the critical values. Substitute in 0.0625 for s^2 and 9 for n based on the sample data. Solve each equation for σ^2. These represent the boundaries to your 95% confidence interval for σ^2.

    c.   Using the chi-squared distribution to model $\frac{(n-1)s^2}{\sigma^2}$ involved assuming that Σz_i^2 is the sum of n squared standard random normal variables. Does this appear to be a limitation to the types of samples for which you are allowed to carry out this procedure? Explain.

    d.   The confidence interval you found in part (b) used the chi-squared distribution. A similar confidence interval was found by repeated sampling in part (c) of problem 13-3. How do the two intervals compare? Which one do you trust more? Which one would be easier to compute without technology? Explain.

13-7.   If you earn one ticket in Ms. Frias's "Caught Being Good" weekly drawing, the probability of winning a prize is 0.08. If you earn one ticket each week for 5 weeks, what is the probability that you will win at least one prize?

13-8.   Psychological issues can affect statistical results. Researchers who conduct experiments need to eliminate sources of bias for their statistical analysis to be meaningful. What are some potential causes of bias in the following samples?

    a.   Super Cola paid for a taste test study comparing it to Amazing Cola. Participants were asked to taste both drinks and pick their favorite. Super Cola was labeled "m" and the Amazing Cola was "q." The majority of participants picked the drink labeled "m," which was Super Cola.

    b.   A survey was conducted in the following manner: *"The Bill of Rights guarantees the right to bear arms so that we can protect our families and our country. Recently, attempts have been made to enact stricter gun controls. Do you want these restrictions?"*

    c.   Another survey was conducted in the following manner: *"Last year over 15,000 people were murdered with handguns, which accounted for 68% of all murders. Recently, attempts have been made to enact stricter gun controls. Do you want these restrictions?"*

13-9.   Kelly is an engineer for a non-profit company that drills wells for impoverished villages in Africa. The cost of drilling a new water well is determined from the amount of drilling needed to find water, plus the fixed costs of the pump. Kelly has collected data on cost versus well depth for a sample of 12 projects:

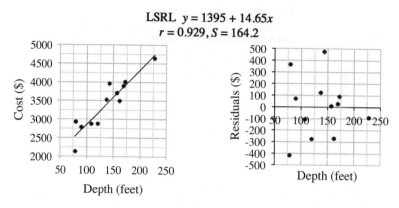

LSRL $y = 1395 + 14.65x$
$r = 0.929, S = 164.2$

a.   Discuss the form, strength, direction and outliers.

b.   Interpret the slope of the least squares regression line in the context of this study.

c.   Calculate R^2 and interpret both it and S in context.

d.   What does the y-intercept represent in this analysis?

e.   Using the LSRL model, estimate the cost of wells that are 80, 150, and 200 feet.

f.   The 80 foot well Kelly measured has a residual of $363. What was the actual cost of the well?

g.   Is a linear model the best choice for predicting well cost using well depth? Support your answer.

13-10. Amina works for an appliance company that produces many different types of blenders, such as bar and kitchen blenders. The amount of time it takes to produce a particular model seems to be quite variable. Amina gathers an independent random sample of 36 blender models, and she finds that $\bar{x} = 6.2$ hours with $s = 1.4$ hours. The distribution of the sampled production times appears mound shaped.

Table entry for p is the probability of lying below χ^2

p

	0.01	0.025	0.05	0.1	0.9	0.95	0.975	0.99
33	17.0735	19.0467	20.8665	23.1102	43.7452	47.3999	50.7251	54.7755
34	17.7891	19.8063	21.6643	23.9523	44.9032	48.6024	51.9660	56.0609
35	18.5089	20.5694	22.4650	24.7967	46.0588	49.8018	53.2033	57.3421
36	19.2327	21.3359	23.2686	25.6433	47.2122	50.9985	54.4373	58.6192

df is labeled along the left side of the table.

a. Use the information from the blender sample to estimate the population standard deviation at 90% confidence. Be sure to verify the necessary conditions are present for a valid inference. (Hint: Find a confidence interval for σ^2 and take the square root.)

b. Amina's boss wants to know if there is evidence, at a 5% level of significance, that the overall standard deviation for this model of blender is higher than one hour. Write out a null and alternative hypothesis. Use the confidence interval from part (a) to make a decision.

c. Explain why a 90% confidence interval is related to a 5% significance level in this context. Why is it not a 10% significance level?

13.1.2 Does one population have more variability?

Introducing the F-Distribution

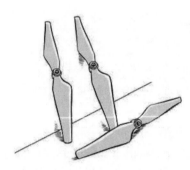

In Lesson 13.1.1, you learned techniques for making confidence intervals of population variance. Today you will discover methods for performing hypothesis tests with variance.

You work for an engineering firm that produces propellers for a new drone. The propellers are designed to be 9 inches in length with a very small tolerance. You seek bids from two companies and need to make a decision about which company to hire with a large, high-volume contract.

As part of the bidding process, each company has provided you with a sample of 20 propellers designed to meet your specifications.

13-11. The lengths of the 20 propellers from each company are recorded and are summarized below and displayed in the following graph.

Company 1: $\bar{x} = 9.0000$, $s^2 = 0.0010$
Company 2: $\bar{x} = 9.0000$, $s^2 = 0.0016$

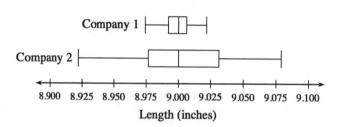

Write a few sentences comparing the distributions of propeller lengths from each company.

MATH NOTES

F-Distribution

The F-distribution is a ratio distribution, calculated as the ratio of two independent chi-squared random variables, scaled by their respective degrees of freedom.

$$F = \frac{\chi_A^2 / \mathrm{df}_A}{\chi_B^2 / \mathrm{df}_B}$$

The F-distribution has two degrees of freedom, one for the numerator and one for the denominator.

Because a chi-squared random variable is centered about its degree of freedom, the ratio of these scaled chi-squared random variables is centered very close to 1. (It is actually centered about $\frac{\mathrm{df}_B}{\mathrm{df}_B - 2}$ for $\mathrm{df}_B > 2$, which is very close to 1 as this degree of freedom increases.)

It has similar properties to the chi-squared distribution in that it is skewed to the right and its values are always non-negative.

13-12.   After briefly analyzing the samples, you informally conclude that Company 1 has the better product. When presenting this to your team, the team is not fully convinced because Company 1 also has a much higher price. They want to be convinced that the samples provide enough evidence that Company 1 does indeed have significantly smaller variability in its product.

a.   Company 1 has a fraction of the variance of Company 2. Make this calculation, and express the fraction as a decimal.

b.   When conducting a hypothesis test, the null hypothesis is usually a statement saying something like, "nothing is going on" or "the two parameters are the same." If you are interested in the population variances as a measure of variability, you use a *ratio* as a measure of equality rather than a difference. Write a null and alternative hypothesis, expressing each comparison using a ratio compared to 1.

Problem continues on next page →

Problem is continued from previous page.

c.   The "test-statistic" for a symmetric distribution usually takes the form of $\frac{\text{statistic} - \text{parameter}}{\text{SD of statistic}}$. The sample variance, after a scale factor, is modeled by the chi-squared distribution and is not symmetric. Instead of using differences centered at zero, you use ratios centered at 1. So you could construct a test statistic like this: $F = \frac{s_1^2 / s_2^2}{\sigma_1^2 / \sigma_2^2}$. See the Math Notes box in this lesson about the F-distribution as a ratio of scaled chi-squared random variables.

Show that this can be re-written as: $F = \frac{\chi_1^2 / df_1}{\chi_2^2 / df_2}$ where $\chi_1^2 = \frac{(n_1 - 1)s_1^2}{\sigma_1^2}$ and $\chi_2^2 = \frac{(n_2 - 1)s_2^2}{\sigma_2^2}$.

d.   If the null hypothesis (from part (b)) is true, what does $F = \frac{s_1^2 / s_2^2}{\sigma_1^2 / \sigma_2^2}$ simplify to? This is the "test statistic." Find the value of this test-statistic for the sample data given in problem 13-11.

e.   The test statistic you found in part (d) will follow the F-distribution, assuming the samples are each independently chosen as independent random samples from normal populations. Since the F-distribution is a family of distributions with shapes depending on the degrees of freedom of the numerator and denominator, a sketch of the specific F-distribution for this setting has been provided. Make a copy of this plot, and find the indicated area using the cdf function on a calculator. This is the *p*-value.

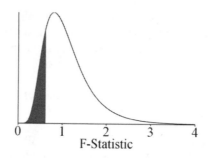

f.   Summarize the results of the hypothesis test in context. Should the null hypothesis be rejected? Use a 5% level of significance.

13-13.   A standard drop of water is supposed to have a volume of 50 μL. Lucas is trying to develop an
          eyedropper that is calibrated to give a precise 50 μL. Lucas is confident that the dropper
          produces drops of 50 μL on average, but he is not sure about how consistent it is. He gathers a
          random sample of 20 drops and records the volume in μL.

          50.00, 49.99, 49.92, 49.98, 49.94, 49.93, 50.01, 50.07, 50.07, 50.03, 49.98, 49.99, 50.04,
          49.95, 50.10, 49.94, 50.01, 50.01, 50.00, 50.04
          checksum: 1000.00

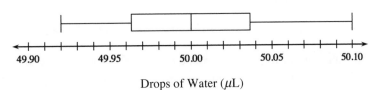

          Drops of Water (μL)

    a.   What does the boxplot above communicate about the shape of the volumes of the drops
          of water?

    b.   Use the chi-squared table below to construct a 95% confidence interval for the overall
          standard deviation of a drop of water from Lucas's dropper.

          Table entry for p is the probability of lying below χ^2

		0.01	0.025	0.05	0.1	0.9	0.95	0.975	0.99
df	19	7.6327	8.9065	10.1170	11.6509	27.2036	30.1435	32.8523	36.1909
	20	8.2604	9.5908	10.8508	12.4426	28.4120	31.4104	34.1696	37.5662

    c.   Lucas wants to give a conservative estimate for the precision of his dropper. He is going
          to advertise it as 50 μL ± tolerance. He decides to use two standard deviations as an
          "error tolerance" for his dropper. To be conservative he also decides to use the upper
          bound for the confidence interval in part (b) as his conservative estimate for σ. How
          should Lucas advertise his dropper?

13-14.   Your water dropper from problem 13-13 was a hit! You have customers asking for an even
          more accurate water dropper with a smaller standard deviation. You redesign the critical
          components of production and create a dropper that produces a random sample of 30 drops
          with $\bar{x} = 50$ μL and $s = 0.03$ μL. The distribution still shows evidence of being approximately
          normally distributed. Is there evidence, at a 5% level of significance, that the standard
          deviation has decreased? Show all relevant steps. You may assume that the conditions for
          inference have been met.

13-15.   North City High School has served the
         following number of lunches since the
         beginning of the school year. The data has
         been sorted.

Number of lunches sold per day

576	605	632	660	671	689	723	774
584	606	636	661	671	695	738	785
594	613	640	663	675	698	745	
595	618	640	665	677	703	755	
603	630	652	666	678	721	774	

checksum: 24711

a.   What are the mean and standard
     deviation number of lunches in the sample?

b.   What is the five number summary of the distribution?

c.   Make a relative frequency histogram of the number of lunches served. Use a scale from
     560 to 800 lunches, with a bin width of 40 lunches. Sketch the histogram and label the
     height of each of the bins.

d.   Describe the distribution. Make sure you consider the center, shape, spread, and outliers.

e.   Using your histogram, determine $P(X < 600)$, where X is a random variable representing
     the number of lunches sold.

f.   Using the histogram, estimate $P(600 < X < 700)$.

13-16.   The carbon content in iron compounds determines the strength and hardness of steel. Hailey is
         an engineering student at University of the Pacific studying valuable inventories of steel.
         Assume an SRS of 27 steels gave the following summary regarding the relationship between
         density and tensile strength.

Regression Analysis: Tensile strength vs. Density

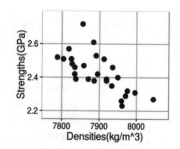

Predictor	Coef	SE Coef	T	P
Constant	11.9655	0.3915	30.561	0.00
Density	−0.0012	0	−24.36	0.00

$S = 0.084$ $R^2 = 47.783\%$ R^2 (adj) $= 45.694\%$

a.   Interpret r^2 and S in context and describe the association between density and tensile
     strength of the steels.

b.   What additional piece of information would make it easier to assess the form of this
     association?

c.   Use the LSRL and S to predict the strength of a steel with a density of 8100 kg/m^3,
     including a reasonable margin of error.

13.2.1 What if I have three or more samples?

One-Way ANOVA

Let's return to Mrs. Hoppenheimer's class. In Chapter 9, Jeremiah, Aliah, and Tobiah tested whether different types of paper had an influence on the shots made during a heated round of trashketball. Their study of different types of paper made these students wonder whether even "standard" paper might differ based on some characteristic such as color.

Mrs. Hoppenheimer provides them with several reams of paper of each color. Each ream is labeled "20-lb bond." They randomly choose a few sheets of paper from each color. Using a digital micrometer, they gather the following data for paper thicknesses (the values are all in μm (micrometers)):

Salmon: 91.0, 90.9, 90.5, 90.5, 90.2, 89.7, 90.9, 89.9, 89.8, 89.5, 89.3 (mean 90.2, sd 0.6)

Green: 90.4, 89.8, 91.0, 90.6, 90.0, 91.6, 91.7, 90.7, 91.3, 90.8, 90.9 (mean 90.8, sd 0.6)

Goldenrod: 89.7, 90.2, 89.8, 90.0, 89.9, 90.6, 89.2, 89.8, 90.3, 90.9, 90.7 (mean 90.1, sd 0.5)

Canary: 90.7, 91.0, 90.6, 91.7, 89.6, 91.7, 90.9, 90.9, 90.2, 90.6, 92.0 (mean 90.9, sd 0.7)

13-17. Before doing any number crunching, Aliah knows that it is helpful to first look at a visual display of the data. She creates the following plot. Write a few sentences comparing the distributions of these data sets.

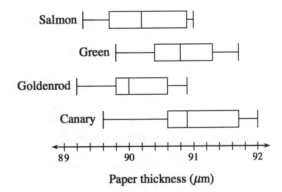

Paper thickness (μm)

13-18.   Jeremiah immediately dives in and starts setting up six two-sample t-tests, one for each pair. Tobiah stops him and says, *"Remember how we were able to carry out one procedure to compare multiple proportions when we learned about the chi-squared distribution? I bet there's a similar procedure we can do here."*

a.   Aliah keeps looking at the list of sample means (90.2, 90.8, 90.1, and 90.9). They seem close to one another, but they are not all the same. Jeremiah says, *"We could calculate some measure of spread, such as the range, IQR, standard deviation, or variance from this list. I can quickly see that the range is 0.8 micrometers. I wonder what the standard deviation is?"* Do it! Find the standard deviation of this list of means.

b.   Tobiah looks at the standard deviation that was just calculated and says, *"Wait—if there is no difference in the population mean thicknesses of these types of paper, we would expect these sample means to be pretty similar. That would cause this standard deviation we just calculated to be small. I just don't know what we should consider to be small."*

Jeremiah has an idea. *"What if we look at the standard deviations from the four samples as a baseline to decide if this is small or not?"*

Aliah likes this idea, but she has a problem with it. *"I think we should be comparing variances, not standard deviations. Remember how the sample variance was an unbiased estimator of the population variance?"* The team decides to go with Aliah's idea. Write down all four sample variances and the variance from the set of means in part (a). Does your variance from the set of means seem "small"?

c.   Aliah is still hesitant. She says, *"I don't think we are making a fair comparison. Aren't sample means supposed to be less variable than individual measurements? Remember how $\sigma_{\bar{x}}^2 = \frac{\sigma^2}{n}$? Each sample had 11 numbers. I think we need to scale one of these sets by 11 to make a fair comparison."* Do it! Multiply your result for the variance of the sample means by 11 so that it has the same "scale" as the other sample variances. Now does it seem "small" compared to the sample variances?

13-19.   Jeremiah is excited. *"We have a scaled variance from our sample means of 1.833. If this number is 'small,' then our four means are likely from populations with the same mean. If this number is 'large,' then it is unlikely that all four population means are the same. This sounds like a hypothesis test."*

a.   Help Aliah, Jeremiah, and Tobiah write a null and alternative hypothesis for this setting.

Problem continues on next page $\rightarrow$

Statistics

13-19.   *Problem is continued from previous page.*

b.   Tobiah thinks that he can calculate a weighted average (based on the size of each sample) of the four sample variances $(0.36, 0.36, 0.25, 0.49)$ to represent the individual variability of paper thicknesses within the samples. Since all of the samples were the same size, this would just be a simple average. However, he realizes that summarizing the variance of individual pieces of paper with a single estimate like this would make the assumption that all four populations have the same variance σ^2. He does some research, and he finds that this is a reasonable assumption as long as the largest sample variance is no more than twice as large as the smallest. Find this average sample variance. Do their sample variances meet the requirement?

c.   Aliah summarizes their information. *"We assume that all four populations have the same variance σ^2. We have four sample means (90.2, 90.8, 90.1, and 90.9) that gave us a variance of 1.833 when we scaled it up based on the sample size. This gives us an estimate for σ^2. We also have our four separate sample variances which give us a weighted average of 0.365. This is also an estimate for σ^2! We have two estimates for σ^2, but one seems much larger."* Calculate the ratio of the two estimates for σ^2. How many times larger is the estimate from the four sample means?

d.   Jeremiah says, *"We have two different estimates for the population variance based on our samples, and we just found their ratio. This is the F-distribution! The numerator degree of freedom will be 3, since there are 4 sample means. The denominator degree of freedom is trickier. We have 44 numbers in all of the samples combined. We usually lose a degree of freedom every time a sample mean is involved in a calculation, and we have four sample means. So I think the denominator degree of freedom is 40. A ratio larger than 5 seems pretty extreme!"* Copy the graph of the F-distribution in this setting. Use the F-distribution cdf function and your ratio in part (c) to find the *p*-value.

F-distribution: $df_1 = 3, df_2 = 40$

F-Statistic

e.   Tobiah is ready to make a conclusion. Help him write a conclusion in context.

13-20.   Mrs. Hoppenheimer was pleased with Aliah, Jeremiah, and Tobia's result. She told them that they discovered the concepts behind the procedure called *"analysis of variance."* She showed them how to use technology to efficiently carry out the procedure.

a.   Aliah thinks that it is strange that a procedure that was designed to test for a difference in three or more population means would be called "analysis of variance." Help explain to Aliah why this procedure was given this name.

b.   Use a calculator or computer to carry out this procedure. Did the F-statistic and *p*-value match your previous calculations?

MATH NOTES

One-Way Analysis of Variance (ANOVA)

The one-way analysis of variance procedure gets its name by analyzing the variance between sample means across different treatment groups (associated with one factor) and comparing it to the variance within the samples. In Lesson 13.2.1, the one factor being studied was the color of paper, and the different samples all corresponded to different colors of paper.

Analysis of variance is useful for testing for a difference in means between two or more samples. It yields an identical result, with two samples, to a two-sample t-test, so in practice, it is typically only used with three or more samples.

This procedure makes familiar requirements of the data that the observations within each sample be randomly chosen and independent, and the samples themselves need to be independent random samples. It is assumed that the population that each sample is drawn from is normally distributed, although this procedure is *robust* against minor violations of this assumption. It is also assumed that the variances of each population are the same, requiring that the largest sample variance be no more than about twice the smallest sample variance in practice.

The F-statistic is calculated as $F = \frac{\text{variance between samples}}{\text{variance within samples}}$.

If all of the sample sizes (n) are the same, the variance between samples is calculated by using the sample means as a small data set and finding the variance of this small data set. It is scaled up by a factor of n so that it is an estimate for σ^2 rather than $\sigma_{\bar{x}}^2$. The variance within the samples, also an estimate for σ^2, is then a simple average of the individual sample variances. These two estimates for σ^2 are compared as a ratio for the F-statistic.

The numerator degree of freedom is one less than the number of samples. The denominator degree of freedom is the total number of values in all samples combined minus one for each sample. The cdf function of the F-distribution is then used to calculate the *p*-value as the tail probability.

13-21.   Junior is studying the effects of diet on the growth of dogs. He chooses a certain breed of dog with very predictable growth and gathers a random sample of puppies. He separates the dogs into three groups and provides each group with a different diet. Each dog begins the diet at four weeks and its weight (in pounds) is measured at the end of one year. Each set of data appears to be symmetric in shape. Junior's data is displayed below.

	Sample size	Mean weight	Stdev
Diet #1	$n = 12$	$\bar{x} = 33.6$	$s = 1.2$
Diet #2	$n = 12$	$\bar{x} = 34.2$	$s = 1.5$
Diet #3	$n = 12$	$\bar{x} = 34.9$	$s = 1.4$

Is there evidence, at a 5% level of significance, that the diet has an effect on the mean weight of the dogs? Show all relevant steps.

13-22.   Anahera is comparing the consistency of battery life for two leading brands of batteries. First, she gathers a random sample of 15 batteries of each brand. Using a small toy that takes one battery, she records how long (in hours) each battery lasts. Anahera's data is displayed below.

Brand 1: 4.8, 4.9, 5.1, 5.1, 5.1, 4.8, 5, 4.9, 5.1, 4.9, 5, 5.2, 5, 5, 5.1 *checksum: 75*

Brand 2: 4.8, 4.8, 4.9, 4.9, 4.7, 4.6, 5, 4.8, 5.1, 4.7, 4.7, 5.1, 5, 4.5, 4.5 *checksum: 72.1*

a.   Construct a parallel boxplot. Compare the distributions.

b.   Is there evidence, at a 5% level of significance, that Brand 1 has a smaller overall standard deviation? You may assume that the assumptions for inference have been met.

13-23.   Matías is interested in how much sleep a high school senior at his school gets. He selected a random sample of seniors and asked them how many hours they slept the previous night. Matías set the threshold at 6 hours of sleep and noticed that 28% of the seniors are below the threshold.

a.   If Matías randomly choses 30 seniors, what is the probability that 5 or less are below the threshold?

b.   If Matías decides to interview students, what is the probability the first student he interviews who is below the threshold is after the 5th student?

13-24. For the spinners at right, assume that the smaller sections of spinner #1 are half the size of the larger section and for spinner #2 assume that the smaller sections are one third the size of the larger section.

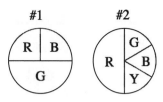

a. Draw a diagram for spinning each spinner once.

b. What is the probability of getting the same color twice?

c. If you know you got the same color twice, what is the probability it was red?

13-25. Meerkat family groups are called gangs or mobs. They are led by an alpha pair, with the female being the most dominant. Sarah is in Gabon collecting data on thriving preserves of meerkats. A cluster sample of 29 meerkats showed the following results regarding the relationship between the length of the alpha female and gang size.

Regression Analysis: Gang size vs. Length

Predictor	Coef	SE Coef	T	P
Constant	-51.3866	1.1237	-45.73	0
Female length	6.9875	0.0903	77.390	0

$S = 3.2$ $R^2 = 88.77\%$ $R^2(adj) = 88.355\%$

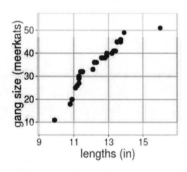

a. Determine the LSRL and interpret the slope.

b. Predict the gang size of an alpha female whose length is 12 in.

c. Calculate the residual for the point (12.9, 39).

d. Explain why the residual of a 12.9 inch meerkat, as calculated in part (c) could never be better than 0.2 meerkats.

13-26. A survey is being designed to determine whether or not people are in favor of legislation that would expand the gray wolf hunting quota and extend the hunting season. Write two poorly worded questions that would result in biased results, one in favor and the other not in favor.

13.3.1 What if my sample is too skewed?

Sign Test: Introduction to Nonparametric Inference

When you cannot meet the all of the conditions for inference, what can be done?

Mariya is a paleontologist who has just discovered a new species of fish. She decides to name this newly discovered species *Pistrix rex*, which means "sea monster king." She is hoping that the name *P. rex* will catch on!

Mariya would like to establish that it is larger than the previously discovered giant megatooth. The largest of these massive sharks was about 60 feet long. She would like to establish that the mean length of the *P. rex* is larger than 60 feet. Mariya has found a sample of 16 incomplete skeletons of *Pistrix rex* from various locations. She is treating this sample as a random sample of independent observations. She has enough of each skeleton to extrapolate the length of each individual. Her data is displayed below:

P. rex length (ft):
74, 70.9, 72.9, 61.1, 69.4, 65.3, 38.5, 48.5, 73.1, 73, 66, 72.7, 75, 57.7, 64.9, 54 *checksum: 1037*

13-27.   Like any well-trained data scientist, Mariya begins with an exploratory analysis of the data.

     a.   Create a graphical display of your choice, and summarize the shape, center, and spread of the *P. rex* data.

     b.   Do there appear to be any outliers in the data? Explain with an appropriate calculation.

13-28.   The strong skew and the potential outlier present a problem. The t-test is robust against violations against the normality requirement, but this sample skewness and outlier are too extreme. It seems as though a t-test is not an option. Determined to establish the *P. rex* as the king of the ocean, Mariya decides to give up on the mean and think about the median.

     a.   If the median *P. rex* length truly is 60 feet, how many individuals from Mariya's sample *should* have been longer than 60 feet?

     b.   How many individuals from her sample *were* longer than 60 feet?

Problem continues on next page →

13-28. *Problem is continued from previous page.*

    c.   Under the assumption that the true population median is 60 feet, establish that the binomial setting applies in this context.

    d.   Use the binomial distribution to calculate what the probability would be of obtaining a sample with 12 or more "success" out of 16 trials.

13-29. The procedure you just carried out in problem 13-28 is called a *sign test* for the median. It is one of the most simple *nonparametric* inference procedures. See the Math Notes box on nonparametric inference procedures in this lesson. Since the *P. rex* data was too skewed to carry out a t-test, a different type of procedure was needed. This procedure made no assumptions about the distribution of the data. The amount of skew was not a problem!

    a.   Write out the null and alternative hypothesis for this test. Use the symbol η (the Greek letter "eta") to represent the population median.

    b.   To see where the name "sign test" comes from, go through the 16 numbers in the sample and subtract the hypothesized median from the null hypothesis. Note the sign (positive or negative) of each number, ignoring any zeros that happen to occur.

    c.   If the population median is higher than 60, you would expect to have a small number of negative signs recorded. The number of negative signs will actually serve as your test statistic. Since you are counting signs, use the symbol S to represent this test statistic. Write down the value of the test statistic.

    d.   The *p*-value (which you calculated in a slightly different way in part (d) of problem 13-28 is the probability of obtaining S or *fewer* signs. Even though you are interested in $\eta > 60$, the evidence for this would be *fewer* negative signs. Use the binomial distribution again to find the *p*-value. How did it compare to your answer in part (d) of problem 13-28?

    e.   Using a standard 5% level of significance, write a conclusion to this hypothesis test.

13-30. Consider the following data set:

91.5, 112.3, 102.3, 105.4, 95.8, 96.5, 109.8, 109.8, 125.4, 109.7, 106.6, 88.2, 117.8, 111.8, 94.3, 102.6
checksum: 1679.8

Median: 106, Mean: 104.99

    a.   Assuming this sample represents an independent SRS, explain why a t-test would be appropriate to test H_0: $\mu = 100$ vs. H_A: $\mu > 100$.

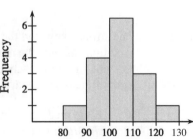

Problem continues on next page →

13-12.   *Problem is continued from previous page.*

b.   Without worrying about all of the details of the test, find the *p*-value for the t-test. At a 5% level of significance, what would you conclude?

c.   For the same data, carry out a sign test for H_0: $\eta = 100$ versus H_A: $\eta > 100$. Again, just find the *p*-value. At a 5% level of significance, what would you conclude?

d.   It is said that, compared to the t-test, the sign test "lacks power." Remember that the power of a test is related to its ability to correctly identify a false null hypothesis. Why might the sign test not be as good at identifying a false null hypothesis?

MATH NOTES

Nonparametric Inference Procedures

Nonparametric inference procedures do not make assumptions about the parameters of a specific distribution such as the normal distribution. The classification of nonparametric is not exactly synonymous with *distribution free*, but many nonparametric procedures have the feature of not being tied to a specific distribution.

Many nonparametric procedures use order, rank (1st, 2nd, 3rd, etc.), or simple counting to calculate a test statistic.

Even though nonparametric procedures are more robust and can often be applied when their parametric counterparts cannot, nonparametric procedures usually lack power. It takes more evidence (larger sample sizes) to recognize a false null hypothesis.

Review & Preview

13-31.   Kostas lives in Chicago, IL, also known as the "Windy City." He has heard that some of the windiest cities in the world have average wind speeds of over 12 miles per hour. He gathered a sample of wind speeds (mph) for 30 random days, and his data is recorded below.

9.7, 8.1, 24.4, 14.1, 18.4, 13.1, 10, 22.5, 10.9, 8.7, 16.8, 17.2, 9.3, 14.2, 16.1, 37.6, 15.7, 16.7, 9.7, 7.2, 30.2, 12.4, 24.5, 16.1, 7.5, 11.9, 12.5, 14.7, 11.9, 8.1

a.   Does the data fit the criteria to be able to carry out a t-test for H_0: $\mu = 12$ versus H_A: $\mu > 12$? Explain.

b.   Is there evidence, at a 5% level of significance, that the median wind speed is higher than 12 mph? Conduct an appropriate test, writing out all relevant steps.

13-32.   Sofía loves to play a card game with her friends. At the end of each round, points are tallied for the cards remaining in the hands of the players, and the sum is awarded to the winner of the round. Sofía has played the game a lot this year, and has been keeping track of the number of points scored each round by three of her friends. A random sample of her data is displayed below.

Friend 1: 76, 51, 56, 61, 55, 45, 63, 41, 45, 41, 72   *checksum: 606*

Friend 2: 46, 28, 39, 57, 33, 60, 65, 48, 59, 40, 52   *checksum: 527*

Friend 3: 50, 80, 57, 63, 73, 50, 69, 56, 62, 71, 72   *checksum: 703*

a.   Write a few sentences comparing (and contrasting) the distributions of scores of the three friends.

b.   Sofía is wondering if there is significant evidence of a difference in the mean scores among her three friends. Conduct an appropriate test at a 5% significance level. You may assume that the assumptions for inference have been met. Carry out all other relevant steps.

13-33.   Sofía continued gathering information based on her favorite card game. She has noticed that some cards, when played, tend to make her friends groan. She chooses four cards and keeps track of whether or not any of her friends groan when they make an appearance. Assume that her observations represent a random sample of independent observations.

	Card 1	Card 2	Card 3	Card 4	
Groan	7	9	18	22	56
No Groan	20	15	17	12	64
	27	24	35	34	120

Does the type of card that is played and the players' response appear to influence one another? Conduct an appropriate test at a 5% level of significance.

13-34.   Benjamin Franklin wanted to make the wild turkey, not the bald eagle, the national bird of the United States. Mary Claire is in Missouri investigating populations of wild turkeys. Mary Claire believes the distribution of turkey lengths are normally distributed with a mean of 3.72 ft and a standard deviation of 0.08 ft. Sketch the normal probability density function. What is the probability of selecting a wild turkey length greater than 3.83 ft?

13.3.2 How do I compare two skewed samples?

Mood's Median Test

As Mariya continues to study the newly discovered *P. rex*, a scientist studying giant megatooths released the following length data:

Giant Megatooth Length (ft): 62.4, 64.1, 54.9, 54.1, 55.1, 30.7, 58.5, 43.8, 64.0, 59.1, 61.8, 62.6, 56.8, 49.9, 30.8, 57.8, 60.4, 54.4, 63.9 *checksum: 1045.1*

This new dataset includes a recently discovered fossil of an individual 64.1 feet long—a record for this species! Mariya fears that *P. rex* may no longer be the uncontested king of the prehistoric ocean. She hopes to make a statistical comparison to the *P. rex* lengths from her sample.

***P. rex* Length (ft):** 74.0, 70.9, 72.9, 61.1, 69.4, 65.3, 38.5, 48.5, 73.1, 73.0, 66.0, 72.7, 75.0, 57.7, 64.9, 54.0 *checksum: 1037*

13-35. Construct a graphical display of the giant megatooth length data and describe its distribution. Do there appear to be any outliers?

13-36. Construct parallel boxplots and compare the distributions of the two species.

13-37. Because you are working with two significantly skewed data sets with outliers, you rule out conducting a two-sample t-test. You focus again on the medians. You set up a test with the following hypotheses: H_0: $\eta_P = \eta_M$, H_A: $\eta_P \neq \eta_M$.

a. If the null hypothesis is true and the medians from both populations are the same, then the overall median could be estimated from the median of both samples combined. Estimate the overall combined median, treating both samples as one large sample.

b. Fill out the following chart of counts:

	P. rex	Giant Megatooth
> hypothesized median		
≤ hypothesized median		

c. Calculate a *p*-value by conducting a chi-squared test for homogeneity of proportions using the table of counts from part (b). Verify that all expected counts are at least 5.

d. Write a conclusion for this hypothesis test comparing the two medians. Use a 5% level of significance.

13-38.   Other than the typical assumptions about the data that each sample represents an independent SRS of the respective populations, this procedure assumes that the populations have similar distribution shapes. Does this condition seem to be met for these two samples?

MATH NOTES

Mood's Median Test

Named after Alexander Mood, this test is designed to test for a significant difference in two or more medians.

H_0: All population medians are equal.
H_A: At least one population median is different.

The samples are all combined into one large data set. The median of this larger combined data set is calculated.

Each sample, then, is organized into two sets of counts: values that are less than the combined median and values that are greater than the combined median. Values that are *at* the combined median could either be ignored or counted with one of the other groups. The "less than" inequality is often used as "less than or equal" to account for this.

The counts can then be analyzed using a standard chi-squared test (assuming expected counts are at least 5 in each category).

This procedure assumes only that the distribution shapes of each population are similar and does not require the data to have a specific shape. It is especially useful if there are significant outliers that prevent other more powerful tests from being used.

13-39.   The depth of the sulcus is the distance from where your gums rest against your teeth to where
           they attach to your teeth. A distance of less than 3 mm is generally considered healthy. Three
           dentists are comparing the depth of the sulcus on randomly selected molars of their clients.
           They each gather a random sample of sulcus depths (measured in millimeters) of 22 clients.

           Dentist 1: 2.8, 2.8, 2.8, 3, 2.9, 2.9, 3, 3, 3, 3.2, 2.9, 3, 3.2, 2.8, 3.2, 3, 2.9, 3, 2.9, 2.8, 2.9, 4
           checksum: 66.0

           Dentist 2: 2.9, 2.9, 3.5, 3.1, 2.7, 3, 2.9, 3, 2.8, 2.8, 3, 3.3, 2.8, 2.9, 2.7, 2.8, 2.8, 2.8, 2.8, 3, 2.7,
           2.8 *checksum: 64.0*

           Dentist 3: 3.6, 3, 3, 4.5, 3.3, 2.9, 3.7, 2.9, 2.9, 3.1, 4.2, 3.5, 3, 2.9, 3.6, 3.1, 3, 3.3, 3, 2.9, 3.5,
           3.5 *checksum: 72.4*

           a.   Explain why it would not be reasonable to carry out an ANOVA procedure to test for a
                  difference in mean sulcus depth.

           b.   Carry out Mood's median test to determine if there is evidence (using $\alpha = 0.10$) of a
                  significant difference in in median sulcus depths between the client populations of the
                  three dentists. Write out all relevant components of the test.

13-40.   The third dentist from the previous problem is concerned that the median sulcus depth for his
           clients is higher than 3 mm. Carry out a sign test at a 10% level of significance.

13-41.   A group of scientists find dinosaur footprints made by a herd of unknown dinosaurs. The
           footprints appear to have a size (measured in square inches) that is normally distributed with a
           mean of 450 in^2 and a standard deviation of 15 in^2.

           a.   Should the scientists be surprised to find a footprint with a size of 485 in^2? Briefly
                  explain.

           b.   Determine the probability of finding 10 random footprints with a mean footprint size less
                  than 444.5 in^2.

           c.   Find the probability of finding four random footprints with a total area (size) of more
                  than 1825 in^2.

13-42.   Nicholas is looking for the proportion of people who have mostly conservative political views. Kaylee claims that "the proportion of people having mostly conservative political views is less than 0.35." Nicholas found a published survey of 57 randomly selected persons which found a 0.4386 proportion of people have mostly conservative political views. Calculate a 98% confidence interval based on Nicholas's survey. Use the results of the confidence interval to evaluate Kaylee's claim.

Index

Many of the pages referenced here contain a definition or an example of the topic listed, often within the body of a Math Notes box. Others contain problems that develop or demonstrate the topic. It may be necessary to read the text on several pages to fully understand the topic. Also, some problems listed here are good examples of the topic and may not offer any explanation. The page numbers below reflect the pages in the student edition. References to Math Notes boxes are bolded.

1.5 IQR Rule, **22**
68-95-99.7 Rule, **203**

A
Alternative hypothesis, 295, **297**, 304
And, *see* intersection, **121**
ANOVA for means, 461, 464
Association, **55**
  as related to causation, 95
  dependent variable, **63**
  describing, **63**
  direction, 55, **63**
  form, **55**, **97**
  independent variable, **63**
  linear, **55**
  negative, **55**
  none, **55**
  nonlinear, **55**
  of categorical variables, 115
  positive, **55**
  slope, **63**
  strength, **55**, **104**
  two-way table, 109, 115
  y-intercept, 63
Average, **20**, **32**

B
Bar graph, 4, **8**
Base rate fallacy, **131**
Bayes' Theorem, **126**
Benford's Law, 339
Bernoulli trial, **242**

Bias, **4**, **155**
  convenience sampling, **155**
  creating, 149
  desire to please, 149
  measurement error, **155**
  nonresponse, **155**
  preface, 148
  question order, 148
  response, **155**
  sampling, **155**
  two questions in one, 149
  undercoverage, **155**
  voluntary response, **155**
  wording, 149
Bin, 7, **9**
Binomial cdf, 237
Binomial distribution
  normal approximation, 244, **250**
  shape, center, and spread, 240
Binomial pdf, 237
Binomial probability density function, 234, **246**
Binomial setting, 231, **238**
Birthday Bonanza, 3, 121, 125
Blind, 172, **174**
Boxplot, **21**, 106
  combination boxplot and histogram, 23, 133
  maximum, **21**
  median, **21**
  minimum, **21**
  modified, **22**
  outlier, **22**
  parallel, **22**
  quartiles, **21**

C
Categorical data, **15**, 109
Categorical variables association, 115
Cats and Dogs, 7
Causation as related to association, 95
Central limit theorem, 374, **375**
Census, **4**
Center of a data distribution, 18
Charity Race Times, 200

Chi-squared conditions for inference
    homogeneity of proportions, **355**
    test for independence, 350
Chi-squared distribution, 335, 336, **337**, 340
Chi-squared goodness of fit test
    applications, 343
    degrees of freedom, 341
    expected count, 340
Chi-squared test
    choosing an inference procedure, 357
    expected count, 347
    goodness of fit, 339, **345**
    homogeneity of proportions, 353, **355**
    independence, 347, **350**
Circle graph, **8**
Claim, 288
    parameter, **290**
Closed question, 150
Cluster sample, **162**
Combination histogram and boxplot, 133
Combining random variables, **228**
Comparing data, **32**
Completely randomized design, **166**
Conclusion, (from a study), 165, 169, 172, 176,
    184
Conditional relative frequency table, 115, **118**
Conditions for inference
    chi-squared test for homogeneity of
        proportions, **355**
    chi-squared test for independence, 350
    experiments, **413**
    one-sample mean, **380**
    one-sample proportion, 271
    proportions
        example, **272**
        independent trials condition, **271**
        large counts condition, **271**
        one-sample proportion, **308**
        random condition, **271**
        two-sample proportions, **322**
            example, **327**
    slope of the regression line, **428**
    two independent means, **409**

Confidence interval, **281**
    evaluating claims with, 288
    for the population mean, 390
    general form, 284
    interpreting, **281**
    one sample mean t-interval, 388
    one-sample mean z-interval, 378
    one-sample proportion, 275, **282**
    population variance, 451
    slope of the regression line, 431
    two-sample proportions, 320, 329
Confidence level, 279, **281**
Confounding variable, **96**
Continuous random varaible, **222**
Control, **182**
Convenience sample, 153, **162**
Convenience sampling bias, **155**
Correlation coefficient, 78, 83, **104**
    in context, 100
Critical value, **282**
Cumulative relative frequency graph, **38**

D
Data, **4**
    categorical, **15**, 109
    extrapolating, **63**
    quantitative, **15**
    representation, **4**
Data analysis
    average, **20**, **32**
    mean, **20**, **32**
    median, **20**, **32**
    range, **20**, **32**
Data display
    bar graph, 4, **8**
    boxplot, **21**, 106
    circle graph, **8**
    dot plot, **9**
    histogram, **9**, 106
    ogive, **38**
    scatterplot, **9**
    stem-and-leaf plot, 6, **9**, 19, 106
    two-way table, **8**
    Venn diagram, **8**
Degrees of freedom, 336
    chi-squared goodness of fit test, 341
    chi-squared test for independence, 349, **350**
    t-distribution, **386**
Dependent variable
    association, **63**
Desire to please, 149
Desired outcome, **112**

Direction of an association, **55**
Discrete, 9
Discrete random variable, 219, **222**
   expected value, **222**
   mean, 219
   variance of a, **222**
Distribution
   geometric, 248
   marginal, **118**
   normal, 200, 202
   standard normal, 210
Distribution shape, **13**
   bell shaped, **13**
   negatively or left skewed, **13**
   outlier, **22**
   positively or right skewed, **13**
   single-peaked, **13**
   symmetric, **13**
   uniform, **13**
Dot plot, **9**
Double-blind, **174**

E

Effect size, 312
Empirical Rule, **203**
Errors in hypothesis testing
   Type I, 310, **312**
   Type II, 310, **312**
Estimating 60 Seconds, 6
Events, **112**
   compound, 134, 138
   intersection, 121
   mutually exclusive, 109, 135
   union, 121
Expected value
   of a discrete random variable, **222**
Experiment, **166**
Experimental design, 176
   completely randomized, **166**
   matched pairs, **178**
   randomized block, **178**
Explanatory variable, 54
Expected count, 340, 347
Experiment
   conditions for inference, 413
Extrapolate, **63**

F

False positive, 131
F-distribution, **457**
First quartile, **21**
Five number summary, **21**, 22

Form
   as related to a residual plot, **97**
   of an association, **55**
Frequency, **9**
   joint, **118**
   marginal, **118**
   relative, **118**, 189, 190
   table, **118**
Frequency table conditional relative, 115, **118**
Function
   inverse normal, 206
   normal probability density, 200, 203
   uniform probability denisty, **196**

G

General form for a confidence interval, 284
General addition rule, **126**
Geometric distribution, 248
Geometric setting, **254**
Given that, **121**
Goodness of fit chi-squared test, 339

H

Histogram, **9**, 106
   combination boxplot, 23
   interval, **9**
   relative frequency, 189, 190
Hypothesis
   alternative, 295, **297**, 304
   null, 295, **297**

Hypothesis test, 295, **297**
  ANOVA for means, 461, **464**
  chi-squared goodness of fit, 339, **345**
  chi-squared independence test, **350**
  chi-squared test for homogeneity of
    proportions, 353, **355**
  fail to accept, **297**
  fail to reject, **297**
  Mood's median test, 471, **472**
  one-sample mean, **394**
  one-sample mean t-test, 392
  one-sample mean z-test, 378, 392
  one-sample proportion, 299, **307**
  population variance, 456
  power of, 315, **317**
  p-value, 296, **297**
  sign test, 467
  slope of the regression line, 432
  two independent means, 406, **409**
  two-sample proportions, 324, **326**
    example, **327**
    pooled sample, **326**
  two-tailed, 304
  types of error, 310, **312**

I
Independence, **123**
Independent variable association, **63**
Independent variables, **123**
Inferential statistics, 259
Interpreting confidence intervals, **281**
Interquartile range, **21**, 24, **26**
Intersection, **121**
Interval histogram, **9**
Inverse normal function, 206

J
Joint frequency, **118**
Jumping Frog Jubilee, 12, 17

L
Law of large numbers, 142
Least squares regression line, 66, 72, **75**, 91
Line of best fit, 53, 58, **60**, **75**
Linear
  association, **55**
  combinations, 224
  regression, 425

M
Margin of error, 259, **281**
  changing, 284
Marginal distribution, **118**
Marginal frequency, **118**
Matched pairs design, **178**
Maximum, 19, **21**
Mean, 17, 18, **20**, **32**
  of a discrete random variable, 219
  of all sample means, 371
Mean absolute deviation, 24
Measurement error, 148, **155**
Measures of central tendency, **20**, **32**
  average, **20**, **32**
  mean, 17, 18, **20**, **32**
  median, 17, 18, **20**, **32**
Median, 17, 18, **20**, **21**, **32**
Midnight Mystery, 129
Minimum, 19, **21**
Model
  line of best fit, 58
  nonlinear, 436, 442, **445**
Modified boxplot, **22**
Mood's median test, 471, **472**
Multistage sampling, **162**
Mutually exclusive, 7, 109, 135

N
Negative association, **55**
Negatively or left skewed, **13**
Nonlinear
  association, 55
  model, 436, 442
Nonparametric inference, 467, 469
Normal distribution, 200, 202
  approximation to the binomial, 244
  approximation to the binomial distribution,
    250
  standard, 210
  test statistic, 384
Normal probability density function, 200, 203
Normalcdf, 201
Null hypothesis, 295, **297**
Nonresponse
  bias, **155**
  errors, 154
Number
  random, 141

O
Observational study, **165**
Ogive, **38**

One-sample mean
   conditions for inference, **380**
   confidence intervals, 390
   hypothesis test, **394**
   t-interval, 388
   z-interval, 378
   z-test, 378
One-sample proportion
   conditions for inference, 271
   confidence interval, 275, **282**
   hypothesis test, 299, **307**
   sampling distribution, **271**
One-way analysis of variance (ANOVA), **464**
Open question, 150
Or, **121**, *See* union
Outcome, **112**
   desired, **112**
   mutually exclusive, 135
   possible, **112**
Outlier, **22**, **55**

P

Paired data, 399
   inference procedures, 402, **404**
Parallel boxplot, **22**
Parameter, **4**
   claim, **290**
   population, **192**
   sampling distribution, estimated, **266**
   unbiased estimate, 364, **371**
Percent as related to probability, **112**
Placebo, **166**
   effect, 174
Point estimate of the parameter, **281**
Pooled sample proportion, 326
Population, 147, 160, **162**
   parameters, **192**
   standard deviation, **192**
Positive association, **55**
Positively or right skewed, **13**
Possible outcome, **112**
Power of a hypothesis test, 315, **317**
Predicted value, **63**
Preface, 148

Probability, **112**
   and, 134, 138
   compound, 134, 138
   event, **112**
   general addition rule, **126**
   normal density function, 200, 203
   outcome, **112**
   sample space, **112**
   simulation, 141
   tree diagram, 134, 135, 138
Probability density function, 194
   uniform, **198**
Probability distribution, 194
Probability mass function, **246**
Probability model, table, 220
Proportion, 190
   pooled sample, **326**
p-value, 296, **297**

Q

Quantitative data, **15**
Quantity, **4**
Quartile, **21**
   first, **21**
   third, **21**
Question
   closed, 150
   open, 150
   order, 148
   two in one, 149

R

R^2, **104**
Random
   number, 141
   variables
     combining, **228**
     continuous, **222**
     discrete, 219, **222**
Randomization, **182**
Randomized block design, **178**
Range, **20**, 24, **26**, **32**
Regression, linear, *See* least squares regression
   line
Relative frequency, **118**, 190
   histogram, 189, 190
Replication, **182**
Representative sample, 160, **162**
Residual, 62, **69**
Residual plot, 90, 91, 92, 95, **97**
Residuals, standard deviation of, 67, **69**

Response bias, **155**
Response variable, 54

S

Sample, 160, **162**, *Also see* survey
  cluster, **162**
  convenience, 153, **162**
  multistage, **162**
  population, **162**
  representative, 160, **162**
  simple random, 153, **162**
  standard deviation, **192**, **196**
  stratified random, **162**
  systematic, **162**
  unrepresentative, 154
  voluntary response, 154, **162**
Sample space, **112**
Sample standard deviation, 28, **29**
Sample variance, 28, **29**
Sampling bias, 153, **155**
Sampling distribution, 260, **261**
  chi-squared, 335, 336, **337**, 340
  of a population parameter, estimated, **266**
  of sample proportions, **271**
  one-sample proportion, **271**
  quantitative data, 363
  sample mean, 363
  sample means, σ is known, **380**
  slope of the regression line, 425
  t-distribution, 384, **386**
  two-sample proportions, **322**
Sampling variability, 259
Scatterplot, **9**
  association, **63**
Shape of a data distribution, 18
Shifty Shauna, 129
Significance level, **297**
Simple random sample, 153, **162**
Simulation, 141
Single-peaked, **13**
Skewed, **13**
Slope
  of an association, 58, **63**
  of linear association, **63**
Slope of the regression line
  confidence interval, 431
  hypothesis test, 432
  inference, 430

Spread
  of a distribution, 18
  describing, **26**
  interquartile range, 24, **26**
  mean absolute deviation, 24
  measuring, 24
  of a data distribution, **21**
  range, 24, **26**
  standard deviation, 24, 25, **26**
  variance, 25
SRS, 153, **162**
Stratified random sample, **162**
Systematic sample, **162**
Standard deviation, 24, 25, **26**
  of the sample mean, **371**
  of the residuals, 67, 69
  population, **192**
  sample, 28, **29**, **192**, **196**
  symbol for, **192**
Standard error of the sample mean, 384
Standard normal distribution, 210
Standardized score, **43**
Statistic, **4**
  t-test, 384
Statistical inference, 259
Statistical testing false positive, 131
Statistics, the field of, 3, **4**
Stem-and-leaf plot, 6, **9**, 19, 106
Strength of an association, **55**, **104**
Study
  conclusions from, 165, 169, 172, 176, 184
  observational, **165**
Subjects, **166**
Survey
  biased wording, 149
  design, 147, 219
  desire to please, 149
  population, 160
  preface, 148
  question order, 148
  two questions in one, 149
Symbol
  standard deviation, **192**
Symmetric, **13**

T

Table
  conditional relative frequency, 115
  frequency, **118**
  two-way, 110, **118**
t-distribution, 382, 384, **386**
  degrees of freedom, **386**

Testing for HIV, 130
Third quartile, **21**
Transformations, 436
Transformations to achieve linearity
   logarithms, 442
Treatment, **166**
Tree diagram, probability, 134, 135, 138
t-test statistic, 384
Two independent means
   conditions for inference, **409**
   confidence interval, 411
   hypothesis test, 406, **409**
Two questions in one, 149
Two-sample proportions
   conditions for inference, **322**
   confidence interval, 320
   confidence interval, 329
   hypothesis test, 324, **326**
   sampling distribution, **322**
Two-tailed tests, 304
Two-way table, **8**, 110, **118**
   association, 109, 115
Type I error, 310, **312**
Type II error, 310, **312**

U
Unbiased estimator, **261**, 364, **371**
Undercoverage, **155**
Uniform, **13**
Uniform probability density function, **196**
Union, **121**
Unrepresentative samples, 154

V
Value, predicted, **63**
Variability, **21**
Variable, 3
   confounding, **96**
   continuous random, **222**
   discrete random, 219, 222
   explanatory, 54
   independent, **123**
   response, 54
Variance, 25
   of a discrete random variable, 219, **222**
   sample, 28, 29
Variance, population
   confidence interval, 451
   hypothesis test, 456
Variation, **4**
Venn diagram, **8**
Visors for Runners, 189, 202

Voluntary response bias, **155**
Voluntary response sample, 154, **162**

W
Wording, biased, 149

Y
y-intercept
   of a linear association, 58
   of an association, 58, **63**

Z
z-score, **43**, 210